Constructions of the Self

A VOLUME IN A SERIES FROM
The Center for the Critical Analysis of Contemporary Culture

◆

Constructions
of the
Self

◆

Edited by

GEORGE LEVINE

Rutgers University Press

New Brunswick, New Jersey

Library of Congress Cataloging-in-Publication Data

Constructions of the self
edited by George Levine.
       p.   cm.
ISBN 0-8135-1772-9 (cloth)
ISBN 0-8135-1773-7 (pbk.)
1. Self (Philosophy)
2. Self.
I. Levine, George Lewis.
BD450.C626   1992
126—dc20   91-27274
                                                                CIP

British Cataloging-in-Publication information available

✦ CONTENTS ✦

Three Reconstructions

✦ ACKNOWLEDGMENTS ✦

More than a year of activity at the Rutgers Center for the Critical Analysis of Contemporary Culture lies behind this volume, which took then two years more. I owe much to many people who helped at different stages. The idea of making the Center's theme for 1988–1989 "Constructions of the Self" came from the Center's Advisory Committee: its members not only helped conceive the program, but provided the language in which it was made public; their suggestions about possible visitors and about the overall shape of the program helped determine the shape of this volume. As director, I get the credit for th committee's ideas, and I would like to right that injustice and thank all of the Center's advisers.

The work of all the Center's fellows, those represented in this volume and those not, contributed to the illumination of the theme of the self and to the essays represented here. I want to thank them all, both for their intellectual contributions and for their generous and friendly support of this project. The fellows for the year, 1988–1989, were: David Axelrod, Sarane Spence Boocock, Heide Fehrenbach, Mary Gibson, Martin E. Gloege, Miriam Hansen, Kali A. K. Israel, Jackson Lears, Jan Lewis, Dennis K. Mumby, Eliza Reilly, Seymour Rosenberg, Louis A. Sass, Joe Thomas, and Linda M.-G. Zerilli.

The work of the Center was enriched by up to week-long visits from distinguished scholars concerned with the issues the fellows were debating. I want to thank them as well: Leo Bersani, Teresa de Lauretis, Agnes Heller, Julia Kristeva, Dominick La Capra, and Richard Poirier.

I would also like to thank Irving Howe whose lecture was delivered not at the Center but as part of his series of Tanner Lectures at Princeton University, March 1990.

This is the first volume in a series deriving from the activities of the Center. Kenneth Arnold, the director of Rutgers University Press, is responsible for what I take to be the imaginative if risk-taking decision to work with the

Center. It is because of his willingness to take advantage of the resources of the Center that this volume exists at all. I am indebted, in particular, to Leslie Mitchner, humanities editor, whose intelligence and energy affected the substance of this book from the very start, and whose editorial commentary led directly to significant improvements.

But to Beryle Chandler, coordinator of the Center, I owe my greatest debt of gratitude. She was not only—as usual—indispensable in the year's work, but she took responsibility for the manuscript from the time it took shape and provided an editorial hand so pervasively and creatively that there is barely a detail of the book's organization that does not owe much to her. She has always been friend and invaluable adviser and assistant; for this, the first volume to issue from the Center, she was in all but name co-editor.

Constructions of the Self

✦ GEORGE LEVINE ✦

Introduction
Constructivism and the Reemergent Self

In his essay in this book, Irving Howe—puzzled, disturbed—touchingly asks why statements deeply hostile to humanism, and particularly to the idea of selfhood, have "become apparently plausible at this historical moment." For many who have stood outside the great wave of French-influenced theory that has engulfed much of literary study and deeply infected all the "sciences of man," Howe's question must resonate powerfully. For many, there does seem something perverse about the current devastation of the idea of an essential selfhood—perverse not because it puts the notion of a stable and coherent self to question, but because it seems to do so with such malice and glee. Modernism had already dramatized the fragmentation of self, but did so gloomily; however, as Martin Gloege notes, "the postmodern narrative enacts a celebratory, or at least resigned, rhetoric toward fragmentation and loss of self." The death of the "self" has, in many areas, become a matter for political and social celebration.

The peculiarity of this intensity of rejection is emphasized by the very difficulties many, probably most of us, have resisting the unselfconscious assumption that we are "selves," that there is something that makes us all of a piece, something beyond the socially constructed personae we play out at our work, in public spaces, even, perhaps, with family and lovers—something "prelinguistic," finally, that makes sense of our very polymorphousness. Even raising this assumption to consciousness can be painful. But the predominant intellectual position within the humanities and some of the social sciences at the moment is *social constructivism*, the view that the categories of human thought, social organization, and psychic (even biological) organization are culturally constructed—not empirically registered aspects of reality but conceptions created by ideology and social and political power. This social constructivism seems to be the weapon most frequently evoked to shatter the

I

category of the "self," to tear off the disguises concealing its naturalized, artificial origins.

The crisis of the self has affected almost every aspect of public and private life—and a vast range of intellectual disciplines. In each of these disciplines, as throughout the arts, questions of individual agency and of the relation between the individual and encompassing systems such as history or society or language have grown to critical importance. Technology seems to be displacing individual agency, authorial intention seems irrelevant to art, political change seems to have little to do with individual effort or personal heroism. The thought of anthropologists has deeply influenced literary study, and that influence has recently been reversed. Psychology, through Freud and Lacan in particular, infects the thinking of social scientists and humanists; philosophy becomes literary theory which becomes cultural study. Discourse theory and semiotics have made the study of language an almost imperial subject, and no discipline can afford to ignore the communicative medium it uses or the methods and assumptions upon which its work is based. With intensified self-reflexiveness in almost every discipline, the questions surrounding the definition, history, ontology, even metaphysics of the "self" have attracted profound, even passionate attention.

No discussion of the self can any longer confine itself to psychology, or to the "internal" conditions of "mind." (The very concepts of "internal" and "mind" are, after all, also in question.) Language and history and social context in fact become psychology, as psychology and anthropology and sociology become language and history. Thus, when the Rutgers Center for the Critical Analysis of Contemporary Culture announced its subject for the academic year, 1988–1989, to be "Constructions of the Self," responses came from almost every discipline in the humanities and social sciences. Everybody's research project seemed to be directly or indirectly about the "self."

Together, everybody recognized that their individual projects reflected a current condition: the idea of the "self" was central to each discipline, and the idea was in crisis. They sought the interdisciplinary dialogues and support the Center could provide because they all recognized that their own disciplinary tools were inadequate to deal with the complexity of the subject. They tended to share an inclination—more or less complete—to some form of constructivism, and they felt strongly the importance of exploring its implications. The very formulation of the Center's subject, "constructions of the self," implied a constructivist bias. But as the year progressed, it became increasingly clear that pure constructivism also posed problems for almost everyone and that the (largely post-structuralist) attack on the self had not sufficiently worked through the losses and limitations as well as the gains of constructivist thinking. In its post-structuralist forms, constructivism depends upon a radical textuality and implicit relativism that several of the fellows resisted in the interests of what seemed a more traditional respect for the authority of the empirical.

It is ironic, then, that the work of the fellows and of several of the distinguished visitors (Julia Kristeva and Agnes Heller, represented in this book, in particular) both emphasized constructivist approaches as distinctively illuminating to their research topics and inched beyond constructivism. The self, in many of the essays here, keeps attempting to reassert itself, even as it is exposed as a naturalized and essentialized construction of cultural forces.

This book makes no claims to definitiveness—either as a summa of constructivist positions or as an articulation of a new critique of constructivism. It is, rather, exploratory, and in several ways: in its efforts, theoretically and empirically, to explain, illustrate, and defend constructivism; and in its attempts to understand how the self is and has been imagined, why it was and continues to be important, how it is and has been shaped across cultures and within the context of the family, society, psyche. Along the way, it makes interesting new contributions to knowledge—about, for example, how the Japanese create and organize childhood, about how an advertising culture developed in America, and about John Stuart Mill's *Autobiography*, Pynchon's novels, and current critical theory. All of these diverse subjects, however, converge on the question of self and self-construction.

I am not, I hope, distorting the beliefs of the contributors to this volume in suggesting that even while it too celebrates resistance to socially rigid conceptions of selfhood and freshly argues some of the terrible consequences of acquiescing in the dominant myth of a naturalized self, it explores the possibility, tentatively, perhaps even anxiously, that some concept of "self" needs to be recognized and reconstructed—one that does not succumb to the political, psychological, and epistemological failures that have plagued the self from the time of its invention in the West. In particular, there is always the difficulty that the social-constructionist, always-already position can be politically enervating. It works well as a critique, as a mode of exposure, but—however much the point is disguised—for effecting or even theorizing social *change* it is useless. It can only show that what seems natural and permanent is in fact a human construction and therefore changeable. Moreover, in this crisis of values, when queried on how to justify certain political positions, *any* political positions, and how to value an individual that is "only" a social construction, it is silent. In the new language of this kind of debate, the "self" has been replaced by the "subject," a term that attempts to use the inevitable sense of individual perspective and individual need and desire, but to avoid the essentializing and metaphysical implications of "self." In the term, "subject," however, the old self may be latent, and that possibility needs to be explored.

None of these issues surrounding the "self" is resolved. And the stakes are high. Thus, despite its often quiet, "objective," scholarly, and muted discourse, this book is doing battle over the very question Howe raises directly in his essay. The question of the "self" is not an academic one: it spills through and over disciplines and out of the academy into the life of our times.

✦ ✦ ✦

Howe's eloquent, moving, and self-consciously untheoretical arguments against the discourse of self-bashing and for the discourse of what might be thought of as liberal "common sense" raise directly the social and political issues latent in all discussion of the "self" these days, and may help open up other, more theoretical, aspects of the subject.

As against the postmodern sense that conceptions of essential selfhood are complicit with conservative and repressive social forces, Howe warmly celebrates the self and through it the possibility of freedom, resistance, and social change. But while he is no postmodernist," neither is he an essentialist—not, at least, by intention; in fact, his essay is useful in making clear that constructivism is not an exclusively post-structural position and that in current battles over the self it is not the decisive issue, after all. Howe argues that the self was indeed constructed, that it has a particular historical origin, and was an aspect of a great enterprise of moral and political renewal, which he associates with "liberalism" and "romanticism." The self is not only the last bulwark against oppression, but a condition of value, for it entails belief in the good and the desirable. Hence the modernist lamentation for loss of the self.

Modernism exerted pressure on the idea of the self, put it to question in a variety of ways, not the least of which being surrealism and dada, parents, surely, of deconstruction. And Howe's modernist history of the self seems largely consonant with the views of the philosopher Charles Taylor, and not really incompatible with Foucault's. The self *is* culturally constructed, a political transformation and affirmation, the condition of a radical shift in power. It is, as Howe puts it, "socially formed even as it can be quickly turned against the very social formations that have brought it into birth."

Belief in the possibility of such turns is one of the marks of Howe's liberal faith and of his difference with post-modernists. Postmodernists are likely to see all individual phenomena as contained within systems, "always already" formed, and incapable of independent and innovative action. Howe's argument that the self is not constrained by the social formations that brought it to birth reflects the traditional liberal reading of the self against which modern theory has been directed, and focuses the political contest latent in contemporary debate. If one were to shift the language to one more compatible with post-structuralist thought, one might say that for Howe the individual "self," unlike Saussure's *parole*—the individual word (or speech)—is *not* entirely determined by its place within a larger system, the *langue* that ostensibly contains it and makes it meaningful.

For Howe, constructivism is no new postmodern phenomenon but a sensible reading of history, fully available to modernists before Foucault. Not only is Howe's "self" culturally constructed, but it is unstable enough to please any post-structuralist. "Once perceived or imagined," he says (and note the evasion of essentialism in the second word), "the self implies doubleness, multiplicity." And he then describes about a dozen possible conceptions of self. (Agnes Heller, as prelude to her own discussion of the "subject," offers a similarly generous list of possible meanings.) In addition, Howe argues that the self in Rousseau's seminal work "*begins* as a state of disintegration," and may well be no essential inner being but mere public performance.

There are some obviously and deliberately unfashionable implications to Howe's argument, and these also throw light on what is at stake in current debates. Howe not only affirms the power of the constructed self to throw off the yoke of its creation and affirm itself against any system, but, after having suggested that the "contrived public self" may be all there is to Rousseau's "self," Howe implies that even yet it may still, in some way, be "authentic." Consistent again with his liberal faith, Howe implies throughout his argument a fundamental belief in authenticity—no matter how complex, no matter how *in*authentic it may seem against the ideal of a transcendent reality. "Authenticity," in current discourse, often carries the weight of essentialism also, because current theory tends to deny that anything can have an absolute intrinsic "nature" that is not largely determined by context. But Howe's commitment to authenticity is based in an important logical argument. Having suggested that the idea of the "self" may be a consequence of the growth of a market society, Howe argues that the discovery does not at all invalidate the concept, for values cannot be determined by imputed origin. The self may yet be authentic in spite of its contrived and rather commercial sources.

On this line of argument (one that must be taken seriously by anyone using constructivist arguments as negative criticism), the fact that all concepts, all knowledge, all apparently "natural" qualities (like selfhood, for example) are culturally constructed does nothing to invalidate them. If all concepts are culturally constructed, no discriminations among them are possible; and this applies as well, of course, to the notion of cultural construction: there is no authentically transcendent reality to measure it against and therefore there are no grounds for rejection of any particular idea found to be culturally constructed. What it can be—and Howe argues that this is one of the functions of the idea of the self—is a heuristic, encouraging us to understand the particular conditions of its historicity. Constructivism does not logically entail negative criticism of what is proved to be constructed. To take an extreme example from this volume: even Jan Lewis's demonstration that American "mother-hood" is an invention serving patriarchy does not, logically, invalidate "motherhood." What is required is an additional argument making use of the discovery for political purposes.

Howe also implies that the validity of a particular social construct can be tested against "experience" (a crucial concept that escapes his otherwise vigilant skepticism and that smuggles in the very ideal of authentic selfhood it is marshaled to affirm). "Experience" is a fundamental category of Western, particularly Anglo-American epistemology: the foundation of knowledge itself. But it is, of course, a category that has been subjected to fundamental questioning in post-structuralist debate, since it implies a pure, positivist, non-linguistic reality that determines the shape of language apart from ideology and culturally systemic shaping. "Experience" implies precisely the essentialist "naturalizing" of linguistic formations that post-structuralism has attempted to call into question. From this perspective, then, a perspective that has dominated discourse about the self, Howe's arguments finally do seem to imply a foundation in an essential selfhood—true, a flexible and multifaceted, but nevertheless an essential one, the condition for change, resistance, growth, ultimately "discoverable," not merely imagined and invented.

Howe needs the "self" for his social and political program as intensely as modern theorists seem to need to reject it. For Howe, the self has a strong history of political liberation, enfranchisement, transformation. For post-structuralists, the history is different, infinitely more repressive and delusive. The urgency of their rejection of the self is derived from these alternative readings of history. Having shown that the idea of the self is almost endlessly multiple, Howe reasonably asks what value there can be in continuing to speak of "the self." His answers are clear: not only is it a condition of thought itself, but "The idea of the self," he says, "has been a liberating and revolutionary step, perhaps the most liberating and revolutionary, toward the goal of a communal self-humanization."

But post-structuralism finds the assumption that the self can be a foundation a moral and political disaster. Moreover, an argument such as this will seem teleological: the invention of the self becomes part of a progress toward the ultimate social and moral goal of "communal self-humanization." Either this *is* teleology, or Howe is simply affirming the political objectives of his historical and literary analysis of the self. That is, politically, we needed to invent the self because the self would become a necessary condition for our ultimate political objective. The rhetoric is evasive on this point, and the touch of teleology is clearly antagonistic to post-structuralism, which, whatever else it does, consistently opposes foundationalism and essentialism. These positions have very complex roots in post-structuralist theory, for they are derived from the positivist science it rejects, from Darwin and Freud, from Nietzsche and Heidegger, and, of course, from Marx (and from the American pragmatism which, as Martin Gloege shows, it so often ignores).

But this opposition to foundationalism is also closely connected to the events of 1968 and their aftermath. Post-structuralism often disguises the high moral line it persistently takes or assumes; the passion of its resistance to humanism, liberalism, individualism—the "naturalized" institutions of Western civilization—derives not from a new epistemology (much of what seems new about it has been available, if not fully employed, since Hume, and is recognizable in Howe's arguments, too), but from the death of the liberal ideals of modernism that lie behind Howe's arguments.

Against the enormous moral failures of modern civilization, from the Holocaust and Stalinist purges, to apartheid and colonialism, to the (now more emphatically argued) global, sexual, and economic repressions of the Other, which Howe has never underestimated, post-structuralism attacks the epistemological foundations of that civilization. What distinguishes Howe's views from those of the post-structuralists is that while both take the destructive power of Western civilization for granted, post-structuralism does not regard it as a flaw in an imperfect but correctable system. Rather, it locates "civilization's" destructiveness in the very structure of Western thought and in the forms of its language: the "horror" of modern Western history is a symptom of its way of knowing. The intense hostility to the self that Howe finds so puzzling is a consequence of the self's participation in the oppressive metaphysics of language. The self is indicted as one of the key naturalized conceptions through which the violence of contemporary "civilization" has been validated.

Since the self is one of those naturalized concepts that passes for the unchangeable real, post-structuralism is out to get it. The simple answer, then, to Howe's question about why the self is now under attack is that the post-1968 intellectuals do not believe in the possibility of resistance on his terms, of liberation on his terms, of moral advance on his terms. They find the conception of a teleological movement of history—as in Howe's ideal "communal self-humanization"—a dangerous one. The shaping forces are not outside us, visible and therefore vulnerable to direct attack or resistance, they are inside us, in the systems, particularly of language, that shape our imaginations and our thought. On this argument, to accept the terms of a foundational language, even if one self-consciously adopts it as a mode of resistance as Howe does, is to surrender to that very oppression Howe has spent his life trying to combat.

Howe tells a story of the self's virtues, of how—as liberating concept, as tool for resisting otherwise uninterrogated forces of political repression—it has made its exuberant and erratic way into the twentieth century, still able to liberate. But there are other stories to tell. Even without accepting the terms of post-structural analysis that I have just described, it is still possible both to discuss what is at stake in the almost overtly political battles about the self, and to intimate another, less optimistic, understanding of it.

It might help to remind ourselves that current attacks on the self have taken place in a sociopolitical context in which the "self," making its "natural" demands for satisfaction, has been the foundation for an extraordinary political reaction all around the West. If one of the great traditions of the self that Howe traces in Wordsworth and, particularly, George Eliot, is its manifestation in consciousness, that consciousness has been moralized or *de*moralized in our own times into psychobabble and psychological self-help; if in its Enlightenment formation the self was a means to resist a brutal traditional autocracy, it has in our own time become the justification for moralized greed on a grand scale, an expression of the right of the individual to reject social demands except on the smallest scale by the nearest at hand. Current history confirms Howe's perception of the link between the idea of the self and the new commercial society. It has produced yuppiedom and magazines like *Self*, television programs like "Lifestyles of the Rich and Famous," junk bonds, and corporate takeovers. Of course, such "selfishness" is much more closely tied to certain aspects of American individualism than to the "subject" as this volume is most obviously concerned to consider it. But I would argue that American individualism of the kind celebrated in Reagan's America, although it might well be analyzed as precisely not evidence of self but of mere free-floating desire, is quickly mystified into "Self." That is, the moral justification for such desire is its identification with an essential self endowed with a fundamental political right to satisfy itself regardless of the larger needs of community and society. From this perspective, self-discipline (as in utilitarian doctrine) is merely self-interest.

The grand romantic-liberal tradition (and nineteenth-century liberalism was, of course, very conservative in our sense of the word), in which the self and an ideal of inner discovery and freedom became ideological weapons for liberation, also became the foundation for bourgeois individualism of a sort that modern corporate buccaneers could only applaud. In such a context, a questioning of the grounds of the self might well seem in order, and a post-structuralist analysis of the incoherences of the self and an insistence on large systems that determine ostensibly individual action might seem salutary. The naturalizing of the characteristics of the "self" has tended to provide almost metaphysical sanction for American individualism: nature itself sanctions selfishness, exclusivity, and exploitation.

The concept of the "self," fully naturalized into a coherent, stable, and normative essence, is precisely what is invoked to dismiss deviations from the norm as symptoms of illness or criminality. In a world society in which difference becomes a condition of everyday life for almost everybody, the self has frequently become a historically constructed ideal for rejection of resistance to authority. "Self-interest" has become normative. The impetus for the theoretical constructions of writers like Lacan and Foucault, for example, must certainly derive from a deeply felt need to affirm polymorphousness, to break down naturalized structures of gender, racial, and even individual differences. If modern theorists were to extend Howe's "history" of the self, they might well show that what began as a construction of bourgeois-liberal political liberation is now a force for bourgeois-liberal political oppression.

Without reducing it to this, I suggest that the post-structuralist critique of the self is historically related to a traditional rejection of the desiring self. It is ironic to be treating as kin a Judaeo-Christian tradition insisting on "self-denial" and a deeply antimetaphysical reaction to Judaeo-Christian metaphysics. But it is equally ironic that the anti-totalizing theory of deconstruction is ultimately totalizing—*nothing* is "*hors de texte*," and the universality of its relativizing is part of its paradoxical being. Its wonderful usefulness as critique depends on its tendency to be a universal solvent. But the special attractiveness of the post-structural critique of the self in our moment is inversely connected to the moralized endorsement of individualist selfishness in modern capitalist society. The emphasis of that critique is on large containing systems that place every ostensibly free individual act in the context of social, political, and epistemological systems.

The ideal of the self, on the other hand, is the foundation of voluntarist, individualist thought that leads, for example, to self-righteous solutions to the drug problem such as Nancy Reagan's "Just say no" campaign; post-structuralism requires a recognition that a slogan such as "Just say no" puts its faith in individual agency while being itself entirely a construction of an ideology that is systemic and apparently beyond individual control. The self as independent actor outside such systems is a chimera of modern Western imagination, an evasion of the social construction not only of ideas but of individual actions as well.

But if the modern idea of the self is a political soporific, a disguise of the individual's total implication in large cultural systems, it does also seem fundamental to any conception of human value. What is it that we seek, after all, if not the well-being of each of us? And what was fascism but a systematic reduction of the importance of the individual self for the good of some larger system, *Volk* or *Vaterland* or moral order. Howe's ideal of communal self-humanization, in which the self and society are somehow both validated, is not, in the end, far off from the ideals of writers as temperamentally and intellectually different as Derrida and Foucault.

It is important, however, to note that rejection of the idea of the self is not in modern discourse inevitably connected with the rejection of the idea of individual agency. It is significant, for instance, that Agnes Heller's discussion is couched in the language of "subject," not self. And in much contemporary argument about the possibilities of resistance to oppressive authority—precisely the kind of authority Howe sees the "self" as having overthrown—writers invoke "subject position." As I have already suggested, such a formulation avoids the implicit foundationalism of the "self" while sustaining the possibility that the "subject" might also be an agent for change. But this question is to be decided on the matter of "agency." Can the "subject" be an agent, or is it also, like "parole," subject to overwhelming systemic power? Thus, although it is important to keep in mind the distinction between "self" and "subject," politically, the question is about "agency," after all. The "self" of contemporary social debate, even transmuted into "subject," remains an agitator for individual action and agency.

The dismissal of the self may well be self-impelled. As Louis Sass puts it in his fine survey of conceptions of the self in the psychoanalytic avant-garde, "many who claim to disbelieve in the self seem to take an inordinate delight in dancing round its burning image." The currently irresistible need to return to the self, if only as disciplinary subject, suggests that Howe's desire to resurrect it is far from chimerical or retrograde.

It is striking, for example, to find Julia Kristeva, in her essay, moving through the "imaginary," the perhaps post-structuralist emphasis on the free play of imagination, to what she concedes may well be a "metaphysical" condition. That is, she seeks a "prelinguistic" reality, a concept that moves her leagues away from the post-structuralist insistence that there is nothing outside the text. Not, of course, that Kristeva is arguing for a traditional, essential, stable notion of self. She explicitly says that commitment to the idea of the prelinguistic is not an opening up to "metaphysics." But it is clear that her *practice* as psychoanalyst, the reality of the pain of her patients and its accessibility through nonlinguistic forms, has moved her to a revised conception both of discourse and of the "self." She leans, indeed, toward religion, and the new conservatism (and one might infer surprising "nonfeminism") of her writing may well confirm post-structuralist suspicions of the "extralinguistic." She tries to imagine a condition in which it is possible to talk both about the linguistic expression and "primal, unnameable, traumatic experiences." Some prelinguistic reality, almost mystical in its intensity and presence, seems a condition of value and health to Kristeva. Perhaps that prelinguistic presence is, indeed, the recuperated self.

And it is an inescapable condition, even for the production of a discourse insistent on abolishing it. This is Agnes Heller's claim as, from another perspective, she explores the ways in which the self has been denied in recent times and demonstrates, like Howe, that it has always been a problematic concept, that it has never been stable, unified, or coherent. Philosophy is contingent on the "subject," and the end of the "subject," according to Heller, would be the end of philosophy. She sees neither end as really possible.

I do not want to claim that the essays here all point toward a quasi-mystical, inescapable, value-laden selfhood, reconstructed from the ashes of the universal critique of knowledge, disciplines, and individualism that has become the dominant discourse of certain aspects of the academy. In fact, many of the essays participate in that discourse and demonstrate its enormous usefulness, if not for politics then at least for scholarship. Rather, I want to establish a context for the varied discussions here, each of which is exploratory in ways I have already suggested. I have tried, by looking at Howe's direct confrontation of the political aspects of the issue, to show that there are reasons for the intense preoccupation with the idea of the self that marks contemporary discourse at almost every intellectual level: those reasons are certainly political, historical, and, consequently, deeply personal, since history and politics significantly shape the way we can imagine ourselves.

They grow not only out of 1968 but out of the worldwide political and social changes that followed 1968. The myth of the Western self has everything to do with almost all of the movements that have marked those changes: with, for example, feminism, which depends in great measure on a disassembly of the polarities of gender built into social usage and ordinary language; with gay liberation, which requires in addition a reimagination of the very concepts of moral and psychological "normality" and "health"; with movements for racial equality, which necessarily entail new concepts of "otherness"; with national liberation movements, often tied to racial stereotypes as well as to conceptions of the normative.

In this context, the urgency of cultural studies that analyze and expose the naturalization in discourse of socially constructed categories cannot be denied. But as the final three essays of this book variously show, that analysis is inadequate to the establishment of moral norms, of critical grounds from which alternative imaginations of value might be constructed. The dominance of constructivism gives almost all participants in this debate mutual points of departure. Yet recognition of the way in which the social has been naturalized is no direct means to change, and certainly, all would agree, we need a conception of change. But we need one that while not merely voluntaristic and individualistic still allows for the efficacy of the will. Systemic analysis can read out the power of anyone using language to say anything not "always already" said, anything not ultimately complicit with the containing system that enables meaning. Against such an increasingly dark notion of the systemic containment of all change within large impersonal and empowered structures—such as language and social organization—the self does seem to remain at least an element in the possibility of change, although an element that needs to be re-thought, reworked, recreated in ways that might bring Howe and his post-structuralist adversaries together in a common movement.

✦　✦　✦

The last three essays of this book—Howe's included—attempt such a rework-ing and constitute a significant restatement, in the context of constructivism, of the necessity of the self in philosophy, psychology, and politics. The other essays here work out the meaning and implications of constructivism from the perspectives of several different disciplines, as they attempt to locate the strengths and weaknesses of constructivist arguments.

So, in the first section, Louis Sass, Martin Gloege, and Dennis Mumby de-scribe and analyze the views about the self held by some of the most influential thinkers of recent times. Sass's masterful overview of the debate in psychoana-lytic theory, including an extremely useful placing of that almost iconic figure, Jacques Lacan, makes clear how integrated the psychoanalytic discussion is with developments beyond psychology—particularly in philosophy. By ex-posing the "unacknowledged presuppositions" of these major theorists, Sass illuminates the dangers and limitations of their ideas.

Martin Gloege shrewdly demonstrates the degree to which the postmodern demonstration of the constructed nature of the self is not complete, and he makes an important distinction between modernist and postmodernist views. But his essay is most interesting when he shows how the postmodernist cri-tique is an American phenomenon, and that its "comfortable" rejection of coherence becomes a form of transcendent explanation, after all. And Dennis Mumby, setting Foucault and Habermas against each other, gives full articula-tion to the problems inherent in Foucauldian analysis and critique. His com-mentary, however, remains above the fray by never entirely endorsing Habermas's commitment to rationality—to a ground that will allow discrimi-nation of differences and ultimately affirmations of value.

In the third section, Jackson Lears, Jan Lewis, and Sarane Boocock provide three case studies—although empirically based—of the ways in which even the most fundamental categories of human nature and relations are con-structed. Jackson Lears provides a forceful analysis of how advertising con-structs a human subject—a normative self particularly useful to corporate society. This disturbing analysis suggests how a careful constructivism can re-veal crucial connections between the ostensibly personal and large systemic class relations. The idea of the advertising self in Lears is the idea of a self con-structed from the ideology of class. For Jan Lewis, the connection is between family and polity. Motherhood itself was constructed in America in part to confirm certain structures of male power, and Lewis's analysis valuably con-nects with Lears's to demonstrate how the private self of family and domesticity connects with the very world from which that private self ostensibly protects its progeny.

These two American examples of historical constructivism are illuminated further by Sarane Boocock's transcultural analysis of the way childhood itself is constructed. The comparison of two cultures' divergent ways of constructing childhood is, by itself, sufficient demonstration of the fact that every culture mystifies and naturalizes its procedures. Boocock is not intent on making a constructivist case but on examining how one culture, the Japanese, actually goes about producing its distinctive patterns of self-definition and socialization. Here a contribution to the sociology of Japanese child rearing becomes part of the larger exploration of the constructions of the self.

The third section comprises two more locally defined and detailed studies of particular people, as opposed to large general considerations of cultural patterns. It seemed appropriate and important to try to see how in very particular lives the problems of the "self" might actually operate. Linda Zerilli studies the famous autobiography of John Stuart Mill to work out the distinction between the self written and the self writing. This complex and original analysis adumbrates a Mill who fits no simple gendered category, who constructs himself through the woman he hyperbolically lauded as the source of his own best thought—Harriet Taylor—and whose life needs to be reconfigured as an expression of a quest for the absent mother. Zerilli's study employs the theoretical tools of a post-structuralist feminism, with particular sophistication about the problems of representation, to provide a remarkable example of the ways in which constructivist analysis can illuminate and transform familiar assumptions about selfhood and familiar texts. And finally, Kali Israel provides an unusual case study of a figure who might be called a Renaissance Woman, Lady Dilke, a woman whose multiple talents and energies allowed her to resist the definition of Woman forced upon her by her culture.

The Self: Modern and Postmodern

✦ LOUIS A. SASS ✦

The Self and Its Vicissitudes in the Psychoanalytic Avant-Garde

The "self," once banished by mainstream psychology to the cloud land of unobservable and irrelevant abstractions, seems to have returned with a vengeance. Not only in psychoanalysis, but also in harder-nosed fields such as cognitive, behavioral, and social psychology, the nature and nurturing of the self has become a central concern—the stimulus for an outpouring of new theories, therapies, and research. Similar trends are, of course, prominent in other disciplines throughout the social sciences and humanities.[1]

It is probably no coincidence that these academic developments should occur at a time when self-involvement seems to pervade society as a whole—when the so-called self disorders fill the practices of psychotherapists, and contemporary fiction makes self-consciousness its central theme.[2] As culture critics like Philip Rieff have pointed out, preoccupation with the self seems to have usurped the role of religion as the central focus of what might, a bit anachronistically, be called the moral or spiritual life of modern man. It is true that, in the more avant-garde fields of the human studies (in literary theory and French psychoanalysis, for example), this modern turn to the "self" has been superseded by theoretical strategies that aim to destroy the claims of this secular god. But even in these quarters—the realms of "postmodernism" and "post-structuralism"—selfhood remains a central obsession: for, as we shall see, many who claim to disbelieve in the self seem to take an inordinate delight in dancing round its burning image.[3]

Previously published in *Social Research* 55, no. 4 (1988) 551–607, under the title "The Self and Its Vicissitudes: An Archaeological Study of the Psychoanalytic Avant-Garde." Reprinted by permission.

New as it may be in empirical psychology, preoccupation with the nature of the self is, of course, hardly a recent development in Western thought. Indeed, according to many historians, concern about the self is *the* central theme of the last several centuries of Western culture—whose spiritual history can be read as a sort of "journey into the interior," marked by such events as the Renaissance "discovery" of individuality and "the dignity of man," the Enlightenment assertion of human freedom and self-determination, the romantic glorification of inwardness and self-expression, and culminating in the dizzying involutions of modernism and postmodernism. In the present essay I want to consider several major positions on selfhood in contemporary psychoanalysis in the light of this history. I hope to show the intellectual roots and underlying "root metaphors" of four of the most influential and creative theorists of recent years: the Freudian analysts, Roy Schafer, Heinz Kohut, and Jacques Lacan, and the Jungian James Hillman.[4]

Since the nature of the self is perhaps the central issue of psychoanalytic debate today, to survey this theme is to cover many of the major issues of contemporary psychoanalysis. Also, it is in the psychoanalytic branch of psychology that views about the self have been most highly elaborated, polarized, and influential. All too often, however, psychoanalysis has tended to be highly insular, ignoring its historical roots in other disciplines and leaving the impression that its theoretical advances have sprung full-grown from the brow of a Kohut or a Schafer. The present essay is in the postpositivist spirit that recognizes the need for the social sciences to consider their own historical-cultural foundations, and, in particular, to acknowledge doubts concerning their putative "independence" from philosophy.[5] What I hope to provide in these pages has some affinities with what the philosopher-historian Michel Foucault has called an "archaeology" or "genealogy" of contemporary thought. Thus, I am not interested in the history of ideas for its own sake, but for the light such a perspective can shed on contemporary conceptions and controversies. (Foucault has described such a study as not "a history of the past in terms of the present" but "the history of the present."[6]) Nor am I concerned to assess the truth-value of the various theories, but, rather, to provide a historical-philosophical perspective which can bring to light the hidden presuppositions and, in particular, the potential problems implicit in each.

By concentrating on problematic aspects of the psychoanalytic approaches, I do not mean to detract from the contributions of these four theorists. All are major figures who have focused on aspects of personality or therapy that may not have been sufficiently appreciated in psychoanalysis. The special contribution of an analysis such as mine is to clarify those deep and usually unacknowledged presuppositions that tend to control a writer's thinking and to show how certain characteristic contradictions and exaggerations are likely to flow from this fundamental position. The point, then (as Foucault has said of his genealogical method) "is not that everything is bad but that everything is dangerous."7

A study such as this is important, not solely for the light it sheds on psychological theories per se, but also for what it may suggest about modern culture and the modern mind in general. With the emergence of the social sciences and the receding of philosophy into more and more technical concerns (at least in England and America), psychology has usurped the role once played by philosophy (and before that by religion), especially in reflecting and in structuring the modes of experience of the present age. It is in the models and metaphors of psychological theory that we can best discover the various aspirations, sometimes conflicting, of modern Western culture, and can observe what Lionel Trilling has called "the moral life in process of revising itself."8

I begin by surveying the history of philosophical notions of the self in modern Western thought, relying here on the historical analyses of the philosopher Charles Taylor.9 After this schematic overview, I will turn to psychoanalysis, considering the theories of the two most influential "humanistic psychoanalysts" of recent years, the "action language" of Roy Schafer and the "self psychology" of Heinz Kohut. My purpose here is to analyze the "root metaphors" of these important theories, and thereby to demonstrate how each is a manifestation of one of the two modern notions of selfhood that, according to Taylor, have emerged in Western thought since the seventeenth-century Enlightenment. After pausing to consider certain self-vitiating dilemmas that both of these alternatives involve (dilemmas that, in a sense, afflict the whole project of modern "humanism"), I will consider, in somewhat less detail, two other approaches that react strongly against "humanism": namely, the "Archetypal Psychology" of James Hillman and the post-structuralist psychoanalysis of Jacques Lacan. Whatever one may think of the cogency of their theories or efficacy of their therapies, these four psychologies have been among the most important sources of innovation and controversy in recent psychodynamic thought. Two of them might, in fact, be thought of as the major heresies of modern psychoanalysis: for, while Kohut's self psychology has recently gained much support in North America, the Lacanian approach has had an enormous influence on European and South American psychoanalysis, as well as on literary theory in North America. While somewhat less influential, Hillman and Schafer are nevertheless figures of considerable importance. Hillman is the most innovative and vital among contemporary Jungian (or post-Jungian) thinkers, while Schafer is the most famous and, perhaps, prototypic representative of a major trend of current psychoanalysis: the rejection of "metapsychology" in favor of a less deterministic and, supposedly, more "hermeneutic" approach.

Before turning to these schools—perhaps the most important representatives of what one might call the contemporary psychoanalytic avantgarde—it is first necessary to consider the major concepts of selfhood in the last several centuries of Western thought.

Notions of the Self: Modern, Protomodern, Premodern

In Taylor's view, the "modern" conception of human subjectivity and its relation to the world is largely based on two conceptions or images of human nature that emerged in the late eighteenth century. One of these conceptions emphasizes as the human essence the exercise of radical freedom, an autonomy unfettered by external constraints of nature or society. The other emphasizes a more complex aspiration: self-expression as the organic unfolding of an innate essence enfolded within the individual human being, an essence that, despite its innerness and its individuality, can be realized only through *communion* with nature and one's fellow man.

Although there are significant differences between these two "modern" conceptions—the "autonomous" and the "expressivist" images of Man—they also have profound affinities: most importantly, an "inward turn" that Taylor sees as the essence of their shared "modernity." Thus, each of these images entails a conception of the human subject as essentially *self*-defining rather than as defined by its relationship to some all-encompassing cosmic or religious order. In Taylor's view (as in that of many historians of Western culture), this inward turn is the *essential* fact about modern Man, and its origins can be traced to a crisis in and subsequent transformation of European thought and experience that occurred somewhat earlier, at the end of the sixteenth and beginning of the seventeenth centuries, and that came to permeate the thought of the Enlightenment (ca. 1670–1770).

♦   ♦   ♦

Central to the "crisis of European consciousness" of the late sixteenth century was the emergence of the Galilean-Newtonian world view of modern science and the undermining of the "premodern" Aristotelian world view that this entailed. In the Aristotelian vision, which had prevailed throughout the medieval and early Renaissance periods, Man could be said to have found his place by looking *outside* himself toward a cosmic order, an order imbued with "value concepts, such as perfection, harmony, meaning and aim."[10] The meanings and values by which one lived were felt not to be emanations from within but reflections of the surrounding cosmos, a

"Great Chain of Being" in which Man himself played a small and pre-destined but secure part. In Alexandre Koyre's description of the earlier conception, the world was then seen "as a finite, closed, and hierarchically ordered whole . . . a whole in which the hierarchy of value determined the hierarchy and structure of being, rising from the dark, heavy and imperfect earth to the higher and higher perfection of the stars and heavenly spheres."[11]

In the world of Galilean or Newtonian science, this looking outward for a source of meaning no longer made sense, for by then a radical separation had been set up between the inner realms of mind or consciousness and the external realm of matter and the physical world. In the Enlightenment the external world of nature came to be understood in a mechanistic and mate-rialist fashion—as a "disenchanted" realm of merely contingent correla-tions utterly devoid of human meaning and subject only to purely causal laws and modes of explanation. The categories of purpose and value, and all associated modes of teleological understanding, tended either to be rejected as illusory projections onto an indifferent universe, or else to be treated as applicable only to the "inner" realm of human experience. Thus, this Galilean-Newtonian world view involved two main ways of understand-ing human nature. To avoid confusion with the two "modern" images of Man already mentioned, and with the "premodern" Aristotelian world view, I will refer to these two Enlightenment views as "protomodern."[12]

According to the first protomodern view, Man was just like any other object in nature—to be studied by the same methods of objective observa-tion and understood as being subject to the same mechanistic and atomistic laws of causation. The associationistic psychologies of Hobbes, Hume, and Bentham (like those of their behavioristic successors) are examples of this homogenizing world view which assimilates mind to matter. The second protomodern conception, by contrast, viewed human consciousness as radically different from the phenomena of the natural world; here the best example is Cartesian philosophy with its famous dualism. Thus, Descartes's well-known method of doubt (the *cogito ergo sum*) involved withdrawing from a supposedly dubious external world and concentrating on a sup-posedly *in*dubitable and secure realm, the subjective domain of one's "own processes of observation and thought about things" (Taylor, *Hegel*, 7).

This inward move was doubly inconsistent with the outer-directed, pre-modern view of the early Renaissance: in Descartes's conception, not only did self-knowledge require turning *away* from the external world or cosmos; it also revealed an "inner" realm, a realm of consciousness that was felt to be more fundamental and meaningful than the ambient universe. From this new standpoint of the "self-defining subject," the old (pre-modern) model, with its orientation to the cosmic order, "looks like a dream of self-dispersal; self-presence is now to be aware of what we are and what we are doing in abstraction from the world we observe and judge."[13]

Taylor points out, however, that this (Cartesian) conception of consciousness as a self-sufficient, inner realm cannot be separated from the antithetical, but ultimately complementary, vision of a purely contingent, meaningless external world: it is only *because* of its sharp contrast with such a deterministic world that the "inner" and "subjective" realm could come to seem so independent of all natural constraints, and thus so totally free to define and control itself. Also, the very comprehensibility and predictability of an external world of contingent correlations and causal laws contributed to the subject's exhilarating sense of having the power of manipulative control over the world. It is for these reasons that, as Taylor puts it, "a disenchanted world is correlative to a self-defining subject" (Taylor, *Hegel*, 8). If we bear in mind these protomodern views, which emerge with the seventeenth-century's scientific revolution and inform the consciousness of the Enlightenment, we can better understand the "modern" images of Man that follow. For, as we shall see, the two "modern" images (the autonomous and the expressivist) both perpetuate and oppose these earlier developments.

♦   ♦   ♦

The first modern view, that of "autonomous" man, seems to be a relatively straightforward descendant of the Cartesian vision of a self-defining subject, but with one important addition. As Taylor explains through the example of Immanuel Kant (1724–1804), the most important exponent of the autonomous view, the (descriptive) notion of self-sufficiency came, in the late eighteenth century, to take on a prescriptive or ethical cast, to be conceived not simply as a fact about human nature but as something it was morally incumbent on man to recognize and to exercise. Kant defended a radical notion of human freedom and argued that morality and determinism were absolutely incompatible, since praise or blame were only relevant to acts freely chosen and performed. To recognize one's fundamental independence of all forms of natural causality was to be "free in a radical sense, self-determining . . . as a pure, moral will." Against Hume's notion that the self was "a mere 'bundle of perceptions' with no visible principle of unity," Kant argued (by means of his famous "transcendental deduction") for the necessity of assuming a unified self, the unity of the "I think" that accompanies and constitutes all possible experiences (Taylor, *Hegel*, 31, 30). This immensely influential doctrine initiated a "cult of moral autonomy"[14] and thereby contributed to a broad current of radical individualism which still pervades Western and perhaps especially North American culture.[15]

Such a conception is consistent with the Cartesian version of the Enlightenment world view in two ways: first, it opts for the notion of the self-defining subject; second, it accepts the dualism of mind and matter. This Kantian vision is a reaction *against* the Enlightenment only insofar as it rejects the other (i.e., the Humean or Hobbesian) side of the Enlightenment view of Man, the homogenizing or naturalizing tendency to treat the human being as just another object in the natural world, amenable to the same modes of objective study and mechanistic explanation.

◆ ◆ ◆

More deeply inconsistent with (protomodern) Enlightenment conceptions is the more complex view that Taylor terms "expressivist," for expressivism rejects not only Newtonian mechanism but also Cartesian dualism as guides to the understanding of subjectivity and its place in the world. Central to the expressivist aspiration, which largely coincides with romanticism (ca. 1780–1830) but is rooted in earlier, counter-Enlightenment thinkers such as Vico (1668–1744), is the attempt to overcome all forms of separation, both those within Man and those that separate Man from the social or natural world, for these are seen as leading to a sterile, devitalized, and alienated sense of human existence. Expressivism reacts against the analysis of the mind into different faculties, against the separation of feeling, will, and the imagination from intellect, against the division of Man into a material body and an immaterial soul, and, finally, against the polarization of consciousness and an objectified physical world.[16]

This expressivist overcoming of all dualisms is intimately bound up with the emergence of a new root metaphor: *organicism*. The Newtonian-Cartesian image of a mechanistic universe of extended substances in external, causal interaction is replaced by that of the biological organism.[17] Since this latter model of the natural world emphasizes qualities that also characterize human experience—unity, wholeness, and purposiveness (but a purposiveness that need not be conscious or volitional)—the Cartesian dualism of mind and matter is undercut. This allows for a reduction or overcoming of the (Cartesian) polarizations both with*in* Man (soul versus body) and *between* Man and the external natural world.

Thus, such an organicist vision holds out hope for achieving a new kind of connection with the physical world, a relation quite different from the manipulative or deterministic ones offered by the autonomous visions of Kant and the Enlightenment. Because of its teleological nature, the biological organism could be seen as akin to consciousness. Insofar as the physical world was conceived on an organismic (rather than physicalistic) model, it was therefore possible to imagine the world as having a certain resonance with the "inner" life of Man—whose own mode of self-experience the expressivists conceived as a vital, organic pulsation felt from within (rather than as the intellective, contemplative, and wholly independent self-awareness of the autonomous Cartesian or Kantian subject, who does not coincide with his body so much as exist *inside* it, like a captain in a ship or a ghost in a machine).[18] The expressivist rejection of Cartesian dualism also had important implications in the realm of methodology and epistemology, for expressivism rejected objectifying vision and insisted that understanding requires the observer to enter empathically into the inner and emotional life of the observed.

In some respect, the expressivist vision might seem to involve a return to the premodern era, when nature was a locus of human meaning. But, given the emphasis on subjectivity in expressionism, "communion with the surrounding world was desired not in the form of the contemplation of a cosmic order of ideas [as in the Aristotelian, premodern world], but rather as a communion appropriate to subjectivities." "What is sought for," writes Taylor, "is interchange with a larger life, not rational vision of order" (Taylor, *Hegel*, 23,25).

Also central to expressivism is the notion of growth. Change is understood on an organic rather than mechanistic model, as involving an inborn and inner essence that initially exists *in potentia* and, as it were, yearns to realize itself through a natural process of self-unfolding. Though it is conceived as an innate teleological process, this self-unfolding can fulfill itself only when it occurs in an environment that harmoniously echoes the self's inner pulsations.

For many expressivists (notably, the German romantic Herder), the unique or individual nature of this inner essence was emphasized: fulfillment for each individual (or for each culture or *Volk*) meant expressing the person's or the culture's own special way of being human (Taylor, *Hegel*, 15). Understandably, discovering this unique essence was extremely important; for not only did the expressivists conceive of the unique inner essence as guiding self-expression (rather like a genetic program), they also considered the very process of discovering this essence to be one of the modes *of* such self-expression. Consequently, just as the aspirations of the radically autonomous conception encouraged the project of self-*control,* that of expressivism valorized self-*exploration* and self-*expression.*[19] Art—understood not as Aristotelian mimesis but, on the romantic model, as organic self-expression—served as the prime example of this process of self-unfolding and thereby took on a quasi-religious function.[20]

This natural and spontaneous self-unfolding was not, of course, seen as inevitable; it could be stifled or go awry. Expressivist theorists have, however, tended to conceive of any distortions of this process of unfolding as necessarily resulting from the negative impact of an unsympathetic environment, not from anything intrinsic to the self. Society as it exists—with its artificiality and rigidity—has generally been seen as distorting the intrinsic organicity of the natural world, and thus as providing a hostile rather than mutually resonating environment for the self-unfolding of the individual.

✦   ✦   ✦

The differences between these two strains of modern humanism seem evident enough. The position of "moral autonomy" accepts a dualistic universe and then enjoins Man to express his essence through an exaggeration of this dualism. As Taylor points out, the separation or "diremption" from nature (both external and internal) that inevitably results is at cross-purposes with the expressivist ideal of wholeness within the self and unity between self and external world. Further, the self-clarity inherent in the exercise of a purpose*ful* Kantian rational will is very different from the purpos*ive,* but not necessarily transparently self-aware, self-actualization inherent in organic unfolding.

And yet, as Taylor emphasizes, we should not forget the important affinities between the autonomous and expressivist perspectives. Both did, after all, arise in reaction against a certain homogenizing materialism and objectivism (i.e., against the first "protomodern" strain); accordingly, both place great emphasis on the ideals of freedom and of individualism. Also, both suggest that the true expression of self will occur in opposition to external forces, whether those of the material universe or of the artificial customs and morals of existing society. Also, since many post-Enlightenment thinkers have been drawn to both these ideals of modern humanism simultaneously, we should not expect to find absolutely pure cases of one or the other aspiration. Nevertheless, current psychoanalytic visions of the self do gravitate toward these alternatives, and they do incur the same problematic consequences as afflict these classical positions. As we shall see, some of these problems can best be understood as involving conflicts *between* the aspirations toward autonomy and toward expression—that is, as ways in which fulfillment of one of these ideals tends to bring with it an undermining or abdication of the other (a problem deeply felt by those many moderns who, while emphasizing one ideal, have actually been drawn to both, often without realizing the incongruence between them). Perhaps even more significant, however, are certain internal contradictions: ways in which pursuit of a single one of these aspirations tends, paradoxically enough, to undermine certain of its *own* deepest yearnings.

✦   ✦   ✦

Now we are ready to turn to the psychodynamic perspectives of Schafer, Kohut, Hillman, and Lacan. Despite their differences, all four of these theorists have at least one thing in common: opposition to the "Ego Psychology" that has become the psychoanalytic orthodoxy of our day. (Ego

Psychology, the immediate successor to Freud's first or "classical" version of his theory, grew out of Freud's postulation of the structural or tripartite model of personality as the interaction of id, ego, and superego. To the classical psychoanalytic concern with instinct, Ego Psychology adds a heavy emphasis on the functions of the ego, especially mechanisms of defense against inner drives and the outer-directed capacity for accurate assessment of the world, "reality-testing.") As we shall see, however, "Ego Psychology" means different things to different people. The humanistic psychoanalysts Schafer and Kohut emphasize Ego Psychology's continuity with classical psychoanalysis, both of which they reject as too deterministic and reifying (for being too closely akin to the homogenizing mechanism of the protomodern position described above). Hillman and Lacan, on the other hand, criticize ego psychology precisely for *deviating* from classical psychoanalysis, and for thereby losing Freud's most valuable insight into the fragmentary, decentered, or illusory nature of the self (and thus for being, in the sense discussed above, too "modern").

Our first example, Schafer's action language, turns out to be a rather straightforward expression of the radically autonomous conception of modern self-defining subjectivity; as we shall see, Schafer accepts not only a Cartesian ontology but also something akin to Kantian ethics.

Schafer's "Action Language"

Schafer criticizes the traditional psychoanalytic modes of discourse (known as "metapsychology," and including both classical psychoanalysis and Ego Psychology) for their tendency to reify psychological processes, thereby treating these processes as events that happen *to* the patient rather than as actions the patient performs—that is, as the doings of "a unitary, fully responsible agent."[21] ("Metapsychological" explanation involves the translation of observable behavior and experience into abstract terms defining the relationship of various hypothesized realms or faculties of the mind, such as "unconscious," "preconscious," "conscious," and "cathexis," or "id," "ego," and "superego.") In contrast with what Schafer calls "the premodern language of mind used by Freud," the primary rule of his "action language" alternative is that all the phenomena of human experience and behavior—not only all thoughts and actions but also all experiences, emotions, desires, and dreams—are to be designated by verbs in the active voice and understood as "actions," as "intentional or goal-directed performances," "for which the analysand accepts some significant measure of responsibility." Only in this way, says Schafer, will we (as, presumably, we should) "unquestionably require there to be a specific author of the action in question."[22]

Like that of Descartes and Kant, Schafer's reasoning tends to be very either/or. In his argument, he presupposes a dualistic ontology with a fundamental rift between two modes or realms of being: a physical world to which natural-scientific and causal-deterministic modes of explanation apply, and a human realm where only the "empathic-introspective method" and teleological-purposive explanations are applicable. In contrast with philosophers like Paul Ricoeur or R. S. Peters who regard psychoanalysis as necessarily a "mixed or even ambiguous discourse," Schafer insists that "the natural science and the experiential rhetorics simply do not mix."[23] Psychoanalysis, he says, must reject Freud's "Newtonian idea of psychodynamics" and adopt "a thoroughly non-mechanistic, non-organismic language," a language of reasons, not causes. He contrasts this action-language approach with the misleading logic of the traditional psychoanalytic "metapsychology"—an approach which supposedly demands "that every psychological process or phenomenon must be located within the realm of psychic determinism or psychodynamics" (Schafer, *New Language*, 196, 120, 207). As Schafer sees it, the traditional approach commits the same error as did the homogenizing mechanism of Enlightenment figures like Hobbes and Hume, the error of importing into the psychological domain modes of understanding appropriate only to the physical world.

Schafer's notion of activity is meant to apply not only to the subject's movements and manipulations of the world, but also to his or her *experience* of the external world. Thus, for Schafer, the point to be emphasized is that experience is always an active construal, never just a passive reflection of a determining external reality.[24] For him, the very fact that the subject contributes to what is experienced indicates that the subject is "active" and "responsible"—even when the subjective contribution would hardly seem to imply that the subject of experience is in any sense in control (e.g., when experience can be shown to be imbued with "phase-specificity," with, say, meanings appropriate to the "oral" or "anal" stage of development).[25] On his action-language reading, therefore, the point of psychoanalysis is not so much that consciousness and action have unconscious and instinctual causes as that people are "authors of their existence," since the realm of "action" includes "all their mental operations and thereby all the circumstances they contrive and all the meanings they ascribe to their circumstances, whether contrived or imposed on them."[26] Such a position assumes not only that subjectivity is self-defining, but that in the most essential sense it also defines—rather than derives from or participates in—the encompassing world or the bodily substrate.[27] "People, thus, are far more creators and stand much closer to their gods than they can bear to recognize," writes Schafer (*New Language*, 153).

Schafer's acceptance of the modern notion of self-defining subjectivity seems clear enough. And, as we have seen, this goes along in his case with an acceptance of the ontology of the second, dualist strain of Enlightenment thought. Obviously, Schafer's rejection of causal or quasi-materialistic explanations regarding human action and experience is not the same as denying dualism itself. Indeed, the very single-mindedness of Schafer's insistence on activity and responsibility in the human or mental domain attests to his unquestioning acceptance of this Cartesian ontology, in which the realm of mind or experience is associated with freedom and contrasted with a domain of mechanistic determinism.[28] (One could, of course, accept the significant role played by consciousness in the "construction" or "interpretation" of the world without assuming that this role is intentionalistic or under the subject's control. Indeed, as we shall see in the case of Kohut, and still more obviously in the cases of Hillman and Lacan, interpretive knowing can, from an organicist, an archetypal, or a structuralist standpoint, be seen as something that, as it were, happens *to* the subject, rather than as something the subject does in any "active" way. The *subjectivity* of experience need not, then, indicate that the individual subject's role is *active* or "responsible.")

Schafer sometimes presents action language as just another creative "construal" of the world—a "narrative" choice no more or less "true" than other such construals[29] (though he will say it has more "consistency, coherence, and transformational effectiveness" [*New Language*, 141]). In fact, however, he is not as relativistic as this sounds. In his view, the causal-deterministic or anthropomorphic descriptions and explanations of traditional psychoanalysis are clearly less valid than intentionalistic ones. (Here, incidentally, we see the two major threads of Schafer's work coming into conflict. The modernist relativism or fictionalism implicit in his writings on the various "visions" of reality—largely informed by his reading of Northrop Frye—is not really consistent with the more positivistic bent of his action language.) Thus, whereas he refers to action language as providing "the locutions of insight" and the accounts of "a more reliable narrator," he constantly reiterates the merely hypothetical and illusory nature of metapsychological, causal descriptions—writing, for example, that "people are fantasizing whenever they disclaim action," and that, "to refer to happenings" rather than actions is to "reinforce certain resistant strategies."[30] Like many Enlightenment thinkers wary of what the empiricist Francis Bacon called the "idols of the mind," Schafer also opposes what he calls "the careless importing of experiential terms into theory"; thus, he criticizes "traditionally evocative or richly metaphoric language"—as, for example, the language Freud used in telling "the tale of an Ego Ideal or Superego measuring the ego, judging it, and shaming or punishing it, as though it were another forceful person or another person's forceful will."[31] With these traditional modes of psychoanalytic description—the causal-mechanistic and the anthropomorphic picture of homunculi in interaction—Schafer contrasts the supposedly less fanciful, less metaphoric action-language account. The following is one of Schafer's examples of an action-language account, in this case of a conflict about overeating: "One might say, 'I ate excessively according to the standards I maintain regarding quantity, and I contemplate what I did regretfully and contemptuously.' . . . In this action version of self-indulgence, rather than two selves being at odds with one another or at least interacting with one another, there is a single agent performing and considering certain of his or her actions in different, more ore less incompatible ways, which is to say performing them, and perhaps consciously considering them, conflictedly" (Schafer, *Analytic Attitude*, 250–251).

Schafer sees action language as "an attempt to describe analytic data with as little use as possible of blatant unsystematized metaphors, especially those metaphors derived from and conducive to a model of a mind-machine or a brute organism with a tamed mind" (*Analytic Attitude*, 87–88). From a non-Cartesian (say, an expressivist) standpoint, however, a description like the above is hardly devoid of metaphoric components: it is just that the prevailing metaphor is a Cartesian one—that of a self-defining subject that seems to survey, as if from a position of detachment, a set of possible courses of actions that are arrayed before it almost like visual objects.

As mentioned, Schafer often backs off from an explicit claim that his approach has more objective truth than does metapsychology; at these times, he often retreats to a more pragmatic justification, arguing that, if not more "true," action language is at least "healthier": it provides "the locutions of insight" (*New Language*, 146). It is in this part of Schafer's argument that the Kantian aspects are clearest, as are the strong if somewhat hidden ethical or value-laden implications of his position.[32]

Schafer seems to regard action language as intrinsically therapeutic since it "changes the mode of constructing experience." "The analysand's switching to action language, when it is not merely compliant, transforms experience rather than merely translates or paraphrases it." Such a shift encourages in the patient "an enhanced and more rational sense of personal responsibility" and agency—the very quality that for Schafer virtually defines psychological maturity and health (*Analytic Attitudes*, 242, 112). Consequently, Schafer claims that action language is the "native tongue" of psychoanalysis, and presumably, of all effective psychotherapy (*New Language*, 361). For example, he writes that it is "a defining feature" of psychoanalytic interpretation to retell happenings as actions, and thus to transform "disclaimed actions" into "claimed actions" (defined as "those for which the analysand accepts some significant measure of responsibility"[33]): "During the progress of an analysis . . . [l]ess and less do analysands present themselves as lived by impulses, emotions, defenses, or conflicts; more and more . . . analysands come to realize how much has always depended on what they have made of these factors, whether they be family constellations, traumas, infirmities, losses, or sexual anatomy" (Schafer, *Analytic Attitude*, 107). In support of his argument that the "person as agent has always stood at the center of psychoanalytic understanding," Schafer refers to Freud's well-known demonstrations of unconscious intentionality in actions previously seen as random or causally determined (slips of the tongue are the most obvious example) (*New Language*, 361).

✦   ✦   ✦

To claim, as Schafer does, that action language is the "native tongue" of psychoanalysis and provides "the locutions of insight" in fact seriously foreshortens both psychoanalysis and psychotherapy, reducing each to what is really but one of its possible modes. For, as seems obvious enough on reflection, psychoanalytic explanations do often move in the opposite direction—as was the case with Freud's equally characteristic demonstrations of the role played by unconscious, quasi-causal factors in acts generally assumed to be purely the result of conscious rationality or volition. There also seems little plausibility to the idea that therapy *should* always bring about a greater acceptance on the patient's part of responsibility for actions. Certainly, this is sometimes and even often true. But there are many patients who come into treatment with an exaggerated or misplaced sense of responsibility or guilt and who need to diminish such a feeling. There are also patients who feel alienated from their emotions and actions precisely because they have too *great* a tendency to experience these emotions and actions as involving volition and arbitrary choice.[34]

That Schafer should be so one-sided in his emphasis can be seen as a reflection of both the Cartesianism and the Kantianism of his assumptions. Whereas the Cartesianism prevents him from imagining a third way between (or beyond) mechanism and voluntarism, the Kantianism makes him embrace, as somehow truer and more virtuous, one of these Cartesian alternatives to the (almost) complete exclusion of the other.[35] Schafer has, in fact, been accused of fostering a subtly moralistic kind of psychotherapy, an implicitly antagonistic relationship in which the patient is likely to feel criticized and held responsible.[36] Though Schafer, naturally enough, has denied this, one can see how his Cartesian-Kantian presuppositions might subtly, and perhaps ineluctably, have led to such a position. Schafer does admit on occasion that agency can be overemphasized, that the relentless use of action language could involve an overly "guilty or omnipotent discourse."[37] But, not surprisingly, he fails to elaborate on this important point, whose implications would call into question the whole thrust of his argument.[38] To understand the possible negative consequences of the stance he espouses, it will be useful to consider some of the classical criticisms that expressivists have directed at the autonomous vision of selfhood.

The negative and, in some ways, self-vitiating potentialities of the autonomous stance emerge most clearly when one recognizes that the natural world exists not just outside but also within the person—in the form of those biological processes that give rise to desires and physical sensations. Hegel, who was strongly drawn to the expressivist ideal, criticized Kant on just these grounds. In his view, the Kantian ideal demanded a kind of self-enslavement, since it enjoined man to assert his freedom not just from the outer world but also from his own inner inclinations. If nature within had to be subjected to rigorous control, this meant that the Kantian "autonomous" man "carries his Lord in himself, yet at the same time is his own slave" (quoted in Taylor, *Hegel*, 60). Such an internal division between a controlling and a controlled part of the self was, of course, anathema to the expressivists; for them, true "freedom" could only inhere in the spontaneous unfolding of a unified organic being.

What is perhaps less obvious is how this mode of selfhood can undermine something central to the autonomous aspiration itself—namely, its own valorizing of the unity of the self (which is implicit in Schafer's concept of the "unitary, fully responsible agent"). Hegel thought that the feeling of being a single, integral self would necessarily conflict with the aspiration to absolute autonomy; he argued that the integral mode of selfhood—he called it "simple, placid consciousness"—would necessarily feel too limiting, too tainted with the kind of substantiality and inertia that characterizes the physical universe. Therefore, argued Hegel, the unchecked press toward the expression of the autonomy of consciousness would lead to a rapid shifting among many different roles, each of them experienced not as a true identity but as a mere mask. For this reason, the aspiration toward total autonomy would lead not to the experience of being "a unitary, fully responsible agent," but to the "self-estrangement" and self-fragmentation of what Hegel called "disintegrated consciousness."[39]

At first glance, Schafer's protests against psychoanalytic reification might seem to place him squarely in opposition to these self-objectifying, self-alienating, and self-fragmenting trends. After all, instead of allowing the patient to treat his own experiences as objects of contemplation that operate independently of the observing or controlling self, Schafer reminds us of the process-like nature of psychological events, and of their intrinsic oneness with the acting subject (*A New Language*, 147). And, against the divided self of, say, the psychoanalytic structural hypothesis (with its id, ego, and superego), Schafer insists on the "unitary, fully responsible agent." On closer consideration, however, one discovers in action language the potentiality for the negative and self-contradictory consequences criticized by Hegel and others of an expressivist persuasion.

Schafer does not overtly argue for the domination of the passions by reason, nor for disengagement from the self or detachment from external moral sources—the elements of the Cartesian-Kantian project; however, his insistence on active over passive modes of experience and on admitting one's nearly hegemonic agency amount to much the same thing. What, after all, is the likely effect of this relentless claiming of responsibility, this denial or downplaying of the automaticity, natural inertia, or objective grounding of action and experience? Is it not something akin to the Cartesian project of self-mastery—a project that, as Taylor says, "calls on me to be aware of *my* activity of thinking or *my* processes of habituation," and that "demands that we stop simply living in the body or within our traditions or habits, and by making them objects for us, subject them to radical scrutiny and remaking"?[40]

Schafer's position encourages the vision of a self in ultimate control, relentlessly "claiming" responsibility even for its dreams, desires, and emotional responses, and becoming explicitly aware of its own role as interpreter in all that it experiences. An expressivist might wonder if any actual increase in self-mastery is likely to come about from this semantic and conceptual shift toward the autonomous vision of the self. (How, for example, could action language make one in *fact* any less the witness and more the author of one's dreams?) It does, however, seem that external reality might come to feel subjectivized, and one's social and physical being alienated, when so much emphasis is put on realizing the extent to which we are, as Schafer says, "authors of our own existence." Thus Schafer, like Kant, may *seem* to be offering a reunification of the self with itself, but the danger is that his aggrandizement of the self-as-agent may actually encourage a *further* isolation and self-alienation, and a sense of the weightlessness and foreignness of the physical and social worlds.

Kohut's "Self Psychology"

If Schafer is the defender of the Cartesian-Kantian concept of selfhood, emphasizing autonomy, self-control, and responsibility, Kohut is the champion of the expressivist self, emphasizing organic wholeness, empathic union, and self-expression.[41] As we shall see, this is apparent in the theoretical presuppositions underlying both the descriptive and prescriptive aspects of self psychology.

Although Shafer and Kohut share an aversion to the traditional psychoanalytic "metapsychology," they differ in the nature of their objections. As we have seen, for Schafer the essential problem is the tendency for metapsychological explanation, in both its mechanistic and anthropomorphic variants, to deny or underplay the role of the patient's intention, volition, and responsibility in favor of deterministic interpretations. Kohut's main criticism, by contrast, derives from his commitment to the ideal of empathy; the issue of freedom versus determinism hardly arises. He faults metapsychology for its tendency, both in theory and in therapy, to slight the empathic *description* of the patient's lived experience in favor of a mode of *explanation* that is abstract, detached, and, in many instances, procrustean—for the fact that its concepts are, as he says, "experience-distant" rather than "experience-near."

As is well known, Kohut sees failures of empathy as the essential source of psychopathology, and the provision of appropriate empathy as the essence of a psychotherapeutic cure. Moreover, in addition to being the *sine qua non* of healthy maturation and effective psychotherapy, empathy is also, for him, the key element in scientific observation. Thus, in the central statement of his later theory, *Restoration of the Self*, Kohut associates the full development of his self psychology with complete acceptance of "the fact that the psychological field is defined by the observer's commitment to the introspective-empathic approach." He criticizes traditional psychoanalysis's adoption of the Enlightenment ideal of scientific objectivity, with its separation of subject from object, and faults Freud for having "gazed at man's inner life with the objectivity of an external observer."[42]

Kohut's dissent from the objectivism of the traditional Cartesian epistemology is firmly in the expressivist tradition, since he calls for overcoming divisions both between subject and object and within the subject itself. For the Enlightenment tradition, knowledge requires distance and the recognition of difference: one must stand back from one's object and refrain from making those anthropomorphizing projections that Bacon called "the idols of the mind." Kohut's views, in contrast, are reminiscent of counter-Enlightenment and romantic claims that man can only know that which resembles him and with which he can identify (e.g., the doctrines of Vico).[43] Thus, Kohut emphasizes that knowledge requires a mutual intertwining or fusion of subject and object, since the observer cannot even "see" his object of study—the consciousness of an other—unless he empathically enters into the other's experience and observes as if from within, a process he calls "vicarious introspection" (Kohut, *How Does Analysis Cure?* 82).

As is characteristic of expressivists in general, Kohut insists that this knowing from within cannot be a purely cognitive process. A confluence of feeling and intellect is required if the observer is to bridge the gap separating him from the other, and to fully appreciate (or, in the case of therapy, to enhance) the essential unity of the other's existence. For this reason, Kohut criticizes the narrowness of the traditional psychoanalytic "commitment to truth" and to "the primacy of knowledge-expansion values."[44] In his view, the goals both of understanding and of curing the patient require the analyst to be "less reserved" and more "emotionally available," to "respond with deeply reverberating understanding and resonant emotionality" (Kohut, *How Does Analysis Cure?* 81–82).

Equal in importance to Kohut's emphasis on empathy is his reliance on organicist and developmental models. Thus, Kohut describes the development of personality as involving a "spontaneously unrolling sequence of transferences" or "the unrolling of a specific epigenetic sequence" of stages of selfhood. Like any biological organism, the Kohutian self supposedly "aims toward the realization of its own specific program of action."[45] And, as with any instance of organic growth, this most fundamental process cannot be understood solely through mechanistic causes operating from behind; a teleological element is clearly involved.[46] We can clarify this expressivist vision, and how it fundamentally differs from the autonomous one, if we consider one of Schafer's criticisms of Kohut.

Schafer has criticized Kohut for not sufficiently emphasizing the agency, responsibility, and unity of the analysand.[47] In his view, "mechanism lingers on" in several aspects of self psychology—such as in Kohut's tendency to reify the "self" by ascribing to it the independence of a drive or a propulsion, and in his tendency to forget the necessary unity of the person by speaking of autonomously acting subselves (such as the "grandiose self").[48] If, however, one bears in mind the organicism central to Kohut's perspective, one can readily understand why Kohut would not emphasize the kind of agency and responsibility implied in action language. After all, in sharp contrast with Schafer's Cartesianism, where the only alternatives are determinism or an at least *quasi*-volitional intentionality, Kohut's emphasis is on precisely those processes that dissolve this dualism: developmental processes that are purposive without necessarily being purposeful, where there is goal-directedness without conscious volition or the responsibility this would imply. It would obviously not be appropriate to speak of such developmental sequences as purposeful actions, to be explained by reference to "reasons" and as the products of a "unitary, fully responsible agent" (Schafer, *Analytic Attitude*, 246). But, to call this "mechanism," as Schafer does, quite misses the point, since it categorizes Kohut's approach in the terms of the dualism of an alien root metaphor—Cartesianism. In an expressivist-organicist universe such as Kohut's, the question of claiming or disclaiming responsibility for actions—Schafer's central issue—either dissolves as conceptually incoherent or recedes to become an issue of minor importance.

✦ ✦ ✦

It should not be thought, however, that Kohut's position is any less value-laden or moralizing than Schafer's. All world views have their ethical dimension, their own notion, explicit or implicit, of what is "normal," "healthy," or "good." In self psychology, however, such notions are not bound up with issues of responsibility and self-control but with the aspiration toward self-expression, toward the organic unfolding or actualization of the inner essence of the individual. The "good," we might say, is this inner essence itself, and anything that fosters its natural unfolding; the "bad" (or the "unnatural") is anything that halts or inhibits this spontaneous process.

Thus, whereas the implicit moralizing of Schafer seems to point a finger back at the self, in Kohut's case, as with all forms of expressivism, the finger of blame points outward, toward the family, the insensitive therapist, or other representatives of the social order. In Kohut's case, in fact, this blaming can be quite explicit and harsh. He indicts the social order for failing to provide "self-cohesion maintaining selfobjects"—that is, interpersonal experiences in which the inner life of the child is mirrored or otherwise responded to empathically.[49] Despite Kohut's idea that "optimal frustration" encourages the "transmuting internalizations" of progressively more mature self-objects, he directs his criticisms overwhelmingly against the dangers of frustration rather than those of overindulgence. Thus, Kohut chastizes therapists who show "even the faintest trace of disapproval" (*How Does Analysis Cure?* 176)—and not, of course, on the classical psychoanalytic grounds that they should be blank screens.

Kohut also criticizes a confrontative approach in psychotherapy as tending to be "trite, superfluous, and experienced as patronizing." In contrast with analysts like Otto Kernberg who would confront the "unrealistic" and exaggerated perceptions of the patient, Kohut claims to have found that the patient is generally right, and he states that one of his patients was correct to insist that Kohut, the therapist, "see things exclusively in *his* way and not at all in *my* way" (*How Does Analysis Cure?* 173, 93–94, 182). For self psychology, then, virtue resides not in "reality-principle morality" but in a biologistically conceived "nuclear self," an expressivist self oriented to the future and free to pursue its own creative aims, to fulfill the "nuclear program . . . determining [its] potential destiny."[50] This faith in the fundamental goodness and health of the nuclear self causes Kohut to reject all forms of manipulativeness in therapy, whether from within (by the patient's conscious design) or from without (by the therapist). In his view, central elements of therapy like transference and termination are "predetermined," and "correct psychoanalytic technique can do no more than allow it to evolve."[51] (The "normal," writes Kohut, is "that which functions according to its [own] design" [*How Does Analysis Cure?* 187].)

Kohut's expressivist biases are clearly evident in this faith in an inner self that seems able to do no wrong. He explicitly states that the productivity, fulfillment, or creativity of the "inner program . . . the pattern of the nuclear self" does "not refer primarily to the values of society."[52] We should not, therefore, be surprised to find Kohut taking as his paradigm of human fulfillment that standard expressivist ideal, the creative artist as conceived by the romantic tradition. By the end of the eighteenth century, the notion of art as essentially mimetic and communicative—a portrayal of external reality for an audience of like-minded individuals—had given way to a new conception; increasingly, art was seen as a form of *self*-expression, an actualization of the artist's inner world, which found its justification simply in manifesting itself, rather than through communication with an audience or through depiction of an outer world. Kohut's critique of Freud's conception of mental health relies on such standard expressivist ideals. And so, while allowing that psychotherapy may increase the capacity for the other-oriented and outer-directed commitments mentioned by Freud—"to love and to work"—Kohut believes that the more essential goal of psychotherapy should be "to establish one sector within the realm of the self through which an uninterrupted flow of the narcissistic strivings can proceed toward creative expression—however limited the social impact of the achievements of the personality might be and however insignificant the individual's creative activity might appear to others. Such a sector includes always a central pattern of exhibitionism and grandiose ambitions."[53]

✦   ✦   ✦

I mentioned above the criticism frequently directed at the autonomous form of modern humanism: its tendency to foster a separation from both inner and outer nature, to lead to what Taylor has described as "the sense of fragmentation within, and of exile in a dead, mechanical universe and society" (*Hegel*, 76). As we saw, Schafer's action language seems prone to these problematic consequences. What is perhaps not so obvious is the potential for a certain isolation of self inherent in the expressivist aspiration, a potential strongly felt by many in the romantic and post-romantic tradition of Western culture and which seems to be implicit in self psychology. (Erich Heller has described "the Romantic malady" as "a severance of mind from world, soul from circumstance, human inwardness from external condition."[54]) To understand this, we must recall that expressivist subjectivity is also self-defining; that, from the expressivist point of view, human fulfillment results from the actualization or expression of a potential that is inner and individual (Kohut's glorified "nuclear self," for example). Consequently, the meaning of the external world is, in a sense, determined by its relationship to this inner essence, which it must either echo or remain estranged from. I have already mentioned how, from the expressivist standpoint, the social world tends, because of its artificiality and its indifference, to be seen as alien from and in opposition to the self. This attitude is likely to be encouraged by self psychology's emphasis on the grievous consequences of the failure of self-objects and its implicit validating of a critical attitude toward the social world. It would seem that such a vision might foster and justify a sense of isolation from those aspects of the environment that fail to "mirror" the patient's inner life.

A common criticism of expressivism is that when this is not the case, when the external world is *not* felt to be somehow in opposition to the self, this is because its very externality or difference has in fact been effaced. Thus, expressivism has sometimes been seen as running a risk opposite to that of Cartesianism—as encouraging not a diremption but a too-easy fusion of the inner and outer or the mental and the physical. Many critics of nineteenth-century romanticism believed, for example, that the romantics had been too eager to overcome the cleavage between man and nature. According to these critics, this led the romantics to indulge the "pathetic fallacy," the naïve, facile, and uncritical "attributing [of] life, emotion and physiognomy to objects of the physical world"[55]—culminating in the loose sentimentality that the anti-romantic critic T. E. Hulme (1883–1917) once derided as "the state of slush in which we have the misfortune to live."[56] As a result, what seemed to be a communion with the external world was really only an illusory projection outward of the inner life, and a failure to grasp nature's reality and externality.

The negative side of this yearning for fusion between man and world was not just a certain scientific and moral weak-mindedness. What we might call an overemphasis on assimilation and neglect of accommodation also had the self-contradictory result of exaggerating one's sense of isolation. For, if the world was too readily humanized, its very otherness was being effaced—and therefore the self of romantic expressivism did not so much commune with the world as subsume it. Any feeling of connectedness would thus be little more than a disguised expression of that essential and all-encompassing inwardness often remarked in romanticism.

A similar overemphasis on assimilation at the expense of accommodation also seems characteristic of Kohut. Often, for example, he is concerned to defend and valorize early infantile states of fusion ("primary narcissism," in the psychoanalytic vocabulary) against those who would see such states as pathological or merely regressive. Thus, Kohut insists that the primal experience of oneness never really ceases, and that, far from being shameful, the yearning for the "old reassurance of a merger bond" or an "oceanic feeling and cosmic narcissism" are human universals and constants, and particularly salient in the glorified "creative" person.[57]

I would not question that Kohut's point is valid in many respects, and that it may serve as a useful corrective to the ego-psychological tendency to glorify separation and realism. But one must also recognize the dangers of this valorization of assimilation and fusion so reminiscent of the romantic rejection of Enlightenment objectivism and scientism. If accepted too uncritically, the insights of self psychology, like those of romanticism, run the risk of degenerating into a rather subjectivist and egocentric world view. For, it would seem that such a vision could easily foster a sense of isolation from those external objects that fail to mirror the inner life of the patient, while, at the same time, making those objects that *do* feel connected with the self seem, in a sense, to have lost their very quality of otherness (since they would be experienced *as* self-objects). One might say, then, that if the danger of action language is that it may entail a burdensome sense of isolation, responsibility, and arbitrariness, that of self psychology is to waver between two states: resentment of an indifferent outer world and a "pathetic" ignoring and assimilation of its Otherness.

Humanistic Psychoanalysis: Schafer and Kohut

The expressivist yearning for unity between the self and the natural world does place expressivism in conflict with radical autonomy, for the latter ideal aims to accentuate and valorize a fundamental distinction between human consciousness and the natural world. As we have seen, this opposition between expression and autonomy is reflected in the rather different conceptions of the goals and processes of psychotherapy espoused by Kohut and Schafer, as well as in the different dangers to which each system is prone.

It would, however, be a mistake to ignore the important ways in which the two projects are similar. After all, both Schafer and Kohut react profoundly against what they perceive to be the oppressive or devitalizing implications of a homogenizing mechanism or quasi-materialism that would deny to man his goal-directedness and his freedom—a position that both theorists associate with the reductionistic and reifying tendencies of classical psychoanalysis and Ego Psychology. Both men are uncomfortable with the postulating of elaborate metapsychological schemas onto which the lived events of the clinical encounter are mapped; and both reject or downplay the role of universal, instinctual forces (especially aggression) that might be seen as the external causes or primal sources of human experience and action. Both deemphasize extensive exploration of a deep and hidden unconscious or of a distant and presumably deterministic past in favor of experiences that are more present and more conscious—"experience-near" in Kohut's phrase. These similarities can be understood as manifestations of their shared commitment to the characteristically modern aspiration toward self-defining subjectivity—an aspiration that, as discussed above, conflicts not only with the (protomodern) mechanistic denial of the relevance or reality of meaning but also with the premodern locating of the source of meaning outside man.

Taylor has described this modern notion of selfhood as involving what he calls "radical reflexivity," a quasi-solipsistic stress on the first-person perspective, on the importance of recognizing that *this* experience is *my* experience.[58] For Kohut, heir to the tradition of self-exploration and self-expression, this emphasis on the first-person quality of experience shows up largely in the importance accorded to the uniqueness and the innerness of experience. For Schafer, heir to the tradition of autonomy and self-control, the first-person quality involves not primarily innerness or uniqueness but rather agency—a sense of doing or having done.

The two theorists are alike in emphasizing the integrity or cohesiveness of the self, the importance of recognizing and fostering one's sense of the self's distinctness and inner unity. Both recommend what Jacques Derrida (an outspoken "post-structuralist" opponent of such a goal) has called "the self-presence of the present in the living present,"[59] a certain coinciding of the self *with* the self, through recognizing and heightening the sense of cohesiveness, of innerness, or of agency. The visions of self psychology and action language seem, then, to be congruent in their tendency to aggrandize the self at the expense of the world. For both schools, the correct attitude— and the one held out as a source of psychological health—directs attention inward, and not toward ideals, realities, or determinants outside the self.

This tendency is apparent in Schafer's frequent stressing of the subject's active participation in his "construing" of his world. Shafer writes that "more and more the alleged past must be experienced consciously [by the patient] as a mutual interpenetration of past and present," and that in psychotherapy "the time is always present. The event is always an ongoing dialogue."[60] Such an emphasis seems likely to subjectivize the sense of reality, both for the analyst or theorist and for the patient in treatment.

Similarly, Kohut's emphasis on "self-objects" encourages one to focus not on the world as it is "in itself," but insofar as it echos or mirrors the self. In interpreting dreams, for instance, Kohut advocates an approach that views dreams as being, in essence, symbols of self states.[61] The radical reflexivity of Kohut's vision of human nature is, however, most apparent in his central concept of empathy, which he variously defines as "vicarious *introspection*" and as "the recognition of the *self* in the other."[62] The essential inwardness of this conception of experience (of the experience one is attempting to grasp) is apparent if one contrasts it with the notion of "being-in-the-world" adopted by existential-phenomenological philosophers like Heidegger, Merleau-Ponty, and Sartre, who do *not* see experience as essentially introspective or self-directed. Sartre has described most vividly the outer-directed, object-intending phenomenological conception of human existence: "If *per impossibile,* you entered consciousness, you would be seized by a whirlwind and thrown outside near the tree in the dust for consciousness has no 'within.' "[63] One wonders whether the self-psychological conception of human existence could actually encourage a certain introversion: might a therapist who empathically hovers over experience, which he conceives as being essentially introspective, not be likely to increase rather than diminish the patient's sense of inwardness, uniqueness, and isolation?[64] The special qualities of both these "humanist" psychotherapies can, incidentally, be foregrounded by contrasting them with the modes of therapy prevalent in many non-Western cultures: for example, the duty-oriented and gratitude-inducing therapies of modern Japan; or the shamanistic treatments practiced (by all accounts, rather successfully) in the Amazon—where the patient's experience is assimilated to the preexistent and shared forms of myth, rather than having its uniqueness or innerness accentuated.[65]

One potential problem with the positions of both Schafer and Kohut is one that afflicts all modern variants of self-defining subjectivity: they can lead to an "unbearable lightness of being," a feeling of lacking any solid grounding in a larger, encompassing, and external world or in transcendent values. For, if one dispenses with, or deemphasizes, the past, the instincts, the unconscious, and the metapsychological apparatus—as do both Kohut and Schafer—what is there to motivate a therapeutic journey? If one no longer moves inward toward a metapsychological schema felt as real, nor backward toward a past felt as solid, nor downward toward the unconscious and the instincts, what is left as the goal of one's exploration? The danger of these psychotherapies, then, is that they will contribute to rather than help overcome the conditions so often depicted in contemporary fiction: the "breakdown of connection between the self and an engageable social milieu, the fading into each other of subjective perception and objective reality." In his book on recent fiction, John Aldridge describes how the "disappearance of all other modes of authoritative measure" beyond the self has left the artist "encapsulated in a bubble of self-awareness afloat in a void."[66] And what another critic has written of Rilke, Stevens, and Valery—three great poets of our age—could as well be said of these modernist psychologies from which all external reference points tend to fall away: "The most immediate datum of experience to be explored appears as an intransitive consciousness, unconcerned with outer objects except as counters in the game of positing the self."[67] One might say, then, that in psychologies like those of Kohut and Shafer, the shadow of the self has fallen on the world.

Subject-centeredness has also been criticized on other grounds: for encouraging a rapacious or possessive individualism and an attitude of selfishness and exploitation toward both the natural and social worlds.[68] It is easier to understand how this could develop from the autonomous position, where, as we have seen, the yearning for absolute freedom sets the self up as against the external and physical world. On such a view, one's relation to the world might well seem to be deterministic or manipulative—as if one had to be either its slave or its master. The holistic emphasis of the expressivist position, on the other hand, might appear to discourage rampant individualism. It must not be forgotten, however, that expressivism is in fact no less subject-centered, that for it too the essential locus of value and meaning is in the self, not the ambient universe. The essential congruence of Kohut's position with the individualism of modern Western humanism emerges in his valorizing of narcissism (both "primary" and "secondary"), and even more clearly in his declaration that "we should not deny our ambitions, our wish to dominate, our wish to shine," and in his defense of the "current materialistic rationalism in Western Culture" for giving "freedom to the enhancement of the self" (as against the value systems of the Orient, which "extols altruism and concern for others and disparages egotism and concern for one's self").[69]

Still other critics of the humanist positions, most notably the French post-structuralists and their followers, have focused on the oppressive potential in the search for the "true self" and in the valorizing of unity and control as attributes of mature selfhood (e.g., Lacan, Foucault, Derrida, Deleuze and Guattari, Lyotard).[70] These critics argue that such a self is really only an illusion; and further, that such a search may actually be a ruse of power—a ruse that, in the guise of liberation, enjoins the person to impose upon himself a consistency that both belies and shackles the actual polymorphousness of human nature.

Thus both projects of self-defining subjectivity, which themselves arose in profound reaction against the oppressive or devitalizing implications of mechanism and materialism, have come in many quarters to be seen as an oppressive orthodoxy; and this has in turn given rise to schools of thought that seek to undercut self-defining subjectivity of both sorts. Despite their profound influence in Europe and in avant-garde thought generally, these *anti*-humanistic developments are not familiar to most American psychologists. I would like to conclude this archaeological tour of the psychodynamic avant-garde with brief discussions of two such thinkers. As we shall see, in both cases, their theories involve strong reactions *against* the devitalizing, burdensome, or isolative implications of the characteristically modern aggrandizement of the self; and, not surprisingly, each incurs problems rather different from those of humanism. One of these antihumanists is Jacques Lacan, the most important of the post-structuralist psychoanalysts, and a major influence on much "postmodernist" thought. The other, whom I shall consider first, is James Hillman, perhaps best described as a post-Jungian. Hillman adopts not a postmodernist but a primitivist vision of the no-self doctrine, calling for a return to a polytheistic and pagan concept of the psyche—or better, of the soul.

Hillman's "Archetypal Psychology"

Hillman's most important book, *Re-Visioning Psychology*, begins with an attack on the separation of subjectivity and matter characteristic of the modern world view.[71] This is one source of the affinity he feels between his own work and that of counter-Enlightenment, romantic, and post-romantic figures like Vico, Schelling, Coleridge, and Dilthey—all of whom also rejected Enlightenment rationalism and dualism. It would, however, be wrong to consider Hillman an expressivist; his position is actually more congruent with the world view that preceded the seventeenth century's scientific revolution. Hillman explicitly associates himself with certain classical, medieval, and early Renaissance thinkers—for example, Plato, Plotinus, and Ficino—and his psychology calls for the emergence of the Renaissance man who lives with us still, in our dreams. Hillman's "Archetypal Psychology" is, as he says, *not* a humanism,[72] and his perspective is antithetical to the positions of Schafer and Kohut—those champions of the unitary, self-defining subject who seeks the source of meaning within.

In Hillman's view, the true basis of human fulfillment is not self-expression or autonomy, but the suppressed yet ever-present yearning outwards toward a disparate assortment of personifications felt as external. He quotes the third-century (A.D.) philosopher Plotinus, the greatest of the neoplatonists, who thought that "those ancient sages, who sought to secure the presence of divine beings by the erection of shrines and statues, showed insight into the nature of the All" (Hillman, *Re-Visioning Psychology*, 14). He believes that what modern man needs is not a liberation *from* graven images and toward the self-presence of radical reflexivity, but the provision of a richer and more vital pantheon in which to lose himself. One might say, in fact, that for Hillman iconoclasm is the height of oppression. "Iconoclasm" here should, of course, be taken in the literal sense—as the breaking of those idols of the mind, the reified paraphernalia of metapsychology found so offensive by Schafer and Kohut, those champions of the "experience-near."

For this reason, the very elements of traditional psychoanalysis that most offend a critic like Schafer are precisely its strength to Hillman. In his view, all psychology is inevitably and appropriately driven by the "will to believe"—"sexuality," "humanism," and "self" are idols like any others. Further, the problem of modern man is that he gives too little, not too much credence to images. What is needed is not, however, the "abstract, quantitative, and topographical concepts" of objectivist or mechanistic psychology, but "an inscape of personified images," a "fostering of images" for the "portions and phases" of a soul in touch with its own disparateness. Therefore, for Hillman, unlike for Schafer, Freud was declaring a strength, not admitting a weakness, when he wrote that "the theory of instincts is, as it were, our mythology. The instincts are mythical beings, superb in their indefiniteness." Hillman praises those independently operating personifications and reifications of traditional psychoanalytic metapsychology: "the Censor, the Superego, the Primal Horde and the Primal Scene" as well as libido and thanatos, projection, sublimation, and condensation—notions that, for him, have the pleasing ring of Greek mythology and medieval alchemy (*Re-Visioning Psychology*, 228, 37, 19, 23, 225; Freud quoted at 19, 17–19). In a display of his powerful if rather purplish prose, Hillman calls for "a pantheism rekindled by the psyche's belief in its personified images . . . space to receive the mass immigration, the resurrection of the repressed, as the Angels and Archons, Daemons and Nymphs, Powers and Substances, Virtues and Vices, released from the mental reservations that restrain such primitivenesses and from the conceptual prisons of small-letter descriptions, now return to enter again into the commerce of our daily lives" (*Re-Visioning Psychology*, 39).

In sharp contrast with Schafer's action-language emphasis on "owning" one's experiences, Hillman says that the "autonomy of fantasy is the soul's last refuge of dignity, its guarantor against all oppressions. . . . If we are willing to accept internal controls upon the imagination, we will have succumbed already in soul to the same authoritarianism that would dominate the body politic" (*Re-Visioning Psychology*, 39).

Hillman might seem somewhat closer to Kohut the expressivist, since, for both these writers, the unconscious has its own telos, which must be respected and given free rein. The crucial difference is that, in Hillman's conception, this telos is not unitary; nor is it some unique or inner process that belongs to *me*. ("[T]his meness is not mine," he writes [*Re-Visioning Psychology*, 49].) Hillman emphasizes, in fact, that the very feeling of individuality is an illusion, the deceiving precipitate of archetypal experiences of "anima" and "soul" (the "personalistic fallacy"). For this reason, he recommends something every different from Kohutian empathy, a technique closer to the shaman's listening through a veil of mythic, transpersonal meaning: "You have to listen for what's going on with an ear that is *not* attuned to the same wavelength as the patient's story. There's a jarring, a discomfort. It's not supportive understanding and sympathetic being in tune. It's more a curious hearing things differently."[73]

It is hard to imagine a more eloquent spokesman for this premodern perspective. But, much as one may admire Hillman's attempt, it must be admitted that his Dionysian flight from modern alienation is, in a way, as unbalanced as Kohut's and Schafer's exaggerated humanism—though the risks it poses are rather different. One danger—difficult to deny given the twentieth century's disastrous experiences with irrationalist ideologies—is that such a perspective can turn into an uncontrolled, destructive, and perhaps authoritarian irrationalism.

The other, rather different flaw in Hillman's approach is one that is likely to keep it from ever taking hold. Archetypal Psychology ultimately founders on the same contradictions as afflict any attempt to foster a religious or magical world view in the modern age of skepticism, scientism, and psychologism. Traditional religious belief does provide a "sacred canopy" of transcendent meanings;[74] but the orienting and protective effect depends on the sense that this "canopy" is a larger, objective reality that preexists and encompasses man, rather than being constituted *by* man and *for* his convenience. Unlike the world views of Schafer and Kohut—Cartesianism and organicism—the essential animism of Hillman's Archetypal Psychology blatantly contradicts contemporary scientific assumptions about both mind and world, and therefore is unlikely to elicit belief, at least among more sophisticated people. Hillman tries to finesse this issue by arguing that explicit *cognitive* belief in his God and Daemons is not required; that it is sufficient if one is *"sensing the soul in the world . . . feeling* the world as personified, as emotional."[75] But, of course, this argument won't do, since modern man is, if anything, even more cut off from this kind of natural, taken-for-granted embeddedness in an animistic world. In a phrase referring to another manifestation of modern primitivism and irrationalism, the poet and critic William Empson perfectly captured this ineluctable dilemma of a modern skeptical mind—namely, the ineffectuality of beliefs that are adopted, always with a certain self-consciousness, for the pragmatic or esthetic purpose they may serve: How can one believe, he asked, referring to Surrealism, "in a nightmare handy as a bike?"[76]

Lacan's Post-Structuralism

The other champion of an antihumanist and Dionysian alternative to self-defining subjectivity, Jacques Lacan, manages to evade this problem of disbelief (though at the expense of other dilemmas no less severe, as we shall see). Unlike Hillman's Archetypal Psychology, Lacan offers not a primitivist but a modernist, or better, a postmodernist alternative. Thus, on the one hand, both his position and his literary style encourage a certain voguish skepticism about truth and reality—leaving the impression that it would be either gauche or naïve to demand a clear or testable account of his views. On the other hand, however, Lacan founds his argument on a rather dogmatic acceptance of a quasi-metaphysical system, the "structuralism" derived from modern linguistics.[77]

It is often forgotten that Lacan was originally a member of the surrealist circle, publishing his first articles in their journal *Minotaure*. As we shall see, his aspirations remained much the same as those of the surrealists. It seems, however, that Lacan sensed the fatal flaw of surrealist irrationalism, for he developed his own irrationalism on the basis of more up-to-date, "scientific" principles. Lacan did not see the unconscious as a cauldron bubbling with archaic fears and desires, nor as a theatre of personified images; he conceived it in the terms of contemporary semiotics, as the crossing-place of vast formal systems. In contrast with Hillman's animism and polytheism, as well as with the primitivism of the surrealists (who were fascinated by alchemy, magic, and "savage" culture, and sought a lost "language of innocence, a renewal of the primordial pact"[78]), Lacan's belief-system is at least superficially consistent with the scientific or scientistic assumptions of modern culture, and is not, therefore, liable to provoke skepticism for being a merely "convenient" belief.

There are two crucial aspects of Lacan's byzantine complex of theories that must be considered. The first, that pertaining to what he calls the "Mirror Stage" and "The Imaginary," is, from our point of view, a negative argument, a way of accounting for the *illusion* of controlled, integral selfhood. The second, concerning "The Symbolic," concerns Lacan's positive, if rather paradoxical, account of the true nature of selfhood (or the lack thereof).[79]

According to Lacan's notion of the Mirror Stage, there is a moment or period of development when the young child, first recognizing himself in the mirror, is thrilled to identify with an image of what looks to be an integral and controlled person. As Lacan conceives it, the infant at this stage (somewhere between the eighth and eighteenth month) does not yet have actual control over its own actions, or an actual sense of the unity of its own sensations: it is still "sunk in motor incapacity, turbulent movements, and fragmentation"—still experiencing what he calls the *corps morcele* (the body-in-parts).[80] Precisely for this reason, the infant is, as it were, seduced into an illusory identification with its own reflection, for only there does it glimpse a unity that it cannot actually live. Lacan sees this moment as the true source of the sense of the unified, authentic self so often glorified by humanistic psychologies and sought by individuals in Western culture. But the ironic truth this Lacanian fable is meant to teach is that the "true self" is both false and inauthentic; not only does the illusion of integral selfhood originate in a masking of an actual fragmentation (the *corps morcele*), it does so by means of a certain *alienation:* for, the source of a sense of self is, after all, a mirrored image at a distance, a being who stands outside the self, like an Other (as a *moi,* not a *je;* self-as-object rather than self-as-subject). According to Lacan, integral selfhood is, therefore, founded on both alienation and illusion: "the assumption of the armour of an alienating identity, which will mask with its rigid structure the subject's entire mental development" (*Ecrits*, 4).

The second crucial element of Lacan's theory is his notion of "The Symbolic"—the phase of development (and later, the mode of being) which the child enters on becoming capable of using language, of accepting and participating in the semiotic system that determines human experience and society by means of its invisible laws. What Octavio Paz has said of modern poetry applies perfectly to Lacan (as well as capturing the difference between him and Hillman): "Language now occupies the place once occupied by the gods or some other external entity or outward reality."[81] Thus Lacan, like most structuralists and post-structuralists, imagines language as a preexisting structure of intersystemic rules so constraining that they deny to the speaker any possibility of freedom or originality, and to the discourse any possibility of reference to a world beyond the system. Language on this account is a kind of Prime Mover or Uncaused Cause—a self-referential, self-generated system that must no longer be seen as man's instrument but as the source and limit of his consciousness. This can best be grasped if we consider Lacan's account of how language creates the (in a sense, illusory) feeling of being a *subject* of experience.

As Lacan describes it, the sense of being an active subject of experience is bound up with, and fundamentally dependent on, the use of the word *I.*[82] But, just as the word *I* (known in linguistics as a "shifter") belongs to no one, and moves about among the participants in a conversation, so, in a sense, the feeling of being a self-as-subject is not a transcendent quality that inheres in a person, but a fleetingly elusive and merely "grammatical" reality (an "effect of the signifier")—a reality that, as it were, precipitates out of the conversation in this spot or that, but lingering only for a moment before moving on to the next speaker. According to Lacan, then, the sense of being a controlling center of consciousness or a unified source of causal efficacy is an effect of language, one that, paradoxically enough, can only be experienced if one lets oneself be taken over by this preexisting, transcendent transpersonal system: "I identify myself in language, but only by losing myself in it like an object" (*Ecrits*, 86). And so, just as the irony of the *moi* is that it is born in the self-alienation of visual reflection (in "The Imaginary"), that of the *je* is that it requires one to *lose* oneself in something quite impersonal, the larger system of language. It follows that the only kind of freedom that reigns in "The Symbolic" (the realm of the subject, the *je*) is the somewhat paradoxical freedom of automaticity emphasized by the surrealists—freedom not as a (Kantian) seizing of responsibility and control or as the unfettered self-unfolding of expressivism, but as a giving oneself over to the larger systemic flows.

It seems, then, that the two great heresies of contemporary psychoanalysis, Kohut's American heresy and Lacan's continental one, are at polar extremes on the question of the self. For Lacan, the "Self" is the central illusion of "The Imaginary," poised as a fictive moment between the fragmentation of the *corps morcele* and the infinite elusion of "The Symbolic." In Lacan's view, "The ego is structured exactly like a symptom. Interior to the subject, it is only a privileged symptom. It is the human symptom *par excellence,* it is the mental malady of man."[83] From such a standpoint, self psychology and action language would be but the playing-out and reification of the delusion of the Mirror Phase—a form of experience that is also self-alienated, though without recognizing this fact at all. The humanistic therapies of Kohut and Schafer are, on this account, doomed to the continuing reification and petrification of this "privileged symptom"—and all this, ironically enough, under the guise of liberation and an overcoming of estrangement. From Lacan's standpoint, as from Hillman's, these psychoanalytic revisionists would, in fact, be the perpetrators of an even more extreme ego psychology—a psychology that, by jettisoning the mechanisms and anthropomorphisms of the "metapsychology" (with its warring part-selves and its cathexes colliding eerily in the dark) rejects all that would allow psychoanalysis to grasp the truly nonvolitional and nonunified aspects of human existence.

Lacan, who has said that he is not at all sure man even *has* an interior, is committed to overcoming the illusion of integral, controlled selfhood, to showing "the self's radical ex-centricity to itself" (*Ecrits,* 171). He interprets Freud's line, "Where id was, there ego shall be" (which he translates as "La ou c'etait il me faut advenir"),[84] not as meaning that the ego should replace the id (the standard reading), but that the ego should come to exist in the *realm* of the id—that it should shed the illusion of integral, controlled selfhood and dissolve into those associative chains normally repressed into the unconscious (and perhaps also into the fragmentary existence of the *corps morcele*). In espousing this vision of human nature, Lacan has stayed surprisingly close to his roots in surrealist irrationalism. For, it was Andre Breton, the high priest of surrealism, who believed that poetic practice demanded the surrender of the ego, and who, in 1928, declared the "crucial inadequacy . . . of any action which requires a continuous application and which can be premeditated" and celebrated the "great victory of the involuntary over the ravaged domain of conscious possibilities," over the "tremulous ennui" of normal consciousness.[85] Like Lacan, the surrealists believed that mind was, in a sense, *both* all-powerful *and* passive[86]—a view that obviously disrupts the accepted polarities of the Cartesian world view (and that conflicts with Schafer's view, as discussed above).

Lacan's borrowings from modern semiotics and linguistics do, however, give his psychology a somewhat different, and rather odd, flavor. Like that of many post-structuralists, his position has a quality that seems somewhat paradoxical in the context of the history of Western thought—what one might call a "high-tech irrationalism" or a "Dionysian mechanism." Such post-structuralists imagine the self as dissolving not into an animist demiurge or biological pulsation but into a quasi-linguistic labyrinth or a mechanical process: into the "host of networks and relations, of contradictory codes and interfering messages" of Jean-François Lyotard,[87] or the "desiring-machines" of Deleuze and Guattari—the tenor of whose influential book, *Anti-Oedipus*, can be gleaned from its first several lines: "It is at work everywhere, functioning smoothly at times, at other times in fits and starts. It breathes, it heats, it eats. It shits and fucks. What a mistake to have ever said *the* id. Everywhere *it* is machines—real ones not figurative ones: machines driving other machines, machines being driven by other machines, with all the necessary couplings and connections."[88]

This passage from Deleuze and Guattari (who, like Lyotard, have been deeply influenced by Lacan) brings out a somewhat surprising aspect of the post-structuralist perspective—the fact that it is, in certain respects, an application to the human domain of mechanistic or, at least, quasi-mechanistic metaphors.[89] I would argue, in fact, that, just as Hillman can be viewed as escaping modern humanism by returning to the "premodern" world view, Lacan can be seen as taking a position akin to the homogenizing mechanism of the "protomodern" era.

It is true that, in emphasizing language as the crucial locus or medium of human existence, Lacan opts for a middle realm, neither inner nor outer, neither spirit nor matter; in this sense, his position is unlike one that would assimilate mind *to* matter. Still, Lacan's opposition to any form of humanism is so intense that he ends up emphasizing only the automatic, deterministic aspects of language, as if language lived itself in man and the reverse were not at all true—and this *is* akin to a homogenizing mechanism.[90] I will leave aside the conceptual problems inherent in this sort of post-structuralism—for example, the unwarranted leap of reasoning from the *existence* of deep structures to the conclusion that *all* sense of conscious control is illusory or trivial. Let us instead consider some of the consequences such a world view is likely to have.

As with Hillman's system, there seems in Lacanian post-structuralism to be a disturbing potentiality for irrationality and authoritarianism—potentialities that, given the obscurantism and the autocratic ways that have characterized the Lacanian movement, seem already to have emerged.[91] A second problem is, in a way, the opposite of what we found in Hillman's primitivist psychology. It is not that a sophisticated modern cannot believe in Lacan's attempt to transcend the estrangement and isolation of modern humanism (witness the widespread popularity of Lacan and other forms of post-structuralism among intellectuals), but, rather, that his doctrines actually seem liable to *exacerbate* certain characteristic problems of modernity. For, Lacan's version of structualism would seem to offer at most a pyrrhic victory: if it overcomes the division between man and world, it does so by effacing both these poles, and thereby giving up most of the aspirations of the modern Western tradition. Instead of being reconciled, self and world simply disappear into the middle term, the language-like structures that replace these supposedly outmoded polarities. Thus, freedom and self-expression are given up since the volitional and individual self turns out to be an illusion, a deceiving epiphenomenon of "The Imaginary" and "The Symbolic";[92] truth is illusory, since there is no world but what the structures allow to appear; further, as we have seen, the unity that is achieved is a unity devoid of vitality—since it is that of a mechanical rather than organic system. And so, perhaps the most that such a perspective could promise is (to borrow Fredric Jameson's suggestion about postmodernism in general): not to overcome alienation but "to make ourselves at home in our alienated being."[93]

Conclusion

In concluding, let me consider a question that may have arisen for many readers. Given the different forms of excessive emphasis that characterize all avant-garde schools, one might well ask if psychoanalysis has a more balanced world view to offer—a psychological-philosophical vision that understands the roles of both freedom and constraint, and that leavens its inward focus with a sufficient appreciation of the necessary, and potentially salutary, role of external constraints and values.

Ironically enough, Freud in his own formulations may have come closer to achieving such a balance than have those successors who have tried to improve or modernize the theory by overcoming its inconsistencies. This seems to be implied by the thought of some philosophers (R. S. Peters and

Paul Ricoeur among them) who see the essential value and raison d'être of psychoanalysis as lying in the very fact that it is essentially a double discourse—the application to the human domain of two quite different forms of understanding, both of which are equally necessary and valid, even though they are mutually incompatible in a strict logical sense. For Ricoeur, these are the languages of hermeneutics and of energetics; for Peters, a philosopher in the Wittgensteinian tradition, these are the languages of reasons and of causes (the "purposive" and "mechanical" models).[94]

There seem to be two possible reactions to this realization of the simultaneous necessity and logical incompatibility of two perspectives. One reaction is to accept a contradictory discourse as the best possible alternative. Perhaps the essence of human understanding just *is* to compare the infinitely complex, multifaceted, and mysterious nature of reality to simplified, and therefore better understood, models or analogies.[95] Perhaps the best one can do is to recognize this propensity of the act of understanding even as one indulges it. Given such a view, the tendency to think in overly simplistic models—like pure causality and pure intentionality—is intrinsic to the human mind, something without which we would lapse into obscurity and confusion. Perhaps, then, the error to be avoided is not *using* such models, but losing sight of their metaphorical nature, or of the need to shift readily between them as necessary. On this view, Freud's switching between the languages of cause and of reason is not something to be deplored or overcome. The second alternative would be to attempt to develop a new vocabulary or mode of understanding that somehow manages to transcend the exaggerated and simplistic models. Such a route does not seem as yet to have been seriously pursued by psychoanalysts (with the possible exception of George Politzer, the teacher of Merleau-Ponty and Sartre who was killed during World War II).[96]

The first position seems consistent with the approach of the philosopher Wittgenstein—that archenemy of all "metaphysical" thinking who wrote that "ordinary language is all right," so long as one doesn't take its (often contradictory and overly simple) metaphors too literally.[97] The second is closer to the thought of Martin Heidegger, that other seminal philosopher of the twentieth century who attempted, at the inevitable risk of obscurity and incomprehensibility, to transcend standard conceptual structures and develop a new vocabulary that avoids the all-too-familiar polarities that have informed Western thought for centuries (e.g., inner versus outer, freedom versus determinism, or body versus soul).[98] Here I can do no more than mention these alternatives: to consider in any detail a Wittgensteinian or Heideggerian approach to the self is, of course, far beyond the scope of the present essay.[99]

NOTES

I would like to thank Shira Nayman, James Walkup, and Fred Wertz for their comments on earlier versions of this essay which appeared in *Social Research* 55 (Winter
1988): 551–607.

In this essay, I often use "Man" to refer to human beings in general. Given the
nature of my subject matter—the history of ideas—I decided to adopt this usage to
avoid confusion when citing examples from the philosophical traditions I summarize.

1. The following are some examples of the trend in psychology: Ruben Fine,
Narcissism, the Self, and Society (New York: Columbia University Press, 1986); K. J.
Gergen, "Theory of the Self: Impasse and Evolution," in *Advances in Experimental
Social Psychology, Theorizing in Social Psychology*: Special Topics, vol. 17, ed. Leonard
Berkowitz (New York: Academic Press, 1984), 49–115; K. J. Gergen and K. E.
Davis, eds., *The Social Construction of the Person* (New York: Springer Verlag, 1985);
and Roy F. Baumeister, ed., *Public Self and Private Self* (New York: Springer
Verlag, 1986). For examples from outside psychology, see James Walkup and Arien
Mack, eds., *Social Research* 54 (1987), "Special Issue: Reflections on the Self"; T. C.
Heller, Morton Sosna, and D. E. Wellbery, eds., *Reconstructing Individualism: Auton-
omy, Individuality, and the Self in Western Thought* (Stanford: Stanford University
Press, 1986); Richard Schweder and Robert LeVine, eds., *Culture Theory: Essays on
Mind, Self, and Emotion* (Cambridge: Cambridge University Press, 1984); Paul
Heelas and Andrew Lock, *Indigenous Psychologies: Anthropology of the Self* (New
York: Academic Press, 1981); Marshall Berman, *The Politics of Authenticity: Radical
Individualism and the Emergence of Modern Society* (New York: Atheneum, 1980);
Stephen Greenblatt, *Renaissance Self-Fashioning* (Chicago: University of Chicago
Press, 1980); Richard Sennett, *The Fall of Public Man* (New York: Vintage Books,
1978); and Theodore Mischel, ed., *The Self: Psychological and Philosophical Issues*
(Totowa, N. J.: Rowman & Littlefield, 1977).

2. On the prominence of "self disorders," see Christopher Lasch, *The Culture of
Narcissism* (New York: W. W. Norton, 1979); and Alice Miller, *Prisoners of Childhood*
(New York: Basic Books, 1981; reprinted as *The Drama of the Gifted Child* New
York: Basic Books, 1981). On recent fiction, see Linda Hutcheon, *Narcissistic Nar-
rative: The Metafictional Paradox* (New York: Methuen, 1984); and Patricia
Waugh, *Metafiction: The Theory and Practice of Self-Conscious Fiction* (New York:
Methuen, 1984).

3. Very recently, however, "the self" seems to be making a comeback in French
intellectual circles—see "La grande lessive: Ou en sont nos intellectuels?" *Le nouvel
observateur* 13–19 June 1986, 112–126.

4. On the notion of "root metaphors," see Stephen Pepper, *World Hypotheses*
(Berkeley and Los Angeles: University of California Press, 1942).

5. See Sigmund Koch, "Afterword," in *A Century of Psychology as a Science,* ed.
Sigmund Koch and D. E. Leary (New York: McGraw-Hill, 1985), 944–945. On the
"postpositivist spirit" in psychology, see Uri Bronfenbrenner, Frank Kessel,
William Kessen, and Sheldon White, "Toward a Critical Social History of Developmental Psychology," *American Psychologist* 41 (1986): 1218–1230; and Marx
Wartofsky, "The Child's Construction of the World and the World's Construction
of the Child: From Historical Epistemology to Historical Psychology," in *The Child
and Other Cultural Inventions,* ed. F. S. Kessel and A. W. Siegel (New York: Praeger,
1983).

6. Michel Foucault, *Discipline and Punish: The Birth of the Prison* (New York: Vintage Books, 1979), 31. Also see Foucault, *The Order of Things: An Archaeology of the Human Sciences* (New York: Random House, 1970). I am obviously not doing precisely what Foucault means by "archaeology" or "genealogy." Foucault contrasts both these methods with more traditional studies of the history of ideas, to which my approach in this essay is in fact closer, though the greater concern with implicit or hidden assumptions and with unrecognized affinities between thinkers may bring it somewhat closer to Foucault's "archaeology."

7. Quoted in Martin Jay, "In the Empire of the Gaze," in *Postmodernism*, ed. Lisa Appignanesi, ICA Documents, vol. 4 (London: Institute of Contemporary Arts, 1986), 25.

8. Lionel Trilling, *Sincerity and Authenticity* (Cambridge, Mass.: Harvard University Press, 1971), 1.

9. Charles Taylor, *Hegel* (Cambridge: Cambridge University Press, 1975), especially 3–126. Henceforth cited by title in both text and notes.

10. Alexandre Koyre, *From the Closed World to the Infinite Universe* (Baltimore: Johns Hopkins University Press, 1957), 2. Also see A. O. Lovejoy, *The Great Chain of Being* (Cambridge: Harvard University Press, 1936).

11. Koyre, *From the Closed World*, 2.

12. Intellectual historians have dated the origins of the "modern" era in a number of different ways. I use the terms "modern," "protomodern," and "premodern" only as heuristically useful labels for an otherwise confusing progression of ideas.

13. Taylor, *Hegel*, 7. See Foucault, *Order of Things*, for another description of the epistemic and cosmological shift from the Aristotelian to the mechanistic view, and also for discussion of the inherent contradictions of modern notions concerning "Man."

14. Isaiah Berlin, "The Counter-Enlightenment," in *Dictionary of the History of Ideas*, ed. Philip Wiener (New York: Charles Scribner's Sons, 1973), 107.

15. See Robert N. Bellah, Richard Madsen, William Sullivan, Ann Swidler, and Steven M. Tipton, *Habits of the Heart: Individualism and Commitment in American Life* (Berkeley and Los Angeles: University of California Press, 1985).

16. Thus Coleridge wrote that the objective of his philosophy was to substitute "life and intelligence . . . for the philosophy of mechanism, which, in everything that is most worthy of the human intellect, strikes *Death*" (quoted in M. H. Abrams, *The Mirror and the Lamp: Romantic Theory and the Critical Tradition* [New York: W. W. Norton, 1958], 65).

17. See Abrams, *Mirror and Lamp*, 204–208; Pepper, *World Hypotheses*, 280–316.

18. One of the clearest expressions of this vision of essential unity between man and nature, consciousness and matter, is contained in Henri Bergson's comment on the phenomenon of habit: "Now, our inner experience shows us in habit an activity which has passed, by imperceptible degrees, from consciousness to unconsciousness and from will to automatism. Should we not then imagine nature, in this form, as an obscured consciousness and a dormant will? Habit thus gives us the living demonstration of this truth, that mechanism is not sufficient to itself: it is, so to speak, only the fossilized residue of a spiritual activity" (quoted in Heller, Sosna, and Wellbery, *Reconstructing Individualism*, 6).

19. In a recent article, Taylor associates this project with the counter-Enlightenment essayist Montaigne, who was a major influence on the Western tradition of autobiography. See Charles Taylor, *The Moral Topography of the Self,*" in *Hermeneutics and*

Psychological Theory, ed. Stanley Messer, Louis A. Sass, and Robert Woolfolk (New Brunswick: Rutgers University Press, 1988), 298–320.

20. Cf., Abrams, *Mirror and Lamp*; Taylor, *Hegel*, 21.

21. Roy Schafer, *The Analytic Attitude* (New York: Basic Books, 1983), 246. Henceforth cited as *Analytic Attitude* in both text and note.

22. Roy Schafer, *A New Language for Psychoanalysis* (New Haven: Yale University Press, 1976), 8, 139 (henceforth cited as *New Language* in both text and notes); *Narrative Actions in Psychoanalysis* (Worcester, Mass.: Clark University Press, 1980), 4; and *New Language*, 208.

23. Schafer, *New Language*, 117. Also see Schafer, *Analytic Attitude*, 234; Paul Ricoeur, *Freud and Philosophy* (New Haven: Yale University Press, 1970); and R. S. Peters, *The Concept of Motivation* (New York: Humanities Press, 1958).

24. Schafer, *Narrative Actions*, 4; *Language and Insight* (New Haven: Yale University Press, 1978), 197; and *Analytic Attitude*, 89.

25. Schafer, *Analytic Attitude*, 99–100. Thus Schafer reasons from the premise that "strictly speaking, there are no phenomena accessible to us in which the subject has not already played a part" to the conclusion that "every action must be located within the realm of reasons" (*New Language*, 201, 207), and from the "recognition that bodily categorizations play a great part in the child's construction" of situations to the conclusion that "a situation corresponds to an action" and indicates that one "author[s] one's own life" (*Analytic Attitude*, 100). Incidentally, this kind of reasoning belies Schafer's occasional claims that action language "does not exclude necessity" in the human domain (*Analytic Attitude*, 84).

26. Schafer, *New Language*, 153; *Analytic Attitude*, 107. Also cf. *Analytic Attitude*, 233.

27. As Schafer realizes, such an argument is reminiscent of Sartrian existentialism, with its radically dualistic ontology and its emphasis on the absolute freedom of human consciousness (*New Language*, 8, 153). But, as Sartre himself came to realize, such a view is seriously one-sided since it fails to grasp the ways in which consciousness itself is, if not determined, at least profoundly influenced by factors beyond its own ken—cf., the summary in R. D. Laing and David Cooper, *Reason and Violence* (New York: Vintage Books, 1971).

28. Schafer does admit that there are circumstances where the action concept does not apply: e.g., severe brain damage and early infancy (*Analytic Attitude*, 84, 99, 112). This does not, however, mitigate his essential dualism, since he treats these conditions, where determinism applies, as existing on the other side of an ontological divide. They do not make him question the applicability of his action concept to the rest of human experience and behavior.

29. Schafer, *Narrative Actions*, 35; *Analytic Attitude*, 212, 268, 277. Also see Roy Schafer, "Narration in the Psychoanalytic Dialogue," in *On Narrative* ed. W. J. Thomas Mitchell (Chicago: University of Chicago Press, 1980).

30. Schafer, *New Language*, 146; "Narration in the Psychoanalytic Dialogue," 44; and *Analytic Attitude*, 243, 93. This is apparent in the following passage where Schafer criticizes the (metapsychological) statement "He can't control his sexual drive": "We must appreciate that 'can't' is a hypothetical inability-word that is often used carelessly or defensively in place of the more exact and simply descriptive words 'don't' and sometimes 'won't'. . . . The idea that one is powerless is a common variation of the inexact word 'can't'" (*New Language*, 208). It should be obvious that for Schafer to assert that "won't" is more exact and descriptive, and less

hypothetical, than "can't" amounts to saying that the former, intentional statement is the more correct or true.

31. Schafer, *Narrative Actions in Psychoanalysis*, 34, 35; *Analytic Attitude*, 250–251.

32. In recent writing, Schafer claims that he never intended to prescribe action language as something to be used "explicitly and consistently in the clinical dialogue" ("A Response to Meares," *Contemporary Psychoanalysis* 21 [1985]: 445–448). Rather, he says, action language is meant to provide only a "theoretical language." Actually, his writings do imply that the therapist should use action language whenever possible: "When we make optimal interpretations, we avoid any suggestion that we are speaking of happenings in the mind. . . . Rather . . . we want to refer . . . to the analysand's being engaged in . . . actions" (*Analytic Attitude*, 93). Also, Schafer does claim that it is an empirical fact that, as patients improve, they begin to speak of their lives in ways that claim action.

33. Schafer, *Narrative Actions in Psychoanalysis*, 4.

34. Such patients, who often have significant "schizoid" traits, may need to feel that their experiences are grounded in something more substantial than their own choices or whims; contrary to Schafer's general recommendation, they hardly need to recognize even their emotions as being "actions" in Schafer's sense (*Analytic Attitude*, 102). Such a therapeutic approach would run into the problem described by Johnson: "The alienated person has already 'solved' the problem of subject-object relatedness by reducing everything to a fusion of subject and object within himself. Regrettably, an existentialist procedure which reinforces this solution only leads to the reification of separateness, despair and hopelessness" (Frank Johnson, "The Existential Psychotherapy of Alienated Persons," in *The Narcissistic Condition*, ed. M. C. Nelson [New York: Human Sciences Press, 1977], 149). Also see Heidegger's essay, "The Age of World View," which argues that this subjectivization of reality is one of the most pervasive and problematic themes of modern culture (in Martin Heidegger, *The Question concerning Technology and Other Essays*, trans. William Lovitt [New York: Harper & Row. 1971]).

35. Despite Schafer's claims (in *New Language* and *Analytic Attitude*) of a deep affinity with the thought of the later Wittgenstein, both Schafer's implicit Cartesianism and the one-sidedness of his action language set him apart from this antimetaphysical philosopher. For an excellent discussion of this point, see Russell Meares, "Metaphor and Reality: A Response to Roy Schafer," *Contemporary Psychoanalysis* 21 (1985): 425–448; and also Schafer's wholly inadequate reply, "A Response to Meares."

36. See Donald Spence, "On Some Clinical Implications of Action Language," *Journal of the American Psychoanalytic Association* 30 (1982): 169–184. Also see W. W. Meissner, "Critique of Concepts and Therapy in the Action Language Approach to Psychoanalysis," *International Journal of Psychoanalysis* 60 (1979): 291–310.

37. *New Language*, 146; *Language and Insight*, 199.

38. Schafer tries to save his system from the accusation that it makes no place for healthy passivity by saying that passivity, when healthy, is also chosen and felt as chosen. But isn't it equally important to acknowledge that activity should, in a way, be felt as passive, that healthy activity often just seems, as it were, to happen, rather than to be willed? On this point, see William James's famous discussion of willing oneself to get out of bed in *Principles of Psychology* (New York: Henry Holt, 1890), 524; and also Maurice Merleau-Ponty's penetrating critique of the notion of freedom in *The Phenomenology of Perception* (London: Routledge & Kegan Paul, 1962), 434–456. In an attempt to capture this truth about human existence, the hermeneutic phi-

losopher Hans-Georg Gadamer, a disciple of Heidegger, uses the image of being caught up in and, in a sense, controlled by, a game that one plays (*Truth and Method* [New York: Crossroad, 1984], 91–98).

39. Hegel's phrases are quoted in Trilling, *Sincerity and Authenticity*, 45; also see 26–53.

40. Taylor, "The Moral Topography of the Self."

41. Heinz Kohut's most important works are *The Analysis of the Self* (New York: International Universities Press, 1971); *The Restoration of the Self* (New York: International Universities Press, 1977); and *How Does Analysis Cure?* (Chicago: University of Chicago Press, 1984) (henceforth cited by title in text and notes).

42. Kohut, *Restoration*, xiii; *How Does Analysis Cure?* 174; and *Restoration*, 67. Kohut quotes a letter to Ludwig Binswanger in which Freud wrote that "consciousness is after all only a sensory organ"—a statement which Kohut sees as "the statement of the man who has become all vision and vision-explaining thought . . . of the man of clear-eyed empirical observation whose mental processes are engaged in the service of his proud realism" (*Restoration*, 66, 67).

43. See Berlin, "The Counter-Enlightenment"; also Abrams, *Mirror and Lamp*.

44. Kohut, *Restoration*, 65, 66.

45. Kohut, *How Does Analysis Cure?* 6; *Restoration* 35; and Heinz Kohut and E. S. Wolf, "The Disorders of the Self and their Treatment," *International Journal of Psychoanalysis* 59 (1978): 414.

46. Kohut contrasts Self Psychology with classical psychoanalysis on this issue of a teleological emphasis: "Classical psychoanalysis discovered the despair of the child in the depth of the adult . . . self psychology has discovered the despair of the adult in the depth of the child—the actuality of the future. The child whose self is stunted by the selfobject's failure is, in his depression, mourning an unlived, unfulfilled future" (*Self Psychology and the Humanities* [New York: W. W. Norton, 1985], 74–75).

47. Roy Schafer, "Action Language and the Psychology of the Self," *Annual of Psychoanalysis* 8 (1980); 86, 90.

48. Incidentally, Schafer ("Action Language and the Psychology of the Self") says that this lingering "mechanism" keeps Kohut from attaining his own goal of being truly "experience-near"; here Schafer seems to assume that action descriptions more accurately capture the feel of lived experience, as if experience were generally felt as intentional; however, when faced with the fact that, in everyday life, people often spontaneously describe themselves in ways that disclaim action (*Analytic Attitude*, 92), Schafer takes the position that we should *not* feel any obligation "to use unsystematically the terms of experience to explain experience"; rather, he claims, one should opt for an action-language description, which, supposedly, is more valid than the person's own spontaneous self-description. Here we clearly see Schafer's metaphysical biases overriding his phenomenological predilections.

49. See Robert Ehrlich, "The Social Dimensions of Heinz Kohut's Psychology of the Self," *Psychoanalysis and Contemporary Thought* 8 (1985): 346.

50. Heinz Kohut, "Reflections on Advances in Self Psychology," in *Advances in Self Psychology*, ed. Arnold Goldberg (New York: International Universities Press, 1980), 543. Also see Ehrlich, "The Social Dimensions," 334, 337.

51. Kohut, *Restoration*, 49. Several aspects of Kohut's expressivism are evident in his defense of "action-thought," activities which more traditional analysts would see as mere "acting-out"—as ways of "regressing" to motor activity in an attempt to avoid the insight that, for them, is the true source of a cure. In Kohut's view, such actions "are not regressive steps; they constitute a not-quite-but-almost-completed

forward movement" (*Restoration*, 37). Kohut's position on this issue illustrates his expressivist faith in the spontaneous processes of the self; also it represents a refusal to valorize consciousness as against physical activity, which is typical of the Cartesian-Kantian position.

52. Kohut, *Self Psychology and the Humanities*, 75.

53. Kohut, *Restoration*, 54. Morris Eagle has remarked on Kohut's abiding "interest in geniuses and the 'great man'" (*Recent Developments in Psychoanalysis* [New York: McGraw-Hill, 1984], 48).

54. Erich Heller, *The Artist's Journey into the Interior and Other Essays* (New York: Harcourt Brace Jovanovich, 1976), 103.

55. Abrams, *Mirror and Lamp*, 291.

56. Hulme quoted in W. J. Bate, ed., *Criticism: The Major Texts* (New York: Harcourt, Brace, and World, 1952), 560.

57. Douglas Kirsner, "Self Psychology and the Psychoanalytic Movement: An Interview with Dr. Heinz Kohut," *Psychoanalysis and Contemporary Thought* 5 (1982): 491; Heinz Kohut, *How Does Analysis Cure?* 191; and "Forms and Transformations of Narcissism," *Journal of the American Psychoanalytic Association* 14 (1966): 266.

58. Taylor, "The Moral Topography of the Self."

59. Jacques Derrida, *Speech and Phenomena and Other Essays on Husserl's Theory of Signs* trans. David Allison, (Evanston, Ill.: Northwestern University Press, 1973), 9.

60. Schafer, "Narration in the Psychoanalytic Dialogue," 32, 49.

61. Kirsner, "Interview with Kohut," 487.

62. Kohut, *How Does Analysis Cure?* 82; and "The Psychoanalyst in the Community of Scholars," *Annual of Psychoanalysis* 3 (1975): 355.

63. Jean-Paul Sartre, "A Fundamental Idea of the Phenomenology of Husserl: Intentionality," in *Situations, I* (Paris: Gallimard, 1947), 32–33 (translated by R. A. Cobb, York University Philosophy Dept., mimeographed).

64. Another possible problem with the modern emphasis on radical reflexivity is captured by Nietzsche in *Twilight of the Idols*: "Experience as the *wish* to experience does not succeed. One *must* not eye oneself while having an experience: else the eye becomes an evil eye" (*The Portable Nietzsche*, ed. Walter Kaufman [New York: Penguin Books, 1977], 517).

65. D. K. Reynolds, *Naikan Psychotherapy* (Chicago: University of Chicago Press, 1983); and Claude Lévi-Strauss, "The Effectiveness of Symbols," in *Structural Anthropology* (Garden City, N. Y.: Doubleday, 1967), 181–201.

66. Quoted in Christopher Lasch, *The Minimal Self: Psychic Survival in Troubled Times* (New York: W. W. Norton, 1984), 158.

67. Ellman Crasnow, "Poems and Fictions: Stevens, Rilke, Valery," in *Modernism: 1890–1930*, ed. Malcolm Bradbury and James McFarlane (New York: Penguin Books, 1976), 373.

68. See, e.g., C. B. McPherson, *The Political Theory of Possessive Individualism* (Oxford: Clarendon Press, 1962). Recently a similar argument has been made concerning modern psychology; see Michael A. Wallach and Lise Wallach, *Psychology's Sanction for Selfishness: The Error of Egoism in Theory and Therapy* (San Francisco: W. H. Freeman, 1983).

69. Kohut, "Forms and Transformations of Narcissism"; "Thoughts on Narcissism and Narcissistic Rage," in *The Search for the Self: Selected Writings of Heinz Kohut: 1950–1978*, ed. Paul H. Ornstein (New York: International Universities Press, 1978), 619.

70. A useful brief overview of the structuralist and post-structuralist positions

can be found in John Sturrock, ed., *Structuralism and Since: From Lévi-Strauss to Derrida* (Oxford: Oxford University Press, 1979).

71. In Hillman's opinion, this vision is rooted not only in Cartesianism but also in Christianity's rejection of pantheism and insistence that the only carrier of soul is the human person.

72. James Hillman, *Re-Visioning Psychology* (New York; Harper & Row, 1975), xi, 224, 29–30, 171, 173. Henceforth cited by title in both text and notes.

73. James Hillman, *InterViews* (New York: Harper & Row, 1983), 49–50.

74. Phrase from Peter Berger, *The Sacred Canopy* (Garden City, N. Y.: Doubleday, 1967).

75. Hillman, *InterViews*, 91, emphasis added. Also cf. *Re-Visioning Psychology*, 16–17.

76. William Empson, *Collected Poems* (New York: Harcourt Brace, 1935, 1940, 1949), 79. I have slightly recast Empson's phrase about "superrealistic comp.," which, according to Denis Donoghue, refers to Surrealism. See Denis Donoghue, "Deconstructing Deconstruction," *New York Review of Books*, 12 June 1980, 41.

77. Jacques Lacan's most important translated works are *Ecrits: A Selection*, trans. Alan Sheridan (New York: W. W. Norton, 1977); and *The Four Fundamental Concepts of Psychoanalysis*, trans. Alan Sheridan (New York: W. W. Norton, 1978). Henceforth *Ecrits* is cited both in text and notes.

78. Octavio Paz, *Alternating Current* (New York: Viking, 1973), 50.

79. For discussions of these notions in Lacan, see Fredric Jameson, "Imaginary and Symbolic in Lacan," *Yale French Studies* 55/56 (1977): 338–395; and Ellie Ragland-Sullivan, *Jacques Lacan and the Philosophy of Psychoanalysis* (Urbana: University of Illinois Press, 1986).

80. See Lacan, *Ecrits*, 1–7; and W. J. Richardson, "The Mirror Inside: The Problem of the Self," *Review of Existential Psychology and Psychiatry* 16 (1978/79): 98.

81. Paz, *Alternating Current*, 4.

82. See W. J. Richardson, "Lacan and the Subject of Psychoanalysis," in *Interpreting Lacan*, ed. J. H. Smith and William Kerrigan (New Haven: Yale University Press, 1983).

83. Quoted in J. P. Muller, "Ego and Subject in Lacan," *Psychoanalytic Review* 69 (1982): 240.

84. See Zvi Lothane, "Cultist Phenomena in Psychoanalysis," in *Psychodynamic Perspectives on Religion, Sect and Cult*, ed. David A. Halperin (Boston: J. Wright, 1983), 216.

85. André Breton, *Nadja* (New York: Grove Press, 1960), 59, 16. Also see Paz, *Alternating Currents*, 47–59.

86. See Maurice Nadeau, *The History of Surrealism* (New York: Penguin Book, 1973), 28–29.

87. Fredric Jameson, "Foreword," in *The Postmodern Condition: A Report on Knowledge*, by Jean-François Lyotard (Minneapolis: University of Minnesota Press, 1984), xviii–xix.

88. Gilles Deleuze and Felix Guattari, *Anti-Oedipus: Capitalism and Schizophrenia*, trans. Robert Hurley, Mark Seem, and Helen Lane (New York: Viking, 1977), 1.

89. I am aware that Deleuze and Guattari are also reacting *against* Lacan, in particular against his view of desire as a purely social product. But this does not gainsay the shared quasi-mechanism of their various views of human nature.

90. According to the French philosopher Bouveresse, the essential message of structuralism (and to this one could certainly add post-structuralism) is "Where I

was, there the It shall be" (*Le Philosophe chez les Autophages* [Paris: Les Editions de Minuit, 1984], 160).

91. See the accounts in Sherry Turkle, *Psychoanalytic Politics: Freud's French Revolution*, trans. Ned Lukacher (New York: Basic Books, 1978); and François Roustang, *Dire Mastery: Discipleship from Freud to Lacan* (Baltimore: Johns Hopkins University Press, 1982).

92. In a letter (August 5, 1987), Charles Taylor has kindly pointed out to me that, in addition to the criticism of Lacan offered in this paper, an opposite one also applies. This has to do with the paradoxical fact that the Lacanian position often attracts people who are looking for a kind of unsituated freedom, a fact that Taylor explains as follows: "Being the subject 'in the know,' grasping a theory of iron necessity, is having a certain disengagement from all those things which ordinary subjects take with ultimate seriousness. The whole poststructuralist vogue partly draws people by the radical freedom it seems to offer. This is more evident, of course, with people like Derrida, and all the talk of 'play' than with Lacan. But I think it also true of him." The radical freedom to which Taylor refers is, of course, not the same as what I, in my discussion above, called the "somewhat paradoxical freedom of automaticity emphasized by the surrealists . . . giving oneself over to the larger systemic flows." It is, I assume, rather more akin to the kind of freedom that is possible for a Cartesian mental substance that has recognized, and therefore distanced itself from, the realm of causal necessity.

93. Jameson, "Foreword," xix. For another critique of the postmodernist attempt to efface the self, see Lasch, *The Minimal Self*, chap. 4.

94. Ricoeur, *Freud and Philosophy*, 65; Peters, *Concept of Motivation*, 94.

95. See, e.g., Pepper, *World Hypotheses*.

96. Georges Politzer, *Critique des fondements de la psychologie* (Paris: Rieder, 1929). Also see: Amadeo Giorgi, "Psychoanalysis as a Concrete Psychology: The Vision of Georges Politzer" (Paper delivered at the meeting of the Eastern Psychological Association, New York, 17 April 1986).

97. Ludwig Wittgenstein, *The Blue and Brown Books* (Oxford: Basil Blackwell, 1958), 28.

98. Martin Heidegger, *Being and Time*, trans. John Macquarrie and Edward Robinson (New York: Harper & Row, 1962). Also see Merleau-Ponty, *Phenomenology of Perception*, especially 434–456.

99. For preliminary discussion of a Heideggerian approach to the self, see Louis A. Sass, "Humanism, Hermeneutics, and the Concept of the Human Subject," in *Hermeneutics and Psychological Theory*, ed. Stanley Messer et al. (New Brunswick: Rutgers University Press, 1988), 222–271. A slightly expanded version of this paper appeared in *Psychoanalysis and Contemporary Thought* 12 (1989).

✦ MARTIN E. GLOEGE ✦

The American Origins of the Postmodern Self

It has become a commonplace of contemporary literary and critical theory to think of the "self" as a "construction," as counterfeit and artificial as opposed to authentic and natural, as a product of society, as a narrative or rhetorical device, trope, or strategy of and within language. Thus, to approach the narratives of the self and expose their constructed nature is to trace the history of the self as a linguistic and social formation.

In much contemporary theory and criticism there is a sense that the exposure of the constructed nature of the self has already taken place. The most recent chapter in the history of the self is the story of its debunking, its fragmentation, its dismemberment, its explosion, dissolution, destruction, its scattering or dispersal, and, finally, its annihilation. Although modernist and postmodern narratives share a formal concern with the fragmentation of the self, the rhetoric of such narratives changes radically after World War II. Modernist texts mourn the loss or fragmentation of the self; the poet or author holds or attempts to hold the self together despite threats of fragmentation. But what modernist narrative mourned, postmodern narrative accepts, sometimes with resignation, sometimes with celebration.

One Postmodern Self:
Cotton Mather and Gravity's Rainbow

One such positive postmodern narrative is the conclusion to Thomas Pynchon's 1973 novel *Gravity's Rainbow*, where the novel's hero (or antihero), Tyrone Slothrop, disappears, is transformed, and reappears in fragmented forms all over post–World War II Europe:

Some believe that fragments of Slothrop have grown into consistent personae of their own. If so, there's no telling which of the Zone's present-day population are offshoots of his original scattering. There's supposed to be a last photograph of him on the only record album ever put out by The Fool, an English rock group—seven musicians posed, in the arrogant style of the early Stones, near an old rocket-bomb site, out in the East End, or South of the River. . . . There is no way to tell which of the faces is Slothrop's: the only printed credit that might apply to him is "Harmonica, kazoo—a friend." But knowing his Tarot, we would expect to look among the Humility, among the gray and preterite souls, to look for him adrift in the hostile light of the sky, the darkness of the sea.[1]

In short, Slothrop has been transformed from a self into a sign. Unlike the typical gestures of modernist texts, however, Pynchon's text offers no rhetorical or narrative gestures that bemoan this conversion, or indicate that this dispersal of the self signifies loss.

This description of Slothrop's fragmentation is cited at the beginning of Michael Sprinker's 1980 essay "Fictions of the Self: The End of Autobiography," in which Sprinker reads Slothrop as an example of the problem of the subject. Slothrop's fragmentation raises questions about the concept of the author and authorial subject, "about the ways texts are constituted, and about notions of consciousness, of self, of personality, and of individuality as categories applicable to authors of texts."[2] After citing examples from Vico, Kierkegaard, Nietzsche, and Freud, Sprinker concludes by noting the linguistic and textual nature of concepts of self in autobiographical writing: "The origin and the end of autobiography converge in the very act of writing . . . for no autobiography can take place except within the boundaries of a writing where concepts of subject, self, and author collapse into the act of producing a text."[3] For Sprinker, the moment of production of the autobiographical text is the center and circumference, the origin and the end, of autobiography. By announcing the end of autobiography and pronouncing the death of the self as a category of the real, Sprinker's essay reveals the impact of postmodernism on contemporary American literary criticism's discussion of the self.

In his discussion of the self, Sprinker argues that Pynchon's text reveals the "constructed" nature of the self insofar as it depicts Slothrop's conversion from self to sign. But when Sprinker quotes Pynchon's *Gravity's Rainbow* he neglects to include the sentence, "But knowing his Tarot, we would expect to look among the Humility, among the gray and preterite souls, to look for him adrift in the hostile light of the sky, the darkness of the sea." By ignoring Slothrop's dispersal among "the Humility"—the humble masses and the unchosen, passed-over "preterite souls"—Sprinker overlooks a number of important rhetorical repetitions. Pynchon's description of the common people of the 1940s echoes the vocabulary and values of New England Puritanism.[4] One echo of that language can be heard in the use of the term "Humility" itself, which repeats a discussion of the self in Cotton Mather's sermon on "Humiliations follow'd with Deliverances." In this 1697 sermon, Mather advocates a general "humiliation" among the people of New England, for

> Were such an *Humiliation* obtained, Then would our God say, *I see, they have Humbled themselves, I will not utterly Destroy them!* The Land of *Canaan,* is as much to say, in English, The Land of the *Humbled.* Oh! if we were universally thus *Humbled,* our Land would soon be a *Canaan,* for the Rest, the Peace, the Plenty, which would be therein vouchsafed unto us.[5]

Mather's sermon is a response to Hannah Dustan's captivity by Indians. Here, Mather explains the captivity as a sign of New England's need for repentance. Such repentance would, if universal, lead to a New Canaan—a return of New England to its "original" destiny.

Sacvan Bercovitch's *The American Jeremiad* explores the suggestion, made in this occasional sermon and elsewhere in colonial Puritan writing, that this mission of the self is also the mission of New England and America. Not simply Dustan, but all of New England, would be saved by her repentance. As Bercovitch points out, this linkage of individual and national destiny marks the difference between American and European Puritanism. The linkage also forms the basis of future American rhetoric in which "character" constitutes the ground of politics. American writing from Mather to Pynchon is marked by the notion of representative character— the destiny of the individual character is read as the destiny of America as a whole.

Crucial to Mather's jeremiad is the idea that a return to New England's original plan is predicated on the loss of self: "You will seriously consider, *What you shall render to the Lord for all His Benefits?* And you will sincerely *Render* your very *Selves* unto the Lord."[6] Mather advocates a universal Humiliation of self, but also says that

> Now, who can tell, how far one *Humble Soul,* may prevail, that shall put in Suit, the *Sacrifice for the Congregation?* The Faith of one *Moses,* of one *Samuel,* yea, of one *Amos,* of one poor, obscure, honest Husbandman, Oh! how far, may it go, to obtain this Answer, from the Great God, *They have Humbled themselves, I will not destroy them, but grant them some Deliverance!*[7]

For Mather, Humiliation—the rendering of one's self to God as a recognition of Divine authority—by one individual can also bring about a universal deliverance.

If we ignore Pynchon's reference to the Humility, we fail to read the novel as an ironic repetition of Mather's narrative of the loss or sacrifice of the Self leading to spiritual deliverance. Pynchon's Slothrop is the postmodern figure of Mather's "one *Humble Soul*" who sacrifices his self for the rehabilitation of society. In Mather's text, the self is portrayed as a possession, as property, as something that can be owned, and hence, given up to God or dispersed among the preterite. While Mather advocates that the self be made subordinate to God, he also, following Locke, gives quarter to the notion of selves as proprietors of themselves. In Locke, self-possession becomes the basis for a capitalist society whose role is "protection of the individual's property in his person and goods, and (therefore) for the maintenance of orderly relations of exchange between individuals."[8] Pynchon repeats Mather's story of self-sacrifice by characterizing the self as something owned, and whose individual destiny is of grandiose social and national significance. Crucial to a reading of both texts is the notion of America's unique historical mission recast in terms of the private self.

By arguing that Pynchon exposes the textual basis of the self by transforming Slothrop from self into sign, Sprinker tells only part of the story. Pynchon also demonstrates that the connection between the self and its "textual" basis is history itself. In *Gravity's Rainbow*, the discovery of the self as a textual construct is simultaneously a discovery of America and its historical construction.

The Postmodern Theory of the De-Centered Self in Historical Context

As the title of this essay suggests, my exploration of the postmodern self in American fiction begins as a quest for origins. I do not pursue this quest, however, in ignorance of Derrida's critique of the naïve quest for origins as a desire for mastery. Rather, I intend to historicize that critique—to place the critique of the desire for mastery into question and account for it in historical terms. By historicizing Derrida's renunciation of mastery, I do not abandon his critique, but rather align it with certain expressions of postmodernism that it attempts to categorize, but also repeats.

By demonstrating a link between the postmodern fragmentation of "national" identity engendered by multinational capitalism, and the fragmentation of the self in prior American philosophical and cultural traditions, postmodern American fiction makes connections between self, history, and literary text. For example, Pynchon's fiction presents a case of de-centering that exemplifies continuities between the colonial American tradition of piety by "humiliation" and postmodern notions of identity. In *Gravity's Rainbow*, Slothrop's fragmentation both rehabilitates Cotton Mather's notion of humiliation and explores the nature of identity in the postmodern United States.

A postmodern humiliation could certainly be found in a number of Western and Christian traditions, but what makes Mather's notion unique is the emphasis placed on national, along with personal, fragmentation. Bercovitch has argued that this connection is uniquely American. There is, however, a larger question regarding the origins of postmodernism that is, so far as I can tell, unanswerable. There are undoubtedly some "American" elements in Western postmodernism, in Borges, or Brecht, or Beckett, for instance, but I would not argue that these non-American authors derive their postmodernism from exclusively American sources. At the very least, however, the role of specifically American traditions active in postmodernist texts—even in American texts—has been underestimated. Indeed, part of my argument here is that one can indeed find materials in the American tradition that would account for the post-structuralist emphasis on fragmentation and humiliation without reference to European sources.

I also argue that postmodern humiliation cannot be said to derive from a stable and continuous American tradition. It must also be linked to the situation in which it emerged—the events of the 1960s. The 1960s not only marked the manifestations of the de-centered subject in literature, but also the birth of a global subject in the position to manage, or contest, the global division of labor. And although virtually all theorists of postmodernism are quick to acknowledge the international aspects of postmodern aesthetics, few consider the place of professional American intellectuals in relation to this international aesthetics and to the international division of labor.

Two of the most prolific American theorists of postmodernism are Ihab Hassan and Fredric Jameson; both describe postmodernism as an international phenomenon. For them, postmodernism is the cultural effect of radical, global changes in economic conditions and libidinal desires. Yet when they refer to global change, to capitalism, to the West, and to postmodernism itself, they are more properly speaking of America and American culture, and, even more specifically, about American "middle class" culture. Their postmodernism is an American thing.

Hassan and Jameson represent two poles of the discussion in that part of American literary criticism which addresses the United States's singular and contradictory position of world dominance following World War II. Although it is impossible to ignore the impact of European theory (particularly French post-structuralism and the Frankfurt School) on American literary criticism, these two influential American critics define the poles of

the current debate for a number of reasons. Each has a clearly defined relationship to the American tradition, which I take to be one of the intellectual
origins of postmodernism. Hassan uses the language of American pragmatism by assuming the position of the Western One, looking (with some
anxiety, I think, but in the name of pragmatic pluralism) to the world's
Many. Jameson eschews any connection to American tradition and assumes
the position of the displaced continental critic who looks to redeem America from without.

From a desire to appear cosmopolitan, American critics are quick to treat
non-Western cultures as unique and consistent, but they forget or deny that
the United States also has its own peculiar cultural identity (in the anthro-
pological sense). By cultural identity I mean a set of traditions, attitudes,
and rituals that are not necessarily common to all Americans, but can be
linked to a dominant American culture.[9] By suggesting that the term "postmodern" can be used to name our dominant culture, I concur with Myra
Jehlen and Sacvan Bercovitch and their employment of Raymond
Williams's notion of a "dominant culture"[10] to describe the values, customs, thought, and behavior that have achieved ideological hegemony
throughout the United States, cutting across divisions of class, religion
race, ethnicity, and gender.

Postmodernism is in part a product of the American middle class which
has established a hegemonic relationship over American culture production
and consumption. Even though minority, alternative, or oppositional cultures do play a role in American cultural production, the hegemonic or
dominant culture appropriates and translates nondominant and even oppositional cultural ideas into its own discourse. This appropriation does
not, however, rule out the possibility of the dominant class being, under
certain conditions, oppositional toward existing structures, both cultural
and material. Hassan can maintain the traditional politics of the American
middle class, even as he adopts a culturally radical persona. Nor does
Jameson escape this middle-class ideological hegemony, even as he takes an
openly oppositional stance toward American power structures.

Hassan uses the (William) Jamesian discourse of "the One and the Many"
to consciously rehabilitate the American pragmatic tradition of conflating
pragmatism with pluralism.[11] Jameson appropriates the "foreign" discourse of Max Weber and European Marxism to lament the extension of
America into foreign territory. He portrays "the advanced world" (the
United States and the West) as the site of the origin of "late" capitalism."[12]
Hassan and Jameson thus represent two different but familiar American literary critical strategies: Hassan, a conscious reliance on or a "return" to tra-
ditional modes of American thought—modes such as Emersonian
Transcendentalism, Pragmatism, the ideas of the "Founding Fathers,"
New World Puritanism, Franklin's notion of Self-creation, Jeffersonian

Democracy, or the regenerative powers of "The Land" itself—in order to identify a *native* critical tradition; and Jameson, a recourse to "foreign" modes of thought and practice—everything from Frankfurt School Marxism to French Psychoanalysis and post-structuralism—in order to sustain a critical "outsider" position.

Hassan participates unreflectively in an American tradition of "self-creation." The idea of America—the land itself—as the absolute origin of American culture has contributed to an unwillingness among critics like Hassan to recognize the actual differences between American and non-American discourses.[13] The net effect is to render the unfamiliar as altogether too familiar. A representative statement can be found in Hassan's recent work, where he describes postmodernism as a form of cultural innovation. Hassan calls attention to a fundamental contradiction of the postwar West—the "rising standard of living in the West," on the one hand, and the West's anxiety about terrorism and its loss of respect in other parts of the world (what he calls "secession") on the other:

> The epistemic factor proves to be only one of many. The force of the antinomian and indeterminate tendency derives from longer dispositions in society: a rising standard of living in the West, the disruptions of institutional values, freed desires, liberation movements of every kind, schism and secession around the globe, terrorism rampant—in short, the Many asserting the primacy over the One.[14]

Hassan paints a picture of the West as a unified, homogeneous "One," and the rest of the world is a heterogeneous, anarchic "Many."

While I agree that much of postmodernism in the United States is brought about by a sense of disruption, conflict, and decline in the West and the rise of non-Western peoples and ways of thought, his use of James's famous formulation of "The One and the Many" reveals his rhetorical lineage. He speaks as a Western subject in the language of the pragmatic American, welcoming, it would seem, the assertion of multiplicity against unity. By fixing his position within the American pragmatic, pluralist tradition, Hassan sounds more as if he's saying that we Americans, some of us anyway, have always affirmed multiplicity. "The Many" becomes less tangible. The assertion of multiplicity becomes the assertion of an old American idea whose time has come. Hassan represents one pole in the postmodernism debate—a pole that locates itself firmly in an American tradition that claims its origins in Emerson, is recuperated in James, and which Hassan ultimately echoes in his reading of the global relations of postmodernism. For Hassan, postmodernism is really American with a vengeance—he represents the United States as the absolute origin and end, the center and circumference, of postmodernism.

Jameson represents himself as the other, nonpragmatic or anti-American pole of the American postmodernism debate:

> Late capitalism in general (and the 60s in particular) constitute a process in which the last surviving internal and external zones within and outside the advanced world—are now ultimately penetrated and colonized in their turn. Late capitalism can therefore be described as the moment in which the last vestiges of Nature which survived on into classical capitalism are at length eliminated: namely the third world and the unconscious. The 60s will then have been the momentous transformational period in which this systemic restructuring takes place on a global scale.[15]

He depicts the West as an economic force of totalizing, colonizing capitalism; postmodernism is the "cultural logic" of this new economic situation.[16]

Latent within his Marxian narrative, however, is another story altogether. Jameson's intellectual roots are tied as closely to Max Weber as they are to the later German Marxist tradition expressed through the Frankfurt School. Jameson employs Weber's story of "Nature" as a transformative force in conflict against the rationalizing forces of the West and capitalism. He shares with Weber a sense of Nature as a regenerative, though doomed, force for the West.[17] But when he sets up an opposition of the "advanced world" to the so-called third world, the equation of Nature with both "the third world" and "the unconscious" radically undermines the reference presumably intended by both these terms. "Nature" begins to sound less like a Weberian concept than something traditionally American, something more Emersonian—a Nature that is regenerative, transcendent, and distinctly American.

Although the third world is broadly imagined to be a group of "real" and concrete geographical and political entities, Jameson equates these entities with two highly theoretical and abstract ideas. Perhaps he is attempting to render a higher degree of materiality to Nature and the unconscious, but the rhetorical effect is one of greater unreality and abstraction. If these terms are as abstract and interchangeable as they appear to be, we can rewrite the formulation "the advanced world" versus "the third world" as: the advanced world versus Nature and the unconscious. But if the unconscious is (also) part of the advanced world (as Jameson purports), we can rewrite this once again as: the advanced world versus itself. Thus we can also rewrite the Emersonian narrative of the regeneration of America by Nature as Jameson's narrative of the regeneration of late capitalism by its own unconscious (from within) and by the third world (from without). Jameson's rhetoric reveals the unspoken content of his own "political unconscious" to be an Emersonian narrative of hope and despair in the regenerative powers of America and Nature, as well as of America *as* Nature.

While both Hassan and Jameson are cosmopolitan, internationally known literally critics, there is an inescapable American-ness to their language—a language intrinsic to American postmodern theory and fiction. This American-ness has its roots in the pragmatic tradition that officially begins with James, C. S. Peirce, and John Dewey, but can be traced to Emerson; however, as I argue above, if postmodernism has its philosophical roots in the Emersonian tradition, its narrative structures take shape in a much earlier American literature.

The Internationalization of America

I want neither to reproduce Hassan's pragmatic and American description of the postmodern United States nor to join Jameson in looking to an Emersonian narrative of regeneration, but instead to explore the aspects of American cultural traditions both latent and manifest in American discourses on and of postmodernism. I am not abandoning Marxism or pragmatism, however, so much as I am abandoning those aspects of Marxist and pragmatic philosophies which move too quickly away from the idea of group conflict and class struggle toward totalization or a pluralism rooted in individualism. We can move differently by recognizing one unexamined assumption shared by Hassan and Jameson—the "event" or "hard fact"[18] of the "internationalization" of America in the period following World War II. Here I am not speaking of the nation-state per se, but of the the geographical, political, economic, and ideological, idea of America.

The internationalization of America can be described in two different ways. The first is the extension of U. S. and Western multinational corporations into the third world—particularly Asia, Brazil and other parts of South and Central America, and the Caribbean. This internationalization also includes the widespread use of woman as cheap labor in these "*comprador*" countries—countries with a bourgeois class whose members act as native agents for international business. Women are also the chief source of "cheap labor" in international subcontracting—labor-intensive manufacturing wherein the product is returned to be sold to the developed country instead of to the local market.[19] This process of economic expansion entails the "Americanization" of the local bourgeoisie through the expansion of consumer markets and ideologies throughout the "developing" nations.

The global model for international relations between capital and labor is an American one. This includes "Taylorized" or "Fordist" production models,[20] profit systems, the loss of agrarian subsistence modes of existence, and runaway and "footloose" shops that come and go like the wind with changes in the business or political climate. Likewise, we can see the creation of consumer cultures and their requisite ideological practices— education, advertising, the invention of "leisure" time—to which the "lowest end" of the international division of labor, "females of the urban subproletariat," are denied access. As Gayatri Chakravorty Spivak notes, "In their case, the denial and withholding of consumerism and the structure of exploitation is compounded by patriarchal social relations."[21]

In this class—the third-world urban subproletariat—we can see something akin to the traditional working class of classic Marxist theory: a class of physical laborers engaged in local and national struggles with the bourgeoisie, but with the potential to form international working class movements and distinct party organizations. Because this class does not exist as such in the United States, some critics are quick to reject any domestic application of Marxist theory. By viewing the division of labor as an international phenomenon, however, we can see that some aspects of the Marxist notion of "class struggle" still obtain: this new class struggle is also an international struggle. But as Spivak also notes, this struggle is compounded, and complicated, by gender stratification.

A second aspect of the internationalization of America is an outgrowth of U.S. economic expansion into the third world: America itself is transformed internally by the shift to an international division of labor. In the emphasis they place on the imperialist model, American Marxists generally overlook the domestic effects of U.S. imperialism. At the very moment when Western Marxists are looking at the Americanization of the third world, America as it has heretofore imagined itself is no longer possible. Once described as a determinate economic and cultural unity, the nation has been taken apart and put back together as an indeterminate multiplicity. Accompanying this largely economic transformation is an apparent and essentially conservative "return" to the supposedly foundational ideologies and texts of this national myth in postmodern literature. This "return to origins" is brought about by an America in "crisis" or a process of transformation—a social and ideological crisis that began in the 1960s and continues today. Jameson reads the 1960s as a period of crisis followed by a totalizing transformation of capital and consciousness into a world system controlled by multinational corporations.[22] I prefer to keep this question open and to avoid prematurely closing off the possibility of another, later crisis, or even one continuing crisis.

This crisis whatever its duration has brought a certain kind of pressure to bear on the foundational ideologies and myths that sustain American national power structures. This pressure can be seen as an attempt both to extend the power of those ideologies and to challenge them. When a culture is in crisis, one strategy is to invoke basic ideological myths as a defense against change. Some aspects of the ideology of Reaganism and its success can be explained as a reaction to broad economic changes such as deindustrialization, but this explanation is complicated by the fact that

Reaganism itself ushered in a great deal of change. And when a culture is undergoing a profound crisis and transformation, it gets out its basic, foundational narratives and mythologies and plays with them. Postmodernism is the way America is presently playing with its foundations.

The pressure of crisis that encourages us to question foundational ideologies is not entirely absent from "modernist" or "realist" literature. Rather, this pressure has manifested itself differently in postmodernism, reflecting the shift to a multinational economic system. An overemphasis on the newness (even while denying the possibility of newness) of postmodernism by critics has led them to overlook the continuities of postmodern American literature with earlier American texts. The shift to a corporate capitalism in the late nineteenth century created a crisis and a need to redefine national character and individual selfhood. This shift is exemplified in the career of Henry James, who began as a self-proclaimed "realist" and ended as a protomodernist, caught up in his own crisis of representation. This crisis of representation extends through high modernism in the earlier twentieth century, and much of aesthetic modernism is simply repeated in postmodernism. What marks postmodern American literature as different from nineteenth and earlier twentieth-century American literature is that for the first time the idea of national identity or selfhood is reconstructed in international terms.

Put another way, the texts of American postmodernism (such as the theories of Hassan and Jameson or the novels of Thomas Pynchon) can be seen as experiments in or examinations of the power of American ideologies of the self. In each text, a "postmodern" model of American selfhood is explored and put to the test. I refer to these texts as experiments, examinations, exploration, or tests, rather than as the cultural "effects" of an absent cause (capitalism, in this case), because one element of these texts is that they invoke an ideological narrative of the American self at precisely that historical moment when that self has taken on a transformed identity. The American self has itself become a subject of experimentation and exploration.

"The 60s in Particular"

Gravity's Rainbow looks backward to the Puritans outward to its own present—the events of the 1960s, to the counterculture and the political paranoia of the times. As I noted earlier, Jameson characterizes the 1960s thus: "Late capitalism in general (and the 60s in particular) constitute a process in which the last surviving internal and external zones of precapitalism . . . are now ultimately penetrated and colonized in their turn."[23] When I evaluate the relative importance of the 1960s to the postwar period, I agree with Jameson; however, I believe that his emphasis on the pre-postmodern period as a period of survival for "precapitalist zones," and his critique of postmodernism in general, reveal a certain nostalgia for the lost heroes of high modernism.

In marked contrast to Jameson's nostalgia, postmodern notions of subjectivity usually begin with the rejection of "modernist" definitions of the self. Postmodernism rejects not only the (re-)identification of the poet with the romantic hero or savior, but also rejects the valorization of the professional, scientist, manager, or engineer that characterizes much of modernism. Slothrop is not a modern hero, but a postmodern antihero. The rejection of heroism is often given in the language of a rejection of mastery and of masculinity.[24] One postmodern "condition" is the loss of power for the group of people who became heroes in the era of high modernism—the "Professional-Managerial" or "New" class of mediators between labor and capital, the offspring of the nineteenth century's "traditional Middle Class."[25]

As Cecelia Tichi points out in *Shifting Gears*, it is not only the authors and heroes of modernist fiction who are part of the professional-managerial class.[26] Likewise, the very stylistic values of modernism—of Ernest Hemingway's "nuts and bolts" prose or William Carlos Williams's high-speed, "rapid-transit poetics"—correspond to the values associated with engineers and other professionals—values of efficiency, speed, and stability against waste and fragmentation. Since World War II, this class of managers and professionals has been transformed from the producers of efficient miracles into the consuming subjects of postmodernism. Fred Pfeil has cogently argued that rather than representing a broad mass of the American population, the audience for postmodern culture is made up of this growing middle strata of professionals and managers.[27] Most of the reading public for postmodern American fiction is also made up of members of this expanding middle strata. Born with the development of corporate capitalism at the end of the nineteenth century, this class now finds its position redefined in terms of its relationship between labor and capital, as the dominant *consumer* class.

Doctors, lawyers, technicians, managers, teachers, and those about to join them—students—went through a profound crisis in the 1960s, and the language of this crisis was one of autonomy, freedom, and community versus the expanding state, military, and corporate apparatuses themselves, primarily the university. A 2 December 1964 speech by Berkeley Free Speech Movement leader Mario Savio is a good illustration of the language of this crisis:

There's a time when the operation of the machine becomes so odious, makes you so sick at heart, that you can't take part, you can't even tacitly take part. And you've got to put your bodies upon the gears and upon the wheels, upon the levers, upon all the apparatus, and you've got to make it stop. And you've got to indicate to the people who run it, to the people who own it, that unless you're free, the machine will be prevented from working at all.[28]

Against the expanding corporation and state, American students maintained a rhetorical alliance with the nation's and world's oppressed. But the demands were made in the name of their own needs for "autonomy" and freedom of expression, demands made before and since by professional and managerial elites.

As John and Barbara Ehrenreich argue in their description of the professional-managerial class, although it could "apologize" for capitalism on "objective," "rational" grounds, those very values, as they applied to the newly created roles performed by this class as "technical innovators, social mediators, culture producers, etc. , . . . required a high degree of autonomy, if only for the sake of legitimization. Claims to 'objectivity' cannot be made from an objective position of servility."[29] But "objectivity" also meant a certain elitist distance from the oppressed whom the student left claimed to represent. The 1960s rebellion in the United States was less part of an international movement for liberation than a period of national redefinition.

This national redefinition of identity manifests some interesting parallels with the simultaneous development of Free Trade Zones in Puerto Rico, Haiti, the Dominican Republic, the U.S.-Mexican border, and elsewhere. Annette Fuentes and Barbara Ehrenreich, in *Women in the Global Factory*, describe the free trade, or "export processing," zone as

> a colonial-style economic order, tailormade for multinational corporations. Customs-free import of raw materials, components and equipment, tax holidays of up to 20 years and government subsidization of operating costs are some of the enticements to investment. National firms are usually prohibited from operating in the zones unless they invest jointly with a foreign company. . . .
>
> A special police force is on hand to search people and vehicles entering or leaving the zones.[30]

Like the zone of *Gravity's Rainbow*, the Free Trade Zone lacks national identity. It represents a truly multinational space, with systems of discipline independent of national legal structures and outside national jurisdictions, and hence capable of repressing trade unions, strikes, and of exploiting third world poverty by legally guaranteeing corporations a large pool of "cheap labor." The parallel between the language of the American national identity crises in the 1960s and the loss of national identity in Free Trade Zones is more than coincidental.

While Free Trade Zones deny workers the right to strike, they also mark one path for the entrance of some third world subjects into the world economy—most as producers, some as managers and consumers. The Western response to the entry of third world voices into heretofore first world conversations—the "death of the subject"—is not a death at all, but rather the West's recognition of the authority and power of *some* third world subjects inherent in the internationalization of heretofore national economies. And it is this recognition that is experienced by some Western subjects as a kind of death.

Evidence of this perception is borne out in a quotation from Dick Hebdige's *Subculture: The Meaning of Style* (1979)—a book that appears in most postmodernism bibliographies as seminal in the delineation of the relation between postmodernism and popular culture. With a self-critical gesture, Hebdige ends his book by suggesting that he is

> producing analyses of popular culture which are themselves anything but popular. . . . The study of subcultural style which seemed at the outset to draw us back towards the real world, to reunite us with "the people," ends by merely confirming the distance between the reader and the "text," between everyday life and the "mythologist" whom it surrounds, fascinates and finally excludes.[31]

Hebdige feels deeply the distance between himself and the punks and Rastafarians he studies, and wants to erase the divide, but knows it is impossible.

Finding solace in the metaphorically homeless situation of the intellectual, Hebdige quotes a passage from anthropologist Claude Lévi-Strauss cited in Susan Sontag's 1966 essay "The Anthropologist as Hero." Hebdige writes: "Like the anthropologist proper, camping out in an alien culture . . . 'he can never feel himself "at home" anywhere; he will always be, psychologically speaking, an amputee.'"[32] For Lévi-Strauss the condition of psychological amputation is not a source of powerlessness, but instead a source of a great deal of power. Sontag quotes Lévi-Strauss further that "the anthropologist is not simply a neutral observer. He is a man in control of, and even consciously exploiting, his own intellectual alienation."[33] For Hebdige, alienation is not something to be exploited, but something to which one is passively resigned. He concludes that the only conceivable subject-position is one of submission to the (imagined) authority of the other. Hebdige overlooks the way in which the description of psychological amputation and powerlessness in Lévi-Strauss is rather more the description of a troubled conscience posing as powerless. The pose effectively preempts actual powerlessness because the intellectual manages and profits from his own "amputation."

Definitions of a so-called postmodernist selfhood or subjectivity are attempts to "cope" with, or even rally behind, a perceived loss of power—a reduction or reconfiguration of power that for some is experienced as a total loss. This coping can take the form of a rejection of mastery and the "embracing of powerlessness." Such an embrace can invoke, for example, a story about how "our failure is triumphant," in the words of Barthesian critic Paul Smith, in which powerlessness involves the carnivalesque "fiasco" of *jouissance* itself. For Smith, this fiasco finally allows a glimpse of "the subject as he might exist outside of ideology and culture" altogether.[34] Far from taking us "beyond ideology," however, such a position merely reflects a crisis in meaning brought on by the recognition of new subject-positions.

Part of the message of the 1960s was that a power struggle that had heretofore been thought in *national* terms of dominant/submissive (e.g., manager/managed, white/black, male/female, rich/poor, right/left, etc.) had now become an *international* phenomenon. The borders had been violated and transgressed. Postmodern texts (like Pynchon's) speak from and to the "New" or professional-managerial class about strategies for coping with the redefinition of self and nation brought on by this change, which is felt as both a source of great exuberance and as a profound loss. At the same time, postmodernism can also be seen as a cultural practice that draws on the American tradition in an attempt to define an oppositional or contestatory self. Such a self would be able to understand, criticize, and even work progressively to change the global system of oppression and exploitation. The very word "self" as a sign for the subject has shifted from having national to having global significance.

Perhaps it is appropriate to assert that the middle-class self (the bourgeois self or self-under-capitalism) and the traditional American self maintain only a tenuous relationship.[35] While American middle-class identity could once have been seen as virtually synonymous with capitalism, this is no longer the case. National economies (including that of the United States) no longer function *as* national economies in the world marketplace.[36] Likewise, national mythologies begin to fail. Postmodern texts can be seen as the site or stage for the construction or enactment of a new subjectivity capable of the kind of cultural relativism necessary to function in, manage, or even contest a global economy. Postmodernism marks the transformation from national corporate ideologies of selfhood to global multinational ideologies—from a national character, for example, to a supposed global "selflessness" (a nationless, homeless self[37]). Thus, the postmodern self appears to both emerge from and contest national mythologies.

Conclusion

American postmodernism, which critics emphasize as a radical break from the past and the radical de-territorialization of geographical boundaries, is, at the same time, an American discourse rooted in long-standing, specifically American notions of identity and selfhood. While postmodernism and its proponents argue that there can be no claims to radical originality, such assertions themselves are often, paradoxically, represented as radically original themselves, and are often coupled with definitions of postmodernism as avant-garde—as boldly new in the sense of high modernism.

The internationalization of the marketplace after World War II transformed America and threatened traditional American notions of identity. Certainly there is no such thing as a unitary American identity, but the idea of such a unitary American selfhood has long had a certain ideological status among the American middle class. Although American identity has been transformed by changes in America's relationship to the rest of the world, it remains grounded in American history and ideologies. In the postwar period we saw the transformation of the American middle, or "professional-managerial," class into a consuming class in the global marketplace. In a global economy, only the global, politicized, critical subject is able to effectively contest the effects of this globalization of the economy. But those in a position to "see" the international division of labor—the members of the professional-managerial class—are in a self-interested ethical position in which they can easily substitute the word "manage" for "contest." This global subjectivity is an ideal vantage from which to maintain a privileged position in the status quo. If members of this class cannot immediately decide this substitution, our indecision at least reveals that the debate about the ethics of postmodern subjectivity is one that is still open.

Postmodernism can be seen as the rehabilitation of traditional American national master-narratives and their revision into an international frame. By focusing on the repetition of certain traditional American discourses of the self in postmodern texts, we can see the durability of these traditions in their continuity and discontinuity with present theories and fictions of postmodern subjectivity. Post-structuralism represents history as "repetition with difference." This theory of history argues against cause and effect or simple continuity, since it sees these as mystifying metaphors or fictions. Instead, history is thought to be the repetition of a series of set pieces, tableaux, or structures, in which radical discontinuities are revealed by difference.

My focus on repetition, as opposed to difference exclusively, raises certain doubts about the discontinuity of postmodernity with earlier forms and makes a case against theories of a "new" humility unique to postmodernism. The incidence of repetition also raises certain doubts about the necessary resistance of the postmodern subject to the new world system, and points up questions about the resistance of the postmodern novel to order and stability, a resistance supposedly inherent, by definition, in postmodern fiction. While critics of postmodernism emphasize the importance of repetition with difference, this emphasis too frequently brackets postmodernism into an abstract, de-historicized, self-contained system. I want to stress the importance of locating these postmodern repetitions in history, and by seeing the repetition—the congruities between early and contemporary American literature—we necessarily also see the differences, since postmodern narratives change what they repeat.[38]

Likewise, while deconstruction has effectively brought the naïve search for origins into question as a logocentric desire for mastery, I wish to reopen the possibility of an origin that has less to do with genius and invention than with ideological and cultural formations. That is, by calling this essay "The American Origins," I do not wish to imply that America is the intellectual or artistic "birthplace" of postmodernism as a form of "expression." There are countless "origins" for the postmodern aesthetic, from French surrealism to the Frankfurt School to Borges and Beckett and Roland Barthes. Still, purely aesthetic genealogies do not explain why postmodern narratives, and particularly narratives of postmodern subjectivity and selfhood, have become meaningful at this particular time (after World War II, especially in the 1960s and later) and in this particular place (the United States).

As Dominick LaCapra has written of the power of the novel in relation to history:

> One way a novel makes challenging contact with "reality" and "history" is precisely by resisting fully concordant narrative closure (prominently including that provided by the conventional well-made plot), for this mode of resistance inhibits compensatory catharsis and satisfying "meaning" on the level of the imagination and throws the reader back upon the need to come to terms with the unresolved problems the novel helps to disclose.[39]

While it has been argued that all of modern, or at least modernist, literature resists closure, postmodern literature *defines itself* as resisting order, stability, and closure. In our search for closure and a "satisfying meaning" to postmodern texts, LaCapra assumes that history is the privileged text of our search.

As in the case of Pynchon, even though the subject-position explored in the character of Tyrone Slothrop is marked by extreme passivity or paranoia, or both, the historical text is useful in identifying an explanatory context in which to frame this passivity and paranoia. Indeed, Pynchon's novels call out for the historical text as the reader is forced to go outside the literary *to* the historical in order to find coherence and some form of "satisfaction" in the narrative. But the idea that the literary critic would not seek answers in an autonomous aesthetic realm of artistic genius, a comparative psychology, a biological determinant, or simply posit an "indeterminacy" or "postmodern sublime" as the ultimate explanation of the postmodern text is far from certain.

Although it may be increasingly untenable to argue that historical and economic factors are the ultimate and absolute determining causes of postmodern culture, it is equally difficult to ignore them. Jacques Derrida writes in *Of Grammatology*:

> There is a short-of and a beyond of transcendental criticism. To see to it that the beyond does not return to the within is to recognize in the contortion the necessity of a pathway [*parcours*]. That pathway must leave a track [or wake, *sillage*] in the text. Without that track, abandoned to the simple content of its conclusions, the ultra-transcendental text will so closely resemble the precritical text as to be indistinguishable from it.[40]

In her essay, "Value," in which she cites this passage from Derrida, Gayatri Spivak claims that "following Marx, it is possible to put the economic text 'under erasure,' to see, that is, the unavoidable and pervasive *importance* of its operation and yet to question it as a concept of the *last resort*."[41] By this comment, Spivak indicates how much is consistently ignored in critical theories and historical studies that limit their vision and frame of reference to exclude the international division of labor. She consistently calls attention to the specificity of that which is left out—the "epistemological violence" of imperialism and the importance of the international division of labor and "the imperialist project" in the production of the West and the Western subject.[42] Spivak's point is that the West itself can only be understood in terms of its operations in the imperialist "elsewhere," and that attempts to ignore the role of imperialism will inevitably be haunted by the return of the repressed.

Although I do not claim that we should see our "selves" as strictly determined by economics and history, I wish to work against a tendency on the part of left critics to ignore the history of production and reproduction, both textual and economic, for the sake of an "indeterminant" or "post-" Marxism that effectively censors the economic and historical text. LaCapra's point could be rewritten to say that narratives of history help us see and understand things—they form what might be called a "strategy of coherence"[43] with which to understand a group of otherwise incoherent texts. Any history of the postmodern subject must take rhetorical, narrative, and ideological formations into account. The apparent alternative, the self-sacrifice involved in renouncing narrative coherence, is precisely the critical activity I wish to bring into question.

NOTES

1. Thomas Pynchon, *Gravity's Rainbow* (New York: Viking, 1973), 742.

2. Michael Sprinker, "Fictions of the Self: The End of Autobiography," in *Autobiography: Essays Theoretical and Critical*, ed. James Olney (Princeton: Princeton University Press, 1980), 322.

3. Ibid., 342.

4. I am certainly not the first to note the parallels between *Gravity's Rainbow* and Puritan rhetoric. Marcus Smith and Khachig Tololyan characterize the redemptive moment in *Gravity's Rainbow* as the assertion of the "chronometric Now." Although they note critically the valorization of the chronometric—the utopian vision of Puritanism—in Pynchon's novel, they are also uncritically compelled by that vision to reject history in favor of the "reimagining of the possibilities open to us in a secular age" and so read *Gravity's Rainbow* as a successful novel of protest (Marcus Smith and Khachig Tololyan, "The New Jeremiad: *Gravity's Rainbow*," in *Thomas Pynchon*, Modern Critical Views series, ed. Harold Bloom [New York: Chelsea House, 1986], 146).

In a footnote to *The American Jeremiad*, Sacvan Bercovitch lists *Gravity's Rainbow* among other "anti-jeremiads." The anti-jeremiad is a form of protest that criticizes America but only in the name of America. The American anti-jeremiad protests America's failure to live up to its promise. This strategy was destined to fail to bring about fundamental social change because "the radical energies [the writer] celebrated served to sustain the culture, . . . the same ideal that released those energies transformed radicalism itself into a mode of cultural cohesion and continuity" (Sacvan Bercovitch, *The American Jeremiad* [Madison: University of Wisconsin Press, 1978], 204–205).

Bercovitch also assumes that *Gravity's Rainbow* is a novel of protest. I do not share this assumption, in part because the novel itself undermines any ground on which to base such a protest. I argue that the novel is (like Bercovitch's book) highly critical of American "jeremiad" rhetoric itself—more critical than Bercovitch or Smith and Tololyan seem to recognize.

5. Cotton Mather, "Humiliations follow'd with Deliverances" (1697), in *Days of Humiliation: Times of Affliction and Disaster: Nine Sermons for Restoring Favor with an Angry God (1696–1727)*, ed. George Harrison Orians (Gainesville, Fla.: Scholars' Facsimiles & Reprints, 1970), 102.

6. Ibid., 135.

7. Ibid., 125–126.

8. C. B. Macpherson, *The Political Theory of Possessive Individualism* (Oxford: Oxford University Press, 1962), 264; Bercovitch, *American Jeremiad*, 107n. Bercovitch cites Perry Miller's reading of Jonathan Edwards as "a central figure in the movement toward the values of liberal free enterprise and 'possessive individualism'" (Bercovitch, *American Jeremiad*, 107). Much of the cultural and intellectual reinforcement for the theory of possessive individualism can be found in American writing prior to Edwards, although heavily mediated by Puritan doctrine. The term "possessive individualism" is from C. B. Macpherson. See also Perry Miller, *Jonathan Edwards* (1949; reprint Westport, Conn.: Greenwood Press, 1973).

9. According to Edward B. Tylor in *Primitive Culture* (1871), culture is "that complex whole which includes knowledge, beliefs, art, morals, laws, customs and any other capabilities and habits acquired by man as a member of society" A. L. Kroeber and Clyde Kluckhohn, *Culture: A Critical Review of Concepts and Definitions* (New York: Random House, 1952), 11; quoted by Alan Trachtenberg, "American Studies as a Cultural Program," in *Ideology and Classic American Literature*, ed. Sacvan Bercovitch and Myra Jehlen, Cambridge Studies in American Literature and Culture series (Cambridge: Cambridge University Press, 1986), 173.

10. Bercovitch, *American Jeremiad*, xiii; Myra Jehlen, "New World Epics: The Novel and the Middle Class in America," *Salmagundi* 36 (1977): 50–51.

11. William James, "The One and the Many," lecture 4 of "Pragmatism," in *Pragmatism and Other Essays* (New York: Washington Square Press, 1963), 57–72; Ihab Hassan, "Pluralism in Postmodern Perspective," in *The Postmodern Turn: Essays in Postmodern Theory and Culture* (Columbus: Ohio State University Press, 1987), 167–187; and "Fictions of Power: A Note on Ideological Discourse in the Humanities," *American Literary History* 1, no. 1 (Spring 1989): 131–142.

12. Jameson uses "late capitalism," a term invented by Ernest Mandel, a German Marxist, to describe multinational capitalism in its contemporary form. As the term implies, late capitalism is the form of capitalism that comes after corporate capitalism and before socialism—it is the form capitalism supposedly takes in its historic decline. Late capitalism is marked by rapid technological growth, an expanded state and a permanent arms economy, neo-colonialism, an expanded service sector and consumer culture, and permanent inflation. See Ernest Mandel, *Late Capitalism,* trans. Joris De Bres (London: New Left Books; Atlantic Highlands, N.J.: Humanities Press, 1975).

13. One sees this obsession with an originary America in Thomas Jefferson's *Notes on the State of Virginia*, especially in his discussion of shells in the Andes and his argument with Buffon in which he makes the case for a prior and better America. See Thomas Jefferson, *Notes on the State of Virginia* (1787), ed. William Peden (New York: W. W. Norton, 1974), 31–33 and 43–64. See also Myra Jehlen's discussion of this tradition in *American Incarnation: The Individual, The Nation, and the Continent* (Cambridge: Harvard University Press, 1986), 43–59.

14. Ihab Hassan, "Ideas of Cultural Change," in *Innovation/Renovation: New Perspectives on the Humanities*, ed. Ihab Hassan and Sally Hassan (Madison: University of Wisconsin Press, 1983), 29.

15. Fredric Jameson, "Periodizing the 60s," in *The 60s without Apology*, ed. Sohnya Sayres, Anders Stephanson, Stanley Aronowitz, and Fredric Jameson (Minneapolis: University of Minnesota Press, 1984), 207.

16. See Fredric Jameson, "Postmodernism, or The Cultural Logic of Late Capitalism," *New Left Review* 146 (1984): 53–92.

17. See Fredric Jameson, "The Vanishing Mediator; or Max Weber as Storyteller," in *The Syntax of History*, vol. 2 of *The Ideologies of Theory: Essays 1971–1086*, Theory and History of Literature series, vol. 49 (Minneapolis: University of Minnesota Press, 1988), 3–34.

18. See Philip Fisher, *Hard Facts: Setting and Form in the American Novel* (New York: Oxford University Press, 1985), 3–21.

19. See June Nash and Maria Patricia Fernandez-Kelly, *Women, Men, and the International Division of Labor* (Albany: State University of New York Press, 1983); Gayatri Chakravorty Spivak, "Can the Subaltern Speak?" in *Marxism and the Interpre-*

tation of Culture, ed. Cary Nelson and Lawrence Grossberg (Urbana: University of Illinois Press, 1988), 271–313; and "Scattered Speculations on the Question of Value," in *In Other Worlds: Essays in Cultural Politics* (New York: Methuen, 1987), 154–175; Annette Fuentes and Barbara Ehrenreich, *Women in the Global Factory* (Boston: South End Press, 1983); and Mike Davis, "The Political Economy of Late-Imperial America," *New Left Review* 143 (January/February 1984): 6–38.

20. "Taylorization" and "Fordism" are methods of industrial or technological production based on principles of "scientific" management whose goals are to "maximize efficiency" in the labor process. Some European Marxists (e.g., Aglietta) have noted the extension of Fordist mass-production methods into mass consumption. See Michael Aglietta, *A Theory of Capitalist Regulation* (London: New Left Books, 1979); Harry Braverman, *Labor and Monopoly Capitalism: The Degradation of Work in the Twentieth Century* (New York: Monthly Review Press, 1974); and Davis, "The Political Economy of Late-Imperial America," 6–38.

21. Spivak, "Can the Subaltern Speak?" 288.

22. Jameson, "Periodizing the 60s," 178–209.

23. Ibid., 207.

24. See, for example, Paul Smith, "We Always Fail—Barthes' Last Writings," *Sub-Stance* 36 (1982): 34. In his brief essay, Smith discusses Barthes's important late works: *Le Plaisir du Texte* (1973), *Roland Barthes par lui-meme* (1975), and *La Chambre Claire: Note sur la photographie* (1980).

25. John Ehrenreich and Barbara Ehrenreich, "The Professional-Managerial Class," in *Between Labor and Capital*, ed. Pat Walker (Boston: South End Press, 1979), 5–45.
See also Cecelia Tichi, *Shifting Gears: Technology, Literature, Culture in Modern America* (Chapel Hill: University of North Carolina Press, 1987); T. J. Jackson Lears, "From Salvation to Self-Realization: Advertising and the Therapeutic Roots of the Consumer Culture, 1880–1930," in *The Culture of Consumption: Critical Essays in American History 1880–1980*, ed. Richard Wightman Fox and T. J. Jackson Lears (New York: Pantheon, 1983), 1–38; and Thorstein Veblen, *The Engineers and the Price System* (New York: Viking, 1932).

26. Willa Cather's *Alexander's Bridge* (1912) and Edith Wharton's *Ethan Frome* (1911) present two examples of protagonists who are engineers. Tichi, *Shifting Gears*, 173–180, 217–219.

27. Fred Pfeil, "Makin' Flippy-Floppy: Postmodernism and the Baby-Boom PMC," in *The Year Left: An American Socialist Yearbook, 1985*, ed. Mike Davis, Fred Pfeil, and Michael Sprinker (London: Verso, 1985), 263–295; and Fred Pfeil, "Postmodernism as a 'Structure of Feeling,'" in *Marxism and the Interpretation of Culture*, ed. Cary Nelson and Lawrence Grossberg (Urbana: University of Illinois Press, 1988), 381–403.

28. Quoted in Hal Draper, *The New Student Revolt* (New York: Grove Press, 1965), 98.

29. Ehrenreich and Ehrenreich, "The Professional-Managerial Class," 22.

30. Fuentes and Ehrenreich, *Women in the Global Factory*, 10–11.

31. Dick Hebdige, *Subculture: The Meaning of Style*, New Accents series (1979; reprint, London: Methuen, 1982), 139–140.

32. Ibid., 168 n. 8.

33. Susan Sontag, "The Anthropologist as Hero," in *Against Interpretation and Other Essays* (1966; reprint New York: Farrar, Straus & Giroux, 1986), 74.

34. Smith, "We Always Fail—Barthes' Last Writings," 38.

35. Which is not to say they ever really did intersect very well. As Sacvan Bercovitch has argued about Melville's fiction, "The same Puritan myth . . . encouraged . . . Melville, in *Moby Dick*, to create an epic hero who represents in extremis both the claims of Romantic isolation and the thrust of industrial capitalism." As with Melville's attempt to combine opposing ideologies, the classic nineteenth-century American novel can be read as an attempt to resolve the contradictions between industrial capitalism and the Puritan vision of America (Sacvan Bercovitch, *The Puritan Origins of the American Self* [New Haven: Yale University press, 1975], 185–186).

See also Philip Fisher's *Hard Facts*, especially the chapter on Dreiser's *Sister Carrie*, for an account of the early twentieth-century novel's role in developing American identity to conform with corporate capitalism's need for consuming subjects.

36. For example, an advertisement for the Irving Trust, (reprinted in Fuentes and Ehrenreich, *Women in the Global Factory*, 6):
U.S. business knows no boundaries.
The profit motive has propelled it on a
fantastic journey in search of new opportunities.

37. One example of the use of the term "homeless" in a similar context can be found in the work of Edward W. Said. See *Beginnings: Intention and Method* (New York: Basic Books, 1975), 11, where he refers to the modern critic as "transcendentally homeless" when confronted by texts, like those by James Joyce, for which he has "no recourse to tradition."

See also Bruce Robbins, "Homelessness and Worldliness," *Diacritics*, 13, no. 3 (Fall 1983): 69–77, a review of Said's work; and Catherine Gallagher's response to Robbins, "Politics, The Profession, and the Critic," *Diacritics*, 15, no. 2 (Summer 1985): 37–43.

38. This is basically the argument put forth as a critique of the "new historicism" in Frank Lentricchia, *Ariel and the Police: Michel Foucault, William James, Wallace Stevens* (Madison: University of Wisconsin Press, 1988), 86–102, especially 99.

39. Dominick LaCapra, *History, Politics, and the Novel* (Ithaca: Cornell University Press, 1987), 14.

40. Jacques Derrida, *Of Grammatology* (1967), trans. Gayatri Chakravorty Spivak (Baltimore: Johns Hopkins University Press, 1976), 61.

41. Spivak, "Scattered Speculations on the Question of Value," 168.

42. Spivak, "Can the Subaltern Speak?" 291.

43. See Teresa De Lauretis, "Strategies of Coherence: Narrative Cinema, Feminist Poetics, and Yvonne Rainer," in Teresa De Lauretis, *Technologies of Gender: Essays on Theory, Film, and Fiction*, Theories of Representation and Difference series (Bloomington: Indiana University Press, 1987), 107–126.

◆ DENNIS K. MUMBY ◆

Two Discourses on Communication, Power, and the Subject
Jürgen Habermas and Michel Foucault

In recent years contemporary European philosophical thought has become increasingly influential in the work of many communication scholars. The move away from the hegemony of neopositivism toward more critical modes of inquiry has forced researchers to confront the challenges to received notions of communication set by philosophers and social theorists such as Hans-Georg Gadamer, Jürgen Habermas, and Michel Foucault.[1] In particular, the works of Habermas and Foucault focus our attention on the need to develop theories of communication that are contextualized within broader theories of knowledge and power. Communication scholars have become interested in such issues in part because they recognize that questions of the relationship between communication, knowledge, and meaning are intimately connected with political structures and forms of domination.[2] In this sense, communication is not a neutral vehicle for the conveyance of messages, but rather an inherently political practice that constitutes the site of the struggle over what defines knowledge in our society.[3]

This essay takes up this issue by comparing and contrasting two different ways of representing the relationship between power and knowledge as articulated by Habermas and Foucault. I am primarily concerned with what they can tell us about this relationship and the role that it plays in the constitution of human subjectivity.[4] In brief, each author represents positions, whether defined as modernist (Habermas) or postmodernist (Foucault), that articulate very different conceptions of the relationship between knowledge and power and the positioning of the subject within that relationship.[5] My intent, however, is not to gloss over their differences, but rather to highlight some of the important overlaps and tensions between them, and thus suggest some fruitful ways of theorizing about human communication.

Habermas and Foucault on Power and Knowledge

Habermas's writings champion the modernist argument in its development of a theory of society that focuses on the rational grounds for human thought and action. His theory of communicative action is predicated on the development of a linguistic model of rationality that provides the normative basis for the examination of knowledge claims.[6] One of the consequences of such a model is the claim that knowledge or truth emerges only in situations that are free from the constraints of various extralinguistic coercive factors. For Habermas, then, power and knowledge are diametrically opposed.

Foucault, on the other hand, represents the postmodern attempt to deconstruct the very notion of rationality and its constitutive role in the development of the contemporary human condition. His goal is to "get rid of the subject"[7] in its transcendental form and to situate it in discourse and history. His evocative image at the very end of The Order of Things, in which he likens the appearance of "man" to a face drawn in the sand that may soon be washed away, clearly speaks to this postmodern frame of reference in which the individual is viewed as a discursive, historical construct.[8] Foucault is concerned with explicating the process by which a certain human discourse emerges in a particular historical period. He contends that by examining such discourses one can genealogically trace "the constitution of the subject within a historical framework" (Foucault, Power/Knowledge, 117).

In this context there is no attempt, as with Habermas, to somehow bifurcate the knowledge that a discourse constitutes on the one hand, and the existence of certain power relations on the other. On the contrary, for Foucault power and knowledge are inextricably linked in the production of the human subject:

> Perhaps we should abandon the belief that power makes mad and that, by the same token, the renunciation of power is one of the conditions of knowledge. We should admit rather that power produces knowledge . . . that power and knowledge directly imply one another; that there is no power relation without the correlative constitution of a field of knowledge, nor any knowledge that does not presuppose and constitute at the same time power relations. These "power-knowledge" relations are to be analyzed, therefore, not on the basis of a subject of knowledge who is or is not free in relation to the power system, but on

the contrary, the subject who knows, the objects to be known and the modalities of knowledge must be regarded as so many effects of these fundamental implications of power-knowledge and their historical transformations.[9]

Clearly, then Habermas and Foucault hold extremely divergent positions on the relationship between power and knowledge, and the concomitant positioning of the subject within this relationship.

One of the important points of disagreement is the question of whether knowledge serves the purposes of critique and emancipation, or whether the entire knowledge-based orientation toward autonomy, reciprocity, and dignity is simply one body of discourse within a particular, dominant, power-knowledge regime. At stake here is the place that the subject occupies within any system of knowledge. Foucault's rejection of any "metaphysics of subjectivity"[10] is seen by many commentators as an antihumanist turn insofar as he reduces the individual to a derivative of certain historical conditions and discourses.[11] Within this framework there is no room for a model of critique centered on the individual as the wellspring of rationality and autonomy. Although Habermas would concur with Foucault in the rejection of any transcendental notion of the subject, his project is an avowedly humanist one involving the explication of the very conditions Foucault denies; that is, the circumstances under which individuals are able to produce rational, consensually derived knowledge claims about the world, free from the distorting effects of power and domination.

For both Habermas and Foucault, knowledge is produced through discourse. For Habermas, knowledge is the product of certain modes of rationality embedded in human interests that predispose individuals to act toward the world in particular ways.[12] These interests manifest through various discursive practices that have different referential domains. For Foucault, knowledge in its modern form is the product of a "disciplinary regime" that has isolated the subject-individual as its domain of study. In this context, knowledge is produced through the multitude of discursive practices that delineate and normalize the individual in a particular way.[13] Each of these positions merits detailed consideration.

Power, Knowledge, and Communicative Action
Habermas's earlier work, particularly *Knowledge and Human Interests*, is devoted to deconstructing the epistemological assumptions underlying the work of philosophers and social theorists such as Hegel, Marx, Comte, and Peirce, and showing how each has, in his own way, contributed to the rise of positivism and the emergence of an objectivistic, technological rationality that masquerades as a commitment to value freedom. Habermas

challenges the hegemony of positivism-scientism by reconstructing the systems of rationality and knowledge formation inherent in prior philosophy and social theory. He moves beyond positivism and its legacy by producing an alternative conception of rationality, one which constructs an appropriate relationship between the different forms of cognitive interests and knowledge formation. These knowledge-constituting interests, according to Habermas, are rooted in the natural history of the human species and produce different modes of inquiry.

Habermas divides the types of human interests and their concomitant knowledge systems into three domains. The technical interest he associates with the empirical-analytic sciences (the natural and social sciences aimed at the production of nomological knowledge); the practical interest he links to the hermeneutic sciences insofar as they are oriented toward interpretive understanding of human social formations; and the emancipatory interest he associates with the critically oriented sciences (psychoanalysis and critical social theory), which aim at deconstructing the quasi-natural constraints that are imposed upon self-reflection and limit the movement toward autonomy and responsibility. Habermas makes it clear that the relations between knowledge-constituting interests and modes of human inquiry are foundational ("quasi-transcendental"[14]) qualities of human existence:

> These cognitive interests are of significance neither for the psychology nor for the sociology of knowledge, nor for the critique of ideology in any narrower sense; for they are invariant . . . they result from the imperatives of a sociocultural life-form dependent on labor and language. Therefore the technical and practical [and emancipatory] interests of knowledge are not regulators of cognition which have to be eliminated for the sake of objectivity of knowledge; instead, they themselves determine the aspect under which reality is objectified, and can thus be made accessible to experience to begin with. They are the conditions which are necessary in order that subjects capable of speech and action may have experience which can lay a claim to objectivity.[15]

Habermas's overall task therefore involves a radical restructuring of both philosophical reflection as it has developed in post-Kantian thought, and self-reflection as developed in the work of Marx and Freud.[16] His development of such a restructuring emerges in his theory of communicative action and its concomitant notion of communicative rationality. The foundations of this theory are laid in his early works,[17] but are not articulated fully until the publication of his two-volume work, *The Theory of Communicative Action*.

Habermas's principal goal in *The Theory of Communicative Action* is to explicate a theory of rationality rooted in language as the primary medium of social interaction. Such an approach, he argues, focuses on the fundamentally communicative grounding for rational thought, while simultaneously exposing the limitations of models of social theory and philosophy that tend to privilege a teleological conception of human action on the one hand, and focus on consciousness to the exclusion of linguistic understanding on the other.[18] In contrast, Habermas attempts to provide a framework for reconsidering and reformulating ideas of reason and rationality by focusing on communicative action as the basis for the process through which individuals reach consensual understandings and make rational claims about the world.

Habermas takes as his starting point the notion developed by J. L. Austin and others that speaking a language involves the performance of an act.[19] Such a claim shifts the focus away from the representational function of language (characteristic of positivist views) and instead thematizes other modes of language use such as self-expression and development of intersubjective understanding. While Austin and J. R. Searle pay considerable attention to the kinds of things that one does by successfully uttering a particular speech act (e.g., promising, threatening, commanding, etc.), Habermas is more interested in the general conditions that undergird all speech acts. Thus by making any utterance, Habermas argues, an individual is putting forth a particular claim about him or herself, the world, or the other (or all three) that can be accepted or discursively challenged.

Habermas suggests that there are three principal validity claims implicitly raised in any given act of speaking, each of which is associated with a specific referential domain. First, a speaker can implicitly or explicitly present the claim that a given utterance is true (verifiable as having some form of correspondence to objective conditions). Such a claim makes reference to "the objective world (as the totality of all entities about which true statements are possible)" (Habermas, *Theory of Communicative Action*, 1:100). Second, a speaker can present claims relating to the legitimacy of the speech act in terms of the normative context in which it is spoken. Such claims take as their object domain the social world defined as "the totality of all legitimately regulated interpersonal relations" (1:100). Third, speakers implicitly or explicitly lay claims regarding the sincerity of their speech acts; such acts take as their referential domain the subjective world, consisting of "the totality of the experiences of the speaker to which he has privileged access" (1:100). In addition, each of these validity claims and their associated object domains are articulated through a particular mode of language use. As such, truth claims are articulated through the representative function of language; legitimacy claims, through the interactive function of language; and sincerity claims, through the expressive function of language.

Taken together, Habermas's validity claims—along with their corresponding referential domains and modes of language use—constitute his theory of communication action, which embodies the principle of action oriented to reaching understanding. In essence, Habermas presents us with a theory of rationality based on the principle of the better argument, played out according to the conditions laid out above: "From this perspective argumentation can be conceived as *a reflective continuation, with different means, of action oriented to reaching understanding*" (1:25; emphasis in original). Habermas is even clearer about the link between communication, argumentation, and rationality in the following:

> Rationality is understood to be a disposition of speaking and acting subjects that is expressed in modes of behavior for which there are good reasons or grounds. This means that rational expressions admit of objective evaluation. This is true of all symbolic expressions that are, at least implicitly, connected with validity claims (or with claims that stand in internal relation to a criticizable validity claim). Any explicit examination of controversial validity claims requires an exacting form of communication satisfying the conditions of argumentation. (1:22)

The importance of Habermas's development of a theory of communicative action, however, lies not simply in his describing a model of human rationality per se, but rather in his situating this framework within a larger theory of society. At this level, Habermas distinguishes between "lifeworld" and "system." The former is "a concept complementary to that of communicative action" (*Theory of Communicative Action*, 2:119) and consists in the shared assumptions that people have about their sense of personal identity and their cultural situatedness. In this sense, the notion of lifeworld refers more to a symbolic than to a physical context. Habermas argues that societies be conceived of as both lifeworlds *and* systems, that is, as "*systemically stabilized* complexes of action of *socially integrated groups*" (emphasis in original).[20] Habermas adapts the notion of "system" from Talcott Parsons to describe the self-regulating, functional contexts that coordinate action in specific ways. (For example, in modern capitalism the market economy is a system that regulates activity through the medium of money.)

Habermas criticizes Parsons, however, for overemphasizing the systemic aspects of society. Under the latter's theory "the structural components of the lifeworld become subsystems of a general system of action" (*Theory of Communicative Action*, 2:153), and communicative action simply becomes one more medium along with money and power. Habermas considers such an approach reductionist and as having pathological consequences. Yet he admits that construing society exclusively from the viewpoint of the lifeworld ignores the degree to which the symbolic world depends upon the material. For Habermas, therefore, "the fundamental problem of social theory is how to connect in a satisfactory way the two conceptual strategies indicated by the notions of 'system' and 'lifeworld'" (2:151).

Habermas's answer to this problem is to provide a complex analysis of the relationship between lifeworld and system in terms of the modes of rationality that characterize each. Through the process of social evolution—from tribal to modern societies—the two domains have become progressively differentiated such that on the one hand the lifeworld is characterized by increasing rationalization in terms of levels of meaning and learning, while on the other hand the system is becoming increasingly complex in terms of expanding markets and utilization of the media of power and money. This process of modernization in late capitalism has, according to Habermas, resulted in the inner colonization of the lifeworld by the system to the extent that genuine communicative action has been replaced by "media-steered" interaction. This inner colonization of the lifeworld is a response on behalf of late capitalism to the crisis tendencies that have developed within it.[21] These crisis tendencies have provoked measures such as increasing state intervention in the market economy, the introduction of mass democracy, and the emergence of a welfare state. In effect, the crisis tendencies that exist in the economic sector have been displaced into other domains, such as the lifeworld. The bottom line, therefore, is that the valorization of capital, which is the driving force of capitalist society, can only be maintained in the modern era by the intrusion of the administrative and economic systems into the domains concerned with social integration. The result is increasingly problematic tensions between system and lifeworld and a concomitant fragmentation of consciousness and individual identity. Habermas's theory of society is therefore (at least) twofold. His goal is to critique the methodological and epistemological assumptions of the contemporary social sciences, *and* "the social reality they are supposed to grasp" (*Theory of Communicative Action*, 2:375). He develops a theory of modernity that replaces the primacy of consciousness with the primacy of communicative action oriented toward intersubjective understanding. It is with this framework that he is able to provide an immanent critique of rationality as it has emerged in advanced capitalist society. Unlike Theodor Adorno and Max Horkheimer, who were ultimately disillusioned with the possibility of emancipation from the debilitating effects of modern capitalism and the culture industry, Habermas calls for yet greater enlightenment and emancipation. For him, the modernist project is not over; it just hasn't gone far enough.

For Habermas, the possibility for emancipation from systematically distorted communication is latent in the conflicts that arise in the connections and overlaps between system and lifeworld:

Earlier I described how the interchange between the private and public spheres, on the one hand, and the economic and administrative action systems, on the other, takes place via the media of money and power, and how it is institutionalized in the roles of employees and consumers, citizens and clients of the state. It is just these roles that are the targets of protest. Alternative practice is directed against the profit-dependent instrumentalization of work in one's vocation, the market-dependent mobilization of labor power, against the extension of pressures of competition and performance all the way down into elementary school. It also takes aim at the monetarization of services, relation-ships, and time, at the consumerist redefinition of private spheres of life and personal life-styles. . . . Finally, certain forms of protest negate the definitions of the role of citizen and the routines for pursu-ing interests in a purposive-rational manner—forms ranging from the undirected explosion of disturbances by youth . . . through calculated or surrealistic violations of rules (after the pattern of the American civil rights movement and student protests), to violent provocation and in-timidation. (*Theory of Communicative Action*, 2:359–396)

I quote this passage at length insofar as it contextualizes Habermas's theory of communicative action not in terms of a philosophical model with epistemological consequences that are distinct from practical activity, but as having genuine consequences.

Habermas is careful to point out that the significance of these reactions to the colonization of the lifeworld becomes obscured "if the communicative rationality of cultural modernity is rashly equated with the functionalist rationality of self-maintaining economic and administrative action systems—that is, whenever the rationalization of the lifeworld is not carefully distin-guished from the increasing complexity of the social system" (*Theory of Communicative Action*, 2:396). It is just this confusion, argues Habermas, that characterizes current debates among the antimodernists (labeled by Habermas the "Young Conservatives")[22] and postmodernists and which "robs a modernity at variance with itself of its rational content and its per-spective on the future" (*Theory of Communicative Action*, 2:396).

Habermas vehemently opposes the project of postmodernity as articu-lated by writers such as Foucault. Not only does postmodernism rob mo-dernity of its rational content, it also undercuts its own legitimacy by arguing that everything is grounded in power relations. Such a position renders rational theory impossible.[23] Habermas would argue that Foucault's very project is self-contradictory because it opposes the privileg-ing of any particular mode of rationality including its own. More impor-tant, whereas Habermas's modernism is an argument for continuous progress toward a rational society characterized by autonomy and responsi-bility, Foucault's postmodernism is a claim that the very notion of such pro-gress is an erroneous one that is shot through with the same kinds of normalizing power formations that it claims to critique. For Foucault, the articulation of a mode of rationality freed from structures of power is an illusion.

I want to examine these issues more closely by focusing on Foucault's representation of his postmodern project, paying particular attention to his conception of questions of truth, power, and subjectivity. It is in this context that one can best see the overlaps, tensions, and aporias that characterize the relationship between his project and Habermas's.

Power/Knowledge and the Subject

Charles Taylor points out that at first glance Foucault's work appears to be an Enlightenment-inspired attempt to unmask the systems of power and domination that insidiously disguise themselves from the view of the modern social actor, and thus rescue us from their grip. This is not the case. Although at one level Foucault is concerned with unmasking or exposing "regimes" of power, he repudiates the idea that there is a way out from them:

> The idea of a liberating truth is a profound illusion. There is no truth that can be espoused, defended or rescued against systems of power. On the contrary, each such system defines its own variant of truth. And there is no escape from power into freedom, for such systems of power are coextensive with human society. We can only step from one to another. [24]

Foucault's project is therefore to delineate the process by which particular "regimes of truth" come into play through the emergence of particular bodies of discourse. In short, his entire oeuvre, particular in its later stages, involves an explication of the relationship between power and knowledge (Foucault, *Power/Knowledge*, 109). He attempts to describe the process by which knowledge becomes defined (that is, what is true and false) through the emergence of a particular system of power, or disciplinary regime. For Foucault, while power and knowledge may presuppose each other, they are not one and the same thing:

> When I read—and I know it has been attributed to me—the thesis "knowledge is power," or "power is knowledge," I begin to laugh, since studying their *relation* is precisely my problem. If they were identical, I would not have to study them and I would be spared a lot of fatigue as a result. The very fact that I pose *the question of their relation* proves clearly that I do not identify them. [25]

Given Foucault's assertion that knowledge and power are always impli-
cated in each other, what is the nature of their relationship? Foucault insists
that power is not merely a constraint on knowledge; rather, power incites
knowledge and creates its very possibility. It is through the disciplinary
practices that have emerged over the last two hundred years that our modern conception of knowledge has been formed. The principal concern of
Foucault the historiographer is therefore the "problem of the regime, the
politics of the scientific statement" (*Power/Knowledge*, 112). Thus many of
Foucault's *genealogies* are explications of the process by which scientific discourse comes to constitute a particular body of knowledge about the individual and thus subject him or her to a particular disciplinary regime. "This
regulated and polymorphous incitement to discourse" (Foucault, *History of
Sexuality*, 1:34) is a product of the power-knowledge relation.

For example, in his analysis of the birth of the prison, Foucault argues
that the shift from sovereign power to disciplinary power was fundamental
to the constitution of industrial capitalism and the accompanying bourgeois
conception of the individual. The rise of industrial capitalism required as its
concomitant system of societal regulation not the public display of sovereign power on the body of the transgressor, but rather the pervasiveness
of panoptical surveillance; that is, the development of a system of disciplinary techniques so ubiquitous and all-encompassing that the individual becomes a model of self-surveillance. Whether it be the prison, the school, the
factory, or the hospital, the individual is subjected to power in its capillary
form. The emergence of such disciplinary forms is coextensive with an explosion of scientific discourse associated with the disciplining of the body.
The discourse on sexuality, for example, produces not a sexually liberated
individual but rather an individual whose very identity is framed sexually.
Thus in analyzing discourse on sex, Foucault is constituting "the political
economy of a will to knowledge" (*History of Sexuality*, 1:73) in which he
shows that "what was formed was a political ordering of life, not through
an enslavement of others, but through an affirmation of self" (1:123).

Foucault articulates a conception of the power-knowledge relationship
that is in direct opposition to traditional Marxist equations of power with
domination or repression. Foucault considers this equation as inadequate
because it is unable to capture the productive aspect of power. He calls any
view that equates power with domination a "Repressive Hypothesis" (*History of Sexuality*, 1:15–49) and notes that such views adopt a purely juridical
conception of power-as-prohibitive. According to Foucault, "What makes
power hold good, what makes it accepted, is simply the fact that it doesn't
only weigh on us as a force that says no, but that it traverses and produces
things, it induces pleasure, forms knowledge, produces discourse" (*Power/
Knowledge*, 119). Foucault is equally critical of the Marxist notion of ideol-

ogy that is used to explain the process by which repressive practices are continually played out and reproduced in society:

> The notion of ideology appears to me to be difficult to make use of, for three reasons. The first is that, like it or not, it always stands in virtual opposition to something else which is supposed to count as truth. Now I believe that the problem does not consist in drawing the line between that in a discourse which falls under the category of scientificity or truth, and that which comes under some other category, but in seeing historically how effects of truth are produced within discourses which in themselves are neither true nor false. The second drawback is that the concept of ideology refers, I think necessarily, to something of the order of a subject. Thirdly, ideology stands in a secondary position relative to something which functions as its infrastructure, as its material, economic determinant, etc. For these three reasons, I think that this is a notion that cannot be used without circumspection.[26]

For Foucault, of course, the bifurcation between science and ideology is erroneous insofar as science is no different from ideology; that is, both ideological and scientific discourses function to subject the individual to various disciplinary practices that constitute his or her identity.[27] Foucault thus substitutes truth and power for science and ideology because the issue is not one of separating what is true (science) from what is false (ideology) but rather of uncovering the "ensemble of rules" according to which a "politics of truth" is constituted through the power-knowledge relationship.

How does Habermas fit into this schema? It is certainly not the case that he makes a simple bifurcation between science and ideology; for him, it is the (ideological) cooptation of practical and emancipatory reason by instrumental reason (science and technology) that is responsible for the inner colonization of the lifeworld. One of the goals of his critical theory of society is to explore the ideological functioning of instrumental reason (through systematically distorted communication) and to articulate the conditions under which the decolonization of the lifeworld (through communicative action) can occur. For Habermas, however, ideology is still opposed to truth and, indeed, becomes equated with systematically distorted communication. In effect, then, Habermas chooses to shift the focus of his analysis away from the traditional Marxist bifurcation of infrastructure and superstructure (in which ideology is seen as a product of the mode of production) and root it instead in a theory based in communicative action and knowledge-producing human interests.[28]

Of course, Habermas's project must be considered within the context of his humanist ideals of autonomy and independence from the coerciveness and asymmetry of systematically distorted communication. But Foucault would argue that such humanist ideals are themselves internal to, and cannot escape from, the disciplinary regime that humanism itself articulates. As such, Habermas's critical theory is, by Foucault's definition, devoid of any emancipatory force. For example, Foucault's analysis of the emergence of the penal system rests on the notion that humanist ideals have not produced a carceral society that is in any real sense more "humane" than the system of torture and repression that functioned in the Middle Ages. Rather, modern punishment takes the form of an "infinitely minute web of panoptic techniques"[29] that provides for an ongoing multiplication of disciplinary power through the never ending accumulation of new forms of knowledge about the subjected individual-as-criminal.

Foucault therefore makes the case that even under the conditions of a perfectly realized autonomous subjectivity (Habermas's ideal speech situation) in which the individual is ostensibly free from all forms of power and domination, what actually exists is the ultimate form of normalizing, disciplinary domination. Habermas's humanist ideal of autonomy and responsibility (*Mündigkeit*) is, in effect, the realization of the perfectly panoptical society; it is self-surveillance in its ultimate form. The realization of the humanist ideal therefore represents for Foucault the complete penetration of social control into all corners of society. It is Jeremy Bentham's panopticon fully universalized.

But what it is that Foucault offers in the place of the humanist ideal of a society characterized by rational thought and action, free from the influence of power and domination? If, indeed, there is no foundation for critique, then how does Foucault maintain any kind of critical force in his deconstruction of humanism and his argument for a *post*humanist political discourse? What would a posthumanist discourse look like? Foucault provides us with at least a partial clue in his description of the notion of genealogy:

> Let us give the term *genealogy* to the union of erudite knowledge and local memories which allows us to establish a historical knowledge of struggles and to make use of this knowledge tactically today. . . . [I]n contrast to the various projects which aim to inscribe knowledges in the hierarchical order of power associated with science, a genealogy should be seen as a kind of attempt to emancipate historical knowledges from that subjection, to render them, that is, capable of opposition and of struggle against the coercion of a theoretical, unitary, formal and scientific discourse. (*Power/Knowledge*, 83, 85)

Genealogies, according to Foucault, are "anti-sciences" that entertain the claims of discontinuous, illegitimate knowledge in opposition to the claims of the unitary, totalizing body of scientific discourse. But what forms of knowledge does Foucault consider to be local, discontinuous, and illegitimate, at least from the perspective of scientific discourse? Nancy Fraser suggests that the answer lies in Foucault's appeal to "bodies and pleasures" (*History of Sexuality*, 1:157) as the mode of counterattack against the modern deployment of discourse on sex as a disciplinary regime (Fraser, "Foucault's Body-Language"). "Sex" for Foucault is an illusory epistemic object that channels protest in ways that confine it within the extant disciplinary regime of bio-power. Thus protests in the name of sexual freedom simply reaffirm the power-knowledge relationship that identifies sex as an object of knowledge: "We must not think that by saying yes to sex, one says no to power; on the contrary, one tracks along the course laid out by the general deployment of sexuality" (Foucault, *History of Sexuality*, 1:157).

The focus on resistance in the name of "bodies and pleasures" instead of sex is, Fraser argues, consistent with Foucault's view that ultimately it is always the body that is contested within the power-knowledge regime. In *Discipline and Punish,* for example, Foucault presents the historical movement from torture to a carceral system not as a shift in the object of punishment from the body to the mind, but rather as an increasingly complex set of disciplinary practices that constitute a political technology of the body. Thus Foucault's project focuses on "the distinctive ways in which various successive power/knowledge regimes institute the body as an object within their respective techniques and practices" (Fraser, "Foucault's Body-Language," 63). It is because of this that the body takes on a special significance for Foucault and can function as a means of resistance to the extant regime of power-knowledge in a way that "sex-desire" cannot.

But what would such a posthumanist discourse of resistance look like? Foucault gives us no real clue, and Fraser admits that she "can form no concrete picture of what resistance to the deployment of sexuality in the regime of bio-power in the name of the body and its pleasures would be like" ("Foucault's Body-Language," 66). One answer might lie in Foucault's assertion that genealogy involves the activation of local knowledges against the unitary body of theory that constitutes the prevailing power-knowledge regime. In this context, feminist theory might fit the profile of a local counterdiscourse of resistance meeting Foucault's criteria for a body of knowledge that escapes the normalizing discourse of science. Although the relationship between Foucault and feminist theory is a topic for another essay, it could be argued that feminism and feminist scholarship articulates a discourse that is discontinuous with the androcentrism characteristic of normal(izing) scientific discourse. Feminist theory reappropriates the female body, not as an object(ification) of male desire, but as a means of (en)gendering political consciousness in a way that reconstructs social norms in a non-androcentric manner. This involves, for example, defining gender politically rather than sexually such that gender is deconstructed as an epistemic object in the same way that Foucault might deconstruct sex.[30]

The issue of the kind of posthumanistic rhetoric that the Foucauldian project implies as an alternative to the discourse of humanism leads me to the next issue; that is, what is the humanist (and in this context, what is Habermas's) response to Foucault and his ilk?

Habermas contra Foucault

The Foucauldian model of disciplinary power comes under particular attack from Habermas because he sees it as both totalizing and reductive: totalizing because, according to Foucault, nothing escapes the normalizing effects of power; reductive because meaning (truth-validity) is "functionistically reduced to the effects of power" (Habermas, *Philosophical Discourse*, 276). Habermas maintains that such a conception of power places Foucault in some aporias from which he cannot escape. If, as Foucault maintains, validity claims are merely the effects of power, then the genealogical project itself comes under question: "If the truth claims that Foucault himself raises for his genealogy of knowledge were in fact illusory and amounted to no more than the effects that this theory is capable of releasing within the circle of its adherents, then the entire undertaking of a critical unmasking of the human sciences would lose its point" (*Philosophical Discourse*, 279).

Foucault's project is to develop a system of thought that moves beyond the difficulties inherent in the human sciences, but his genealogy cannot be deemed superior on the grounds that it is more convincing than the human sciences. Foucault handles this difficulty by "turn[ing] genealogical historiography upon itself" and establishing its superiority through the history of its own emergence. It is in this context that Foucault invokes the disqualified, subjugated "erudite knowledge" the established human sciences have rejected. He claims to have secured the preeminence of genealogical historiography by establishing it as a counterpower that "is supposed to be able to transcend all validity claims that are only constituted in the enchanted circle of power. This link with disqualified popular knowledge is supposed to give to the genealogist's labor of reconstruction its superiority" (Habermas, *Philosophical Discourse*, 280).

According to Habermas, this conceptual turn by Foucault does not ameliorate the difficulties that he faces, For Foucault's concept of power does not allow a Lukácsian privileging of a particular, historically located class consciousness that frees critique from ideological bias. On the contrary, Foucault's theory of power dictates that every counterpower is located within the purview of the disciplinary power that it struggles against and, in turn, becomes the prevailing power regime against which new counterpowers emerge. Consequently, "genealogy only confirms that the validity claims of counterdiscourses count no more and no less than those of the discourses in power—they, too, *are* nothing else than the effects of power they unleash" (Habermas, *Philosophical Discourse*, 281). Ultimately, the genealogical method becomes a tool for assailing the unassailable regimes of power that constitute society. The question then becomes, of course, why engage in any form of resistance against the domination of the extant power-knowledge regimes?

> But if it is just a matter of mobilizing counterpower, of strategic battles and wily confrontations, why should we muster any resistance at all against this all-pervasive power circulating in the bloodstream of the body of modern society, instead of just adapting ourselves to it? Then the genealogy of knowledge as a weapon would be superfluous as well. It makes sense that a value-free analysis of the strengths and weaknesses of the opponent is of use to one who wants to take up the fight— but why fight at all? (*Philosophical Discourse*, 283–284)

Habermas finds the ultimate relativism of Foucault's position unacceptable. His own theory of communicative action provides a rational grounding for critical, emancipatory activity. Habermas maintains that Foucault's genealogical historiography privileges the power-knowledge relationship to such a degree that he has "erased all traces of communicative actions entangled in lifeworld contexts" (*Philosophical Discourse*, 286). In effect, according to Habermas, the Foucauldian subject has become a pure effect of power from which there is no escape. Habermas sees Foucault as having eliminated the subject as a conscious, autonomous individual in favor of a docile body created by the normalizing force of the disciplinary regime.

Habermas himself moves beyond the paradigm of the subject, but not by eliminating it. Instead, Habermas decenters the subject but at the same time retains it as a participant in communicative action. Thus he preserves an intrinsic relationship between communicative action and reason through the relationship between communicative action and validity claims that makes rationality possible and allows for the critique and transformation of society.

So although Habermas may agree that the decentering of the subject appropriately moves the focus of philosophical attention away from consciousness per se, he cannot accept the postmodern totalizing critique of reason. Such a critique negates the ability of reason to be critical of itself. For Habermas, postmodernism is fatally flawed because it has refused to acknowledge the emancipatory conditions of the modern, humanist tradition. It is to these critical emancipatory possibilities inherent in the Enlightenment tradition that Habermas's philosophical project is devoted.

Communication and the Power/Knowledge Relationship

How, then, does this discussion of Habermas and Foucault inform our conception of communication? Lawrence Grossberg provides a context for answering this question when he states:

> If discursive subjectivity is required for the reproduction of the contemporary social formation, then the fact that discourse and, increasingly, communication have come to define the essence of human nature, social life and the real locus of our subjectivity is itself a further ideological representation. Thus the very importance and power of communication is a form of domination, for particular interests, articulated within a context of ideological practices. It is this question—the ideological role of communicative practices and the ideological production of the status of communication—that has resisted and blocked philosophical interrogation.[31]

Although they approach the issue in very different ways, both Habermas and Foucault interrogate the "ideological role of communicative practices" and demonstrate the extent to which communication is a constitutive element in the production and reproduction of power relations in society.

For Habermas, this process of interrogation is conducted through the reconstruction of social theory around his theory of communicative action. In this sense, his deconstructive project operates on two levels. First, he is concerned with showing how the emergence of contemporary social theory is the product of certain epistemological turns taken via the Cartesian dualist legacy (manifesting itself in various forms in the works of Hegel, Marx, Comte, Weber, Parsons, Mead, and so on). This deconstructive process then gives way to a reconstruction of social theory based on his linguistic model of communicative understanding—a model which attains its fullest articulation in *The Theory of Communicative Action*. From a communication-theory perspective, this reconstructive process is important because it positions the analysis of communication at the very heart of

Habermas's theory of society. Communication is therefore conceived not as one variable among others (a conception framing most positivist communication research), but rather as that which makes the very existence of a lifeworld possible.

At the second level, Habermas's project informs our understanding of communication as a social and political practice. In other words, by situating communication at the center of his theory of society, Habermas forces us to conceive of the act of communication as indissoluble from the politics of everyday life. From this perspective, communication becomes *praxis*; that is, the individual actor-as-communicator is situated within a complex interplay of meaning systems and power relations that both enable and constrain social action.[32] In this context, the analysis of communication involves an exploration of the processes through which it functions ideologically to produce and reproduce certain interests and power relations in society.

For Habermas in particular, communication functions ideologically through the dominance of technological rationality and the colonization of the lifeworld by the system. His theory of communicative action therefore represents an attempt to reclaim the lifeworld as a sociocultural context freed from the dominance of systematically distorted (that is, ideological, techno-rational) forms of communication. Ultimately, Habermas's conception of communication is important to communication scholars because it articulates both the repressive and the emancipatory potential of social interaction and meaning formation, and the role of communication therein. Just as important, Habermas provides us with a rational, well-grounded theoretical perspective from which we can systematically deconstruct this ongoing process.

Foucault's impact on the interrogation of the "ideological role of communicative practices" is somewhat more difficult to assess, both because of his disavowal of emancipation as an explicit goal of critical inquiry, and because of his rejection of the notion of ideology and ideology-critique as an important critical tool. In addition, Foucault's ostensible antihumanism appears to militate against any conception of communication familiar to communication scholars. Yet, as Blair and Cooper indicate, this apparent antihumanism can actually be reconfigured as emancipatory and as a reaffirmation of the humanist ideal:

> Although Foucault turned his method of analysis onto humanism as it has been actualized as a positive ideology, his analysis functioned so as to explore the constraints that operated within the humanist perspective and to offer the possibility of freeing humankind from those constraints. In this way, Foucault celebrated the humanist ideal. Although

Foucault suspended the idea of a founding subject, his view of symbolic action implies a human agent and his method of critique focuses on the nature of that human agent.[33]

From this perspective, Foucault becomes less peripheral to a critical model of communication and society. In this context his work is interpreted as a deconstruction of the various structures and institutional modes of domination that characterize modern social systems.

But of course, Foucault's own particular configuration of the relationship between power and knowledge makes it much more difficult for us to imagine a Foucauldian view of communication fitting comfortably into a theory of society, as is the case with Habermas. The epistemic quality that Habermas attributes to communication is also present for Foucault, but in a very different form. The latter's conception of a productive relationship between power and knowledge makes the privileging of certain, so-called noncoercive forms of communication impossible. Whereas for Habermas the engagement in communicative action within the lifeworld context represents the humanist ideal of autonomy and responsibility, for Foucault such a mode of communication is just as derivative of the normalizing, repressive systems of humanist thought as any other. As such, it is devoid of any genuine emancipatory force.

How, then, can Foucault's oeuvre provide us with critical insight into the relationship between communication and power-knowledge? I argue that Foucault's work is best viewed from the perspective of "perpetual critique," in which no single discourse is afforded a privileged normative or epistemic status. From this point of view, Foucault exemplifies Richard Rorty's notion of "continuing the conversation" in which philosophical discourse is evaluated not in relation to some foundational truth criteria, but rather in terms of its ability to find "new, better, more interesting, more fruitful ways of speaking."[34] For Rorty, Foucault's work is "abnormal" or "edifying" in that it has the therapeutic goal of opening up new possibilities for ways of conceiving of the world. Most important, it problematizes received notions of the relationship between discourse and knowledge, and provides us with a new perspective on the ways in which communicative practices structure subjectivity in social and political contexts.

If nothing else, Foucault provides an important and necessary counterpoint to the Habermasian privileging of an evolutionary view of knowledge as moving smoothly and coherently toward the completion of the modernist project. As Rorty states:

> Maybe we *cannot* put together a history of thought which is both honest and continuous. Foucault might just possibly be right in saying that the stories we tell about how our ancestors gradually matured into our-

selves are *so* "Whiggish," *so* anachronistic, as to be worthless. . . . We can be grateful to Foucault for doing another of the things that philosophers are supposed to do—reaching for speculative possibilities that exceed our present grasp, but may nevertheless be our future.[35]

Conclusion

I have tried to address some of the philosophical, theoretical, and political concerns associated with conceptualizing the relationship between subjectivity and power, particularly as it is contextualized in the debate between modernist and postmodernist systems of thought. Although there is a degree of arbitrariness in constructing the argument in terms of a "debate" between Habermas and Foucault, such a framework does allow us to explore some of the central issues involved in constructing an adequate theory of the subject.

As a communication scholar, my principal concern is how adequately to conceive of the relationships among communication, power, and subjectivity, and this essay is an attempt to explore some of those relationships. As a field, however, communication has been so preoccupied with Quintilian's conception of rhetoric as "the good man speaking well" that it has neglected questions of subjectivity and power. Such a perspective essentializes the (primarily white, male) subject, and reduces questions of power to the rhetorical force of the better argument. In this sense much of the field of communication is largely unable to address the processes through which subjectivity is constituted in structures of discourse and power, precisely *because* subjectivity is taken as unproblematic (that is, as the essential, already constituted wellspring of reason and rhetoric).

Habermas and Foucault clearly offer possibilities for moving beyond such difficulties, albeit in different ways. Habermas is concerned with how subjectivity is constructed through communicative action grounded in certain knowledge-constituting interests, while Foucault shows how subjectivity is produced via the discursive practices of certain power-knowledge regimes. One could argue that Foucault articulates the more powerful critique of the "metaphysics of subjectivity," and therefore provides the more fruitful means by which to reconceptualize issues of communication, power, and subjectivity.

Specifically, Foucault's decentering the subject allows communication scholars to move beyond a naïve conception of communication as the product of a coherent, already formed subjectivity. By examining the processes through which various discursive formations constitute (and are constituted by) regimes of power-knowledge, we can develop a more radical theory of the subject that at the same time is not "subjectivist." That is, analyses must focus on the ways in which communication practices create "objective" conditions for the construction of the identities of social actors. Such a position does not conceive of subjectivity as a pure "effect" of discourse, but rather argues for a complex, contradictory, shifting relationship among discursive practices, subjectivity, and power. In this way we can move toward explanations of the ways in which individuals are structured into systems of domination on the one hand, and of the possibilities for transformation of these systems by social actors on the other.

It can therefore be argued that Foucault's decentering of the sovereign subject is not antihumanist at all, but rather that "in turning his critical method on humanism, Foucault turned toward a humanist ideal."[36] In other words, by deconstructing humanist discourse, Foucault exposes the constraints that are placed on human freedom, and by so doing simultaneously serves a critical (and potentially emancipatory) function. The critique of humanism does not therefore necessarily entail the complete rejection of humanist ideals; rather, it involves the critique of a "Whiggish" form of humanist idealism that falsely privileges the sovereign subject as the embodiment of bourgeois principles, which are in turn seen as universal characteristics of subjectivity.

By describing the emergence of particular power-knowledge regimes and the concomitant articulation of certain modes of subjectivity, Foucault creates the discursive space within which we can begin to talk about alternative ways of being. An important task for the field of communication is therefore to explicate how discursive practices constitute forms of subjectivity in different ways. Through the examination of what Foucault refers to as "erudite knowledge," we can gain a better understanding of the complex interplay of dominance and resistance that emerges in the intersection of discourse, subjectivity, and power-knowledge relations.[37]

NOTES

1. Contemporary European thought does not begin to exert any real influence on the field of communication until the 1970s. For example, Stanley Deetz's "An Understanding of Science and a Hermeneutic Science of Understanding," *Journal of Communication* 23 (1973): 139–159, is one of the earliest articles to be published in a communication journal that explicitly adopts a hermeneutic approach to communication theory and research. Similarly, Brant Burleson and Susan Kline's "Habermas' Theory of Communication: A Critical Explication," *Quarterly Journal of Speech* 65 (1979): 412–428, appears to be the first piece to examine systematically the impact of Habermas's work on contemporary communication theory. Foucault's impact on the field is even more recent and perhaps more tenuous, although examples of studies that adopt a Foucauldian perspective abound: Carole Blair and Martha Cooper, "The Humanist Turn in Foucault's Rhetoric of Inquiry," *Quarterly Journal of Speech* 73 (1987): 151–171; Raymie McKerrow, "Critical Rhetoric: Theory and Praxis," *Communication Monographs* 56 (1989): 91–111; and David J. Sholle, "Critical

Studies: From the Theory of Ideology to Power/Knowledge," *Critical Studies in Mass Communication* 5 (1988): 16–41:

2. See, for example, Dennis K. Mumby, *Communication and Power in Organizations: Discourse, Ideology, and Domination* (Norwood, N.J.: Ablex Publishing, 1988); and "The Political Function of Narratives in Organizations," *Communication Monographs* 54 (1987): 113–127; Lawrence Grossberg, "The Ideology of Communication: Post-Structuralism and the Limits of Communication," *Man and World* 15 (1982): 83–101.

3. See, for example, Stuart Hall, "Signification, Representation, Ideology: Althusser and the Post-Structuralist Debates," *Critical Studies in Mass Communication* 2 (1985): 91–114; Fredric Jameson, *The Political Unconscious: Narrative as a Socially Symbolic Act* (Ithaca: Cornell University Press, 1981); and Lawrence Grossberg, "Strategies of Marxist Cultural Interpretation," *Critical Studies in Mass Communication* 1 (1984): 392–421.

4. For excellent discussions on the notion of "the subject" in the context of contemporary philosophical thought, see Rosalind Coward and John Ellis, *Language and Materialism: Developments in Semiology and the Theory of the Subject* (London: Routledge & Kegan Paul, 1977); and Paul Smith, *Discerning the Subject* (Minneapolis: University of Minnesota Press, 1988). In this context I refer to the notion of "subject" or "subjectivity" in the Althusserian sense as the process by which individuals are interpellated, or addressed, by various discursive-political practices and thus ideologically inserted into social formations in certain ways. But I differ from Althusser in that my understanding of "subjectivity" also embodies a notion of "agency"; that is "a form of subjectivity where, by virtue of the contradictions and disturbances in and among subject-positions, the possibility (indeed, the actuality) of resistance to ideological pressure is allowed for (even though that resistance too must be produced in an ideological context)" (Smith, *Discerning the Subject*, xxxv). See also, Goran Therborn, *The Ideology of Power and the Power of Ideology* (London: Verso, 1980); and Anthony Giddens, *Central Problems in Social Theory* (Berkeley: University of California Press, 1979), for conceptions of subjectivity incorporating a notion of agency.

5. The critical commentary on both Habermas and Foucault concerning their modernism and postmodernism is voluminous, but see, for example, Richard J. Bernstein, ed., *Habermas and Modernity* (Cambridge: MIT Press, 1985); and Gilles Deleuze, *Foucault* (Minneapolis: University of Minnesota Press, 1988).

6. See Jürgen Habermas, *Communication and the Evolution of Society*, trans. Thomas McCarthy (Boston: Beacon Press, 1979); *The Theory of Communicative Action*, vol. 1, *Reason and the Rationalization of Society*, trans. Thomas McCarthy (Boston: Beacon Press, 1984); and *The Theory of Communicative Action*, vol. 2, *Lifeworld and System*, trans. Thomas McCarthy (Boston: Beacon Press, 1987). *The Theory of Communicative Action* is also cited in the text.

7. Michel Foucault, *Power/Knowledge*, ed. Colin Gordon, trans. Colin Gordon, Leo Marshall, John Mepham, and Kate Sopher (New York: Pantheon, 1980), 117. This source is also cited in the text.

8. Michel Foucault, *The Order of Things: An Archaeology of the Human Sciences* (New York: Vintage Books, 1973), 387.

9. Michel Foucault, *Discipline and Punish: The Birth of the Prison*, trans. Alan Sheridan (New York: Vintage Books, 1979), 27–28.

10. Nancy Fraser, "Foucault's Body-Language: A Post-Humanist Political Rhetoric?" *Salmagundi* 61 (Fall 1983): 56. This source is also cited in the text.

11. See, for example, Nancy Fraser, "Michel Foucault: A 'Young Conservative'?" *Ethics* 96 (1985): 165–184; and "Foucault's Body-Language"; and Jürgen Habermas, "Modernity versus Postmodernity," *New German Critique* 22 (1981): 3–14. For a more sympathetic reading of Foucault's antihumanism, see Blair and Cooper, "The Humanist Turn."

12. Jürgen Habermas, *Knowledge and Human Interests*, trans. Jeremy Shapiro (Boston: Beacon Press, 1971).

13. See Foucault, *Discipline and Punish*; *The History of Sexuality*, vol. 1, trans. Robert Hurley (New York: Vintage Books, 1980); and *Madness and Civilization*, trans. Richard Howard (original English language publication 1965; reprint New York: Vintage Books, 1988). *The History of Sexuality* is also cited in the text.

14. Jürgen Habermas, *Theory and Practice*, trans. John Viertel (Boston: Beacon Press, 1974), 8.

15. Ibid., 8–9.

16. See Thomas McCarthy, *The Critical Theory of Jürgen Habermas* (Cambridge: MIT Press, 1981), 55 and *passim*.

17. In addition to *Knowledge and Human Interests* and *Theory and Practice*, see also Jürgen Habermas, *Communication and The Evolution of Society* (Boston: Beacon Press, 1979); and *Legitimation Crisis* (Boston: Beacon Press, 1975).

18. See John. B. Thompson, "Rationality and Social Rationalization: An Assessment of Habermas's Theory of Communicative Action," *Sociology* 17 (1983): 278–294.

19. J. L. Austin, *How to Do Things with Words* (Oxford: Basil Blackwell, 1962). See also J. R. Searle, *Speech Acts: An Essay in the Philosophy of Mind* (Cambridge: Cambridge University Press, 1969).

20. Habermas, *Theory of Communicative Action*, 2:152. See chapter six for a full discussion of the relationship between lifeworld and system.

21. See also Habermas, *Legitimation Crisis*.

22. In Habermas's essay "Modernity versus Postmodernity," *New German Critique* 22 (1981): 13, he writes:

> The Young Conservatives recapitulate the basic experience of aesthetic modernity. They claim as their own the revelations of a decentered subjectivity, emancipated from the imperatives of work and usefulness, and with this experience they step outside the modern world. On the basis of modernistic attitudes, they justify an irreconcilable anti-modernism. They remove into the sphere of the faraway and the archaic the spontaneous powers of imagination, of self-experience and of emotionality. To instrumental reason, they juxtapose in manichean fashion a principle only accessible through evocation, be it the will to power or sovereignty, Being or the Dionysiac force of the poetical. In France this line leads from Bataille via Foucault to Derrida.

23. Habermas's most extensive critique to date of postmodernism can be found in *The Philosophical Discourse of Modernity*, trans. Frederick Lawrence (Cambridge: MIT Press, 1987). For a critique of Foucault specifically, see chaps. 9 and 10. (*The Philosophical Discourse of Modernity* is also cited in the text.) For a discussion of some of the principal issues in the Habermas-Foucault debate see, for example, Peter Hohendahl, "Habermas' Philosophical Discourse of Modernity," *Telos* 69 (1986): 49–65; Stephen White, "Foucault's Challenge to Critical Theory," *American Political Science Review* 80 (1986): 419–432; Tom Keenan, "The 'Paradox' of Knowledge and Power: Reading Foucault on a Bias," *Political Theory* 15 (1987): 5–37; and Alexander

Hooke, "The Order of Others: Is Foucault's Anti-Humanism against Human Action?" *Political Theory* 15 (1987): 38–60.

24. Charles Taylor, "Foucault on Freedom and Truth," *Political Theory* 12 (1984): 152–153.

25. Quoted in Keenan, "The 'Paradox' of Knowledge and Power," 12.

26. Foucault, *Power/Knowledge*, 118. For a Foucauldian critique of Marxist approaches to critical studies, see Sholle, "Critical Studies: From the Theory of Ideology to Power/Knowledge."

27. In recent years the most fully developed Marxist conception of this bifurcation is provided by Louis Althusser in his *For Marx*, trans. Ben Brewster (London: Verso, 1977).

28. It is interesting that John B. Thompson criticizes Habermas for not fully exploring the relationship between communication, ideology, and the inner colonization of the lifeworld. Thompson argues that he employs an overly restrictive conception of ideology:

> By restricting the notion of ideology to the totalizing conceptions of past decades and centuries, Habermas leaves us without the theoretical and methodological means to examine critically the forms of language which serve *today* to sustain relations of domination. That such forms of language often operate by fragmenting consciousness in various ways, that they can be conceived as ideology and analyzed with the help of specific methods—these are claims which I have defended elsewhere. Suffice it to say here that few tasks seem more urgent than the continuation of that project of a *critique of ideology* which appears to have faded into the background of Habermas's work. ("Rationality and Social Rationalization," 293)

Also see John B. Thompson, *Studies in the Theory of Ideology* (Berkeley and Los Angeles: University of California Press, 1984), for an explication of the relationship between language, ideology, and domination.

29. Foucault, *Discipline and Punish*, 224.

30. There is some debate about the degree of compatibility between Foucauldian discourse and feminist theory. In a sense, one has to be careful to distinguish between Foucauldian theory per se, in which Foucault has little to say about the way in which female bodies specifically are rendered docile by a particular disciplinary regime (Foucault speaks of power as subjugating everyone equally), and the ways in which feminist theory is sympathetic to and hence utilizes a Foucauldian perspective. Thus Isaac Balbus argues that "the discourse of the mother looks like a paradigm case of what Foucault would call a 'disciplinary true discourse,' while from a feminist psychoanalytic standpoint the Foucauldian deconstruction of true discourse betrays assumptions that can only be characterized as a classically male flight from maternal foundations. If feminism necessarily embraces these foundations, then a Foucauldian feminism is a contradiction in terms" (Isaac D. Balbus, "Disciplining Women: Michel Foucault and the Power of Feminist Discourse," in *After Foucault: Humanistic Knowledge, Postmodern Challenges*, ed. Jonathan Arac [New Brunswick: Rutgers University Press, 1988], 138). In the same collection of essays, Jana Sawicki makes the following counterclaim:

> Is Foucauldian feminism a contradiction in terms? I would not have thought so. After all, Foucault and feminists both focus on sexuality as a key arena of political struggle. Both expand the domain of the political to include forms of social domination associated with the personal sphere. And both launch critiques against forms of biological determinism, and

humanism. Finally, both are skeptical of the human sciences insofar as they have participated in modern forms of domination. Indeed, rather than link the growth of knowledge with progress, both describe how the growth of specific forms of knowledge—for example, in medicine, psychiatry, sociology, psychology—has been linked to the emergence of subtle mechanisms of social control, and the elision of other forms of knowledge and experience.

("Feminism and the Power of Foucauldian Discourse," in *After Foucault*, 161).

31. Grossberg, "The Ideology of Communication," 100.

32. For an elaboration of the notion of enablement and constraint as applied to social action, see Anthony Giddens's theory of structuration as articulated in *Central Problems in Social Theory* (Berkeley: University of California Press, 1979); and in *The Constitution of Society* (Berkeley and Los Angeles: University of California Press, 1984).

33. Blair and Cooper, "The Humanist Turn," 168.

34. Richard Rorty, *Philosophy and the Mirror of Nature* (Princeton: Princeton University Press, 1979), 60.

35. Richard Rorty, "Foucault and Epistemology," in *Foucault: A Critical Reader*, ed. David Hoy (Oxford: Basil Blackwell, 1986), 48.

36. Blair and Cooper, "The Humanist Turn," 159.

37. Examples of communication studies that explore the constitution of subjectivity within specific sites of discursive dominance and resistance (and which either implicitly or explicitly suggest transformative possibilities) are Henry Jenkins III, "*Star Trek* Rerun, Reread, Rewritten: Fan Writing as Textual Poaching," *Critical Studies in Mass Communication* 5 (1988): 85–107; Marc J. LaFountain, "Foucault and Dr. Ruth," *Critical Studies in Mass Communication* 6 (1989): 123–137; and Charles Conrad, "Work Songs, Hegemony, and Illusions of Self," *Critical Studies in Mass Communication* 5 (1988): 179–201.

Social Constructions

✦ JACKSON LEARS ✦

The Ad Man and the Grand Inquisitor
Intimacy, Publicity, and the Managed Self in America, 1880–1940

T
he rise of national advertising promoted new rhetorical strategies in the emergent discourse of a managerial ruling class. All the cute new business icons—the Gold Dust Twins, the Campbell Soup kids—were enmeshed in developing forms of corporate power. This observation seems uncontroversial: who, after all, was paying the ad agencies' bills except the emergent national corporations? Yet any attempt to link advertising and power tends to provoke rancorous and unproductive debate, with one side lamenting that advertisers have seduced whole populations into serving the false gods of commodity civilization and the other side asserting that ordinary folk are too shrewd to be manipulated. Inquiries into the impact of advertising tend to fall into rigid bipolar categories: accommodation and resistance, submission and freedom—each in some sense a mirror image of the other. To get beyond this stalemate, we might begin by reconsidering a classic parable of modern power—a tale that seems to confirm the model of a manipulative elite and a stupefied populace, but actually leads us in more productive directions.

The Problem of Power and the Production of the Subject

Little more than a century ago, Fyodor Dostoyevsky wrote a chapter of *The Brothers Karamazov* (1880) called "The Grand Inquisitor." Christ returns to earth and is jailed by a withered cardinal who tells him that he must be burned as a heretic: his gospel's emphasis on moral choice is unsuited to the frailties of human flesh. "I tell Thee," says the churchman to Christ, "that man is tormented by no greater anxiety than to find someone quickly to whom he can hand over that gift of freedom with which the ill-fated creature is born." The genius of modern church administrators, according to the grand inquisitor, has been to recognize that anxious need, to offer humankind earthly bread in exchange for abject submission. The exchange involves a kind of shell game between the powerful and the powerless, a process recalling Marxian accounts of alienated labor.

> Receiving bread from us, they will see clearly that we take the bread made by their hands from them, to give it to them, without any miracle. They will see that we do not change the stones to bread, but in truth they will be more thankful for taking it from our hands than for the bread itself! For they will remember only too well that in old days, without our help, even the bread they made turned to stones in their hands, while since they have come back to us, the very stones have turned to bread in their hands. Too, too well they know the value of complete submission! . . . Then we shall give them the quiet humble happiness of weak creatures such as they are by nature. . . . We shall show them that they are weak, that they are only pitiful children, but that childlike happiness is the sweetest of all. . . . They will marvel at us and be awe-stricken before us, and will be proud at our being so powerful and clever. . . . Yes, we shall set them to work, but in their leisure hours we shall make their life like a child's game, with children's songs and innocent dance. . . . And they will have no secrets from us. . . . The most painful secrets of their conscience, all, all they will bring to us, and we shall have an answer for all. And they will be glad to believe our answer, for it will save them from the great anxiety and terrible agony they endure at present in making a free decision for themselves.[1]

The scene is a deft reversal of Enlightenment convention: the cardinal is not a representative of an outmoded reactionary order but rather a harbinger of a new kind of administrative state—a modern bureaucratic system whose leaders command allegiance by claiming an unrivaled capacity to meet the physical and psychic needs of their subjects. Through a mystifying sleight-of-hand the administration persuades the people that the fruits of their labor are instead the largesse of an omnicompetent productive mechanism. The administrators remain inquisitors; they seek to know "the most painful secrets," the most intimate details of private lives, in order (they assert) to relieve those lives of pain. They construct an authority structure that fosters fawning dependency rather than hostile servility, that surfeits the body but suffocates the soul.

This view of the future seems indistinguishable from the nightmare vision that has haunted critics of mass society for generations. Yet the passage also raises issues that complicate any such formulaic reading. In the speech of the grand inquisitor, Dostoyevsky anticipated by many decades the influential assertions now associated with Michel Foucault: modern authority has not been merely negative, repressive, and juridical, but positive and productive—animated by a "will to knowledge" that has generated more than a vast apparatus of surveillance and classification; it has unleashed as well a flood of "expert opinion" that brought intimate experience into the arena of public commentary. Private matters previously ignored by the state have become topics of intense political debate, symptoms of health or disease in the body politic. Like earlier rulers, but more systematically and intrusively, the architects of the administrative state have constructed notions of human subjectivity that conform to their needs and interests. In the process of investigating and publicizing the private self, Foucault observed, modern inquisitors have created new patterns of dependency and new forms of cultural power.[2]

Foucault's most original contribution was his argument that power under modern administration was neither monolithically institutionalized nor straightforwardly expressed. Rather than a centralized regime, Foucault envisioned a multitude of sites (schools, hospitals, prisons) where power relations were enacted under the banners of modernity and rationality. Like Dostoyevsky, he turned Enlightenment wisdom on its head: he asserted that the precondition for these new forms of domination was a humanist mythology that placed the autonomous individual subject at the center of history. The celebration of the individual's freedom from old constraints coincided with the preparation of new and subtler systems of dependency and coercion. The owl of Minerva flew at dusk.

Yet whiggish notions die hard. Despite the skeptical shafts of doubters like Melville, faith in the autonomy and centrality of the human subject weathered storms of revolution and reaction, pervading the liberal and Marxist traditions and surviving to our own time. It underlies contemporary debates over advertising and mass culture, joining the critics of accommodation with the celebrants of resistance. Whatever their disagreements, the two sides share an unspoken prior commitment to an essentialist ideal of individual autonomy. However morally admirable, that commitment has concealed the contingent, historically constructed character of the autonomous subject; it has also obscured the ways that this cultural construction, the central myth of the Enlightenment, serves the interests of modern inquisitors who are interested in promoting anything but autonomy.

The problem for the historian is to relate this schematic and abstract set of propositions to the messiness of actual experience. One way is to look at the rise of sorting and categorizing institutions—the army, the schools, the prisons—in various bureaucratic nation-states. But I have in mind a less obvious example of a modern inquisition, the development of national advertising in the United States during the late nineteenth and early twentieth centuries.

At first glance it seems absurd to suggest that American advertising could have anything to do with the claustrophobic worlds of Dostoyevsky or Foucault: advertisers have often been condemned or celebrated (and have celebrated themselves) as agents of personal liberation.[3] Yet that celebration is precisely what should give us pause. National advertising, more systematically and pervasively than any other institution, has produced the dominant ideals of human subjectivity under advanced capitalism. (Indeed one could argue it has produced little else.) This production of the subject has not been a monolithic process run by a central administration; it has occurred in a variety of cultural sites—visual and verbal texts in magazines, newspapers, and other mass media. Yet it has been sponsored by some of the most powerful bureaucratic hierarchies in the modern world, the national and later multinational corporations.

To explore the links between the ad man and the grand inquisitor, then, is not merely to make literal-minded sport of market research. Nor is it to indulge in the time-worn and unprovable charge that advertisers "brainwash the masses," or even merely manipulate their audience to do their bidding. It is to make a more modest but maybe more interesting claim: national advertisers, by arrogating the prestige of production, bringing publicity to areas of intimacy, and projecting their own world view into a mass-produced commercial rhetoric and iconography, participated in the construction of what one might call a managed subject—a normative self that suited the emerging corporate structure of power relations in the early twentieth-century United States. By exploring the construction and reconstruction of that self in advertising, we may be able to get a firmer grasp on some previously neglected relationships: those between supposedly apolitical notions of personal well-being and the public realm of class relations, and those between the mass dissemination of imagery and the actual exercise of corporate power.

The developing discourse of selfhood was sponsored by public as well as private institutions. Advertisers were by no means the only group involved in the construction of a managed subject. They were part of a larger historical bloc of educated managers and professionals coming to prominence around the turn of the century—a loose coalition of doctors, lawyers, and college professors (especially social scientists) as well as business executives; people who traded in information rather than things and spoke a common idiom that could be called imperial rationality.

The idiom of imperial rationality was a streamlined version of nineteenth-century impulses to control the unsettling cultural impact of expanding commerce. Victorian moralists, drinking deep from the springs of the plain-speech tradition, had sought to stabilize the epistemological sorcery inherent in market exchange by developing various idioms of control—ideals of sincerity in personal conduct and mimesis in the arts, doctrines of legal rationality in the realm of social relations—all sanctioned faith in linguistic transparency and unified selfhood. During the later nineteenth century, the growing prestige of positivistic science and the rise of photography provided more secular bases for the belief in unproblematic communication; the swelling numbers of immigrants from Eastern and Southern Europe and the rising intellectual respectability of racism tied that belief more firmly to an imperial ideology of Anglo-Saxon supremacy; and the beginnings of bureaucratic structure in business, government, and education provided an institutional home for a developing technocratic idiom of control.[4]

Where did advertising men fit into this picture? As products of a common Protestant culture, they embraced both the older and newer versions of linguistic transparency. Yet for many the claim to provide a transparent window on a particular commodity was a superficial gloss; they continued to behave as if they were involved in a rhetorical performance intended to mesmerize their audience. They remained wedded to the carnivalesque contentions of the nineteenth-century peddler: the promise of magical self-transformation through the ritual of purchase. If the ethos of imperial rationality prized predictability and control, the older language of the market traded on novelty and discontent. Advertising executives struggled to merge two incompatible discourses. Seeking to appropriate the idiom of imperial rationality, they remained hampered in the project by their own carnivalesque traditions. From the carnivalesque view, language is not transparent but opaque, an opportunity for clever performance that conceals rather than reveals the speaker's motives. The self is not coherent and controlled but ambiguous and fragmented.

So it should come as no surprise that advertising men were never fully at ease with the other groups in the professional-managerial bloc—despite the interests and values they held in common. Debates were most acrimonious during the agitation for pure food and drug legislation in the 1900s and 1910s, then again with the rise of the consumer movement in the 1930s. At other times, particularly during the world wars, the professional-managerial bloc closed ranks, assuming the captaincy of what Edward Bellamy (a favorite managerial author) had called "the industrial army." This move granted the advertising industry unprecedented legitimacy as a vehicle of prowar propaganda. When demands for national conformity were at their height, the ad man and the grand inquisitor grew closer in spirit.

Still, it remains an open question how successfully their managerial powers were exercised. As Lizabeth Cohen and other historians have demonstrated, there were many working-class Americans who clung to traditional ways, who refused to conform to the standardized models held out to them by national advertising. And David Thelen has shown how middle-class reformers could use consumer consciousness as a basis for challenging the assertion of corporate power. Raymond Williams put the matter succinctly in his unwittingly post-structuralist comment: "There are no masses, there are only ways of talking about people as masses."[5]

By talking about people as masses, national advertisers and other managerial professionals participated in a dramatic reconstitution of the human subject. If advertisers did not officiate at the marriage of intimacy and imperial rationality, they at least posted the banns. And if the new norms failed to stabilize the quiverings of discontent, that was less the fault of management than of the unquiet human heart.

Institutions and Ideology: The Managerial Demiurge

Mid-nineteenth-century entrepreneurs did without advertising agencies. They wrote and designed their own advertisements, and bought their own space in newspapers and magazines. If they wanted more elaborate artistic effects, they could hire a chromolithography firm to produce them. By the 1850s, chromolithographers had become the chief producers of a burgeoning vernacular tradition in commercial iconography. Many though by no means all were recent German immigrants (gentile or Jewish), and they tended to proliferate in cities with large German populations; among the best-known and most influential were Louis Prang in Boston and the partnership of Major & Knapp in New York. They worked in small shops with a rudimentary division of labor, cranking out sentimental genre prints, interchangeable images that could be used as trade cards by various retailers, and specialized work designed for particular advertisers. Without question the most vigorous and innovative of those advertisers, and the first to try to reach a national market, were the patent medicine companies. The men who bottled and sold Hood's Sarsparilla, Ayer's Cherry Pectoral, and dozens of like remedies developed their own advertising departments (often using the bulk of the budget for the entire firm), which flooded newspapers and country store counters with increasingly sophisticated sales appeals.[6]

The patent medicine companies were also among the earliest and most important customers of the first national advertising agencies. Beginning as space brokers, agency heads soon followed George H. Rowell's example of trying to provide a sounder basis for the troubled client's choice of media. This sort of marketing service soon expanded into the makeup and design of the advertisements themselves. By the turn of the century, J. Walter Thompson, Calkins & Holden, and others were describing themselves as "full-service agencies" and supervising every detail of the advertising process from layout and copy to final insertion.[7]

The rise of advertising agencies marked a major change in the social conditions of commercial image production. The independence of the chromolithographer, always problematic at best, disappeared in the interdependent, bureaucratically organized operations of the advertising agency; illustrations and copy were subject to revisions at the hands of art directors, copy chiefs, account executives, and clients. Advertising agency staffs were from more affluent and ethnically homogenous backgrounds than those of the chromolithographers. All available evidence indicates that by the early twentieth century, if not earlier, the most influential agencies with the biggest accounts were staffed by a remarkably similar group of Anglo-Saxon males—college-educated, usually at prestigious northeastern schools; Protestant, often the sons of Presbyterian or Congregationalist ministers; midwestern or northeastern, commonly from small towns or suburbs. The experience of working for a national advertising agency in New York separated them ambiguously from their own past and decisively from the vast majority of their fellow Americans.[8]

After several decades this insulation from the common life led to some soul-searching. Wallace Boren of J. Walter Thompson, conducting an in-house survey of New York copywriters for the company in 1936, discovered that not one belonged to a lodge or civic club; only one in five went to church except on rare occasions; half never went to Coney Island or any other popular public resort, and the others only once or twice a year; more than half had never lived within the national average income of $1,580 per family a year, and half did not know anyone who ever had. While 5 percent of American homes had servants, 66 percent of J. Walter Thompson homes did. The profile was affluent, metropolitan, secular, and (superficially) sophisticated. And this was typical of the copywriters of the most prominent agencies with the largest accounts.[9]

These institutions were part of the burgeoning "service sector" of an emerging oligopolistic economy. Between the Civil War and World War I, the making and distribution of consumer goods as well as more "basic" forms of production and processing came under the unprecedented direction of national corporations. To take an example that reflects the values as well as the economic structures of the new corporate system, wristwatch manufacturers, who had done $2.8 million dollars of business in 1869, quadrupled that amount to over $14 million by 1914; yet the number of firms making watches decreased from thirty-seven to fifteen—eleven of which were brand-name advertisers in the national magazines.[10]

The magazines themselves (*Saturday Evening Post, Ladies Home Journal,* and the like) were expressions of the managerial order as well: they were cheaper than the great maiden aunts of quality journalism—magazines like *Atlantic* or *Harper's Monthly*—largely because they were supported by advertising revenues rather than subscriptions. And their advertisers were nearly all large corporations aiming their goods at a national market. "There is still an illusion to the effect that a magazine is a periodical in which advertising is incidental," the advertising executive James Collins told a congressional committee in 1907. "But we don't look at it that way. A magazine is simply a device to induce people to read advertising. It is a large booklet with two departments—entertainment and business. The entertainment department finds stories, pictures, verses, etc. to interest the public. The business department makes the money." Small wonder that the editorial matter and even the fiction in many of the magazines came to resemble the advertising copy. National brand-name advertisements were a key cultural expression of the hegemonic professional-managerial bloc that was hesitantly emerging out of the wreckage of the war between labor and capital.[11]

While advertising agencies were consolidating control over nationally distributed commercial information and imagery, other professionalizing elites were laying claim to different sectors of the culture. Among the most successful was the allopathic medical establishment. (Allopathy referred to the orientation toward fighting specific disease entities rather than a more holistic approach—as in homeopathy.) In two decades around the turn of the century, mainstream medical practitioners acquired unprecedented legitimacy, largely due to the popularization of the germ theory of disease and such therapeutic breakthroughs as the development of rabies vaccine (1885) and diphtheria antitoxin (1891). Doctors' efforts to weed out charlatans and standardize credentials suddenly bore fruit. Advertising executives, attempting to duplicate the procedure, struggled to sanctify "the legitimate agent who has a scientific, definite, and above-board knowledge of advertising." By 1909, the N. W. Ayer agency was solemnly advising its clients to "choose your [advertising] agent as you would your lawyer or your doctor"—then leave the rest of the work to him.[12]

There was more going on here than just a clumsy effort to appropriate the prestige of professionalism. By enfolding themselves in the mantle of expertise, advertising claimed the same sort of authority that was passing to other managerial elites both in government and business. During the first two decades of the twentieth century the development of regulatory agencies cemented the partnership between oligopolistic capital and the administrative state, insulating public policy from popular influence as never before. Perhaps the most striking example of this was in the realm of monetary policy: the defeat of the Populist campaign for a democratically managed currency and the formation of the Federal Reserve System signaled official government support for the most powerful central bankers—men with cultural as well as economic ties to the WASP elites in national advertising.[13]

Like other managerial professionals, agency executives believed they were playing a key role in lubricating the mechanisms of economic growth and moral progress. They identified their national outlook (and the national brands they promoted) with a cosmopolitan "new American tempo"; they dismissed local custom as sluggish provincial reaction. Especially when addressing an audience other than their clients, they dropped their salesman's baggage and embraced a secular missionary role consistent with their Protestant past. "We advertising writers are privileged to compose a new chapter of civilization," a senior copywriter named James Wallen wrote in 1925. "It is a great responsibility to mold the daily lives of millions of our fellow men, and I am persuaded that we are second only to statesmen and editors in power for good." The definition of publicity as education was a common "progressive" reflex during the early twentieth century; advertisers stressed not the exposure of corruption bred in filthy places (as muckrakers and other reformers had done) but the dissemination of a modernized standard of physical well-being. The nature of advertisers' "power for good" was nowhere more visible, they claimed, than in the sanitation of Americans' daily lives and personal appearances: the plumbing of bathrooms from Maine to California, the elimination of the American carnivore's traditional greasy breakfast; the disappearance of beards and expansive stomachs among men, of body hair and facial blemishes among women. Historically contingent fashion, as at other points in modern cultural history, was endowed by advertisers with universal moral significance. As early as 1910, a contributor to the advertising trade journal *Printers Ink* noted "the spick-and-spanness of American people as compared with people abroad" and concluded that "without any doubt the advertising artist is responsible for it." Implicitly rejecting the ancient Protestant distrust of appearances, national advertisers equated the smooth face with the regenerate heart.[14]

Advertisers' claim to be key agents of progress was part of a broader managerial reworking of postmillennial thought. For many "progressive" reformers the exercise provided them with moral legitimacy in a culture still largely wedded to Protestant habits of mind; for advertisers it served the added purpose of distancing them further from their carnivalesque origins. Far from contributing to the centrifugal confusions of the marketplace, as their entrepreneurial predecessors had done, they claimed to be stabilizing a steady movement toward a secular millennium. In moments of hubris (or desperation) they professed the ultimate managerial faith: a belief in their own capacity to flatten the curves in the business cycle. From this view, even in hard times advertising could entice enough customers through the turnstiles to keep a manufacturer's profitability afloat.[15]

The intellectual assumptions behind this sort of hubris were part of the outlook I am calling imperial rationality. Like other aspiring professionals of the era, advertising men participated in the regnant fantasy that "we" (the managerial elite in question) had acquired the capacity to predict and control human behavior through "social science." The epistemological basis for this world view was a radical disjunction between observer and observed—an assumption that the observer could analyze the object of study without intruding his own attitudes and prejudices. It was this world view that led advertisers, along with many other managerial professionals, to probe intimate areas of life more systematically than had been done before.

But the imperial rationalist outlook could take a variety of forms. One of its softer versions was the faith that "the laws of human nature" had been discovered and could be used to promote valuable social goals, a faith that led to what the historian William Graebner has ironically (and accurately) dubbed "democratic social engineering." This oxymoron was the "group process" method of manipulating consensus; a persuasive group leader, often possessing scientific expertise, would foster a sense of spontaneity, experimentation, and participation while leading the group toward an "appropriate" goal. The method was hailed (or used) by men as various as John Dewey, Dale Carnegie, Walter Lippmann, and Edward Bernays. By the 1920s, it was employed in settling "labor relations" disputes (indeed the very term was a social engineer's euphemism for class struggle), promoting effective salesmanship, and devising schemes for personnel management and progressive education. It was a way of rendering coercion invisible.[16]

Advertising men thought they had a knack for it too—though they practiced a more impersonal and literary version. In public forums their tribunes spoke the language of consumer sovereignty, as in this 1930 *Collier's* editorial:

> The old Kings and aristocrats have departed. In the new order the masses are master. Not a few, but millions and hundreds of millions of people must be persuaded. In peace and in war, for all kinds of purposes, advertising carries the message to this new King—the people.
> Advertising is the King's messenger in this day of economic democracy. All unknowing a new force has been let loose in the world. Those who understand it will have one of the keys to the future.[17]

It was still too early in the depression for the tone to be defensive. Nevertheless, there were certain revealing strains in the argument. It is never

clear, first of all, who this message is from: by 1930 the shift from highly
visible robber barons to faceless managers has already occurred; the invis-
ibility of corporate leadership will become one of the keys to its hegemony.
In this particular text, after the old forms of oppression have made their
ritual departure, the masses are molded into a single master. Then the voice
shifts to passive: the master does not act, though he has to "be persuaded."
Advertising, meanwhile, metamorphoses rapidly from a mere messenger
to "a new force . . . let loose in the world," and finally, by the final sentence, "one of the keys to the future." Despite all the talk of "economic democracy," from the 1890s to the 1930s advertisers increasingly assumed
that their audience constituted an extraordinarily pliable mass of putty, and
that their own power to mold it was almost unlimited.

This was especially apparent when they spoke among themselves in their
trade journals. John Lee Mahin, an agency head from Chicago, captured
much of the conventional wisdom in 1910 when he wrote that the "consumer nearly always purchases in unconscious obedience to what he or she
believes to be the dictates of an authority which is anxiously consulted and
respected." The key word was "unconscious," and the point is not that advertisers ever acquired any real understanding of Freud (they did not), but
that along with many other middle- and upper-class Americans during the
first decade of the twentieth century they were trading in the catchwords of
"the new psychology." For them the new psychology was not psychoanalytic theory; it was a general tendency to view the mind as an instrument
engaged in assisting human beings to adapt to their environment, rather
than as a static collection of faculties. The new psychology's Darwinian
emphasis on adaptation was fundamentally conformist; it flowed easily into
later normative psychologies that preached the virtues of "adjustment." It
also fed the ad man's faith in a malleable mass of consumers. In 1903, Walter
Dill Scott, a professor of advertising at the Northwestern University
School of Business, began publishing the articles that became his influential
book *The Psychology of Advertising* (1908). Dozens of similar works appeared during the first four decades of the twentieth century. Nearly all
were simpleminded and mechanistic; they contained lists of "instincts"
("the home instinct," "the herd instinct," etc.) and depended on an associa-
tionist notion of causality that was compatible either with behaviorism (as
John B. Watson, the "father" of that wretched child, demonstrated during
his career at J. Walter Thompson), or—more commonly—with "suggestion psychology."[18]

This body of thought revealed the continuities between national advertisers and nineteenth-century peddlers, mesmerists, and other practitioners
of "influence." In 1892, a contributor to the trade journal *Fame* compared
advertising to hypnotism, observing that "the public is obeying a 'suggestion,' not acting upon reason." As late as 1905, one of the early agency

heads, Joel Benton, was still suggesting that the advertising writer had to cultivate an occult capacity for mind reading: "He must know how to fathom human traits and premises of thoughts."[19]

By the late nineteenth century, however, the doctrine of influence was clothed in respectable academic garb. The psychology of suggestion presented the consumer as an easy mark for the informed marketing strategist. Arthur Holmes, marketing professor at Northwestern, summarized (and up to a point inflated) the conventional wisdom in 1925.

> People unacquainted with psychology assume that men have the power to say "Yes" or "No" to an advertisement. The assumption is only partly correct. A man has the power to decide in the first stage of the game, not the last. . . . If the printed word can seize his attention, hold him chained, drive from his mind all other thoughts except the one "Buy this!" standing at the head of an organized sentiment from which every opposing idea, perception, feeling, instinct, and disposition have been driven out or smothered to death, then HE CANNOT SAY "NO!" His will is dead.[20]

This extraordinarily violent statement suggests some of the imperial impulses behind the positivistic "science of human nature." An "organized sentiment" holds the consumer's attention chained, then drives out or smothers to death everything else in his mind including finally "his will" itself. The drive to predict and control human behavior could lead to intoxicating fantasies.

Yet even Holmes's fantasy was prefaced by the acknowledgement that "in the first stage of the game" consumers were free to choose whether or not they would attend to the advertisement. A major part of the copywriter's task was tailoring the appeal so that it would fit the predispositions of the audience. Not even the most chuckleheaded buyer could be persuaded unless you caught his notice first. The problem of attracting attention led advertisers to another scientific tool for discovering and directing consumers' attention, the statistical survey—a little less thrilling than psychology, but in the end more influential.

Market research began around the turn of the century. By the 1920s it was being hailed as a major achievement of the national advertising agencies. The most recent leap forward in advertising, according to J. George Frederick's whiggish account, "The Story of Advertising Writing" (1925), occurred when " 'Arm-chair' copy-writing gave way to market-survey built copy. Intuitive insight into the public mind began to be supplemented by research-backed judgments of consumer-reactions." In 1930 a *Printer's Ink* contributor summarized three decades of development toward a marketing orientation: "I prefer knowing my consumer to knowing my product," he announced. To know consumers one counted them, categorized them by income, neighborhood, ethnicity, and religion, correlated these data with their brand preferences, and tested their reactions to specific ads. This last was first done systematically by the J. Walter Thompson Company in 1903. The bureau of design in their Chicago office solicited reader reactions to full-page advertisements that had been inserted in twenty-five national magazines: they received over thirty-thousand responses, discovering that "the [middle and upper class WASP] public" did not like ads without illustrations, or for beer. This sort of survey suggested that market research involved not only the measurement of objectifiable data like income and place of residence, but also the slippery task of investigating cultural attitudes.[21]

And that returned the researcher to the problem of mind reading. As Frederick saw it, advertising copy was "the apex of a solid merchandising plan" that included data questions for the manufacturer as well research into consumer types, preferences, and influences. The copy analyst would use proofs of varied copy to "conduct a carefully graded test on consumers (so planned that their unconscious judgment and not their conscious judgment be obtained)." Despite the reassuring impersonality of numbers, market surveys were still energized by the researcher's eagerness to catch the consumer unawares and penetrate the inner sanctum of his motivation. And this required as many intimate details of his or her life as could be assembled. A *New Yorker* cartoon from the early 1940s only partially exaggerated the practice: a well-dressed man appears before a housewife on an affluent suburban doorstep and says "Good morning, madam, the J. Walter Thompson Company would like to know if you are happily married." (Characteristically, JWT used the free publicity as part of a new business presentation.) Just as private corporate welfare schemes predated and set the pattern for government programs like workmen's compensation and social security, market research pioneered the management of public opinion later practiced more openly by political pollsters—George Gallup, to take just one example, cut his intellectual teeth at the Young & Rubicam agency during the early 1930s. *Fortune* magazine caught the broader applications of market research in 1935: "No one—and least of all the journalists—seems to have remarked that what the advertisers had developed was a mechanism adapted not only to the selling of toothpaste but to the plumbing of the public mind." No one, that is, until *Fortune* pointed the way with its first public opinion survey, conducted that same year.[22]

This was a key moment in the developing alliance between the ad man and the grand inquisitor. Statistical sampling, whether sponsored by business or government elites, soon became an instrument for rendering public opinion more manageable and predictable—another force against which people had to struggle to maintain alternative visions of reality. And yet survey research advanced under the banner of popular sovereignty. Through opinion polling and market research, government and business were supposed to become more responsive to their masters, the people. But what actually happened, as Tocqueville had predicted, was that the more responsive huge organizations seemed to be, the more masterful they became. Advertising executives and other practitioners of the "human sciences" promoted this convergence of corporate and government interests, as they shared not only an objectivist cognitive style but a preoccupation with the management of public opinion.[23]

They were also joined by a common cultural style of clinical frankness. Advertisers often congratulated themselves on leading the charge against Victorian prudery and hypocrisy; and (especially after the increasing use of photography in the 1920s) they joined the allopathic medical establishment as well as sundry sexologists, neurologists, and "scientists" of the psyche in developing a common denatured discourse on sexuality and other bodily functions. This "repeal of reticence" is usually treated as a rejection of Protestant moralism, but it can also be seen as a secular reworking of one of the profoundest impulses in Calvinist tradition: the demand that life be all of a piece, unified into a single systematic whole; the rejection of any notion that life could be fashioned into various planes of existence, the transfigured world of theater, sport, or ritual, for example, versus that of everyday life. That impulse toward systematic unification of meaning lay behind the entire tradition of plain speech. Despite its frequent invocation in nineteenth-century Protestant culture, the ideal of plain speech was actually a countercultural antidote to the Victorian knack for dividing life into spheres of privacy and publicity, sincerity and theatricality. Victorian morality juxtaposed rigid propriety and peep-show prurience; national advertising aimed to dissolve both in clinical frankness. Like other practitioners of imperial rationality, advertising executives claimed to be pioneers of honest talk about the body—a discourse of absolute transparency, complete with photographs. This was a major change, they believed, from what had gone before. And they were right.

Institutions and Images: The Incorporation of the Body

Nineteenth-century entrepreneurial advertising dramatized the contrarieties of Victorian culture. During the era when manufacturers hired chromolithographers directly to design advertisements, the commercial discourse of the body sought to tame the beast within and tap his vital powers; it celebrated the triumph of a "civilized morality" of self-control even as it revealed a powerful fascination with the exotic and the primitive.

1. Detail, 1888 pamphlet, Warner's Safe Remedies
Warshaw Collection of Business Americana
National Museum of American History
Smithsonian Institution, Washington, D.C.

Until after the turn of the century, patent medicine advertising was steeped in herbalist lore—incantatory references to the product's magical effects and closeness to nature. An overwhelming number of patent medicines claimed a primitive tribal origin—kola from the heart of Africa, coca from the mountains of Peru, "sagwa" from the North American Indian herb doctors: elixirs that cured everything from impure blood to sexual debility to indigestion. In 1893, for example, the Kickapoo Medicine Company promised its customers "a stomach like an Indian—*he* never worried about dieting. Why can't we live like the Indian, in a healthy, hearty, natural way?" Kidney Cure Company made common assumptions explicit in an 1896 pamphlet for Church's Kava-Kava Compound ("Nature's Cure for Diseases of the Kidneys Blood and Urinary Organs"): "There is no doubt whatever but that many of the best botanical remedies used in medical science have first become known through their use by savage or semi-barbarous people."[24]

The construction of an ideal of naturalness followed a pattern one might call imperial primitivism: the white man enters the dark interior of a tropical land, extracts mysterious remedies, and puts them to the service of Anglo-Saxon civilization. One clear example of this formula was a pamphlet describing the discovery of Peruvian Catarrh Cure (1890). The story was allegedly told to the narrator by Dr. Edward Turner, "an adventurous and daring Englishman," on the eve of his death by ambush at the hands of "black devils" in Zululand, Africa. Troubled with catarrh since boyhood, Turner had endured the failures of "medical men, with whom I got disgusted" until he learns of Mosca, a red root that could be ingested in powdered form. Having acquired some Mosca from a Catholic missionary in Indian Territory (now Oklahoma), Turner is thrilled by its effects and heads for the source: the Cotahuasi Indians of Peru. The chief of the Cotahuasi likes Turner's pluck and even more, his apparent desire to help others. Turner, he believes, is not like the other "palefaces," who care only for money. The irony is that Turner wants to make a business of the cure but conceals his aim because he fears the chief might want too many presents in exchange for the secret ingredient. "I therefore left him with the idea that I was one of the few palefaces who don't care for money. That, you know, may work among the Indians, but not with us." The narrator rescues the secret from the dying Turner, and it brings relief to millions. The convoluted path of discovery, the aura of mystery and secrecy, the key moment when the shrewd Caucasian outwits the natives—the narrative pattern was repeated often. It was captured visually in an 1888 advertisement for Warner's Safe Remedies, which shows a respectable white man's head on a muscular brown body, paddling a canoe toward the heart of primitive darkness (fig. 1).[25]

Cosmetics as well as food and even laxative advertising wallowed in exoticism during the last three decades of the nineteenth century. Breath and body perfumes, talcum powder and toilet water, all were placed in settings redolent of luxuriant sensuality (fig. 2). There was a strikingly overt eroticism about many of these images, in specific icons (fig. 3), and more generally in the air of languorous ease displayed by the mature and voluptuous woman—whom historians of fashion have identified as the belle ideal of the late nineteenth century (fig. 4). She was hardly a sexless Victorian, and her origins lay in a subculture of sensuality inhabited by actresses, prostitutes, pimps, and gamblers.[26]

Even the corset, long since dismissed as an emblem of patriarchal domination, could be associated with explosive fecundity and female sexual energy, as well as with voyeuristic fantasy (figures 5 and 6). The removal of the corset could be an occasion for protracted foreplay, the demonstration of amatory skills, and the erotic buildup of tension. Even before the Civil War, a print called "The Wedding Night" caught the parodic potential of those possibilities by showing a bride looking demurely behind her at her husband who is popeyed, flushed, and on his knees unfastening her corset; clearly, despite the parody, the process is intended to look exciting for both of them. Opponents of the corset recognized this and attacked its capacity to stimulate sexual excitement. Tightlacing could be as much an emblem of exotic decadence and rebellion against female quiescence as a sign of submission to prudery.[27]

It is difficult if not impossible to infer any particular set of power relations from the imagery surrounding the body in entrepreneurial advertising. The voyeuristic trade card for Warner's corsets (see figure 6), for example, demonstrates how chromolithographers could assemble a bizarre amalgam of

2. Cover, 1882 Almanac, Warner's
Safe Remedies

Warshaw Collection of Business Americana
National Museum of American History
Smithsonian Institution, Washington, D.C.

3. Trade card. c. 1880, Love's
Incense Perfume

Warshaw Collection of Business Americana
National Museum of American History
Smithsonian Institution, Washington, D.C.

4. Trade card, c. 1890, London Toilet Bazaar Cosmetics

Warshaw Collection of Business Americana, National Museum of
American History, Smithsonian Institution, Washington, D.C.

hieroglyphs. One of the Cupids photographing the corset is holding St. Joseph's staff, with lily attached—a traditional emblem of male virginity. The corset is an object of prurient fascination, yet it is set in a hard, dry desert landscape. It is giving birth to vegetation (as in figure 5), but the growth is cactuslike, not luxuriant or inviting. The stone barrier suggests the parallel function of the corset—a barrier to be overcome, a fetishistic aid to excitement. The whole picture seems animated by a muddle of male fears and anxieties. In its surrealist yoking of dissimilar images as well as in its voyeurism, this trade card typifies the vernacular tradition of commercial iconography.

The coming of corporate advertising brought major changes. Exotic and primitive icons persisted in the entrepreneurial tradition, inscribed on the walls of fashionable restaurants and metropolitan movie theaters; but in national advertising those images were sanitized and transmuted. The advertisers who promoted the early twentieth-century vogue of tanning, for example, detached dark skin from its overtones of lush tropicality and linked it instead with bracing outdoor vigor (fig. 7). Imperial primitivism gave way to imperial rationality—a dualistic rather than a dialectical relation with the nonhuman world as well as with the humans supposedly "closer to nature" than the Anglo-Saxon. This attempt to draw sharper boundaries between the civilized world and brute creation was in part a response to the popularization of Darwinian biology and paleontology as well as to the increased knowledge of the nonwhite world gained through imperial adventures. If one had to accept apes for ancestors and Hottentots for cousins, one did not have to acknowledge that there was anything of value to be learned from them. The resulting cultural pattern, at least as expressed in advertising iconography, was less an attempt to extract regenerative secrets from mysterious interiors than an effort to impose civilized values on "inferior" native populations.

And those values were invariably defined in terms of cleanliness and good grooming. In an Ivory Soap series from 1900, for example, an assembly of Plains Indians recall their old ways of dirt and disorder:

> Our blankets smeared with grease and stains,
> From buffalo meat and settlers' veins . . .

Then:

> Ivory soap came like a ray
> Of light across our darkened way
> And now we're civil, kind, and good
> And keep the laws as people should
> We wear our linen, lawn, and lace
> As well as folks with paler face.

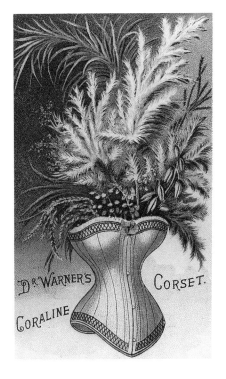

5. Trade card, c. 1890, Dr. Warner's Corsets

Warshaw Collection of Business Americana
National Museum of American History
Smithsonian Institution, Washington, D.C.

6. Trade card, c. 1890, Warner Bros. Coraline Corset

Warshaw Collection of Business Americana, National Museum of
American History, Smithsonian Institution, Washington, D.C.

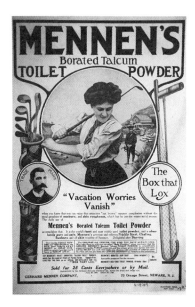

7. Advertisement, 1908, Mennen's
Borated Talcum Powder

*Warshaw Collection of Business Americana
National Museum of American History
Smithsonian Institution, Washington, D.C.*

This newer imperial rhetoric was nothing if not universal in its ambitions, as B. T. Babbitt's soap announced "Soap is the Scale of Civilization" and Gillette proclaimed its razors' predominance "from Boston to Bombay" (fig. 8).[28]

In one sense this was nothing new. A preoccupation with cleanliness, often carrying racial overtones, had been a central theme in bourgeois culture for at least half a century. It intensified as technological advances made soap and water more widely available. Cleanliness became a crucial piece in the puzzle that upwardly mobile strivers were constantly trying to assemble. As early as the 1850s, clean hands joined white skin, white bread, and white sugar as emblems of refinement.[29]

By 1900, though, soap had begun to imply not cleanliness per se but a certain kind of cleanliness, purged of any decadent, hedonistic associations, oriented toward productive activism and a broader agenda of control. In 1899 the *Yale Review* noted that the "philosophy of modern advertising" was beginning to elevate soap and water over "perfumery and enervating pleasures."[30] What the *Review* failed to note was that for most of the nineteenth century, earlier advertising had celebrated "enervating pleasures"— it was only with the corporatization of advertising that the iconography of the body began to be sterilized and submitted to the ethos of rationalization.

The sweep of an idea is not a matter of geography. Start something in Boston and you get the echo in Bombay. It is an idea that makes neighbors of us all.

In the farthest corner of the world you find the Gillette Safety Razor—introduced by Army and Navy officers, tourists, capitalists, business men.

The Gillette now has great sales agencies in India and China. Men there have been stropping and honing for five thousand years. It's time they were awakening. How long will *you* cling to obsolete shaving methods?

Seven hundred thousand men bought Gillettes last year. We expect a million new customers in 1910.

Wake up! Get a Gillette! Make a good front. Look the world in the face. A Gillette shave every morning is more than a material comfort—it's a moral brace—gives you a new grip on the Day's work.

The Gillette is for sale everywhere. It costs $5, but it lasts a lifetime.

Write and we'll send you a pamphlet—Dept. B.

King C Gillette

8. Advertisement, 1910, Gillette razors

Warshaw Collection of Business Americana, National Museum of American History, Smithsonian Institution, Washington, D.C.

The most striking change was the growing emphasis on standard images of physical perfection—"perfect specimens of the human type"—on the Anglo-Saxon model. In this area as elsewhere, developments in advertising were reinforced by changes in the wider culture, especially the growth of statistical definitions of normality and the popularization of mechanistic metaphors representing the body as an engine. The voluptuous woman and the portly, bearded man yielded to smoother, cleaner, more athletic and more obviously youthful models of beauty. Exotic settings faded in favor of the more immediate and familiar—the soda fountain and the suburban neighborhood (see figure 8).[31]

The form of these images changed as well: surrealist pastiche yielded to literalist realism, often assisted by photography and linked to didactic narrative. In general, pictures were more thoroughly intermeshed with words, more commonly illustrations of a particular text, than they had been in the days of free-lance chromolithography (fig. 9). This "editorial-style" advertising, which J. Walter Thompson claimed to have introduced in the early 1920s, came closely to resemble the fiction and advice literature in the slick-paper national magazines. In its visual and literary forms, managerial culture was becoming all of a piece, in keeping with the universalist assumptions of imperial rationality.

9. Cover for Howard Way, "The Coca Cola Girl," 1927

Warshaw Collection of Business Americana
National Museum of American History
Smithsonian Institution, Washington, D.C.

10. Advertisement, Ipana toothpaste
Saturday Evening Post, 1936.

In the advertisements themselves, behind the streamlining of bodies and magazine formats, there was an almost panicky reassertion of culture over nature, most evident in the growing intolerance of odors. With the coming of an urban society and the increase in person-to-person contact, there was growing concern about offensive breath, perspiration odors, and the like. One can find scattered advertisements for breath and body perfumes from the 1830s on, but in general, genteel folk put up with a lot more in the nine-teenth century than in the twentieth. Dress and suit shields, marketed in the 1880s, were designed to stop perspiration stain but not odor. Yet by the 1930s, odor was virtually an obsession. Popular magazines were full of faces (male and female) contorted with disgust over everything from "sneaker smell" to "smelly hands" (fig. 10). And more and more people had shown themselves willing to submit to the demanding and cumber-some procedure of applying deodorant to their underarms. The best selling product, Odorono, was "pretty hard on sensitive skins," John B. Watson told a JWT staff meeting in 1928—not to mention clothing; the user had to hold his or her arms aloft for ten minutes after applying the ruby red paste, taking care not to let it touch any article of clothing as it would eat into the fabric.[32]

Within national advertising's symbolic universe, the recoil from odor was part of a general revulsion against biological processes—an attitude encouraged by the popularization of germ theory and by the allopathic medical establishment's assumption that treatment of disease involved a war against nature rather than a cooperation with it. A Kleenex advertisement from 1934, for example, presented a nearly nauseated housewife who declares that washing dirty handkerchiefs is "the worst job on earth!"—but it was no longer necessary thanks to throwaway tissues. Much advertising copy seemed animated by an itch to extirpate all signs of organic life from a sterile home environment, and an assumption that the audience felt a similar urge. As a copywriter for Zonite antiseptic (also peddled as a contraceptive douche) claimed in 1931, "The feminine world now demands an absolute cleanliness of person, a real surgical cleanliness." And a long-running Lysol ad from the early 1930s presented a cellophane-wrapped guest at the front door: "If callers also arrived in sanitary packages, we wouldn't need Lysol." What had once been a set of pious maxims about cleanliness and godliness had become an almost obsessive desire for a sanitized environment—a desire that extended to death's door and beyond, as Guardian Memorials claimed of their mausoleum: "The thought of its clean, dry, airy above-ground crypt is a constant consolation to those still living."[33]

The preoccupation with bodily purification and control linked advertising executives with both the Protestant past and the professional-managerial present by translating ancient longings for self-transfiguration into the secular rhetoric of personal efficiency. "Progressive" crusades against alcohol and prostitution, which drew on a familiar evangelical ethos of self-control, nevertheless also dovetailed with an emergent managerial faith that all of social and personal life could be organized on principles of bureaucratic rationality. Frederick Winslow Taylor's *ur*-test of time-and-motion study, *The Principles of Scientific Management* (1911), helped to make "the elimination of waste in industry" the chief preoccupation of employers by providing them with a new legitimating language for labor discipline. Advertising played a major role in accelerating the pursuit of efficiency, extending it into the most intimate areas of life and unwittingly laying bare its psychoanalytic meanings. Not only did executives seek to transform their agencies into smoothly functioning bureaucratic mechanisms, but copywriters made "regularity"—in every sense—the basis of successful selfhood. From the 1910s through the 1930s, with intensifying shrillness, advertisers warned that behind every broken marriage or failed career lay the spectre of "auto-intoxication" or "intestinal fatigue," which kept men and women from maintaining peak performance. The chatter about intestines resonated with political as well as personal significance. The obsession with expelling "alien filth" neatly caught the rhetorical connection between bodily purification and national purification: the eugenic dream of perfecting Anglo-Saxon racial dominance in the United States through judicious breeding and immigration restriction.[34]

But the self-parodic quality of those warnings about constipation should give the historian pause. It is not merely a consequence of our distance from the sources; contemporary observers, too, found it difficult to take national advertising as seriously as its spokesmen demanded. Even inside the agencies, as early as the 1920s, horse-laughs of derision and self-satire could be heard. There were awkward moments when earnest young pups had to be told what the agency was really up to. At a JWT staff meeting on 13 February 1930, for example, a naïve new copywriter named Wengler questioned an old hand about the scientific basis of intestinal fatigue:

> **MR. WENGLER:** "At what age do people become liable to this intestinal fatigue? Do very young people have it?"
>
> **MR. DAY:** "People have it at all ages."
>
> **MR. WENGLER:** "Do people in their early 20s suffer from this condition at all?"
>
> **MR. DAY:** "Fatigue is universal; we simply have to credit it to the intestines, that's all."[35]

Despite their drive toward professionalism, advertising executives could never cast aside their Barnumesque inheritance, could never make common cause with the clinicians of society whose ideology they emulated. Part of the problem was the limited nature of their authority: unlike doctors and lawyers, they claimed professional expertise but always bowed to the opinions of the client, however inexpert he might be. Yet a deeper difficulty was embedded in the very nature of the advertising business: at bottom it had always involved the clever orchestration of surface effects in a fashion that undermined all pretensions to sincerity and claims to objective truth. Straining to stabilize meanings with resort to imperial rationality, advertisers remained surrounded by the epistemological ambiguities of their trade.

Tensions and Resolutions: Mass Man at Peace and War

Advertising executives and copywriters were confronted with a fundamental conflict. The professional-managerial world view put a scientific gloss on Protestant plain speech: in epistemological matters it created a vast apparatus for falsifying and verifying universalist truth-claims; on ethical questions it encouraged the welding of private and public *personae* into a single systematic life. Yet ad men themselves came out of a carnivalesque tradition that subverted unified meaning and promoted the pursuit of success through persuasion, theatricality, and outright trickery.

Conditions of work in advertising reflected this conflict. Despite the efforts of agency executives to rationalize their organizations into smoothly functioning arms of business productivity, everyday life inside the agency remained chaotic and unpredictable even in flush times. An advertising agency, one copywriter observed in 1926, "is a place of swift movement— of constant shifts—of things finished at the last possible gasp—of seconds grabbed from eternity—of huge presses stopped to make a last minute change—of superhuman rush jobs—of hurrying and joshing and smoking and swearing. Something happens every minute—some triumph or some disaster. There are no middle tones, for all is colored by the fury of creation." The importance of creativity was constantly emphasized as an antidote to smooth professionalism and an alternative to bureaucratic notions of expertise. When an anonymous contributor to *Profitable Advertising* in 1893 defined an advertising expert as "one who knows the value of words," he spoke more prophetically than he knew: despite the effort to embrace an objectivist cognitive style, "mere word-slingers" remained essential to the success of every advertising agency. The getting and keeping of clients also required more than objectivist cognition and clinical frankness. The furious competition for accounts made the advertising world a Hobbesian jungle as early as the 1890s: "There is altogether too much copying of ideas," a writer in the trade journal *Fame* complained in 1894, "as though the world of thought were fast becoming a howling wilderness." The trade press early on realized the importance of flattery and complaisance—the seductive arts of "influence"—in selling to clients as well as to consumers. Despite the panoply of statistics, charts, and graphs that accompanied nearly every new business presentation by the 1920s and 1930s, executives and copywriters alike privately acknowledged that their authority with clients rested on little more than "bootlegging and bootlicking." Yet in talking to clients, ad men could at least point to the bottom line as a quantitative index of success; in talking to consumers their authority was even more precariously based—not on precise knowledge but on the mere appearance of it. The ghost of Barnum was not easily exorcised.[36]

The difficulty of reconciling professional pretensions with a Barnumesque inheritance first became apparent during the pure food and drug agitation of the early 1900s. The allopathic medical establishment, having consolidated its authority through a series of therapeutic breakthroughs, joined with "progressive" reformers in journalism and government to challenge the patent medicine advertisers—still a major source of income for many national advertising agencies. The reformers' demands for precise labeling revealed the persistence of the plain speaker's faith that all would be well if communication could be rendered transparent. Yet the attack, led by muckrakers like Samuel Hopkins Adams in *Collier's* magazine, focused almost exclusively on the most flagrant and marginal offenders, allowing the biggest corporations to play the role of "reputable advertisers." Still, ad men were stung. They formed the Associated Advertising Clubs of America and at their first meeting in 1911 they launched the Truth-in-Advertising movement. Their immediate aim was to promote the passage by state legislatures of *Printers' Ink*'s model statute. Under the proposed law, the advertiser responsible for "any assertion, representation, or statement of fact which is untrue, deceptive, or misleading shall be guilty of a misdemeanor." Spokesmen for the movement preached a gospel of bureaucratic rationality, attacking the "waste" and "unfair competition" promoted by deceptive advertising. Prosecutions focused on loan sharks, real-estate speculators, and mail-order frauds—confidence men on the margins of business respectability. Corporate offenders went virtually unscathed.[37]

The Truth-in-Advertising movement offered national advertisers a chance to reaffirm their ethnic solidarity as well as their commitment to managerial conceptions of efficiency. Many of the men prosecuted had Jewish surnames, and anti-Semitic stereotypes sometimes surfaced at campaign committee meetings. In 1916 one New York organizer explained his group's approach to the false advertiser: "We appeal to his selfishness if not his morals—you can't get by with that on the average 'kike'—you can't do it." Patterns of prosecution comported well with the durable belief that Anglo-Saxons had a unique claim on sincerity and plain speech. Ethnocentrism reinforced professionalism.[38]

The coming of World War I provided agency people with an even better opportunity to demonstrate their respectability and reaffirm their ties to WASP managerial elites. Ad men participated in George Creel's Committee on Public Information; but what was perhaps more important was their participation in the politics of morale—a word that was acquiring unprecedented power in work of the psychologist G. Stanley Hall and other reform-minded therapeutic professionals. From their view, morale merged the psychic health of the individual with the social vitality of the nation. The doctrine of morale was a corporatist version of "influence" in the guise of "democratic social engineering"—a manipulative model of social control through the simulation of self-actualization. It depended on the idea that through some alchemy of desire, each individual could most efficiently serve the public needs of a reified "society" by pursuing her or his private emotional fulfillment. This was a psychological version of Mandeville or

Adam Smith, and indeed some of its advocates positioned themselves as correctors of classical economics. In *Social Process* (1902), the sociologist Charles Horton Cooley charged that the "economic man" model "is false even as economics, and we shall never have an efficient system until we have one that appeals to the imagination, the loyalty, and the self-expression of the men who serve it." (The word "system" no longer referred to static classificatory schemes but to a fluid "social process" that at peak efficiency remained in dynamic equilibrium.) The new conditions of interdependence—always a talismanic word for managerial-professionals—led to a symbiotic emotional relationship between society and the individual. People yearned to serve some higher goal for the sheer emotional thrill of it; the state needed willing soldiers and loyal civilians. What better solution than to marry desire and duty in obedience to what Luther Gulick (founder of the Campfire Girls) called "the corporate conscience that is rendered necessary by the complex interdependence of modern life." By arrogating the authority of educators, advertising men could claim to be among the keepers of that conscience. By "speaking humanly" to the multitudes, advertisers could truly become "the cheerleaders of the nation"—as the president of Eastman Kodak claimed they had become in 1918. Touching the crowd's imaginations with dreams of fuller expression in a better world, advertising could meet popular and corporate needs at the same time. That was a major implication of morale.[39]

Yet there was a harder side to advertising's role in the war, just as there was a harder side to government repression than the milk-and-water doctrine of morale. The sorting of deviants and defectives became a cottage industry after the declaration of war, and a knowledge of national advertising was officially included as part of the national norm. On the Army intelligence tests, recruits and draftees were required to puzzle out questions like these:

Revolvers are made by
    Swift & Co.   Smith & Wesson   W. L. Douglas
    B. T. Babbitt

"There's a reason" is an "ad" for a
    drink   revolver   flour   cleanser

The Pierce-Arrow car is made in
    Buffalo   Detroit   Toledo   Flint[40]

Rarely has the category of "knowledge" been so obviously constructed. Not to fit in it was to risk being labeled another mediocrity with a "fourteen-year-old mind"—the "mental age" of the average American, according to the journalistic view of the test results. As a crucial part of the new managerial model of normality, national advertising flourished during and after the war years. Advertisements for bodily purification subtly reinforced a broader agenda of national purification, an agenda that included the deportation of aliens as well as the drive to restrict immigration.

After the war, advertisers reaffirmed their sense of superiority to their audience by dabbling in the rhetoric of "mass man." By the 1920s and 1930s, advertising spokesmen had developed their own version of a world view expressed in more elegant form by Ortega, T. S. Eliot, and other fastidious observers of the emergent urban societies in the early twentieth century. Advertising's version of the typical consumer, if not quite Eliot's "young man carbuncular," was just as much a vacant-eyed straphanger, stupefied by monotonous work, craving instinctual release and a sense (however fleeting) of personal autonomy. This view required that ad men emphasize the social and intellectual chasm separating themselves from their audience. The same publicists who celebrated "the people, our masters" were privately dismissing the common man as an intellectual cipher. Let us not mince words, William Esty told his colleagues at J. Walter Thompson in 1930, "We say the Hollywood people are stupid, the pictures are stupid; what we are really saying is that the great bulk of people are stupid." Unlike the advocates of "democratic social engineering," advertising people were occasionally honest enough—at least among themselves—to abandon any pretense that they were promoting democracy. Yet in their eagerness to embrace a social engineer's role, they departed from pessimists like Eliot and preserved fundamental ties with managerial professionals. All shared a belief that ordinary folk could not negotiate "the complexity of modern life" without the aid of people like themselves.[41]

Advertising spokesmen married mass consumption to bureaucratic rationalitiy in yet another way as well. They argued that the spread of installment buying and the incessant propaganda of commodities, far from undermining commitments to hard work, actually reinforced a new and more systematic form of labor discipline. "The American conception of advertising is to arouse desires and stimulate wants, to make people dissatisfied with the old and out-of-date and by constant iteration to send them out to work harder to get the latest model—whether that model be an icebox or a rug, or a new home," the agency head Bruce Barton told a radio audience in 1929. If "the bulk of the people are stupid" but can be led to progressive goals by experts, then advertising men could play a legitimate role in the emergent managerial culture despite their dubious parentage.[42]

Yet even in the 1920s there were critiques of advertising from the technocratic left wing of the professional-managerial bloc, characterized by Stuart Chase's *The Tragedy of Waste* (1925). Under the impact of the depression, Chase and other positivist heirs of the plain-speech tradition reasserted their demands for accurate labeling in the food and drug industry, as well as their accusations that advertising was a wasteful drain on an over-burdened "distribution system." Advertising executives and copywriters, meanwhile, were being laid off by the thousands from agency staffs that had become bloated during the 1920s. The ones who remained were desperate for any share of a dwindling market; they turned to screaming tabloid styles and franker displays of nudity. The rise of radio encouraged an ever more aggressive tone, a mixture of carnival barking and pseudo-intimacy. Annoyed by this return of repressed peddler strategies, upper-class clubwomen and other defenders of good taste lent support to Rexford Tugwell and other would-be regulators of national advertising. Yet consumer protest in the 1930s came to little beyond a mild strengthening of the Federal Trade Commission in 1938.[43]

Perhaps this was partly because advertising men and other managerial professionals continued to share so many fundamental assumptions. Blending the ideology of mass man and the widespread contempt for popular intelligence, the managerial world view of the 1930s assumed that psychic and political health were functionally interrelated. A more passive version of the doctrine of morale was articulated in the many popularized versions of Adlerian psychology that appeared alongside the advertisements in the national magazines. As Warren Susman perceptively observed, the Adlerian prescription that one should overcome one's "inferiority complex" and "adjust" to collective norms was perfectly suited to middle-class Americans during the 1930s. Pervasive economic and emotional insecurity brought feelings of inferiority and the desire to transcend them through a sense of belonging to a larger whole. The advice from *Good Housekeeping* and similar magazines was "don't be afraid to conform," or to encourage your children to. The link between longings for connectedness and a paternalistic material state surfaced with particular clarity in a 1935 article in *Good Housekeeping* called "Uncle Sam Wants Your Mark." The author, Vera Connolly, urged voluntary compliance with J. Edgar Hoover's plan to fingerprint all Americans. The benefit of this program, she believed, was that it would end "a travesty on our modern civilization"—the anonymous burial of decent citizens in potters' fields. "Almost every 'unknown' is known to and loved by someone. Behind almost every commitment to that soil is family heartbreak somewhere. For it is chiefly the decent who are buried here. The criminal seldom is. His fingerprints are on file." The longing to belong could sanction new forms of hierarchy and surveillance.[44]

During the later 1930s, national advertising agencies and the major corporations they represented began to develop a rhetorical response to critiques from the planners on the managerial left. Everyone from William Z. Foster to Archibald MacLeish had been celebrating "The American Way of Life" as a kind of transcendant collective identity; national advertising helped corporate industry appropriate that way of life and redirect its chief connotation from a vague populism to an equally obscure notion of "free enterprise." The coming of the war provided the key opening. "Business Rushes to Government's Aid in Preparedness Crisis," *Printers' Ink* announced in August, 1940, hailing "a new relationship between business and government." Well before Pearl Harbor, advertising and other business executives flocked to Washington to race around town in cheap taxicabs and make the case for deregulated industry. At last the bureaucrats were willing to listen: some had begun to understand Keynes's argument that aggregate demand could be stimulated as effectively through private as through public investment; more probably they shared *Printers' Ink*'s opinion that "in this day of mechanical warfare, national defense and industrial mobilization are nearer than ever before to being synonymous." And even the mobilization brought by Lend-Lease had been enough to send a flurry of increased profits through many ad agencies. War, if not the health of the state, proved again to be the health of the advertising business.[45]

The cooperation among national advertising executives and other managerial professionals was sometimes limited and ambiguous, at other times thorough and straightforward. But one conclusion is permissible: the ad man and the grand inquisitor would not have been altogether at odds. Certainly their meeting would have been more congenial than the one Dostoyevsky imagined. Probably they would have hopped in a cab together and headed for Duke Zeibert's.

NOTES

1. Fyodor Dostoyevsky, *The Brothers Karamazov*, trans. Constance Garnett (1880; New York: Modern Library, 1931), 264, 268.

2. See especially Michel Foucault, *Power/Knowledge*, ed. Colin Gordon, trans. Colin Gordon, Leo Marshall, John Mepham, and Kate Sopher (New York: Pantheon, 1980), 55–62, 109–133, 183–192, as well as his *The History of Sexuality*, vol. 1, trans. Robert Hurley (New York: Vintage Books, 1980).

3. The notion of advertising as an agent of a hedonistic consumer culture lies behind textbook clichés about a "revolution in manners and morals" during the early twentieth century; it pervades historiography as well as industry apologetics. Among the most striking examples are William Leach, "Transformations in a Culture of Abundance: Women and Department Stores, 1890–1925," *Journal of American History* 71 (September 1984): 319–342; Warren Susman, "Introduction" to his *Culture as History* (New York: Pantheon, 1984); and David Ogilvy, *Confessions of an Advertising Man* (New York: Atheneum, 1963).

4. On the relationship between photography and the faith in linguistic transparency, see Allan Sekula, "The Body and the Archive," *October* 39 (Winter 1986): 3–64.

5. Lizabeth Cohen, "Encountering Mass Culture at the Grassroots: the Experience of Chicago Workers in the 1920s," *American Quarterly* 41 (March 1989): 6–33; David Thelen, "Patterns of Consumer Consciousness in the Progressive

Movement: Robert M. Lafollette, the Antitrust Persuasion, and Labor Legislation," in *The Quest for Social Justice: The Morris Franklin Memorial Lectures, 1970–1980*, ed. Ralph M. Aderman (Madison: University of Wisconsin Press, 1983), 19–47; and Raymond Williams, *Culture and Society, 1780–1950* (New York: Harper, 1958), 12.

6. For useful background on the chromolithography industry, see Peter Marzio, *The Democratic Art: Pictures for a Nineteenth Century America* (Boston: Museum of Fine Arts, 1979); and Robert Jay, *The Trade Card in Nineteenth Century America* (Columbia: University of Missouri Press, 1987).

7. George H. Rowell, *Forty Years an Advertising Agent* (New York: Printers Ink Publishing, 1906), 40–102; Ralph M. Hower, *The History of an Advertising Agency* (Cambridge: Harvard University Press, 1939), chap. 1; Daniel Pope, *The Making of Modern Advertising* (New York: Basic Books, 1982), 102; "Some Basic Roots of the J. Walter Thompson Company," typescript in J. Walter Thompson (henceforth, JWT) Archives, Duke University, Durham, North Carolina; "If I Had It To Do Over Again," undated clipping from *Printers' Ink*, box 8, Earnest Elmo Calkins Archives, Knox College, Galesburg, Illinois; Joseph Banister, "The General Advertising Agency," *Printers' Ink* (henceforth *PI*) 12 (6 February 1895): 3–7; and "How the Best Advertising Agencies Operate," *PI* 69 (3 November 1909): 3–7.

8. The relevant data are summarized in Roland Marchand, *Advertising the American Dream: Making Way for Modernity, 1920–1940* (Berkeley and Los Angeles: University of California Press, 1985), 130–138; and Pope, *Making of Modern Advertising*, 177–180. Pope, drawing on survey samples from 1916 and 1931, shows that 97 percent of advertising people were men; not one in either sample came from eastern or southern Europe; in 1916 half had attended college and more than a fourth held bachelor's degrees; by 1931 more than two-thirds had gone to college and almost half had graduated. See also the revealing portraits in the JWT Newsletter for 1930, JWT Archives.

9. Wallace Boren, "Bad Taste in Advertising," *J. Walter Thompson Forum*, 7 January 1936, unpaginated, JWT Archives.

10. "A New Profession," *The Yale Daily News*, 26 May 1919, clipping from house ads file in JWT Archives.

11. James Collins, quoted in Penrose Overstreet Committee, 59th Cong., 2d sess., 1907, *H.R. 608*, xxxvii. I use the notion of a hegemonic historical bloc because I believe the Gramscian vocabulary is more flexible than the language of class, and therefore more appropriate for characterizing the shifting and unstable coalitions of managerial elites during the early twentieth century. See T. J. Jackson Lears, "The Concept of Cultural Hegemony: Problems and Possibilities," *American Historical Review* 90 (1985): 567–593.

12. "The Passing of the 'Expert,' " *PI* 41 (1 October 1902): 3; N. W. Ayer & Co., *Forty Years of Advertising* (Philadelphia: N. W. Ayer, 1909), 60, in Advertising, box 2, Warshaw Collection of Business Americana, National Museum of American History, Smithsonian Institution, Washington, D.C. (henceforth Warshaw Collection). Also see E. E. Calkins, *The Business of Advertising* (New York: D. Appleton, 1915), 198–199. On the consolidation of allopathic medical authority, see Paul Starr, *The Social Transformation of American Medicine* (New York: Basic Books, 1982), especially chaps. 1–3.

13. The two best guides to these developments are Lawrence Goodwyn, *Democratic Promise: The Populist Moment in America* (New York: Oxford University Press, 1979); and James Livingston, *Origins of the Federal Reserve System* (Ithaca: Cornell University Press, 1986).

14. Earnest Elmo Calkins, "The New Consumption Engineer and the Artist," in

A Philosophy of Production, ed. J. George Frederick (New York: Business Bourse, 1930), 114; James Wallen, "Emotion and Style in Copy," in *Masters of Advertising Copy*, ed. J. George Frederick (New York: Business Bourse, 1925), 110–111; L. B. Jones, "Advertising Men as the 'Cheer Leaders' of the Nation," *PI* 102 (7 February 1918): 62–65; and Leon Dabo, "Advertising Art's Influence on National Dress," *PI* 73 (27 October 1910): 92. On moralists' habit of seeking universalist justifications for changes in fashion, see Norbert Elias, *The Civilizing Process: The History of Manners*, trans. Edmund Jephcott (New York: Pantheon, 1977).

15. "Bankers Watch Advertising," *Business Week*, 14 May 1930, 34; Richard Tedlow, *Keeping the Public Image: Public Relations and Business, 1900–1950* (Greenwich, Conn.: JAI Press, 1979), 155.

16. William Graebner, *The Engineering of Consent: Democracy and Authority in Twentieth Century America* (Madison: University of Wisconsin Press, 1987). For a striking example of democratic social engineering applied to the family circle, see William F. McDermott, "I Want My Daughters To Marry," *Good Housekeeping*, December 1934, 169, 170.

17. "Messenger to the King," *Collier's*, 3 May 1930, 78.

18. John Lee Mahin, "Advertising—a Form of Organized Salesmanship," *PI* 70 (30 March 1910): 5; Walter Dill Scott, *The Psychology of Advertising* (Boston: Houghton Mifflin, 1908); and Harry L. Hollingworth, *Advertising and Selling: Principles of Appeal and Response* (New York: Columbia University Press, 1913); Bruce Bliven, "Can You Sell Goods to the Subconscious Mind?" *PI* 102 (28 March 1918): 3–8, 92–97.

19. Will B. Wilder, "Hypnotism in Advertising," *Fame*, September 1892, 196–197; and Joel Benton, "Experiment in Advertising," *Fame*, April 1905, 81–82.

20. Arthur Holmes, "The Psychology of the Printed Word," in Frederick, *Masters*, 344.

21. J. George Frederick, "The Story of Advertising Writing," in Frederick, *Masters*, 27; Allen T. Moore, "I Prefer Knowing My Consumer To Knowing My Product," *PI* 151 (17 April 1930): 57; and George Raymond, unpaginated typescript memoir in JWT Archives. Susan Strasser, *Satisfaction Guaranteed: The Making of the American Mass Market* (New York: Pantheon, 1989) is a useful survey of the rise of market research.

22. J. George Frederick, "The Research Basis of Copy," in Frederick, *Masters*, 152–153; undated *New Yorker* cartoon in "The Largest Clinic of Advertising Experience in the World," JWT New Business Presentation, 1945, JWT Archives; and information on Gallup in JWT Creative Staff Meeting, 4 March 1932, JWT Archives; and "A New Technique in Journalism," *Fortune*, July 1935, 65–68. Also see Frederick Russell, "My Reply To Critics Who Say That Marketing Will Never Be a Science," *PI* 131 (23 April 1925): 105–116.

23. For a fuller version of this argument, see Benjamin Ginsberg, *The Captive Public: How Mass Opinion Promotes State Power* (New York: Basic Books, 1986); and the perceptive review by Mark Crispin Miller, "Suckers for Elections," *New York Times Book Review*, 8 February 1987, 32.

24. The material cited can be found in Patent Medicines, Warshaw Collection: Kickapoo Medicine Company, *Almanac*, 1893, box 18; and Church Kidney Cure Company, box 5. For three among innumerable other examples of primitivism, see Wright's Indian Vegetable Pills, 1844, box 33; Lyon Mfg. Co., *Morning, Noon, and Night*, 1872, box 21; and Centaur Co., *Atlas, Almanac, and Receipt Book*, 1884–1885, box 5.

25. These materials are also stored in Patent Medicines, Warshaw Collection: Pamphlet for Peruvian Catarrh Cure Co., ca. 1890, box 25; and advertisement for Warner's Safe Remedies in *Warner's Artistic Album* (Rochester: Warner's Safe Remedies, 1888), box 34. For other examples of this pattern see advertisements for Oregon Indian Medicine Co., ca. 1890, box 24; and for Church Kidney Cure Company's Kava-Kava Compound, 1896, box 5.

26. The following advertisements can be found at various locations in the Warshaw Collection: for F. J. Taney Co., Angostura Bitters, 1876, Patent Medicines, box 31a; for Taylor's Premium Cologne, 1890, Patent Medicines, box 31a; for Love's Incense perfume, 1880, Cosmetics, box 108; and for London Toilet Bazaar, 1886, Cosmetics, box 108. On the voluptuous woman as belle ideal, see Lois Banner, *American Beauty* (New York: Knopf, 1982), 111. For fin-de-siècle images of devouring women, see the chamber of horrors assembled by Brom Djikstra in *Idols of Perversity* (New York: Oxford University Press, 1987).

27. Advertisements for Warner Bros. Coraline Corsets, ca. 1890, Cosmetics, box 110, Warshaw Collection. On the erotic significance of the corset I follow the argument made by David Kunzle, *Fashion and Fetishism: A Social History of the Corset, Tightlacing, and Other Forms of Body-Sculpture in the West* (Totowa, N.J.: Rowman & Littlefield, 1982).

28. The following advertisements can be found at various locations in the Warshaw Collection: for Mennen's Borated Talcum Powder, 1909, Cosmetics, box 110; for Ivory Soap (pamphlet), "What a Cake of Soap Will Do," Soap, box "Procter & Gamble"; for B. T. Babbitt's Best, ca. 1885, Soap, box A–B; and for Gillette Safety Razors, 1910, Barbering, box 1.

29. Ruth Schwartz Cowan, *More Work for Mother: The Ironies of Household Technology from the Open Hearth to the Microwave* (New York: Basic Books, 1983), 51–53; and Claudia Bushman and Richard Bushman, "The Early History of Cleanliness in America," *Journal of American History* 75 (December 1988): 675–725.

30. "The Philosophy of Modern Advertising," *Yale Review* 8 (November 1899): 229–232.

31. "Woodbury's Advertising," *PI* 22 (23 February 1898): 24–26; Wengarten Bros., *Beauty Book,* ca. 1910, Corsets, box 4, Warshaw Collection; advertisement for Coca-Cola, 1927, Beverages, box 1, Warshaw Collection. On the growth of statistical definitions of normality, see Howard P. Chudacoff, *How Old Are You? Age Consciousness in American Culture* (Princeton: Princeton University Press, 1989); and Lisa Norling, "The Early History of Dieting in America," unpublished manuscript. For one among many examples of mechanistic metaphors for the body, see E. B. Rosa, "The Human Body as an Engine," *Popular Science Monthly* 57 (September 1900): 491–499.

32. Banner, *American Beauty*, especially 39–47; advertisement for Dewey's Dress and Coat Shields, 1887, Corsets, box 2, Warshaw Collection; advertisement for Hood Canvas Shoes in *Good Housekeeping*, May 1933, 175; advertisement for Royal Gelatin in *Good Housekeeping*, March 1934, 150–151; John B. Watson, quoted in minutes of JWT Co. Representatives Meeting 1 June 1928, JWT Archives; and advertisement for Odorono in *Good Housekeeping*, March 1930, 173.

33. Advertisement for Kleenex Tissues in *Good Housekeeping*, July 1932, 160; advertisement for Zonite antiseptics in *Good Housekeeping*, April 1931, 126; advertisement for Lysol in *Good Housekeeping*, April 1930, 143; and advertisement for Guardian memorials, 1926, book 134, N.W. Ayer Collection, National Museum of American History, Smithsonian Institution, Washington, D.C.

34. On the linkage between body and soul in the Puritan morphology of conversion, see John Owen King, *The Iron of Melancholy* (Middletown, Conn.: Wesleyan University Press, 1983), especially 57. On the secularization of this tradition, see David Pivar, *Purity Crusade: Sexual Morality and Social Control, 1868–1900* (Westport, Conn.: Greenwood Press, 1973). For one among hundreds of advertisements detailing the dangers of "intestinal fatigue," see advertisement for Fleischmann's Yeast, *Saturday Evening Post*, 11 October 1930, 62–63.

35. Minutes of JWT Representatives' Meeting, 13 February 1930, 7–8.

36. Helen Woodward, *Through Many Windows* (New York: Putnam, 1926), 200; "Concentration, the Secret of Success," *Profitable Advertising*, 15 November 1893, 170–172; Milton J. Platt, "Ruts and Originalities," *Fame*, November 1894, 345–346; "Confessions of an Advertising Solicitor," *PI* 14 (22 January 1896): 70; and Aesop Glim, "Playboy or Business Man?" *PI* 151 (17 April 1930).

37. "Sensational Attacks upon Proprietary Medicines," *PI* 52 (22 August 1905): 9; "Why Alcohol Is Used in Patent Medicines," *PI* 53 (4 October 1905): 19; "Dr. Wiley on Honest Advertising," *PI* 65 (18 November 1908): 30; "The Campaign against Fraudulent Advertising," *PI* 90 (4 March 1915): 67–79; Joseph Appel, *Growing Up with Advertising* (New York: Business Bourse, 1940), 123–136; and Pope, *Making of Modern Advertising*, 186–218.

38. New York organizer, quoted in Pope, *Making of Modern Advertising*, 318n.

39. Stephen M. Vaughn, *Holding Fast the Inner Lines: Democracy, Nationalism, and the Committee on Public Information* (Chapel Hill: University of North Carolina Press, 1980); Charles H. Cooley, *Social Process* (1902; Carbondale: Southern Illinois University Press, 1966), 136; Luther H. Gulick, *A Philosophy of Play* (New York: Appleton, 1920), 245; and Jones, "Advertising Men as the Cheer Leaders of the Nation." For a more passive version of morale, formulated (significantly) by a woman, see Annie Payson Call, *Nerves and the War* (Boston: Houghton Mifflin, 1918).

40. Clarence S. Yoakum, *Army Mental Tests* (Washington, D.C.: U.S. Government Printing Office, 1919), 260–261.

41. Jose Ortega y Gassett, *The Revolt of the Masses* anon. trans. (1930; New York: W. W. Norton, 1957); T. S. Eliot, "The Wasteland" [1922], in *Collected Poems 1909–1962* (New York: Farrar, Straus, & Giroux, 1970), 53–76; and William Esty, comment at JWT Representatives' Meeting, 30 September 1930, JWT Archives. See also JWT house ads for 5 August 1920, and 9 and 23 December 1920 in *PI*, clippings in JWT Archives; and "People Like to Spend," *People*, October 1937, JWT Archives. There are strikingly Eliotic visions in such unlikely sources as J. M. Campbell, "Some Reasons Why 'Reason Why' Copy Often Fails," *PI* 74 (9 March 1911): 11–14; and Paul Nystrom, a marketing professor at Columbia who wrote of a "philosophy of futility" enveloping modern life in his *The Economics of Fashion* (New York: Columbia University Press, 1928), 66–69.

42. "The New Business World: Number Five in a Series," broadcast transcript, 30 November 1929, Bruce Barton Papers, Wisconsin State Historical Society, Madison, Wisconsin. The pre–Henry Luce *Life* magazine created a character named "Andy Consumer" who reiterated this same argument. See for example, the advertisement for *Life* in *PI* 133 (5 November 1925): 94–95. Advertising executives communicated this sentiment privately as well: see S. L. Meulendyke, letter of 14 April 1926 to Earnest Elmo Calkins, box 1, Calkins Papers Knox College, Galesburg, Illinois. On the growing respectability of installment buying, see "New Wine in Old Bottles," *PI* 39 (16 April 1902): 14.

43. Stuart Chase, *The Tragedy of Waste* (New York: Macmillan, 1925); Marchand, *Advertising the American Dream*, 286–324; and Otis Pease, *Responsibilities of American Advertising: Private Control and Public Influence, 1920–1940* (New Haven: Yale University Press, 1958), 115–166.

44. Susman, *Culture as History*, 150–210; Rita S. Halle, "Can They Pass In Emotion?" *Good Housekeeping*, September 1932, 26–27; Marion Sturges-Jones, "Don't Be Afraid to Conform," *Good Housekeeping*, November 1936; Vera Connolly, "Uncle Sam Wants Your Mark," *Good Housekeeping*, December 1935, 24–25.

45. Donald Wilhelm, "Business Rushes to Government's Aid in Preparedness Crisis," *PI* 192 (16 August 1940): 11–13.

✦ JAN LEWIS ✦

Motherhood and the Construction of the Male Citizen in the United States, 1750–1850

Several years ago, when my son was in kindergarten, he brought home an advertisement for a school-sponsored reading program that carried with it an endorsement of sorts by Abraham Lincoln: "All that I am I owe to my angel mother." What struck me then was the misattribution; the words were those of Daniel Webster.[1] But since that time I have often reflected upon the advertisement and why Lincoln's supposed words were being used to try to sell me and other suburban mothers a bunch of children's books.

The manifest meaning of the text of that advertisement is, I suppose, rather clear: Mothers who buy these books may rear another Lincoln (or, at the very least, another Webster). Yet this seemingly simple statement is rather complex; it yokes at least two different elements. First, there is the statement itself: "All that I am I owe to my angel mother," which is an extraordinary paean to the doctrine of maternal influence. *All* that the child becomes is the responsibility of the mother; there are no other forces at play. Second, the attribution to a leading political figure, whether Webster or Lincoln, who is better-remembered today, links child rearing to politics. The measure of maternal success is rearing a great statesman, or, alternately, it is one's civic duty to be a good mother. Motherhood has a civic dimension. A simple declaration of filial debt, when attributed to one of the nation's greatest leaders, becomes a political statement, and a domestic relationship between a mother and her child is transformed into one with political significance.

It is this particular construction of motherhood, one that exalts and politicizes its influence, that I wish to examine. It should be clear that if a late-twentieth-century advertisement for children's books can invoke the name of Abraham Lincoln and the praise he supposedly bestowed upon his mother, this construction is one with continuing resonance in American culture. Although some may consider this depiction of motherhood as in some ways natural, which is surely the way the advertiser must have seen it, it is, in truth, a cultural construction, and one whose history is rather brief. It dates to the period just before Daniel Webster penned those words of filial devotion that now have outlived even his own once-substantial fame.

The origins of the doctrine of maternal influence can be traced to the decades just after the American Revolution. It was created to address certain problems in democratic thought left unresolved by that upheaval in political life and thought. Put another way, the doctrine of material influence was an expression of liberalism, the political philosophy that provides the basis for the modern, democratic state. Contemporary feminist political theorists have reexamined the classic texts of liberalism and shown how important considerations of gender were to the architects of liberalism such as Locke and Rousseau. The political doctrines they formulated excluded women from the public sphere, while requiring them to serve it in the private, in their capacity as mothers of male citizens. In liberal thought, as Carole Pateman has put it, "the performance of women's duty is vital for the health of the state, yet this duty lies outside citizenship—indeed, motherhood is seen as the antithesis of the duties of men and citizens." As a result, "modern liberal society is," in Susan Moller Okin's words, "deeply and pervasively gender-structured."[2] Historians, however, have not yet followed through on the lead established by political theorists; today we have a much better understanding of how considerations of gender entered formal political thought than how they became part of informal, quotidian practice, particularly on this side of the Atlantic. We do not yet know how the assumptions of the liberal theorists were translated into the vernacular of American habit.[3]

✦ ✦ ✦

If we want to trace the history of the politicization of motherhood in America, we should look back to an earlier period, before motherhood was esteemed and before democracy was in vogue. At the time of the Revolution, ideas about family and government would change, but early-American culture was decidedly patriarchal. Statute, custom, and religious doctrine all established the father as the preeminent authority in the household. Moreover, authority itself was revered, which enhanced paternal dominion at home. As a consequence, well into the eighteenth century most child-rearing literature was addressed to fathers or to parents generally, but with the assumption that the father would take the leading role, and much of the advice was concerned with control, rather than, for example, nurturance.[4] The colonial ideal was, as Cotton Mather put it in 1699, "A Family Well-Ordered," or, in Benjamin Wadsworth's words a few years later, "The Well-Ordered Family." "Good order in any Society renders it beautiful and lovely," observed Wadsworth. "This is true of Families, as well as of other societies."[5] Good order required obedience, wife to husband, and children to parents, much as God's creatures were supposed to follow the commandments of their Lord. And the family was an inherently political institution, for it inculcated the principles of authority and hierarchy upon which early American society and government depended. In this sense, the family represented, as John Demos has suggested, the society in miniature.[6]

That a man in such a society should rule his household was unquestioned. As Wadsworth put it, "The Husband is call'd the *Head of the Woman*, 1 Cor. 113. It belongs to the *Head*, to rule and govern."[7] In a society so concerned with order, it is, perhaps, no surprise that mothers were feared. As Laurel Thatcher Ulrich has observed for northern New England, "Mothers represented the affectionate mode in an essentially authoritarian system of childrearing." In a "patriarchal order . . . mother love or any other form of human love could never be an unqualified good."[8] So, while mothers were assured that "the Fathers are not the only *Parents* obliged . . . to pursue the Salvation of their *Children*," and while they were assigned particular responsibilities, such as breast-feeding their children, they were also warned not to undermine social order by coddling their offspring. Mather, for example, instructed mothers not to "*overlay* them with her Sinful Fondness."[9] Passionate and emotional, mothers and their love had to be subordinated to a higher order.[10] And although historians have debated whether the Protestant Reformation enhanced or diminished the position of women, there is very little indication of reverence for mothers in early America, and considerable evidence for filial neglect, indifference, and even hostility.[11]

Before motherhood could be idealized and its influence exalted, Americans would have to think in radically different ways about both gender and authority. It was, however, thinking about authority that would change first, as part of the transformation in political thought that would make possible the American Revolution. This transformation drew women into the political discourse of the late-eighteenth century almost by accident, but the effect it would have upon ideas about gender would be enormous.

The late-eighteenth century's revolt against patriarchy as a system for both the polity and the family worked to dethrone both kings and fathers, opening the way for more democratic forms of organization at all levels of the society. Intellectual historians have demonstrated that rebellion itself was conceptualized as the overthrow of a tyrannical father. When hierarchy was rejected as a fit model for political and social relations, so also were the images of the citizen as a dutiful son and the ruler as a wise parent. Independence required a different familial metaphor, and, according to Jay Fliegelman, American revolutionaries found one in the "affectionate union" of marriage.[12] Citizens of a republic, the form of government the rebels chose for themselves, were to be bound not by patriarchy's duty nor the hidden hand that would regulate liberalism's self-interest, but by affection, an uncoerced and supposedly natural attachment such as that members of a family manifested for one another. Influenced by Scottish Common Sense moral philosophy, Revolutionary-era American commentators found in marriage the familial metaphor for the society they hoped to create.[13] Marriage, they believed, more than any other institution, trained a citizen in this virtue.

That is why John Witherspoon, who taught his Princeton students from Scottish Enlightenment texts, could proclaim the "absolute necessity of marriage for the service of the state."[14] Other essayists elaborated upon the political function of marriage. One, for example, argued that the pure love of marriage formed the basis for "social virtue," for "while other passions concentrate man on himself, love makes him live in another, subdues selfishness, and reveals to him the pleasure of, ministering to the object of his love. . . . The lover becomes a husband, a parent, a citizen." Another noted that the "marriage institution is the first to produce moral order."[15] In the republican view, marriage was the school of virtue and, hence, the most important institution in society.

It is important to remember that this paradigm was neither patriarchal nor liberal, but republican, and, hence, its vision of the properly functioning society was social or corporate. Although American historians have engaged in heated debates about the sources of republicanism, which individuals and groups should be identified as republicans, and the doctrine's life-span, it is widely accepted that republicanism was one of the main, if not the chief, intellectual currents that fed Revolutionary ideology, and that whatever else it may have implied, republicanism rested upon the principle of self-sacrifice for the common good, which was known as virtue.[16] In retrospect, we may view republicanism as a transitional political doctrine, which attempted to subordinate the individualism unleashed by a rapidly changing society to an older concern for order and the primacy of the community. The challenge republicanism faced was how to maintain order in a society that had renounced coercion without yet embracing individualism or the attendant principle of self-interest. It offered a model of civic behavior patterned after marriage and the sort of renunciation that lovers were supposed gladly to make for the sake of the happiness they might share. Love, not fear, would bind society together.

Although it was anti-patriarchal, this formulation was not, it is important to note, fundamentally feminist. Its object was to fit men to be citizens in a republic, not to change the role of women in the family or the state. Nonetheless, it would have important implications for the conceptualization of woman's role, for it drew women—as partners in the conjugal union—into the political culture. Hence, both male and female were necessary components. As one essayist put it, "That MAN who resolves to live without WOMAN, or that WOMAN who resolves to live without MAN are [sic] ENEMIES TO THE COMMUNITY in which they dwell, INJURIOUS TO THEMSELVES, DESTRUCTIVE TO THE WORLD, APOSTATES TO NATURE, and REBELS AGAINST HEAVEN AND EARTH."[17] In Witherspoon's words, the single life "narrows the mind and closes the heart."[18]

Marriage opened the heart and mind both, and both realms, which later Americans would segregate into separate spheres, must be developed in the mature political personality. Hence the importance of marriage, which fused "virtuous love and friendship, the one supplying it with a constant rapture, the other regulating it by the rules of reason. . . . Reason and society are the characteristics which distinguish us from the other animals[;] an excellence in these two privileges of man, which enter into wedlock, must raise us in happiness above the rest of our species."[19] Both woman's love and man's reason were required; they worked reciprocally, as his intellect moderated passion, while her love socialized reason. Thus it was woman who suited man for society, by awakening his affection. "L," writing in the *Royal American Magazine* in 1774, explained that in marriage "the tender feelings and soft passions of the soul are awakened with all the ardour of love and benevolence. . . . In this happy state, man feels a growing attachment to human nature, and love to his country."[20] For republicans, as much as for Puritans, the family was but "a little commonwealth . . . or schoole wherein the first principles . . . are learned,"[21] but the lesson had been changed: Now it was affection, not subjection, that must be taught. And, significantly, it was grown men, not children, who were to be educated.

We have come quite a distance in defining the place of women in American political thought, but we still have a way to go before we will reach Daniel Webster's idealization of his angel mother. But at this point we should note that by the end of the eighteenth century, women—or, perhaps more accurately, the category woman—had been drawn into the political discourse, and according to that discourse, women were thought capable of enormous influence. Thus, the young man who addressed his classmates at Columbia College's commencement in 1795 believed that "woman can mold the taste, the manners, and the conduct of her admirers, according to her pleasure." Moreover, "she can, even to a great degree, change, their tempers and dispositions, and superinduce habits entirely new." Woman was capable of effecting "miraculous transformations" in masculine character. [22] And so she was enjoined, in the words of one essayist, "to make our young men, not in empty words, but in deed and in truth, republicans."[23]

This was the role assigned women in the early republic. To be sure, it was a domestic role; it was to be performed within the family, in the relationship that a woman enjoyed with her mate. Yet it was also an adult role, one that presumed that women themselves could be moral,[24] and that they made their greatest contribution to the polity by the influence that they exercised over other adults. Yet therein lay its fatal flaw, for woman could be no more powerful than man allowed her to be. The pivot of the paradigm was not feminine morality—which was granted—but masculine susceptibility, which remained problematic.[25] The problem, then, was not with women, but with men.

It may bear repeating that, as I have tried to suggest, early American discourse about the family and about gender was also often a form of political colloquy. Not only was the family a fundamental political and social institution, but political thinkers often found it a convenient and easily grasped metaphor for the polity. Both families and polities have histories, and in the case of the United States, these histories have been intertwined; patriarchy as a form of government came under attack, for example, just when patriarchy within the family was beginning to fall. But we should no more look for or expect a complete and literal congruence of changes in government and the family than we ought to expect ideology to function as description. The metaphors of family offered political theorists a way to think about and work through problems in power arrangements not unlike the way a dream may expound upon problems left unresolved in the waking state.

And the problem for American political thinkers in the years after the Revolution was that men just did not seem to behave. James Madison may have been the first to grasp the dimensions of this dilemma. His solution, expressed in the Constitution and the philosophy that served as its rationale, brought what Gordon S. Wood has called an "end of classical politics." According to Wood, the framers of the Constitution decided that "the people were not an order organically tied together by their unity of interest but rather an agglomeration of hostile individuals coming together for their mutual benefit to construct a society. . . . America would remain free not because of any quality in its citizens of spartan self-sacrifice to some nebulous public good, but in the last analysis because of the concern each individual would have in his own self-interest and personal freedom."[26] Such a concept of politics made republican schemes for the encouragement of virtue profoundly irrelevant. Put another way, women and their influence, like the virtue they were supposed to impart, should no longer have been required.

Nonetheless, long after the ratification of the Constitution supposedly brought an end to classical politics, with its vision of a corporate society and its dependence upon a virtuous citizenry, certain Americans continued to insist that the fate of the nation rested upon the character of its citizenry. Catharine Beecher is a case in point. When in 1841 she invoked this principle as one "conceded by all" in her *Treatise on Domestic Economy*, she also observed that government by the vicious "is much more dreadful than any other form of civil government, as a thousand tyrants are more to be dreaded than one."[27] Her oblique reference to Jefferson's criticism of the democratic Virginia state constitution of 1776 in his *Notes on the State of Virginia* suggests the anachronism of her argument. Jefferson had objected to the concentrating of authority in the legislature. "One hundred and seventy-three despots would surely be as oppressive as one. . . . An *elective despotism* is not the government we fought for."[28] He suggested a system of checks and balances to remedy this defect in republican government, and the Constitution created such a structure at the national level a few years later. In this context, Beecher's use of republican terminology is rather curious; the ratification of the Constitution should have rendered her scheme for the creation of a virtuous citizenry unnecessary.

Catharine Beecher, however, was not alone. As a number of historians have shown, the republican vision persisted well into the nineteenth century. Indeed, although the Constitution, the Bill of Rights, the increasingly capitalist economy, and the emerging two-party system of government surely must be considered manifestations of an ascendant liberalism, recent historians have suggested that many Americans retained elements of the republican vision.[29] So prominent has this historiography become that James Oakes has written that "a 'republican synthesis' is rapidly replacing the older 'liberal consensus.'" Both the Whigs and the Democrats, it has been argued, adhered to certain republican tenets. The same has been said about groups ranging from urban artisans and middle-class female reformers in the antebellum period to upcountry southern farmers at the end of the nineteenth century.[30] The new structure of the American government notwithstanding, the commitment of the American people to liberalism seemed, at best, partial; and republican ways of thinking persisted long after the institution of changes in the government that should have made them unnecessary.[31]

And if historians have disagreed about how far into the nineteenth century the republican vision persisted, so also have they quarreled about who should be called a "liberal" and who a "republican." The disputes over the appropriate labels for Jefferson, Madison, and Hamilton are well known. But even Stephen Douglas and Abraham Lincoln—quintessential nineteenth-century political leaders—have each been described as at least partially classical republicans.[32] Perhaps the terms "liberal" and "republican" are too capacious if they can be applied to all the leading political figures from the Revolution to the Civil War. Or perhaps liberalism itself preserved certain tenets of classical republican thought. If John Stuart Mill, one of the leading theorists of liberalism—and whose works, unlike those of Jeremy Bentham, attracted a wide audience in the United States[33]—could espouse republican principles, perhaps it tells us something about the nature of liberalism.

In his essay "The Subjection of Women," Mill reflected upon the connection between the family and the polity. "Citizenship, in free countries," he wrote, "is partly a school of society in equality; but citizenship fills only a small place in modern life, and does not come near the daily habits or inmost sentiments." The theorist of liberalism identified one of the weaknesses in the system he helped to create. And he pointed to the remedy. "The family, justly constituted, would be the real school of the virtues of freedom. . . . What is needed is, that it should be a school of sympathy in equality, of living together in love, without power on one side or obedience on the other." At the same time that Mill extolled such quintessentially liberal principles as liberty, justice, and equality, he maintained a commitment to the older ideal of affection. Indeed, he yoked justice to sympathy and liberalism to the ideals of the Scottish Enlightenment. "We are entering into an order of things in which justice will again [as in 'former times'] be the primary virtue; grounded as before on equal, but now also on sympathetic association; having as its root no longer in the instinct of equals for self-protection, but in a cultivated sympathy between them."[34] It is this "Common Sense" appreciation of the affections that connects classical republicanism to liberalism, for not even liberals could imagine a society without benevolence. Naked, unsocialized self-interest had no appeal.

So at the same time that Madison and his colleagues were creating a government that would not require men to behave as angels, Americans refused to surrender their hopes. They continued to believe that the fate of the nation rested upon the character of its citizens, and they devised new techniques—manifested in religious revivals and benevolent reforms—to make the new nation moral.[35] The object of these endeavors was the creation of virtuous citizens, that is, the construction of the male citizen-self.

Women, of course, had an important role to play in this mission. Even Mill recognized, however, that the limits of feminine influence were established by masculine susceptibility.[36] If women could not, as wives, effect miraculous transformations in the behavior of grown men, they would simply have to start the work of moral reform earlier, before vicious habits had become ingrained. Thus, in the first decades of the nineteenth century, the paradigm of the republican wife was slowly supplanted by that of the mother who trained her children in benevolence and prepared them for heaven. This new formulation developed naturally out of the republican one, using its terminology and preserving its assumptions; and it represented itself as a counter to emerging liberal-individualist values. Nonetheless, it was not as it seemed. Instead, the idealized antebellum mother would become the agent of the very self-interested liberalism she was designed to counter.

The roles of republican wife and liberal mother are so similar that it is, perhaps, not surprising that their differences have not yet been noticed. Still, if we examine the didactic literature written by men and women and addressed to mothers in the period between approximately 1820 and 1850—the years in which the ideal of motherhood was established—we can see the ways in which this formulation differed from its predecessors.[37] The most obvious of these is in the object of the woman's ministrations—in one case, her husband, and in the other, her sons. (Significantly, the maternal advice literature almost always assumed that children were male.[38]) In each case, however, the woman's assignment was the "education of the benevolent affections."[39] The republican wife's love was called upon to socialize masculine reason, while the nineteenth-century mother's care was required to "cultivate the affections of the child."[40] Thus, an essayist in the *American Ladies' Magazine* wrote in 1829, "If the future citizens of our republic are to be worthy of their rich inheritance, they must be made so principally through the virtue and intelligence of their mothers. It is in that school of maternal tenderness that the kind affections must first be roused and made habitual . . . the sense of duty and moral responsibility unfolded and enlightened."[41] Jacksonian-era advisors, like their republican antecedents, believed that men must be made affectionate; they simply insisted that the work of moral education begin young. This shift reflected two new assumptions, opposite sides of the same coin: on one face, the belief that children's characters are especially malleable, and, on the other, implicitly, that adults' are not. In a significant revision of eighteenth-century orthodoxy, many Protestant ministers now accepted—indeed, advocated—childhood conversion.[42] By the age of eight or ten—when, coincidentally, a boy left his mother's side for his father's masculine world—the character was set.[43]

If the republican marriage paradigm assumed that the male citizen must embody both (feminine) love and (masculine) reason, so also did the new ideal of maternal influence. One essayist, using "The Mother of Washington" as his example, argued that "the talents of the female are the transmitted inheritance of her sons; [by] this wise dispensation of Providence . . . the endowments of the sexes are equalized, and both alike made to participate in the glories of their common nature."[44] Elaborating upon the assumptions of sensationalist psychology, such advisers explained that, in the formation of character, "the mother does the most. *Her* eye and voice–*her* smiles and tears—*her* reproofs and commendations—are the first objects of [her child's] observation, and the latest in his remembrance. Her expressions, her feelings, her passions become *almost* imperceptibly a part of his nature."[45] Thus, the properly reared young man represented a fusion of feminine and masculine, for "the mother must dwell in the heart of the child, and be . . . the soul of its every action."[46] When, finally, he is "thrown" upon the "world of sin, passion, temptation, and trial" where "there must be forbearance, concession, and sacrifice of interest and feeling,"[47] he will carry in him a woman's heart.

Heart, affection, love: these qualities represent, in the Jacksonian, as in the republican, idiom, both a feminine and a communitarian, anti-individualist impulse. In a sense, women—and their sphere—became the heirs of this facet of republicanism. As Mary Beth Norton has put it, "Women became the keepers of the nation's conscience, the only citizens specifically charged with maintaining the traditional republican commitment to the good of the entire community."[48] Those historians who have described the creation of woman's separate sphere have noted its compensatory function. According to Kathryn Kish Sklar, for example, "The male and female spheres were separated to allow men to continue their acquisitive pursuits and to enable women to concentrate on their moral role. . . . Together they gave society an energized labor force and a free conscience."[49] Thus, antebellum Americans could have their cake and eat it too, maintaining simultaneous commitments to disinterestedness and competitive individualism both. In other words, men could be liberals—so long as women weren't.

That, however, is not the way the architects of woman's separate sphere saw it. In fact, they rejected the notion of separate, countervailing interests; to have offered woman's selflessness as a balance for man's vice would have been to concede masculine amorality—and to accept a liberal vision of the world. Instead, those antebellum writers who articulated the ideology of woman's role preserved a republican understanding of social and political relations. Women were supposed to redeem the world not so much by offering men a haven from it as by sending missionaries to it in the persons of their sons. Antebellum maternal advice literature taught women how to instill in their children such quintessentially republican, feminine values as benevolence and disinterestedness. For example, *The Mother's Magazine* advised that "the social affections need to be watchfully and judiciously *educated.* . . . So simple a thing as inducing a little child to say '*Goodnight*' to the family will exert a lasting influence upon its social character."[50] Similarly, Dr. Humphrey, author of "Education of the Benevolent Affections," believed that "a mother . . . can bring her infant of a few months old, to give up anything," for instance, a rattle. The older child would then share his toys, and a grown man be inclined to acts of charity.[51] One mother—a correspondent to the *Mothers' Monthly Journal*—used a similar technique. Whenever her children were given a treat, she required them to share it with "each person present. . . . I have found this an admirable corrective to self-ishness."[52] Lydia Sigourney urged mothers to teach their children to show "kindness to all around. The rudiments are best taught by treatment of animals." She thought it instructive that the young Benedict Arnold "in his boyhood loved to destroy insects, to mutilate toads, to steal the eggs of the mourning bird, and torture quiet domestic animals."[53] Other authors described methods for teaching children to master their anger, their indolence, and their appetites for food and drink.[54] The object of these lessons in benevolence and self-restraint was to assure that, once grown, the child "will stand forth in manhood the high-souled, lofty-minded being [his mother] would have him."[55] The citizen-self would be a man with the heart and soul of a woman.

It was assumed that virtues taught in private would have a public application, that children who shared their toys and loved their pets would become charitable, affectionate citizens. Even Alexis de Tocqueville, that great observer of Jacksonian democracy, believed that the values a man learned at home he would "afterwards carr[y] with him into public affairs."[56] Yet, except for vague descriptions of George Washington as the "benefactor of his country,"[57] no models for adult civic behavior appear in the literature addressed to mothers. To be sure, a drunkard, a blasphemer, a gambler, or an avaricious businessman might indicate maternal failure.[58] But how might a success be recognized? What were the distinguishing characteristics of a "high-souled, lofty-minded being"? How should a benevolent, disinterested character be displayed? On the one hand, antebellum maternal advice literature insisted that "woman holds in her hands the destiny of the world." According to this doctrine, "In a few years [your son] will stand up among his fellows to discharge the duties of a free man in a free country . . . the foundation of our Glorious Republic is VIRTUE . . . the perpetuity of our benign institutions depends upon the *morality* of its citizens."[59] On the other hand, the duties of free men in a free country were never elaborated, and as a consequence, the virtues that mothers taught were defined and confined by the domestic context in which they were instilled.

Thus, in the decades after the Revolution, the words—benevolence, disinterestedness, morality, virtue—remained the same, but the context changed. And it is this new context that altered the meanings of republicanism and gender identity in the liberal age. Charity that began at home surely would end at home, as well, if mothers could not demonstrate how it should be exercised in the public realm. The doctrine of separate spheres lacked both the means and the measures to effect the public good, and thus, it turned in upon itself, finding its validation in private acts of repentance and reform. Incapable of creating good citizens, maternal influence had to settle for turning out good sons. And if the testimonies published in women's magazines can be trusted, here American mothers met with some success. H. W., for example, told the readers of *The Mother's Magazine* that, although he left home at the age of fourteen, "My mother's influence, the remembrance of her example and prayers still followed me, as a guardian angel, to preserve me from the many dangers and temptations which were around my path." That memory enabled him to control his temper and re-frain from swearing.[60] Many was the sinner pulled back from the edge of the abyss by the memory of his mother's prayers.[61]

The measure of a mother's success, then, was the degree to which her son embodied her heart and values—which could only be expressed in ways that had meaning in her sphere. And so, when Stephen Douglas, later to leave his mark upon his nation's history, left home at the age of fifteen to see "what I could do for myself in the wide world among strangers," he carried with him his mother's warning "of the dangers and temptations to which young men are exposed. . . . I promised to comply with her wishes, that is, keep good company, or in other words keep out of bad company, avoid all immoral and vicious practices, attend church regularly, and obey the reg-ulations of my employer; in short I promised everything she wanted, if she would consent to my leaving home."[62] Douglas listened to his mother—and he left.

Lincoln, his great rival, lost his mother before he, himself, was ready to leave home, but he cherished her memory, once confiding to his law part-ner, in words strikingly similar to Webster's, "God bless my mother. All that I am or ever hope to be I owe her."[63] Not Sarah Douglas or Nancy Lincoln or even Abigail Webster, so far as we know, gave their sons any political instruction. Lincoln was so young when his mother died that she could not have taught him very much. But, according to the doctrine of maternal influence, it was not so much the specific content of the training as the impress a mother made upon her child's heart that mattered. Indeed, according to one essayist, "the example and counsel of a living mother could hardly equal in power, upon the filial heart, the silent but thrilling preaching of a departed one."[64] Still, Lincoln and Douglas and Webster all, like many less illustrious antebellum American men, thought of themselves as dutiful sons. Whether the love each received from his mother became part of his political vision—as the doctrine of maternal influence thought it must—is problematic; instead, that love circled around, and was carried home. That, finally, was the mother's gift to the man, and the one he brought home to her. An essayist in the *American Ladies' Magazine* ex-plained "The Influence of Women on Society": Woman was, first of all, the "*mother*, around whom our affections twine as closely and surely, as the young vine clasps itself about the branch that supports it: our love for whom becomes so thoroughly a part and portion of ourselves, that it bids defiance to time and decay. When all other passions have turned to bitterness, when every other feeling is withered and dead, this reaching out of the heart towards our mother . . . remains an imperishable element of our nature."[65] His love for his mother, then, was the measure of the man.

The doctrine of maternal influence, like antebellum evangelical religion, with which it is closely allied, sought to reform society by touching the individual's heart. It left his other parts alone. The American mother was told that she held the fate of the nation in her hands, that her influence knew no bounds, if only she would "develop and mould the character of her children, leaving her own impress, a mental and moral daguerrotype of herself."[66] Women who followed this doctrine may have believed that they were casting their children in their own image, but, as Mary Ryan has noted, middle-class mothers were, in truth, turning out the sorts of persons their economy and society needed, ones who embodied "the usual array of petit bourgeois traits."[67] Because the values of honesty, hard work, and benevolence were taught in the context of the home, they were stripped of all public meaning; citizens schooled in these virtues were freed of all public obligations other than the private practice of the principles of bourgeois morality. This was the sense in which conventional morality, as Tocqueville had pointed out, contributed to political order.[68]

Women, then, created the very world they sought to redeem. The doctrine of maternal influence mystified this process, however, and this mystification, which allowed Americans to profess an allegiance to corporate values in an individualist world, is one of the hallmarks of liberalism. Gordon Wood has noted that, when the Federalists appropriated the language of their opponents in order to advance their own scheme, they established "a hiatus in American politics between ideology and motives that was never again closed." Thus, the liberal tradition uses rhetoric not—as in classical politics—to describe reality, but to obscure it.[69] The antebellum American mother posed as a critic of the very regime she so effectively served. In this sense, she was liberalism's creature and its creator, its artifact and its agent.

✦   ✦   ✦

Daniel Webster's angel mother, then, was constructed by the emergent liberalism of nineteenth-century America. We cannot say whether she truly made her son into what he was to become, although the doctrine of maternal influence suggested more generally that motherly affection and self-sacrifice would be redeemed in the public sphere, which men would enter carrying their mothers' hearts. The doctrine of maternal influence, then, placed women in politics in the persons of their sons; they would not themselves be political subjects, but instead would be represented by their sons. The doctrine of maternal influence aimed at an androgynous political culture, one in which (masculine) self-interest and (feminine) virtue might be joined. Yet most studies of American political life, particularly of the nineteenth century, depict it as rough, boisterous, and aggressively masculine, while analyses of contemporary family life suggest that, at home, at least, men attempted to adhere to feminine standards of gentility and decorum.[70]

Although this picture does not conform to the grand hopes of the doctrine of maternal influence, it is probably true, perhaps to the point of truism, that American mothers generally have reared the children their society has required, performing thereby a crucial social and political function. Moreover, motherhood, as much as "natural rights," "the people," or "interests," or any other of the contested truths whose usage Daniel Rodgers has analyzed in his recent study of American political language, has functioned as a keyword in political discourse.[71] "Motherhood" was constructed as the idiomatic opposite to "interest," the "antithesis," as Carole Pateman put it, of "the duties of men and citizens." Again and again, social commentators described mother's love as disinterested, and her patriotism—in contrast to man's—"a sentiment of the noblest kind," unsullied by a "tinge of egotism."[72] Unwilling to break radically from their republican heritage and its ideal of civic virtue, Americans incorporated virtue and the notion of the common good into their model of liberalism by assigning them to the supposedly private sphere of the home, where, like Nancy Lincoln, Abigail Webster, and Sarah Douglas, they might be praised—and abandoned. In other words, liberalism's construction of motherhood served two functions at the same time. It offered a way of holding onto the ideal of civic virtue in an increasingly ambition-driven culture. And it helped to create a male self appropriate for a modern democratic society, one that seized and subordinated mother's love.

But perhaps I am unfair. Lincoln, Douglas, Webster, and all the other American sons may have loved their mothers as deeply as they claimed and missed them dearly, just as Americans in general often seem to long for a fuller public life and a sense of common purpose. Daniel Rodgers has recently noted that "no other political culture has had a vocabulary of individual liberation quite like [ours]. But what Americans [have] found much harder to come by were clear ways in which to talk about the common bonds and responsibilities of public life."[73]

Surely it is significant that these alternate approaches to politics—the one emphasizing individual liberation and the other, responsibility—echo the different modes of masculine and feminine experience and interpretation that Carol Gilligan has described. Gilligan has noted that men speak in a language of rights and women, in one of responsibilities. Expanding upon the work of Nancy Chodorow, Gilligan suggests that these alternate voices are the product of the different kinds of relationships that a girl and a boy have with their mother: As a boy matures, he must separate himself from his mother, while a girl may maintain her identification with and her attachment to her mother with no threat to her gender identity. As Gilligan puts it, "Masculinity is defined through separation while femininity is defined through attachment."[74] It is but a short distance from this theory of psychological and moral development to the assertion that liberalism, with the premium it places upon rights, is an inherently masculine theory, and one that devalues and excludes a feminine ethic of attachment and responsibility. A number of feminist theorists have made this connection.[75]

Yet those who critique liberalism from this particular feminist standpoint may themselves have been constructed by liberal political discourse. The very notion that women, particularly in their capacity as mothers, stand outside the American liberal tradition, and that they, with their different experience and perspective, offer an alternate vision not only of political and social life, but of selfhood is itself an artifact of liberalism. It is this very doctrine that has defined the principles of attachment and responsibility as feminine and located them within the family. Liberalism has shaped the language with which we talk about rights and obligations, as well as the words we use to discuss gender and the family.[76]

If we cannot talk about the polity without using the language of family, neither are we able fully to discuss the family without calling forth an array of political meanings. Daniel Webster's claim that all that he was—his very identity—was a gift from his angel mother, was a political statement, his way of saying that, although a man, he embodied feminine affection. In this way, the male citizen-self created by liberalism both constructed femininity and appropriated it. Daniel Webster—the male citizen-self of modern democracy—represented both himself and his mother, or rather, in representing her he replaced her. Once he left home, he had no reason to return.

NOTES

Research for this essay was made possible by fellowships from the National Endowment for the Humanities, the Philadelphia Center for Early American Studies, and the Newberry Library. Earlier versions of this essay were presented to the annual meeting of the Organization of American Historians, the Philadelphia Center for Early American Studies, and the Columbia University Early American History Seminar. I thank the members of those audiences for their comments and suggestions, and Norma Basch and Linda Zerilli for valuable advice.

1. "The Influence of Woman," in *The Young Ladies' Reader* (Philadelphia, 1851), 310, quoted in Barbara Welter, "The Cult of True Womanhood," in *The Underside of American History*, ed. Thomas R. Frazier (New York: Harcourt Brace Jovanovich, 1978), 237.

2. Carole Pateman, *The Disorder of Women* (Stanford: Stanford University

Press, 1989), 11; and Susan Moller Okin, *Justice, Gender, and the Family* (New York: Basic Books, 1989), 89. See also, Okin, *Women in Western Political Thought* (Princeton: Princeton University Press, 1979), Jean Bethke Elshtain, *Public Man, Private Women: Women in Social and Political Thought* (Princeton: Princeton University Press, 1981); and Joan B. Landes, *Women and the Public Sphere in the Age of the French Revolution* (Ithaca: Cornell University Press, 1988). Speaking of France, Landes writes, "The Republic was constructed against women, not just without them" (171).

3. An important exception is Linda K. Kerber, who has examined the way in which gender figured in early American political thought and practice. Her works include *Women and the Republic: Intellect and Ideology in Revolutionary America* (Chapel Hill: University of North Carolina Press, 1980); and "The Republican Ideology of the Revolutionary Generation," *American Quarterly* 37 (1985): 187–205.

4. John Demos, "The Changing Faces of Fatherhood," in *Past Present, and Personal: The Family and the Life Course in American History* (New York: Oxford University Press, 1986), 41–67; and Ruth H. Bloch, "American Feminine Ideals in Transition: The Rise of the Moral Mother," *Feminist Studies* 4 (1978): 101–126. I am using the term "patriarchal" here as most political theorists do, to mean a theory of government modeled on the rule of an authoritarian father, rather than as feminist theorists do, to mean the domination of women by men. Carole Pateman has recently addressed this confusion of terminology, arguing that the theory of government modeled on the father's rule, given its quintessential expression by Sir Robert Filmer, should be denominated "classic patriarchalism," one of the forms male domination of women has taken. See Pateman, *The Sexual Contract* (Stanford: Stanford University Press, 1988), 24–25 and *passim*. It seems to me, nonetheless, that the use of the term "patriarchy" to mean rule by literal or figurative fathers does not necessarily deny that subsequent theories of government presume the political domination of women by men. For an elaboration of the relationship between patriarchal theories of government and patriarchal family forms in early modern England, see Lawrence Stone, *The Family, Sex, and Marriage in England, 1500–1800* (New York: Harper & Row, 1977), part 3.

5. Cotton Mather, *A Family Well-Ordered, or An Essay to Render Parents and Children Happy in One Another* (Boston: B. Green and J. Allen, 1699); and Benjamin Wadsworth, *The Well-Ordered Family* (Boston, 1712), preface.

6. John Demos, *A Little Commonwealth: Family Life in Plymouth Colony* (New York: Oxford University Press, 1970).

7. *Well-Ordered Family*, 35.

8. *Good Wives: Image and Reality in the Lives of Women in Northern New England, 1650–1750* (New York: Alfred A. Knopf, 1982), 154.

9. Mather, *Family Well-Ordered*, 36; Wadsworth, *Well-Ordered Family*, 45; Mather, *Ornaments for the Daughters of Zion; or the Character and Happiness of a Vertuous Woman* (Cambridge, Mass.: Samuel Phillips, 1692), unpaginated; and *Ornaments*, unpaginated.

10. See Nancy F. Cott, "Passionlessness: An Interpretation of Victorian Sexual Ideology, 1790–1850," *Signs* 4 (1978): 219–236.

11. See, for example, Carol F. Karlsen, *The Devil in the Shape of a Woman: Witchcraft in Colonial New England* (New York: W. W. Norton, 1987), 216 and *passim*.

12. *Prodigals and Pilgrims: The American Revolution against Patriarchal Authority, 1750–1800* (New York: Cambridge University Press, 1982), especially chap. 5. See

also Jan Lewis, "The Republican Wife: Virtue and Seduction in the Early Republic," *William and Mary Quarterly*, 3d ser., 44 (1987): 689–721; Melvin Yazawa, *From Colonies to Commonwealth: Familial Ideology and the Beginnings of the American Republic* (Baltimore: Johns Hopkins University Press, 1985); Edwin G. Burrows and Michael Wallace, "The American Revolution: The Ideology and Psychology of National Liberation," *Perspectives in American History* 6 (1972): 167–306; and Winthrop D. Jordan, "Familial Politics: Thomas Paine and the Killing of the King, 1776," *Journal of American History* 60 (1973): 294–308.

13. See Lewis, "Republican Wife"; and, for the influence of Scottish moral philosophy, see Fliegelman, *Prodigals*, especially 9–29; Daniel W. Howe, "The Political Psychology of *The Federalist*," *William and Mary Quarterly*, 3d ser., 44 (1987): 485–509; and Garry Wills, *Inventing America: Jefferson's Declaration of Independence* (Garden City, N.Y.: Doubleday, 1978), especially part 4. Consider also Perry Miller, "The Rhetoric of Sensation," in *Errand into the Wilderness* (New York: Harper Torchbooks, 1956), 166–183.

14. "Reflections on Marriage," *Pennsylvania Magazine*, September 1775, 408, later published as "Letters on Marriage," in *The Works of Rev. John Witherspoon*, 2d ed. (Philadelphia, 1802), 4: 161–183.

15. "On Love," *New York Magazine*, June 1791, 311; and "A Second Vindication of the Rights of Woman," *Ladies' Monitor*, 15 August 1801, 12. See also "The Reflector No. 1," *Ladies' Monitor*, 7 November 1801, 92; "On Matrimonial Felicity," *Gentleman and Lady's Magazine*, September 1784, 193–194; "On Love," *Ladies Magazine and Repository*, June 1792, 34–37; "Fashionable Miscellany," *Baltimore Weekly Magazine*, 12 July 1800, 91–92; and "On Marriage," *General Magazine*, July 1798, 41–45.

16. A useful summary of the vast literature on republicanism is provided by Robert E. Shalhope, "Republicanism and Early American Historiography," *William and Mary Quarterly*, 3d ser., 39 (1982): 334–356. Different historians understand the term "republicanism" in different ways; my thinking has been shaped particularly by Gordon S. Wood, *The Creation of the American Republic, 1776–1787* (Chapel Hill: University of North Carolina Press, 1969). Ruth H. Bloch, "The Gendered Meanings of Virtue in Revolutionary America," *Signs* 13 (1987): 37–58, offers a fine discussion of the implications of republicanism for gender and vice versa.

17. "From the Genius of Liberty," *The Key*, 14 April 1798, 105–106.

18. "Reflections on Marriage," 411.

19. "Conjugal Love," *Massachusetts Magazine*, February 1792, 102.

20. "Thoughts on Matrimony," *Royal American Magazine*, January 1774, 9.

21. William Gouge, *Of Domesticall Duties* (London, 1622), quoted in Demos, *Little Commonwealth*, xix.

22. "Female Influence," *New York Magazine*, May 1795, 299. For another analysis of this problem, see Kerber, *Women and the Republic*. In this pathbreaking work, Kerber showed that American women in the Revolutionary era were assigned a peculiar role, at once domestic and political. She dubbed this role "Republican Motherhood," using that term to embrace women's several domestic roles—both rearing sons and influencing husbands. It is my argument that the focus upon the political dimension to marriage is characteristic of the early national period—from 1776 to 1820 or so—and that it gave way to an emphasis upon motherhood. For Kerber's most recent elaboration of her paradigm, see "The Republican Ideology of the Revolutionary Generation."

23. "Female Economy," *The Ladies' Literary Cabinet*, 8 July 1820, 67.

24. This point is elaborated in Lewis, "Republican Wife."

25. I have suggested elsewhere that the late eighteenth century's seduction literature, a body of novels and stories modeled on *Clarissa* and exemplified by the works of Susanna Rowson and Hannah Foster, may be read as an extended commentary upon the possibilities for feminine virtue when confronted by masculine vice. In such seduction stories, virtue always falls. The moral, not merely for women, but for all those who would rest the fate of their nation upon virtue, was grim (Lewis, "Republican Wife," 713–721).

26. Wood, *Creation of the Republic*, 607.

27. Catharine Beecher, *A Treatise on Domestic Economy for the Use of Young Ladies at Home* (Boston: Marsh, Capen, Lyon, and Webb, 1841), 13.

28. *Notes on the State of Virginia*, in *The Life and Selected Writings of Thomas Jefferson*, ed. Adrienne Koch and William Peden (New York: Modern Library, 1944), 237.

29. Recent works that describe the persistence of republican ideas and language into the nineteenth century are noted in Kerber, "Republican Ideology," 491–492. More recent works in this vein include the articles in *American Quarterly* 37 (1985), "Special Issue: Republicanism in the History and Historiography of the United States," especially Jean Baker, "From Belief into Culture," 532–550. Note also Daniel Walker Howe's observation in *The Political Culture of the American Whigs* (Chicago: University of Chicago Press, 1979), 79: "It appears that the 'end of the classical conception of politics,' which at least one historian had dated at the ratification of the Constitution, actually took quite a bit longer in coming." See similarly J. G. A. Pocock, *The Machiavellian Moment: Florentine Political Thought and the Atlantic Republican Tradition* (Princeton: Princeton University Press, 1975), 526–527.

30. James Oakes, "From Republicanism to Liberalism: Ideological Change and the Crisis of the Old South," *American Quarterly* 37 (1985): 552. See Howe, *Culture of Whigs*, 74–80 for the Whigs; and Baker, "From Belief into Culture," for the Democrats. See Sean Wilentz, *Chants Democratic: New York City and the Rise of the American Working Class* (New York: Oxford University Press, 1984), for artisans; Carroll Smith-Rosenberg, "Misprisoning *Pamela*: Representations of Gender and Class in Nineteenth-Century America," *Michigan Quarterly Review* 26 (1987): 9–28, for middle-class women; and Steven Hahn, *The Roots of Southern Populism: Yeoman Farmers and the Transformation of the Georgia Upcountry* (New York: Oxford University Press, 1983), for upcountry yeomen.

31. For an interesting recent discussion of American political thought, see Daniel T. Rodgers, *Contested Truths: Keywords in American Politics since Independence* (New York: Basic Books, 1987). Rodgers notes that the term "interest" was not commonly used or discussed by American political thinkers until the twentieth century. Throughout the nineteenth century, American political language favored abstractions such as "natural rights," and Madison's *Federalist* no. 10 was all but forgotten.

32. For a review of the disputes about how to label the Revolutionary generation, see Lance Banning, "Jeffersonian Ideology Revisited: Liberal and Classical Ideas in the New American Republic," *William and Mary Quarterly*, 3d ser., 43 (1986): 3–19; and Joyce Appleby, "Republicanism in Old and New Contexts," *William and Mary Quarterly*, 3d ser., 43 (1986): 20–34. Douglas is described as partly republican in Baker, "Belief into Culture," 532–534; and Howe, *Culture of Whigs*, 274, notes the republican element in Lincoln's thought.

33. For the American revulsion against utilitarianism, which made Bentham anathema and tainted even Mill, see Rodgers, *Contested Truths*, chap. 1.

34. "The Subjection of Women," in *Three Essays*, ed. Richard Wollheim (Oxford: Oxford University Press, 1975), 478. I am indebted to Linda Zerilli, in particular for pointing out this passage to me, and more generally for sharing with me her rich insights into Mill and his political theory.

35. For the significance of religious revivalism, see Perry Miller's classic analysis, "From the Covenant to the Revival," in James Ward Smith and A. Leland Jamison, *The Shaping of American Religion* (Princeton: Princeton University Press, 1961), 322–368; for a survey, see William G. McLouglin, *Revivals, Awakenings, and Reform* (Chicago: University of Chicago Press, 1978). The literature on benevolent reform is vast. A good starting place is Alice Felt Tyler, *Freedom's Ferment: Phases of American Social History from the Colonial Period to the Outbreak of the Civil War* (1949; New York: Harper & Row 1962), especially part 3.

36. Mill, "Subjection of Women," 470–471.

37. For descriptions of the antebellum maternal advice literature, see Anne L. Kuhn, *The Mother's Role in Childhood Education: New England Concepts, 1830–1860* (New Haven: Yale University Press, 1947); and Mary P. Ryan, *The Empire of the Mother: American Writing about Domesticity, 1830–1860,* published as nos. 2/3 of *Women & History* (1982).

38. That this body of didactic literature typically assumed that children were male suggests both that rearing boys was problematic in a way that rearing girls was not and also that the underlying concern or subtext of this literature was the education of male citizens, not the upbringing of children generally. Although there are exceptions, most of the child-rearing literature published in this period, either as books or magazine articles dealt more with the moral than with the physical development of (male) children. Not until later in the century would the focus shift to the physical care of children, whereupon the rearing of girls receives extensive treatment. See, for example, Marion Harland, *Eve's Daughters: or Common Sense for Maid, Wife, and Mother* (New York: J. R. Anderson and Henry S. Allen, 1883).

39. *The Mother's Magazine*, April 1840, 73–78. See also, "What Can You Do For Your Country," *Mother's Magazine*, June 1834, 94; "Maternal Influence," *Mother's Magazine*, April 1841, 84; "Benevolence," *Mother's Magazine*, March 1842, 64; John A. Bolles, "The Influence of Women on Society," *American Ladies' Magazine*, June 1831, 266; Mrs. C. Sedgwick, "A Plea for Children," *American Ladies' Magazine*, February 1835, 93–95; "Thoughts on the Education of Girls," *Mothers' Monthly Journal*, July 1837; Mrs. H. C. Conant, "Our Children," *The Mother's Journal and Family Visitant* 14 (1849): 339; and Rev. John S. C. Abbott, *The Mother at Home: Or the Principles of Maternal Duty* (Boston: Crocker and Brewster, 1834), 159.

40. "Family Government Essential to National Prosperity," *Mother's Magazine*, March 1833, 36. See also Mill, "Early Essays on Marriage and Divorce," in *Essays on Sex Equality*, ed. Alice Rossi (Chicago: University of Chicago Press, 1970), 75–76.

41. "The Beginning," *American Ladies' Magazine*, January 1829, 4.

42. See "The Conversion of Children," *Mother's Magazine*, November 1835, 161–164, and December 1835, 179–181; "Remarks on the Conversion of Children," *Mother's Magazine*, February 1836, 24–25; C. A. Goodrich, "Hints on the Conversion of Children," *Mother's Magazine*, May 1838, 97; and *Religious Remembrancer*, 20 July 1816, 187.

43. Abbott, *Mother at Home*, 10; "Suggestions to Parents," *American Journal of Education*, October 1826, 603, and November 1826, 674; "The Influence of Mothers," *The Casket*, February 1827, 67.

44. *American Ladies' Magazine*, November 1831, 385.

45. "Extract," *Mother's Magazine*, January 1840, 24. See also "The Mother's Affection," *American Ladies' Magazine*, July 1833, 321; "The Peculiar Faculties Afforded to Mothers for Training up Their Children for God," *Mother's Magazine*, May 1837, 100–105; and Miss Ann Mason, "The Two Visits; or, Home Influence," *The Mother's Assistant*, November 1845, 105.

46. "Extracts from Report of Maternal Associations," *Mother's Magazine*, February 1841, 46.

47. "Hints for Maternal Education," *Mother's Magazine*, August 1834, 113, 114.

48. "The Evolution of White Women's Experience in Early America," *American Historical Review* 89 (1984): 615. See similarly Kerber, "Republican Ideology," 485.

49. *Catharine Beecher: A Study in American Domesticity* (New Haven: Yale University Press, 1973), 163. See similarly Nancy F. Cott, *The Bonds of Womanhood: "Woman's Sphere" in New England, 1780–1835* (New Haven: Yale University Press, 1977), chap. 2. See also Paula Baker, "The Domestication of Politics: Women and American Political Society, 1780–1920," *American Historical Review* 89 (1984): 629–631.

50. "Education of the Social Affections," *Mother's Magazine*, December 1839, 280, 284.

51. *Mother's Magazine*, April 1840, 73–75.

52. "The Golden Rule," *Mothers' Monthly Journal*, February 1837, 31.

53. *Letters to Mothers* (Hartford, 1838), 39. See also Catharine Maria Sedgwick, *Home* (Boston and Cambridge, 1835), 16–17.

54. "For Who Hath Despised the Day of Small Things," *Mothers' Monthly Journal*, July 1837, 102–103; "Family Scenes—The Inflicted Penalty," *Mother's Magazine*, March 1836, 43–45; and Sedgwick, *Home*, 32.

55. Sarah W. Gordon, "It Should be Love," *Mother's Assistant*, March 1849, 53.

56. Alexis de Tocqueville, *Democracy in America*, Henry Reeve text, rev. Francis Bowen, ed. Phillips Bradley (New York: Alfred A. Knopf, 1945), 1: 304.

57. Abbott, *Mother at Home*, 10–11. See also Sedgwick, *Home*, 24; and Sigourney, *Letters*, 37.

58. For example, Abbott, *Mother at Home*.

59. "The Mother," *The Hesperian; or, Western Monthly Magazine*, September 1839, 329; "A Mother's Influence," *The Mother's Journal* 14 (1849): 169–172.

60. "Recollections of a Mother by Her Elder Son," *Mother's Magazine*, March 1842, 54.

61. See "The Mother in Her Closet," *Mother's Magazine*, October 1840, 223–226; "Maternal Influence," *Mother's Magazine*, November 1840, 254–255; "The Pious Mother," *Mother's Magazine*, November 1837, 261; "Peculiar Faculties," *Mother's Magazine*, June 1837, 121–127; *Mother's Journal*, 16 (1851): 210; *Mother's Magazine*, October 1854, 307–309; and Abbott, *Mother at Home*, 16–17.

62. "Autobiographical Sketch," 1 September 1838, quoted in Robert W. Johannsen, *Stephen A. Douglas* (New York: Oxford University Press, 1973), 8.

63. Quoted in Charles B. Strozier, *Lincoln's Quest for Union: Public and Private Meanings* (New York: Basic Books, 1982), 3.

64. "A Mother's Grave," *Mother's Magazine*, June 1837, 138.

65. John A. Bolles, "The Influence of Women on Society," *American Ladies' Magazine*, June 1831, 256.

66. Joseph A. Hanaford, "Friendly Suggestions to Mothers," *Mother's Journal* 20 (1855): 189.

67. *Cradle of the Middle Class: The Family in Oneida County, New York, 1790–1865* (New York: Cambridge University Press, 1981), 161. See also her *Empire of the Mother*.

68. Tocqueville, *Democracy*, 1: 304; 2: 198; 1: 304.

69. Wood, *Creation of the Republic*, 562.

70. For nineteenth-century political culture see, for example, John F. Reynolds, *Testing Democracy: Electoral Behavior and Progressive Reform in New Jersey, 1880–1920* (Chapel Hill: University of North Carolina Press, 1988); Michael E. McGerr, *The Decline of Popular Politics: The American North, 1865–1928* (New York: Oxford University Press, 1986); and Paula Baker, *The Moral Frameworks of Public Life: Gender Politics, and the State in Rural New York, 1870–1930* (New York: Oxford University Press, 1991). For the single standard of behavior at home, see Carol Zisowitz Stearns and Peter N. Stearns, *Anger: The Struggle for Emotional Control in America's History* (Chicago: University of Chicago Press, 1986), especially. chap. 3.

71. See Rodgers, *Contested Truths*.

72. For the use of the term "disinterested," see, for example, "Thoughts on the Education of Females," *American Journal of Education* 1 (July 1826): 401; and "Home," *American Ladies' Magazine*, May 1830, 217–220. For patriotism, see Mrs. Jameson, "Woman's Patriotism," *American Ladies' Magazine*, June 1833, 282. This formulation is reminiscent of Abigail Adams's comment that "patriotism in the female Sex is the most disinterested of all virtues," because, "excluded from honours and from offices," they, unlike their husbands, had nothing to gain. Adams quoted in Mary Beth Norton, *Liberty's Daughters: The Revolutionary Experience of American Women, 1750–1800* (Boston: Little, Brown, 1980), 227.

73. *Contested Truths*, 223.

74. *In a Different Voice: Psychological Theory and Women's Development* (Cambridge: Harvard University Press, 1982), 8.

75. See, for example, Sara Ruddick, *Maternal Thinking: Toward a Politics of Peace* Boston: Beacon Press, 1989); and Karen Offen, "Defining Feminism: A Comparative Historical Approach," *Signs* 14 (1988): 119–157. For the application of such theories see Joan Hoff, *Law, Gender, and Injustice: A Legal History of U.S. Women* (New York: New York University Press, 1991).

76. For the persistence of the familial metaphor, see Martha Minow's very interesting "We, the Family: Constitutional Rights and American Families," *Journal of American History* 74 (1987): 959–983.

✦ SARANE SPENCE BOOCOCK ✦

The Social Construction of Childhood in Contemporary Japan

ecent research in the social sciences has manifested not only a resurgence of interest in the concept of the self, but also a new interest
in exploring that concept across cultures. It is now generally agreed
that the self is a social construct, that we are the result of our interactions
with significant others, and that the nature of these interactions is in turn
shaped by the characteristics, material and nonmaterial, of the settings in
which the interactions occur. Until recently, however, American research
tended to be biased by the assumption that the process by which the self is
constructed is the same everywhere; not surprisingly, that process was usually formulated in terms of the researchers' own knowledge and experience.
As the American author of a recent study comparing psychoanalytic
practices in India, Japan, and the United States pointed out: "Our very way
of conceptualizing human nature is deeply rooted within Western culture.
More than this: when we universalize our findings and assume that everyone has essentially the same nature . . . we take for granted the Western
cultural premise of universalization."[1]

This biased perspective has now been called into question by research
which demonstrates that the self-construction process is *not* the same everywhere, that different cultures and subcultures provide quite different settings for this process. In particular, a growing body of scholarly work on
socialization in Asian societies suggests that the experience of growing up in
Asia may be in certain respects profoundly different from the patterns
found in the United States and other Western societies. To explore this further, I examined the social construction of the self in early childhood in one
East Asian society: contemporary Japan.

Japan seems an appropriate setting for a number of reasons. By virtually any indicator of health, welfare, or educational attainment, the status of children in Japan today is impressive. Japan has the world's lowest infant mortality rate. In Japan virtually no children live in poverty. The Japanese school system produces almost 100 percent literacy and the world's highest high school graduation rate, and on a number of international comparisons of academic achievement, Japanese students score at or very near the top. Japan also has one of the world's most highly developed preschool systems, which includes many types of innovative outside-the-home child care. Indeed, some observers of Japan's recent spectacular economic, educational, and other accomplishments have suggested that they are the result of a value system and modes of child rearing especially well suited to the development of human resources in complex, information-based societies. Japan's unique blend of "imported" ideas (for example, Confucian ethics and Buddhist views of human nature) with indigenous culture and customs have, it is argued, produced a society in which children are more highly valued and more carefully brought up than in most Western societies. At the same time, the kinds of social changes that have special impact on children's lives are present in Japan to such a degree that it provides an excellent laboratory in which to study emerging definitions of childhood and child care. Finally, Japanese scholars and practitioners have produced a large body of research on virtually every aspect of child development and child care, though almost none of it has been translated into English or any other Western language.

For this essay, I shall draw upon the research literature in English and Japanese as well as upon my own fieldwork in Japan.[2] Several shortcomings of this approach should, however, be noted in advance. Any analysis that does not compare either Japan with other societies, or the Japanese experience with itself at two or more points in time, is subject to many forms of bias. In Japan, as elsewhere, there is a great deal of journalistic and pop sociological writing that criticizes the way children are brought up these days, much of it expressing nostalgia for a past when, supposedly, families, communities and schools were stronger and the rules for raising children were clearer and tougher. Despite the many claims about what has been "lost" in contemporary culture, few of these critiques are based upon a systematic analysis of changes over time. Valid cross-cultural comparisons are also in short supply. Much of the research literature relating to Japan refers to other societies only anecdotally or speculatively. In the absence of valid comparisons with other societies, it is difficult to evaluate the extent to which any particular value, attitude, or mode of child care is uniquely "Japanese."[3] Finally, the difficulties of making valid judgements are exacerbated by the dilemma that Robert Merton has identified as the "insider-outsider" problem.[4] Stated most simply, Japanese and non-Japanese scholars studying the same subjects are apt, quite literally, to "see" them differently. Since social science research conducted jointly by Japanese and non-Japanese scholars is still rare, the insider and outsider perspectives are seldom systematically combined in a single study.[5]

Bearing these limitations in mind, let us now turn to the analysis. In the first part, we shall examine Japanese definitions of children and childhood— what one prominent Japanese sociologist has referred to as "the unconscious assumptions that form the basis for an adult's actions when dealing with a child."[6] In the second part, we shall consider how these definitions have been translated into actual child care practices.

Childhood and the Nature of Children

Scholars comparing Japanese and Western modes of child rearing often conclude that they are based upon different views of children and childhood. Perhaps the most profound difference is that in traditional Japanese culture, the child's nature is viewed as not only different from but even superior to that of adults. A number of Japanese proverbs or popular sayings refer to the goodness and preciousness of children, for example: "Ko ni sugitara takara-nashi" (There is no treasure that surpasses a child); "Tsumi mo kegare mo nai kodomo" (In children there is neither sin nor pollution); "Nanatsu made wa kami no uchi de aru" (Until seven, children are with the gods). Nowhere in the Asian traditions (indigenous or imported) that have shaped Japanese cultural values is there any notion parallel to the doctrine of original sin. The presence of evil in the world is acknowledged, but it is connected to adults and events in the adult world that corrupt the originally pure and good nature of children. This conception of children seems to have multiple origins. One study of the belief systems underlying Japanese child-rearing techniques posits Confucian sources, particularly the ideas of Mencius, which took root in Japan by the eighth century.[7] The notion of the innate goodness of children also seems consistent with Buddhism as it developed in Japan as well as with indigenous folk beliefs.[8]

Childhood in the Life Course
Western scholarship has been much influenced by the work of Philippe Ariès, J. H. Plumb, Lloyd de Mause, and other social historians who argue that childhood as we know it is a social invention, and a rather recent one at that. In his often-cited *Centuries of Childhood,* Ariès deduced, from analysis of portraits and other works of art, that until about the seventeenth century, European art "did not know childhood or did not attempt to portray it." If

they appeared at all, children were distinguished from adults only by their smaller size, otherwise resembling their elders in clothing, bodily proportion, and facial expression. Diaries and other written documents turned up many examples of persons under the age of ten employed in offices, workshops, or on the battlefield, or enrolled as university students. In such a world, the period of dependence was brief, nurturance was minimal, and children were absorbed into the adult world early. Not until sometime between the end of the Middle Ages and the seventeenth century, by Ariès's reckoning, did a combination of social and economic forces that changed the organization of the workplace and the community lead also to the creation of the private home, where parents were more deeply and continuously involved in their children's upbringing.[9]

Recently, Japanese scholars have questioned the validity for Japanese society of models developed by Western scholars to describe childhood in Western societies. In particular, they argue that clear distinctions between child and adult, as well as expressions of deep bonds of affection between parents and their children can be found in Japanese literature and art well before the seventeenth century. Expressions of parental attachment toward their young children can be found in Japanese poetry as early as the eighth century.[10] *Emaki* (picture scrolls) dating from the thirteenth and fourteenth centuries show children with plump bodies, childish facial expressions (some downright mischievous), and distinctive hair styles and clothing (short kimono, often awry). Children are shown spinning tops, teasing animals, sprawled on their stomachs drawing, or looking at picture books.[11]

The proverb, "Until seven, children are with the gods," refers both to the divine nature of infants and young children and to the folk belief that infants and young children exist in a kind of limbo between the spirit world and the human world, a particularly vulnerable position in that they are always at risk of being "called back." Traditional child-rearing techniques emphasized maintaining close physical contact between child and caretaker and avoiding any kind of stimulation that might provoke the child into returning to the spirit world whence he came. Contemporary child care practices retain elements of this view of young children as both precious and vulnerable.

Japanese folk culture is rich in celebrations and ceremonies marking the major transitions of the life course, and such ceremonies were especially frequent during the first seven years of life, forming a sequence of ceremonial occasions by which the Japanese child "was gradually led to adulthood through a series of socially systematized stages, established on the basis of age."[12] A number of ceremonies for infants and young children are for the purposes of placating the gods and obtaining their protection of the child during these vulnerable years. For example, during the *Shichi-*

go-san festival in mid-November, parents take three-, five-, and seven-year-olds, elaborately turned out in kimonos or Western finery, to their neighborhood shrines to be blessed. Although there has been a general decline in observance of life-course ceremonies in postwar Japan, research indicates a countertrend with regard to children's ceremonies, several of which (including *Shichi-go-san*), may be practiced by more Japanese parents today than twenty-five to thirty years ago.[13]

In traditional Japanese villages, a major turning point occurred at age seven, when children were believed to be fully human. In ceremonies marking this occasion, children were received as full members of their clan or village and began to participate in the work life of the community. At this time, they also became members of their village's *kodomo-gumi,* or children's group, a peer group of all village children from age seven to age fourteen or fifteen. In present-day Japan, the seventh year also marks the beginning of compulsory formal education. The following description of the opening ceremonies at one elementary school suggests that the elaborateness that characterized traditional life-course ceremonies has been carried over to the secular bureaucratic institutions of contemporary urbanized Japan:

> On the first official day of school, each new first grader comes to school dressed in his best clothes along with his mother or father. While the parents go to the assembly hall, the children line up in their new classrooms, and at the call they solemnly march in to take seats before their parents. The principal introduces the students' teachers and delivers a short speech on the ideals of the school. . . . To complete the ceremony a group of second graders stood before the newcomers to chant a hearty welcome and to extend the hand of friendship.
>
> Following the assembly, each child went to his new classroom, and as the parents stood around the back, the teacher explained the procedures he intended to follow. . . . He emphasized that the classroom is different from the home, and that some might experience problems. . . . He urged parents to come to him for discussion of their child's adjustment, but always in these discussions to keep in mind that their child was not the only member of the class. . . . Then the teacher turned to the students and called out their names, and for the first time each student stood up to say present.[14]

In the 1980s, a number of books were published in the United States with titles like *The Disappearance of Childhood, The Erosion of Childhood,* or *Children without Childhood.*[15] Though the hypothesized causes varied from one study to another, all argued that after a long period of evolution, childhood as a social institution had reached its zenith, and that there is a turning back toward less differentiation between the social roles of adults and children. An occasional Japanese critique warns of a loss of *kodomo-rashi* (child-like) children, of the appearance of children who are *kogata no otona* (small-sized adults),[16] but the "disappearance of childhood" theory has attracted far less attention in Japan, where on the contrary, sociologists seem more concerned with a reverse phenomenon—termed the "moratorium" syndrome—which describes young people (especially males) who refuse to make the transition from childhood to adulthood.[17]

The Changing Social Value of Children
All societies claim to cherish their children. Folk literature throughout the world abounds in proverbs and myths in which children are portrayed as priceless jewels or gifts from the gods. Politicians and advertisers are wont to refer to children as a nation's most precious resource. At the same time, one of the most striking recent trends in industrialized societies has been the sharp decline in birth and fertility rates. Whether or not the dropping birth-rate reflects a commensurate decline in the social value of children is a matter of debate in Japan as in other societies,[18] but it does suggest that the value of children has changed, and that the criteria upon which that value is based have changed as well.

One explanation for the declining birthrate is the loss of children's economic value. While children in the past constituted a much-needed source of labor in the home or income from work outside the home, they now constitute a very large financial burden to their parents and communities. Recent estimates indicate, for example, that it now costs more than $100,000 on the average to raise one American child to age eighteen (not including the expense of any post-secondary education), though the costs vary considerably depending upon family socioeconomic status, wife's employment status, and total number of children in the family.[19] Comparable estimates for Japanese child-rearing costs are not available, but some expenses are even higher there. For example, free public education in Japan ends with the ninth grade, although, as noted earlier, almost all Japanese students now graduate from high school. Moreover, a high proportion of Japanese children are enrolled in private lessons or classes outside of school, and supplementary textbooks and other study aids—a huge industry in Japan—further raise the costs of child rearing for many Japanese parents.[20] Nor do children provide a large or immediate "return on investment" in purely economic terms. Cross-cultural surveys indicate that Japanese children are even less likely than children in other societies to help out with cooking, cleaning, and other household chores, although they are more likely, when they become adults, to provide a home and other kinds of support for their elderly parents.[21]

Research on the reasons for having children in Western societies indicates that the social value of children is now primarily emotional. The author of one such study argues that American children are now viewed as "economically worthless but emotionally priceless."[22] A similar conclusion was reached in a study of Japanese parents, conducted by the East-West Population Institute:

> With regard to the advantages of children, emotional rewards for the parent (such as happiness, love, and companionship), childrearing satisfactions (pleasures from growth and development, children to carry out parents' hopes and aspirations), personal development of the parent (children representing incentives to succeed), and benefits to the family unit were more important to respondents than economic benefits and security or kin group benefits of children. . . .
>
> In citing reasons for wanting and not wanting another child, most respondents ignored traditional reasons (e.g., to continue the family name, inherit property, perform religious duties) while stressing affective values such as love, companionship, and parental incentives. . . . Utilitarian values of children (especially economic and psychological reliance upon children) were not very strong. In other words, parents were rearing children in the expectations of deriving happiness from them.[23]

In a series of surveys conducted by a Japanese governmental agency, mothers in three Asian nations (Japan, South Korea, and Thailand) and three Western nations (France, Britain, and the United States) were queried about the meaning to them of having and raising a child. In Japan, as in the United States and the European nations, the reasons most often given were "to mature and enrich myself" and "to strengthen our family bond." The emotional or personal rewards of child rearing were considered far more important than economic reasons such as "additional work power" in the family, "security in old age," or the importance of carrying on a family line, all of which were cited by large numbers of Korean and Thai mothers. A majority of the Japanese mothers (71.5 percent) agreed that a husband and wife wishing a divorce should remain together for the sake of their children, which was more than double the proportion of American or British mothers who took this position, but considerably less than the proportions among the other Asian societies studied (91.6 percent of the Koreans, 90.2 percent of the Thais). Concerning children's subsequent obligations toward their parents, Japanese respondents were more likely than Americans or Europeans to say they would like to live with their children in their old age, but much less likely than their Korean or Thai counterparts to expect their daily needs to be looked after by their children.[24]

In sum, the cross-cultural evidence available provides some support for distinguishing between East Asian and Western views of the social value of children, but comparisons of contemporary Japanese and American samples point to as many commonalities as differences. Although the definition of children as "economically worthless but emotionally priceless" seems to have permeated both cultures, in some other respects, the Japanese seemed to occupy a kind of middle position, not fully "westernized," but less committed than some other East Asians to the family bonds and filial obligations commonly associated with Confucian ethics.

A number of scholars have argued that a major difference between Japanese families and Western families lies in the relative prominence of the husband-wife relationship versus the parent-child relationship; that is, in the West, the husband-wife relationship now takes precedence, while in Japan (some would argue, in East Asian societies generally), the parent-child (especially the mother-child) bond is the central one.[25] At least since the 1970s, a number of American studies have indicated that the responsibilities and skills involved in caring for young children are, increasingly, in conflict with other activities and roles that adults value, both within and outside of marriage.[26] Until very recently, comparable Japanese research indicated that children and child rearing remain more central to the lives of Japanese parents than to their Western counterparts. A national survey conducted in the 1970s found that in answer to the question "What makes your life meaningful?" a majority of the female respondents (52.6 percent) ranked "children" first, with "family" second but much lower than the first-ranked item (13.2 percent), "occupation" third (9.0 percent), and "husband" last (2.7 percent). Male respondents ranked "occupation" first (43.9 percent), "children" second (28.8 percent), "Hobbies" third (15.9 percent), and "Wife" last (4.8 percent). For both sexes, what was important about their family was the children. Even for men, children were second only to their jobs in giving meaning to their lives. Neither men nor women were likely to mention their spouse as significant, though men were almost twice as likely as women to do so.[27]

More recent cross-cultural comparisons indicate that the traditional sex-role division of labor is still more widely accepted in Japan than in many other societies. For example, a survey conducted by the Japanese Ministry of Labor, comparing respondents in six countries, found that only in Japan did a substantial majority of respondents agree with the following statements:

The husband should go out to work, the wife should stay at home. (Seventy-one percent of the Japanese respondents were in favor of this proposition, followed by 56% in the Philippines, 34% in the U.S.,

33% in West Germany, 26% in the United Kingdom, and 14% in Sweden.)

After marriage, the wife should look after her husband, children and others in the family. (Seventy-two percent of the Japanese respondents were in favor, followed by 58% in the Philippines, 41% in West Germany, 18% in the U.S., 10% in the U.K., and 6% in Sweden.[28]

The proportion of female employees in the twenty-five to thirty-four age bracket, the modal years for childbirth and care of young children, has remained considerably lower in Japan than in the United States and most Western European nations, as has the proportion of women who work full time. Opinion poll data indicate that a high proportion of Japanese still disapprove of divorce, and the divorce rate and the proportion of single-parent families remain less than one-third that of comparable rates in the United States. The three-generation family still holds a place, both as an ideal and in reality, in Japan that it does not hold (some would say has never held) in Western society.[29]

At the same time, however, poll data reveal growing numbers of young Japanese expressing the desire for a lifestyle that suits their own needs and tastes, and declining numbers saying they are willing to sacrifice their identity and their personal happiness for the sake of their children. And for the first time, sizable numbers of young women express the opinion that women can have full and satisfying lives without marriage and children.[30]

A society's beliefs about the nature and value of children have powerful implications for the ways in which children are actually treated in that society. We shall now turn to a consideration of child care practices in Japan.

Bringing Up Children in Japan

Western visitors to Japan, from the earliest explorers and missionaries to the most recent tourists, have been impressed by the mild, patient, even indulgent treatment of children by adults.[31] An American who lived in Japan for several years during the Meiji Period remarked that it is "a rare thing is to hear a baby crying, and thus far I have never seen the slightest sign of impatience on the part of the mother. I believe Japan is the only nation in the world that yields so much to the babies, or in which babies are so good."[32]

Present-day Americans who visit Japanese homes are often struck by an apparent anomaly in the behavior of children and in the responses of adults to children's behavior. In schools, department stores, restaurants, subways and other public places, young children appear, by American standards, remarkably docile. Yet in their own homes these models of decorum often seem transformed into unruly household tyrants. Misbehavior that would provoke a sharp rebuke from an American parent, or more, is treated with extraordinary leniency, even indulgence. The highly disciplined behavior the Japanese display in the classroom as well as in offices and factory assembly lines is not apparently the result of severe demands in the earliest years of life. Weaning, toilet training, being disciplined for temper tantrums, aggression against parents, even for misbehavior in public, all begin on the average later in Japan than in most Western societies.[33]

Creating a Social Self

A content analysis of the two best-selling books on child rearing in Japan and the United States respectively (Dr. Michio Matsuda's *Ikuji no Hyakka* [Handbook of Child Rearing], and Dr. Benjamin Spock's *Baby and Child Care*) shows that although Spock has been accused of fostering permissiveness, in fact his methods involve more rigorous regulation of the child's life than Matsuda's methods. The Spockian parent must make clear to the child who is in charge. Night feedings should be stopped as early as possible, and weaning is best accomplished with the first six months. Thumb-sucking is a sign of developmental "regression" and should be prevented. Sleeping "problems" can be avoided by the child's having its own room and being put to bed on a regular schedule. At bedtime, the parent should put the child to bed, pleasantly but firmly, and leave the room; even if the child cries to the point of vomiting, the parent should not give in, and on no account should the child be allowed to sleep with the parents.

Matsuda's views often sound perilously close to "spoiling" by Spockian standards. It is not terribly important, says Matsuda, when one begins weaning or toilet training. The child's physiological makeup, more than anything the parent does, will determine when these things will be accomplished, and it should be respected. Likes and dislikes in food are to be expected; as long as the child is not suffering from some nutritional deficiency, there is no harm in accommodating its food preferences. Thumb-sucking is a natural and pleasurable activity for most children, not the sign of some underlying problem. If the child has trouble going to sleep, let it sleep near or with a parent.[34]

Discussions of Japanese socialization often refer to the concept of *amae*. The subject of a highly influential book by the Japanese psychiatrist, Takeo Doi, *amae* is based upon the verb meaning to depend and presume upon another's benevolence. Doi believes that the complex mixture of passivity, mutuality, and "feelings of dependency coupled with the expectation of indulgence" that comprise *amae* are at the core of the Japanese psyche. He also argues that the concept is quite distinct from "love" in the Western sense and is in fact alien to Western thinking, "with its exaltation of independence and self-sufficiency."[35]

Amae is built up and reinforced through a number of mechanisms. One such mechanism is "skin-ship," or physical closeness, between children and their caretakers. For example, breast-feeding, co-bathing, and co-sleeping are all more prevalent in Japan than in the United States.[36] Studies by William Caudill and his associates, comparing the socialization of Japanese and American infants, found that Japanese mothers did more things to soothe or quiet their babies—"carrying, rocking and lulling," as Caudill puts it—than their American counterparts, who made more efforts to stimulate their babies, encouraging them to vocalize and to be physically active. Japanese mothers were more likely to be "passively present," that is, in the room physically even when the baby was asleep or when they were not engaged in actual caretaking, than American mothers, who tended to be "in and out," leaving the baby's room when they had completed some act of caretaking.[37]

Amae is also reinforced in many everyday activities, including mealtimes, where, as Ruth Benedict commented, "the baby is always counted in."[38] For example, the discussion of weaning in Matsuda's *Handbook of Child Rearing* emphasizes its social functions more than its nutritional ones. According to Matsuda, it's not so important that the baby learn to eat vegetables, or any other particular food—as a matter of fact, he recommends feeding the child from foods that are *ariawase* (on hand), rather than from a special "weaning-food menu." What is important is that the child *eats with, and from the same menu, as the rest of the family,* preferably by about age one.[39]

One particularly striking characteristic of Japanese modes of upbringing is the relative absence of the use of physical force to control or punish children. Parents may respond to a child's misbehavior by shaming it, pointing out the effects such behavior have on the child itself or the family, or by threatening to abandon or give it away, though direct confrontations with children are avoided if possible. The concept embodied in the Western proverb, "Spare the rod and spoil the child," is apparently quite alien to Japanese attitudes regarding children.[40] As one author puts it, Japanese mothers "tend to 'suffer' their children rather than to forbid or inhibit their behavior by using verbal chastisement or even physical punishment."[41] Harumi Befu, a Japanese-American anthropologist who has studied both societies closely, concluded that the major difference between the disciplinary approaches of Japanese and Americans is that "the former uses solicitude rather than authority, which the latter might use, pleading with or begging a difficult child to do as he is told, rather than standing firm and meting out punishment. . . . An American mother would look ridiculous to bystanders if she begged and pleaded with a three-to-five-year-old, whereas a Japanese mother who took an authoritarian approach would be regarded as lacking in human feeling."[42]

The Importance of Group Life

While strong family relationships are highly valued, socialization in children's groups is also considered both natural and essential for full human development. It comes as a surprise to many people to learn that Japan, a society that is commonly viewed as extremely family-centered and anti-feminist, has one of the world's most highly developed systems of outside-the-home group child care. For example, a 1982 study of child care arrangements of working mothers in six nations (Japan, Korea, United States, Great Britain, West Germany, and France) showed that Japan was the only nation in which the majority of children aged five or younger were enrolled in an organized preschool program.[43] The majority of preschoolers— over 70 percent of all Japanese children between the ages of three and five— are enrolled either in *yochien,* which are under the authority of the Ministry of Education and combine elements of the American kindergarten and nursery school, or *hoiku-en,* which are under the authority of the Ministry of Health and Welfare and are comparable to American day-care centers. Whether public or private, the majority of Japanese preschools are government subsidized and supervised, and a majority of the staff have obtained professional training in early childhood education and child care. While still only a fraction of children under age three are enrolled in group care, the fastest rates of growth are at these younger ages. Overall, the enrollment rates support the contention of one researcher that preschool has acquired the status of "semi-compulsory education" for four- and five-year-olds— and, increasingly, for three-year-olds as well—and even for younger children group care outside the home has become "socially established."[44]

Group care, even for very young children, may be more acceptable in Japan than in the United States, because it is not basically inconsistent with traditional Japanese culture or Confucian ethics, both of which posit a group-centered existence and place great value upon harmonious group relations. In traditional village culture, it was said that "a child cannot be raised by mother's love alone," and the children's peer group was viewed as a major socializer.[45] This may explain why the spread of government-subsidized preschool and after-school programs has proceeded more quickly and smoothly in Japan than in the United States, where day care still raises the specter of maternal deprivation and neglect. It may also explain why Japanese scholars and educators have neither conducted systematic research on the effects of group care on children's cognitive and social development, nor paid much attention to the huge body of American research on this subject.[46] Among parents today, group care outside the home may be viewed as simply reinforcing the group consciousness already acquired in the home.[47] It is probably not coincidental that Dr. Matsuda espouses both prolonged breast-feeding *and* early group socialization, and that many of the photographs in Matsuda's handbook are of children in day-care centers.[48]

Japan has produced some true pioneers in preschool theory and practice, little known outside the country but highly influential within. For example, Saito Kimiko, the energetic, charismatic, and controversial founder of Sakura-Sakurambo Day Care Center, regarded by some specialists as the best in Japan, has created a preschool model that draws from socialist and Marxian theories, from biological research, from the folklore and children's literature of many societies, and from her own critique of contemporary Japanese culture and society. She is particularly concerned about the isolation of so many young families in contemporary Japanese society. Crowded into tiny apartments, far from relatives and without real links to their communities, children "grow up in a vacuum where only mother and child exist." In such a situation, group care in which children are surrounded by many loving adults as well as by a children's peer group, is absolutely essential for their development as human beings.[49]

The daily and seasonal routines at Sakura-Sakurambo are designed to nurture physical vitality, simple and direct interpersonal communication, and the personal qualities—*iyoku* (will power), *shuchu-ryoku* (concentration), and *nebari-tsuyosa* (perseverance)—needed to carry out complex, demanding tasks. Saito claims not to have a fixed curriculum, and children are allowed to roam freely over the four and a half acres of the school grounds. They are, however, responsible for tending gardens and cleaning animal pens and barns as well as their own classrooms, and they also participate daily in a series of rhythmic exercises developed by Saito that call for coordination, concentration, and considerable courage. There are few toys, per se. Rather children collect stones, leaves, twigs, and other things they find outdoors and make their own tops and jump ropes. Art and music are an important part of the curriculum. Each child produces literally hundreds of drawings and paintings; these are carefully studied by staff and parents in order to understand the child's development. There are also joint art projects that require groups of children to work cooperatively for extended periods of time. Though now in her sixties and recently retired as director, Saito still publishes voluminously, conducts workshops attended by teachers from all over Japan, travels widely, and remains deeply involved in the lives of the children who are or have been enrolled at Sakura-Sakurambo.[50]

While there is considerable variation among preschools, certain assumptions about the objectives of child care and the behavior of caretakers do seem to be rather widely shared among Japanese parents and teachers. Because group life and harmonious group relations are highly valued, group tasks that promote sensitivity toward and cooperation with others tend to be emphasized more than individual tasks that promote self-discovery and self-realization. A British anthropologist who has observed a number of Japanese kindergartens describes a number of ways in which teachers inculcate a sense of collective identity in their students:

> First of all, considerable attention is devoted to creating a new inside group for these children to identify with. As children arrive at kindergarten they may play freely in the playground for a while, but at an appointed hour each day the class gathers in its own room and goes through an important greeting sequence. . . . Similar routines accompany the serving of meals, and break, and separation at the end of the day. . . .
>
> Each child in the room will be wearing the same uniform, or at least a smock or apron to make them alike, and every child is provided with identical sets of equipment. During the course of the day, many activities will be carried out together, each child being instructed to make the same preparations as the others, and following the teacher's demonstration . . .
>
> Forms of address and reference used with the children reinforce this emphasis on equality within the group. All the children in the same class are referred to as "friends" by parents and teachers alike, and children are not encouraged to seek out special friends for themselves. There is a collective term of address, *mina-san*. Addressed in this way, the children are expected to chorus their reply. Used in its possessive form, it denotes the collective ownership of classroom and kindergarten equipment, for which everyone is therefore responsible.[51]

Socialization in the home and preschool also teaches children to distinguish between *uchi* and *soto,* which translate roughly as "inside" and "outside" respectively. *Uchi* connotes any group whose members share "we" or "in-group" feelings. It is first learned by the child in association with the security and indulgence of the home. By contrast, the "outside" world is often associated with danger, fear, and punishment. "Thus threats may be made about demons, policemen and passing strangers, and a severe punishment is to put a child out of the house altogether."[52] While the boundaries between *uchi* and *soto* are clear, they are not necessarily permanent. When children enter day care or nursery school, for example, the class forms a new "inside" group for them, where they will soon feel as secure as in their own home.

Foreign visitors to Japanese schools are often impressed by the students' quiet, attentive demeanor and apparently self-disciplined behavior. Cross-cultural comparisons of Japanese, Chinese, and American elementary schools have shown that the East Asian students do spend more time than their American counterparts listening to their teachers, less time in "inappropriate" behavior, such as talking to other students, or wandering around the room.[53] At the same time, recent research indicates that Japanese elementary teachers are less likely than their American counterparts to control students' behavior through the exercise of their adult authority. One observer described a first-grade class where chaos reigned while the student monitor for the day struggled to quiet the class for the morning greetings. The teacher, who was present but made no effort to intervene, later told the researcher: "I could have quieted the children myself by saying one word, but I didn't, because the class needs to learn how to manage itself."[54] Another American observer has characterized Japanese strategies for controlling children as "patient, low-key, but highly consistent," based upon "psychological outmaneuvering" rather than upon harsh words, physical punishments, and other overt displays of adult authority.[55]

Such examples suggest a high degree of congruence between the goals and techniques of parents and teachers. The relatively infrequent recourse to physical force and other displays of adult authority as modes of controlling children also seems consistent with the assumption, described in the previous section, that children are basically good, and that misbehavior is due to inadequate environments or insufficient effort, which can be corrected. One study, based upon observations in fifteen nursery schools, concluded that not only did many teachers tolerate a noise level and a latitude of behavior that American teachers would probably find unacceptable, but they also tended to attribute aggressive or mischievous acts (e.g., one child hiding another's shoes, or several children dropping clay "bombs" on the fish in the aquarium) to *lack of understanding* on the child's part rather than to intentional misbehavior.[56]

While Japanese teachers are generally more lenient than their American counterparts about noise and acting-out behavior, they tend to treat as a more serious behavior problem a child's nonparticipation in group activities. Peak reported several incidents in which a teacher exerted considerable pressure on an individual child who refused to join the group: "Following a number of direct requests, teachers often try to lead the child by the hand toward the activity. If this fails, the teacher frequently warns the child that the group will proceed without him. . . . If a child continues to refuse to participate, the teacher may force the issue, often provoking a tantrum, [which] is faced cheerfully, patiently, and sympathetically. However, the teacher psychologically outflanks the child who ultimately finds himself the loser in a smiling 'battle of perseverance.'"[57]

In sum, Japanese parents and teachers may be more tolerant than their Western counterparts about noise, temper tantrums, and many forms of aggressive behavior, but much more concerned about lack of collective spirit and inadequate group skills—which may explain not only why more Japanese than American preschoolers are cared for in organized group programs, but also why the efforts exerted by Japanese parents and teachers to ensure full group participation often seem excessive to Western observers. A team of anthropologists who compared preschools in Japan, the People's Republic of China, and the United States concluded that Japanese parents send their children to preschool not just for child care, but, "more profoundly, to facilitate the development of a group-oriented, outward-facing sense of self."[58] A study of life-course patterning in Japan reached a similar conclusion, that the American way "seems more attuned to cultivating a self that knows it is unique in the cosmos, the Japanese archetype to a self that can feel human in the company of others."[59]

How Children Learn
Orderliness, correctness, and hard work are important elements of the Confucian model of education, which taught that there is a correct way to carry out any task and that a learner shown the correct way will follow it freely, without external constraints. The Confucian model continues to influence Japanese schools today, where children are constantly reminded to do their best and to do things correctly. Indeed, differences in children's behavior and accomplishments are generally viewed as stemming not from significant differences in natural talent, but from differences in effort. It is not unusual for first grade teachers to devote much time during the first weeks of the school year to instructing students to sit properly. Even in preschools, a great deal of time is spent in showing children the "correct" way to do many things—how to hold a fork or chopsticks, to fold up a *futon* after a nap, or to arrange chairs for an assembly. Compared to Western preschool and elementary classes, a relatively greater portion of time is given to activities that require concentration and attention to details for fairly long periods of time. Japan's Nobel Prize winner, Yukawa Hideki, is often held up as a role model to Japanese school children, not so much for his natural talents and the originality of his work, but for his comment that success in any endeavor comes through continuous repetitive practice until one masters every detail.[60]

It is also believed, however, that children learn better through observation and imitation than through abstract verbal instruction. This mode of teaching, also based upon Confucian principles, is known as *minarai* in Japanese, and has been the major mode of teaching many traditional arts and crafts. The Suzuki method of music instruction is exemplary in this regard. This method requires the beginning student of the violin or piano simply to observe more experienced students' lessons, quietly but with full concentration, for a period of weeks or even months, then to spend more weeks or months learning to stand in front of the teacher and to bow properly, before even touching the instrument let alone attempting to play it. When the student finally does begin to make music, he will already have correct habits as well as tremendously high motivation, and progress will be rapid.[61]

Conclusions

Although Japanese culture has absorbed a host of different, sometimes conflicting theories of child development and child rearing throughout the twentieth century, and although the sheer pace of social change in Japan today makes it difficult to characterize current modes of upbringing with great precision, several themes emerge from the preceding review of research findings. One is the favorable position of children in Japanese society. However one defines and measures children's health, welfare, and educational accomplishments, Japan ranks at or very near the top. Ruth Benedict's characterization of the years up to age seven as "the privileged life of little children" seems as applicable to present-day Japan as it was to the prewar society she examined in *the Chrysanthemum and the Sword*.[62] The perception of children as "special," especially vulnerable, and worthy of concern and affection, seems to have appeared relatively early in Japanese culture. The early years of childhood still seem to contain more, and more clearly delineated, life-course transitions, providing a more uniform, gradual, and clearly marked path toward adulthood for Japanese children than for their Western counterparts.

The indulgent treatment of young children may also be related to the view, still stronger in Japanese culture than in Western culture, that children in general and young children in particular are inherently good, and that misbehavior is caused by external forces (inadequate training or bad experiences), not to any evil within children themselves. Thus it may be easier for Japanese adults to treat children's noise and physical activity as "natural" rather than as something to be restrained. In fact, from the Japanese point of view, too much control may even destroy the child's nature.

The high degree of dependency and the group orientation fostered by Japanese upbringing have important consequences. On the one hand, they may contribute to the impressive academic performance of many Japanese students. *Amae,* suggests one prominent Japanese psychologist, "helps the child assimilate the hopes and values of the parents, thus enhancing the child's educability."[63] On the other hand, development of a sense of personal autonomy may be difficult; the Japanese child may have to struggle hard "to separate his identity from what he is only in relation to others—at first in the family, later in school, and still later in his occupation and marriage."[64]

Another theme emerging from the preceding analysis has to do with the boundaries of the self. As one analyst has put it: "The Japanese tends to include within the boundaries of his concept of self much of the quality of the intimate social groups of which the individual is a member," as opposed to the American self-concept, which is "apt to stop at the skin."[65] Some scholars have characterized this view of self as "interactionist," distinguishable from more individualistic Western models by its assumption that the self and other, like the individual and the group, are basically complementary rather than potentially conflicting. For the scholar accustomed to viewing the self as having clear ego boundaries and a sharp differentiation between self and other, the nonseparation—some would say fusion—of self and other(s) that characterize many Japanese interpersonal relations seems to violate fundamental premises of self-construction. At the same time, the more diffuse ego boundaries characteristic of the Japanese model of self, in combination with the sensitivity to *uchi-soto* distinctions learned in early childhood—distinctions that, as we have seen, are likely to shift over time—may allow individuals to move more easily from one setting to another and to play a broader range of social roles than individuals whose sense of self is based upon a more unitary and static model.[66]

Whether these distinctive patterns of self-definition and socialization will survive current and projected social trends is a matter of debate among social scientists. However much their conceptions of childhood and child care may differ from the rest of the industrialized world, Japan too has shifted from being a society in which children routinely went to work and were active participants in if not full members of the adult world, to a society in which raising a child requires a huge financial investment and the rewards are primarily emotional. Changes in the social value of children have been accompanied by changes in their social status. Although the Japanese do not yet subscribe to the "fun morality" that some analysts have attributed to American child-rearing norms,[67] the definition of children as "economically worthless but emotionally priceless" seems to have permeated Japanese culture as deeply as it has several Western cultures. Whether such shifts in attitudes and values will bring about greater congruence in Japanese and Western child care practices remains to be seen. The Japanese have in recent years been engaged in a national debate over the social institutions responsible for the care and education of children, and a number of critiques have called attention to the harmful effects of excessive *shudan-shugi* (group-ism), and the need to promote more autonomy and creativity in a society in which the group generally takes precedence over the individual.[68] Meanwhile Japan continues to provide their scholar with an excellent laboratory in which to study the effects of rapid social change upon definitions and constructions of the self.

NOTES

The research reported in this essay was supported by a Fulbright research fellowship and by grants from the Spencer Foundation, the Social Science Research Council, and the Rutgers University International Center. I am deeply indebted to Professor Yamaguchi Hiroko, of Shiraume Gakuen College, Tokyo; to Professor Yamamura Yoshiaki, of Rikkyo University, Tokyo; to Professor Kuse Taeko, Aichi University of Education, Aichi Prefecture; and to President Shimada Tadashi, Professor Tsuyoshi Kobayashi, and the late Professor Aisei Yamazaki, of the University of Fukui, for facilitating my work during the data-gathering phase. I am also grateful to Nobuo Shimahara, Koya Azumi, Ryoko Kato Tsuneyoshi, John Gillis, Jan Lewis, and the other members of the 1988–1989 CCACC Seminar for their helpful comments on earlier versions of this chapter.

1. Alan Roland, *In Search of Self in India and Japan* (Princeton: Princeton University Press, 1988), xvi.

2. My data gathering in Japan was carried out during four periods of field work between 1983 and 1987, during which I visited some fifty child care facilities and attended a number of conferences and meetings, formal and informal. I interviewed preschool personnel, parents, government officials, university scholars and research institute staff, and journalists and publishers. I also gathered statistical data; governmental and other reports; research studies; the published work of pioneers in child care and early childhood education in Japan (some of whom I also interviewed); stories about children and child care from national and local newspapers; statements of purpose, curriculum, and other materials prepared by individual child care facilities; and journals, pamphlets, and promotional materials put out by citizens' groups engaged in political action on behalf of children.

3. Ethnocentrism has always been a problem in the field of Japanese studies, particularly when comparing Japanese and Western cultures. In recent years this problem has manifested itself in a heated debate over what has been termed *Nihonjinron,* or "Japan Theory," which argues that "Japanese culture is unique and therefore, by implication, incomprehensible to the outside world" (Herbert Passim, "Preface" to *The Challenge of Japan's Internationalization: Organization and Culture,* ed. Hiroshi Mannari and Harumi Befu [Tokyo: Kodansha, 1983], 17). Passim points out that Japanese "exceptionalism" is fueled as much by Western stereotypes about the "inscrutability" of the Japanese as by the admittedly great concern of the Japanese themselves over their national and cultural identity. The *Nihonjinron* controversy is also discussed in Peter N. Dale, *The Myth of Japanese Uniqueness* (New York: St. Martin's Press, 1986).

4. Robert K. Merton, "The Perspectives of Insiders and Outsiders," in R. K. Merton, *The Sociology of Science* (Chicago: University of Chicago Press, 1973).

5. The studies by Harold Stevenson and his associates, and by Joseph Tobin, David Wu, and Dana Davidson—to be discussed later in the essay—are among the few exceptions in this regard. Tobin, Wu, and Davidson address the insider-outsider problem in a particularly ingenious fashion. By videotaping preschool sessions in three countries, and then having adults and children in each country view and discuss tapes from all three countries, the authors are justified in claiming that they produced "an ongoing dialogue between insiders and outsiders" (Joseph J. Tobin, David Y. H. Wu, and Dana H. Davidson, *Preschool in Three Cultures: Japan, China, and the United States* [New Haven: Yale University Press, 1989], 4).

6. Yoshiaki Yamamura, "The Child in Japanese Society," in *Child Development and Education in Japan*, ed. Harold Stevenson, Hiroshi Azuma and Kenji Hakuta (New York: W. H. Freeman, 1986), 28.

7. Hideo Kojima, "Child Rearing Concepts as a Belief-System of the Society and the Individual," in Stevenson, Azuma, Hakuta, *Child Development and Education in Japan*, 28–38.

8. Hiroko Hara and Hiroshi Wagatsuma, *Shitsuke* (Tokyo: Kobundo, 1974); Yuki Oto, *Kodomo no Minzoku-gaku* (Tokyo: Sodo Bunka, 1982); and William Caudill and Carmi Schooler, "Child Behavior and Child Rearing in Japan and the United States: An Interim Report," *Journal of Nervous and Mental Disease* 157, no. 5 (1973): 323–338.

9. Philippe Ariès, *Centuries of Childhood* (New York: Alfred A. Knopf, 1962), 33 and *passim*.

10. For example, in Ian Hidao Levy, *The Ten Thousand Leaves: A Translation of the Man'yoshu* (Princeton: Princeton University Press, 1981), 1: 348. See also, Yamamura, "The Child in Japanese Society."

11. Tanio Nakamura, Sadeo Kikuchi, and Iwao Murai, *Nihon Kaiga Meisakusen* (Tokyo: Dentsu, 1981), plates 10, 20, 21, 23, 24, and 26, and accompanying documentation; and Kojima, "Child Rearing Concepts," and personal communication.

12. Yamamura, "The Child in Japanese Society," 30.

13. Hara and Wagatsuma, *Shitsuke*, chap. 2; and Takeo Sofue, "Childhood Ceremonies in Japan: Regional and Local Variations," *Ethnology* 4, no. 2 (April 1965): 148–164.

14. William K. Cummings, *Education and Equality in Japan* (Princeton: Princeton University Press, 1980), 108–109.

15. For example, David Elkind, *The Hurried Child* (Reading, Mass.: Addison-Wesley, 1981); Neil Postman, *The Disappearance of Childhood* (New York: Lauren Books, 1982); Valerie P. Suransky, *The Erosion of Childhood* (Chicago: University of Chicago Press, 1982); Vance Packard, *Our Endangered Children* (Boston: Little, Brown, 1983); and Marie Winn, *Children without Childhood* (New York: Pantheon, 1983). Note that all of the books listed here were published within a three-year period.

16. For example, Yoshiaki Yamamura, *Kawaikunai Kodomo-tachi* (Tokyo: Hiroji Shupan, 1983), 26–31.

17. Keigo Okonogi, *Moratoriamu Ningen no Jidai* (Tokyo: Chuo Koronsha, 1978). For a brief discussion of Okonogi's thesis in English, see Winston Davis, "The Hollow Onion: The Secularization of Japanese Civil Religion," in Mannari and Befu, *The Challenge of Japan's Internationalization*, 212–231.

18. Samuel Coleman, *Family Planning in Japanese Society* (Princeton: Princeton University Press, 1983).

19. Thomas J. Espanshade, *The Cost of Children in Urban United States* (Berkeley: University of California, Institute of International Studies, 1984).

20. NHK Hoso Seron Chosa-jo, *Nihon no Kodomo-tachi: Seikatsu to Ishiki* (Tokyo: NHK Books, 1980); Nihon Kodomo o Mamoru-Kai, *White Paper on Japanese Children* (Tokyo: Sodo Bunka, 1985).

21. Youth Development Headquarters, *International Comparison: Children and Their Families, Summary of Findings* (Tokyo: Prime Minister's Office, Youth Development Headquarters, 1982).

22. Viviana Zelizer, *Pricing the Priceless Child: The Changing Social Value of Children* (New York: Basic Books, 1985).

23. Toshio Iritani, *The Value of Children: A Cross-National Study*, vol. 6, *Japan* (Honolulu: East-West Population Institute, East-West Center, 1979), 79–81.

24. Youth Development Headquarters, *International Comparison: Japanese Children and Their Mothers* (Tokyo: Prime Minister's Office, Youth Development Headquarters, 1981).

25. Harumi Befu, "The Social and Cultural Background of Child Development in Japan and the United States," in Stevenson, Hazuma, and Hakuta, *Child Development and Education*, 13–27; Takie Sugiyama Lebra, *Japanese Women: Constraint and Fulfillment* (Honolulu: University of Hawaii Press, 1984); George DeVos, "Dimensions of the Self in Japanese Culture," in *Culture and Self: Asian and Western Perspectives*, ed. Antony J. Marsella, George DeVos, and Francis L.K. Hsu (New York and London: Tavistock, 1985), 141–183; Hiroshi Azuma, "Why Study Child Development in Japan?" in Stevenson, Hazuma, and Akuta, *Child Development and Education*, 3–12; and Suzanne H. Vogel, "Professional Housewife: The Career of Urban Middle Class Japanese Women," *Japan Interpreter* 12 (Winter 1978): 17–43.

26. Yankelovich, Skelly, and White, Inc., *Raising Children in a Changing Society* (Minneapolis: Consumer Center of General Mills, 1977); and Angus Campbell, Philip E. Converse, and Willard L. Rodgers, *The Quality of American Life* (New York: Russell Sage Foundation, 1975).

27. Kazoku Tsurumi, *Women in Japan: A Paradox of Modernization* (Tokyo: Sophia University, Institute of International Relations, 1977).

28. Japanese Ministry of Labor, *Summary of Actual Labor Market for Women in 1983* (Tokyo: Foreign Press Center, 1983).

29. Economic Planning Agency, *40 Years since the End of World War II: On the Threshold of the Age of Maturity* (Tokyo: Ministry of Finance Printing Bureau, 1986); Susan O. Long, *Family Change and the Life Course in Japan*, East Asian Papers, no. 44 (Ithaca: Cornell University, China-Japan Program, 1987); and Mary Brinton, "Gender Stratification in Contemporary Urban Japan," *American Sociological Review* 54 (August 1989): 549–564.

30. NHK Hoso Seron Chosa-jo, *Nihonjin to Amerikajin* (Tokyo: NHK Books, 1982), appendix table 11; H.I.L.L, *Japanese Women in Turmoil* (Tokyo: Hakuhodo Institute of Life and Living, 1984); and *Asahi Evening News*, 24 June 1987, 3.

31. The Japanese language contains a number of words for upbringing. The term in common usage until after World War II was *shitsuke,* a compound of the characters for "body" and "beautiful," which means, literally, training the child to behave beautifully. *Shitsuke* can also be translated as "discipline," and it originally connoted the teaching of correct behavior and the passing on of traditional values, beliefs, and customs as well as training in the specific skills necessary for participation in community life. The centrality of discipline in traditional upbringing is underscored in the folk saying: "Shitsuke to kyoiku" (First discipline, then education. Or, if you don't discipline them, you can't teach them). In the postwar period, other terms have been introduced, in particular, *ikuji* and *kosodate,* both of which can be translated as child rearing or child care. The former is somewhat more commonly used, in scholarly discussions as well as in child-rearing manuals for parents; the latter is more likely to be used in connection with the nurture of infants. In current debates on child rearing, there are occasional calls for a return to *shitsuke,* or "true" Japanese ways of upbringing, and the word began reappearing in the titles of child-rearing books in the 1980s (Hara and Wagatsuma, *Shitsuke,* 2; Hirosho Wagatsuma and Betty B. Lanham, "Childhood and Child Rearing," in *Kodansha Encyclopedia of Japan* [Tokyo: Kodansha, 1983], 1: 278; Hendry, *Becoming Japanese,* 11–14; Hiroo Suzuki,

Oya to Ko no Shitsuke Dokuhon [Tokyo: Shitsuke Daihyaka, 1985]; and Hiroko Yamaguchi and Yoshiko Okuda, personal communications).

32. Quoted in Kojima, "Child Rearing Concepts," 3.

33. Takie Sugiyama Lebra, *Japanese Patterns of Behavior* (Honolulu: University of Hawaii Press, 1976), chap. 8; DeVos, "Dimensions of the Self"; and Robert J. Smith and Ella Lury Wiswell, *Women of Sure Mura* (Chicago: University of Chicago Press, 1982).

34. Keiko Hosotsuji, "Ikuji-shu ni Yoru Hikaku Shakaikaron no Kokoro— Supokku to Matsuda Michio," *Soshioroji* 28, no. 1 (May 1983): 97–117.

35. Takeo Doi, *The Anatomy of Dependence* (Tokyo: Kodansha, 1981), 54. Doi's claim that the notion of dependence embodied in the word *amae* is unique to Japanese culture has been contested on the grounds that it ignores the pervasiveness of this concept in other cultures. One critique, for example, argues that the Korean language contains at least two equivalents to the Japanese *amae,* and that "the concept of dependence plays such a crucial role in child rearing in Korea that one could say dependence is even more inextricably bound up with the Korean psyche than it is with the Japanese" (O-Young Lee, *Smaller Is Better: Japan's Mastery of the Miniature* [Tokyo: Kodansha, 1984], 11). See note 3.

36. Lebra, *Japanese Patterns of Behavior,* chap. 8; William Caudill and David W. Plath, "Who Sleeps by Whom? Parent-Child Involvement in Urban Japanese Families," in *Japanese Culture and Behavior: Selected Readings,* ed. T. S. Lebra and W. P. Lebra (Honolulu: University of Hawaii Press, 1974), 277–312.

37. William Caudill and Carmi Schooler, "Child Behavior and Child Rearing in Japan and the United States: An Interim Report," *Journal of Nervous and Mental Disease* 157, no. 5 (1973): 323–338; and William Caudill and Helen Weinstein, "Maternal Care and Infant Behavior in Japan and America," in Lebra and Lebra, *Japanese Culture and Behavior: Selected Readings,* 225–276. Caudill's studies are acknowledged classics in the field, though it is difficult to assess their current validity.

38. Ruth Benedict, *The Chrysanthemum and the Sword: Patterns of Japanese Culture* (Boston: Houghton Mifflin, 1946), 258.

39. Hosotsuji, "Ikuji-shu ni Yoru Hikaku Shakaikaron no Kokoro," 104.

40. Comparative research indicates that rates of abuse, in home or school, are several times higher in the United States than in Japan, although some reports indicate that "teacher violence" is a growing problem in Japanese middle schools (Yoshiko Ikeda, "Child Abuse in Japan," *Child Welfare Quarterly* 5, no. 2 [December 1984]; Keji Tamura, "A Study on Intrafamilial Child Abuse Conducted at Child Guidance Centers throughout the Nation," in *Child Welfare Annual Report from Japan* [Tokyo: Japan Research Institute on Child Welfare, 1985]; and Tamiko Bjerner, "School Violence," *Tokyo Journal* 7, no. 6 [September 1987]: 26–27). At least one study (Lebra, *Japanese Patterns of Behavior,* 150) claims that Japanese mothers are also less likely than either Korean or Chinese mothers to use corporal punishment, though I have not located any empirical evidence for this claim.

41. DeVos, "Dimensions of the Self," 155.

42. Befu's conclusions as summarized in Joy Hendry, *Becoming Japanese: The World of the Pre-School Child* (Honolulu: University of Hawaii Press, 1986), 105. A similar point is made in DeVos, "Dimensions of the Self," 151; and Wagatsuma and Lanham, "Childhood and Child Rearing," 278.

43. Youth Development Headquarters, *International Comparison,* 26–27.

44. Yuichi Murayama, *Gendai no hoiku-sho/yochien* (Tokyo: Aoki Shuten, 1983), 16–17; see also S. S. Boocock, "Controlled Diversity: An Overview of the Japanese Preschool System," *Journal of Japanese Studies* 15, no. 1 (Winter 1989): 41–65.

45. Hara and Wagatsuma, *Shitsuke*, 5–15; Mitsuo Akada, "Mura no Ningen Kankei," in *Mura to Mura-jin*, ed. Hirobumi Tsuboi (Tokyo: Shogakukan, 1984), 83–101.

46. Interviews with Nakanishi Koji, Japanese Ministry of Education, 9 December 1985; and Matsuda Shiketaka, Japanese Ministry of Health and Welfare, 16 December 1985.

47. Robert C. Christopher, *The Japanese Mind* (New York: Simon and Schuster, Linden Press, 1983), 76.

48. While both Spock and Matsuda cite independence as one of the components of a desirable personality or character, they seem to mean rather different things by independence. Dependence on mother is viewed by both men as necessary for the baby's sense of security, but for Spock, full personal development requires the child to overcome and slough off that very dependence. For Matsuda, independence and dependence are not mutually exclusive, but run parallel to each other. Indeed, it is from the baby's powerful desire for companionship with other people that the first glimmerings of self-reliance can be seen. True independence, in Matsuda's conceptualization, is achieved not in the self but in the group (Hosotsuji, "Ikuji-shu ni Yoru Hikaku Shakaikaron no Kokoro," 106).

49. Kimiko Saito, *Kosodate* (Tokyo: Rodojuno-sha, 1982), chaps. 1 and 2.

50. Description based upon the author's field notes of a visit to Sakura-Sakurambo, attendance at a Sakura-Sakurambo workshop for preschool teachers, and an interview with Mrs. Saito, July and October, 1985. A fuller exposition of Saito's philosophy can be found in: Saito, *Kosodate*; Kimiko Saito and Hirosho Kawahima, *Asun o Hiraku Kodomo-tachi* (Tokyo: Ayumi Shuppan, 1976); and Hiroshi Kawashima and Kimiko Saito, *Hito ga Ningen ni Naru* (Tokyo: Ayumi Shuppan, 1984).

51. Joy Hendry, "Kindergartens and the Transition from Home to School Education," *Comparative Education* 22, no. 1, (1986): 55. Catherine C. Lewis, "Cooperation and Control in Japanese Nursery Schools," *Comparative Education Review* 28 (1984): 69–84, also contains examples of the sort of cooperative group activities favored in Japanese preschools.

52. Joy Hendry, *Understanding Japanese Society* (London and New York: Croom Helm, 1987), 40–41.

53. Harold W. Stevenson, "Making the Grade: School Achievement in Japan, Taiwan, and the United States," in *Annual Report 1983* (Palo Alto, Calif.: Center for Advanced Study in the Behavioral Sciences, 1983); Harold W. Stevenson, James W. Stisler, and Shin-Ying Lee, "Achievement in Mathematics," in Stevenson, Hazuma, and Hakuta, *Child Development and Education in Japan*, 201–216.

54. Catherine C. Lewis, "From Indulgence to Internalization: Social Control in the Early School Years," *Journal of Japanese Studies* 14, no. 1 (Winter 1989): 151.

55. Lois Peak, *Learning to Go to School: The Transition from Home to Preschool*, Ph.D. diss., Harvard University, 1987. See also Ryoko Kato Tsuneyoshi, *The Structural Basis of Social Relations in Japanese and American Elementary Schools*, Ph.D. diss., Princeton University, 1989, chaps. 3 and 4.

56. Lewis, "Cooperation and Control." Similar anecdotal evidence is reported in Tobin, Wu, and Davidson, *Preschool in Three Cultures*; and Mariko Fujita and Toshiyuki Sano, "Children in American and Japanese Day Care Centers: Ethnography and Reflective Cross-Cultural Interviewing," in *School and Society: Learning Content through Cultural Context*, ed. Henry T. Trueba and Concha Delgrade-Gaitan (New York: Praeger, 1989).

57. Lois Peak, "Learning to Become Part of the Group: The Japanese Child's

Transition to Preschool Life," *Journal of Japanese Studies* 15, no. 1 (Winter 1989): 93–124.

58. Tobin, Wu, and Davidson, *Preschool in Three Cultures*, 58.

59. David Plath, *Long Engagements: Maturity in Modern Japan* (Stanford: Stanford University Press, 1980), 218.

60. Peak, *Learning to Go to School in Japan*; Cummings, *Education and Equality*, 108; and author's field notes.

61. Lois Peak, "Training Learning Skills and Attitudes in Japanese Early Educational Settings," in *Early Experience and the Development of Competence*, ed. William Fowler (San Francisco: Jossey-Bass, 1986), 111–123; and Susan Grilli, *Preschool in the Suzuki Spirit* (Tokyo: Harcourt Brace Jovanovich Japan, 1987).

62. Benedict, *The Chrysanthemum and the Sword*, 279.

63. Azuma, "Why Study Child Development," 8.

64. William Caudill, "Around the Clock Patient Care in Japanese Psychiatric Hospitals: The Role of the *Tsukisoi*," *American Sociological Review* 26, no. 2 (1961): 211.

65. Christie Kiefer, quoted in Robert J. Smith, *Japanese Society: Tradition, Self, and the Social Order* (New York: Cambridge University Press, 1983) 70.

66. I am grateful to John Gillis for pointing out that the "unitary self" is probably a rather recent development in Western culture, and that prior to about 1800, many Westerners too were able to "put on many masks without feeling disoriented."

67. Martha Wolfenstein, "Fun Morality: An Analysis of Recent American Childtraining Literature," in *Childhood in Contemporary Cultures*, ed. Margaret Mead and Martha Wolfenstein (Chicago: University of Chicago Press, 1955).

68. For analysis of recent discussions on "liberalizing" the Japanese educational system, see Mamoru Takahashi, *Discussions on Educational Reform in Japan* (Tokyo: Foreign Press Center, 1985); and Nobuo Shimahara, "Japanese Educational Reform in the 1980s: A Political Commitment," in *Education in Japan: An Overview*, ed. Edward R. Beauchamp (Westport, Conn.: Greenwood Press, forthcoming). It is interesting to note that the Japanese debates over group-ism are occurring in a period that is also marked by renewed criticism of excessive *individualism* in American culture and upbringing.

Two Nineteenth-Century Examples

◆ LINDA M.-G. ZERILLI ◆

Constructing "Harriet Taylor"
Another Look at J. S. Mill's Autobiography

But if I were to say in what above all she is preeminent, it is her profound knowledge of human nature. To know all its depths and elevations she had only to study herself.

—*John Stuart Mill*

Readers of John Stuart Mill will recognize this passage as but another expression of his homage to Harriet Taylor, a woman of exceptional character and superior intellect. "The knowledge and contemplation of her," Mill wrote, was itself the study of humankind—a study that, for him, "so inferior in nature," involved a "long course of education."[1] Mill's timeless and genderless portrait of his wife was simultaneously a rebuke of English society, of a petty world far too "insipid" to appreciate a nature as lofty and poetic as hers: "Such a woman could not be otherwise than alone in the world," lamented Mill, "especially in a world like England," where sensibility is commonly dismissed as "madness" (EDRL, 618). Thus, he wrote to Thomas Carlyle, it fell to the "man of speculation," to Mill himself, to translate the intuitive truths of the artist into the language of practical politics.[2] The innovative ideas found in his writings, Mill reiterated in his *Autobiography*, "originated" not with him but Taylor; they were "emanations from her mind" (146).

In wielding the pen that affixed his name to an extensive body of writings, then, Mill claimed that he was but a mediator between "original thinkers" such as Taylor and otherwise uncomprehending English readers (*Autobiography*, 146). He noted in his diary that his self-appointed task "as the interpreter of the wisdom of one whose intellect is as much profounder as is her heart nobler" was difficult if not daunting: "I do not wish that I were so much her equal as not to be her pupil, but I would gladly be more capable than I am of thoroughly appreciating and worthily reproducing her admirable thoughts."[3] But if Taylor was the author and Mill was her scribe, this representation of intellectual collaboration is itself mediated by another image of his wife as the beautiful muse, whose "influence" and "prompting" inspired Mill to write on the "great questions of feeling and life" (*Correspondence*, 199). Indeed the ambiguity if not the anxiety of authorship is evident in the following diary entry, in which we find a doubled figure of woman as both the origin and the addressee of the theorist's language: "Neibuhr said that he wrote only for Savigny: so I write only for her when I do not write entirely *from* her" (*Correspondence*, 198).

I propose to examine the question of gender identity and authorship in Mill's writings and to suggest one interpretation of the highly contested representations of the Mill-Taylor intellectual relationship.[4] Rather than speculating whether Mill's superlatives paint a historically realistic picture of Harriet Taylor, I am concerned both to point out how such language works against its purported claim to establish Mill's companion as a speaking subject and an intellect in her own right and to suggest possible reasons for this paradox. Specifically, I am interested in the construction of the written self in Mill's work as an attempted reconfiguration of sexual identity. "Harriet Taylor," as Mill portrays her in his writings, is best understood as part of his larger effort to challenge conventional gender distinctions by incorporating into himself a traditionally feminine sensibility—an effort, as I have argued elsewhere, that bears directly on the politics of his feminism.[5] Indeed Taylor, in Mill's self-representation,[6] was the preeminent figure in that distinguished community of androgynous "higher natures," in whom morality and inclination coincided: "If all resembled you, my lovely friend," wrote Mill in an early essay on marriage, "it would be idle to prescribe rules for them."[7] Unfortunately, in Mill's view, the world was populated by the "lower natures," whose desires, specifically sexual desires, were an obstacle to that complementary wholeness of the sexes coveted by Romantic poets and embraced by Mill in his lifelong struggle to free himself from the emotional straitjacket of his father's utilitarianism.

The problem of signature and gender, however, which goes far beyond the documented disbelief with which readers have responded to presumably exaggerated accounts of Taylor's contribution, character, and intellect, cannot be addressed meaningfully without some attention to the haunting figure of Mill's mother, née Harriet Burrows. Although mention of Mrs. James Mill is missing entirely from her son's *Autobiography*, as Christine Di Stephano has written, she looms large by virtue of the "sheer excess of her absence."[8] And it is to the absent mother that "the Life" is addressed.[9] "Harriet Taylor," the central figure on the Millian narrative landscape, bears more resemblance to the maternal figure than the Christian name which they share: as a core trope in Mill's writings, Taylor is one of many substitutes for the maternal desire that his prose both evokes and manages. Notwithstanding Mill's insistence that his work but "fixed in writing" Taylor's unique voice, his tributes to her, I will argue, work to return her to the position of the lost maternal object, that is, to "the feminine" in language.

The mother's absence in Mill's exalted portrait of his father and of Taylor has special significance for Mill's multiple self-representations as dutiful son, as political champion of women, and as an androgynous "higher nature"—"Harriet Taylor Mill." Mill's explicit claim to androgyny needs to be read through its far more disturbing subtext of rememoration—a symbolic reworking of the past that creates the possibility of authorship by allowing Mill to be both son and father, father and mother, male and female at once.[10] "Harriet Taylor," in short, is a self-constituting trope in Mill's written self; a trope deployed in Mill's effort to master his own genealogy: both his personal genealogy as a son born into a nineteenth-century family organized around patriarchal authority, and his intellectual genealogy as a political theorist educated according to the principles of utilitarianism.

His Construction of Their Union

"When two persons have their thoughts and speculations completely in common," wrote Mill in the *Autobiography*, "it is of little consequence in respect to the question of originality which of them holds the pen" (145). Had Mill lived a hundred years longer, he might have been surprised to discover just what a difference it made that he held the pen. But if Harriet Taylor has been blamed for everything that Mill's readers find inconsistent or undesirable in his writings—ranging from his "naive socialism" to his "excessive liberalism"—the problem of distinguishing her contribution from that of the acknowledged author must, at least in part, be blamed on Mill himself. For if Mill was obsessed with giving Taylor her due in his writings, his tributes to her function instead fused two distinct identities into one; merged Mill into Taylor and Taylor into Mill such that later generations of readers would have difficulty in disentangling them, and, consequently, those who were hostile to the figure of "Taylor" would have little trouble in dismissing her contribution entirely.

One example of this blurring of identities is suggested by Mill's own problematic relationship to his wife's historical past. In a letter to an American feminist, Pauline Wright Davis, Mill, as F. A. Hayek writes, "emphatically denied that a proper memoir of his wife could be written":

> Were it possible in a memoir to have the formation and growth of a mind like hers portrayed, to do so would be as valuable a benefit to mankind as was ever conferred by a biography. But such a psychological history is seldom possible, and in her case the materials for it do not exist. All that could be furnished is her birth-place, parentage, and a few dates, and it seems to me that her memory is more honoured by the absence of any attempt at a biographical notice than by the presence of a most meager one. What she was, I have attempted, though most inadequately, to delineate in the remarks prefaced to her essay, as reprinted with my *Dissertations and Discussions*.[11]

Harriet Taylor Mill died at the age of fifty-one. That Mill, who knew her intimately for a period of twenty-eight years, could not provide Davis with any more biographical information than her "birth-place, parentage, and a few dates" casts more doubt on his willingness to disclose such knowledge than it convinces us of his own ignorance of Taylor's past. The gesture, however, was not unusual: Mill was notoriously secretive about his relationship with Taylor and was quick to disown those friends whom he suspected of spreading rumors about the impropriety of their long friendship before the death of Taylor's husband in July 1849 and their subsequent marriage in April 1851. Not surprisingly, then, George Makepeace Towle, who in 1869 had requested materials for a biography of Mill, received a response similar to the one sent to Davis: once again, all that could be provided were a "few dates."[12] Hence Mill's unwillingness to cooperate with the American feminist might be read as nothing more than an extension of the veil of confidentiality that has frustrated scholars in search of the "truth" of that self-proclaimed *Seelenfreundschaft*.

This reading of Mill's reply to Davis, however, begs the question of the veil itself. What, we might ask, is being concealed by the claim to ignorance? Students of Mill need not be reminded of the speculative literature that has vigorously pursued precisely this question. Perhaps the metaphor of the veil is itself misleading; for it suggests that the scholar, through persistence and close study of archival materials, might someday lift the shroud of secrecy that envelops the Mill-Taylor relationship, thereby revealing its historical "truth." This approach, however, undertaken by those who are eager either to prove or, more often, to disprove the validity of Mill's account of his wife, founders on the problem of representation: in this case, the uncritical assumption that Mill's *Autobiography* and his personal correspondence offer the reader access to a life unmediated by language.

Further, when the written is assumed to be the writing self, it matters not whether one reads Mill's words skeptically or literally; for the effect is to reduce the constitutive act of writing to a debate polarized around two possible meanings: deception or description. I suggest that if we think about the letter to Davis less as a ploy intended to hide the "facts" of Taylor's past from a voyeuristic community of readers and more as a constructive strategy deployed (consciously and unconsciously) in the larger project of self-invention, Mill's curious reply to Davis is not so much a biographical ruse as it is a mode of self-presentation.

Whatever the "truth" of Mill's intentions in keeping "Taylor," and, by extension, himself, from her would-be biographers, his response to Davis is telling in yet another way that relates to the issues of writing the self noted above. For in the absence of an independent biography, we are left with Mill's personal account: a sketch of a life in which Harriet Taylor's "history" begins with her "introduction" to Mill in 1830, when he "was in his twenty-fifth and she in her twenty-third year":

> It is not to be supposed that she was, or that anyone, at the age at which I first saw her, could be all that she afterwards became. . . . Up to the time when I first saw her, her rich and powerful nature had chiefly unfolded itself according to the received type of feminine genius. . . . Married at a very early age, to a most upright, brave, and honourable man, of liberal opinions and good education, but without the intellectual or artistic tastes which would have made him a companion for her . . . ; shut out by the social disabilities of women from any adequate exercise of her highest faculties in action of the world without; her life was one of inward meditation, varied by familial intercourse with a small circle of friends, of whom only one (long since deceased) was a person of genius, or of capacities of feeling or intellect kindred with her own. (*Autobiography*, 111–112)

The movement of this passage, which locates Mill first as an outsider and then quickly establishes him as privileged soul mate, perfunctorily acknowledges Taylor's social position as the wife of another (honourable) man only to separate her through a kind of intellectual divorce. Similarly, in portraying her as the friend of dear but mentally inferior (or deceased) persons, the enigmatic figure of Taylor before 1830 is recuperated through language as a product of Mill's own life trajectory. As if she were a sleeping princess waiting to be awakened by a man of similar feeling and intellect, Taylor is introduced to the reader as part of the theorist's second birth: a reinvention of self, as will shortly become apparent, that released Mill from the prison of his ratiocinative utilitarian education.

"To be admitted into any degree of mental intercourse with a being of these qualities," Mill tells the reader, "could not but have a most beneficial influence on my development" (113). Still, it took many years "before her mental progress and mine went forward in the complete companionship they at last attained" (113). Of course, he adds, the benefit he gained from the friendship "was far greater" (113) than any that he could give her. Nevertheless, Mill qualifies, since he and Taylor developed their opinions in different ways—she through "moral intuition" and "strong feeling" and he through "study and reasoning" (113)—it is not unjust to note that in "the rapidity of her intellectual growth, her mental activity, which converted everything into knowledge, doubtless drew from me, as it did from other sources, many of its materials" (113).

In many ways, of course, the description of Taylor's emergence as a thinker in the *Autobiography* is classic Mill. The story of his education, as is often noted, carries traces of self-deprecation that suggest that the writing is not even worth the ink spilled over the selective recollections of "so uneventful a life": "I do not for a moment imagine that any part of what I have to relate can be interesting to the public as a narrative, or as being connected with myself" (3), Mill writes in his first sentences. Instead, we are told from the start, the subject at hand is not John Stuart Mill the person but John Stuart Mill the pupil: "I have thought that in an age in which education, and its improvement, are the subject of . . . study, it may be useful that there should be some record of an education which was unusual and remarkable" (3).[13] Likewise, the author, who makes no claim to originality, proposes merely to record the "debts" his "intellectual and moral development owes to other persons" (3). Some of these individuals are well known, for example, Jeremy Bentham; some are less known than they ought to be; "and the one to whom most of all is due," as it turns out, is the "one whom the world had no opportunity of knowing" (3).

The *Autobiography*, then, proposes to present this "one" to society at large—a society whose patriarchal conventions have rendered her, like all women, invisible as subjects and authors in their own right. The decision to describe "what I owe to you *intellectually*," Mill wrote to Taylor in 1854, "is the most important to commemorate, as people are comparatively willing to suppose all the rest" (*Correspondence*, 194). The attempt to pay his "debt" to Taylor, however, raised the question of how to negotiate the pedagogical and personal aspects of the *Autobiography*: that is, how to write what Mill referred to in his letter as "the Life" and "*our* life" (194). The two, of course, were inextricably linked, since Taylor's "effect" on Mill was central to the instructive purposes of writing an autobiography; however, the problem of what constitutes a "fair representation" preoccupied Mill as he struggled to imagine himself as a reader of his own life story: "Of course one does not, in writing a life, . . . undertake to tell everything—& it will be right to put something into *this* which shall prevent any one from being able to suppose or to pretend, that we undertake to keep nothing back" (194). But Mill's concern in writing his/their life, I would argue, has less to do with concealing the "facts" of his relationship with Taylor, noted above, than it does with a specific anxiety of authorship—with a fear of being rewritten by the reader.[14] Stated somewhat differently, what Mill called his "sacred duty of fixing in writing" (*Correspondence*, 189; see also 199) a life that would "be of use to the many" (198) was fraught with the problems of authorial control. For what was to prevent readers of the *Autobiography* from producing their own meanings for Mill's "Life," from reconstructing his written self?

To grasp the complexities of reader and author, however, as well as the positioning of "Harriet Taylor" in Mill's self-representations, we must first turn to the issues of enunciation and address encoded in the narrative structure of the very text that, as we have seen, was presumably of no interest as a personal narrative.

The Book and the Boy

"I was born in London, on the 20th of May, 1806, and was the eldest son of James Mill, the author of the History of British India" (*Autobiography*, 4). So begins Mill's account of his life—a touching story of creation, as Bruce Mazlish has argued, in which the mother is missing. Instead, writes Mazlish, "we have the book and the boy."[15] Significantly, I would add, the *Autobiography* ends with the following: "I have written various articles in periodicals . . . , have made a small number of speeches on public occasions, especially at the meetings of the Women's Suffrage Society, have published the "Subjection of Women," . . . and have commenced the preparation of matter for future books, of which it will be time to speak more particularly if I live to finish them. Here, therefore, for the present, this Memoir may close" (185). These two passages, which frame the autobiographical account of what Mill called his "education" and his "self-education," are linked by more than the seemingly random event of his birth and the authorial need for narrative closure. John Stuart's figurative reinstatement of himself within Oedipal law, as the son of James Mill, a self-proclaimed Malthusian whose wife would bear him nine children, is itself transfigured in the final passage of "the Life," in which the son's signature is annexed to his own textual creations. Of the latter, the one that is named is the book that defended women against the "brute instinct" of male sexual desire and the debilitating demands of maternity. What began as a tribute to the father and to paternity, then, in which the pen that signs the scholarly book inscribes as well the identity of the boy, ends as a radical intervention into the field of heterosexuality and eighteenth-century gender relations. In authoring a Life that concludes by putting his name to "The Subjection of Women," Mill, as we shall see, distances himself from the project of his father—a project that stamped both sons and women as the mere re-presentations of paternal identity—and constructs an alternative self that is intimately bound up with questions of power and sexual difference.

It is worth lingering for a moment over the very project of writing one's life. For, as noted above, the distinction between the written and the writing self is crucial to my reading of Mill. Since an autobiography culls its materials from the author's memory, a brief caveat on the meaning of memory is in order. Notwithstanding Mill's claim to have merely recorded the events of his past, a radical reading of the *Autobiography* must begin with the insight that, as Freud argues, memories of one's past cannot be understood as simply emerging from the multiplicity of childhood experience; instead all memories are formed in relation to the psychic needs of the present.[16] Hence rememoration is a process in which the past is not so much recol-lected as it is worked over—a process in which the "I" of childhood, for example, constitutes and is constituted in relation to the "I" of the locutor. Understood in this manner, then, memory, as Patricia Spacks has written, is a means of possessing one's past,[17] of transforming it in the urgency of the present. Like Harriet Taylor, then, the personages encountered by a reader of Mill's Life are best understood as figures deployed in the construc-tion of the author's subjectivity.

To substantiate these claims I return to the Oedipal issues raised in Mill's self-introduction. The "debt" to his father is repaid with interest, so to speak, by a painful presentation of self as the pedagogical utilitarian "exper-iment," whose seven-chapter autobiography consists of at least two devoted entirely to his father's ideas on politics, education, and social re-form. More significant, however, is the manner in which John Stuart con-stitutes himself in relation not only to the *History of British India* but also to the closed world of books in which he was immersed until the age of four-teen. As he recollected his life, we have seen, Mill was unable, or unwilling, to distinguish his own birth from that of a book. It is not surprising, then, that the first chapter of Mill's Life situates him exclusively in relation to the numerous texts his father made him read. Cut off from "intercourse with other boys" (22), Mill, in short, is subjected to a rigorous educational pro-gram, which, among other things, has him learning Greek at age three un-der his "father's tuition." That tuition, however, was invasive for reasons that went beyond the fact that, as Mill writes, "I went through the whole process of preparing my Greek lessons in the same room and at the same table at which he (the father) was writing." Not only did he read in the pres-ence of his father, but "as in those days Greek and English lexicons were not, . . . I was forced to have recourse to him for the meaning of every word which I did not know. This incessant interruption he, one of the most impatient of men, submitted to, and wrote under that interruption several volumes of his History and all else that he had to write during those years" (6).

Under the tutelage of James Mill, the otherwise private practice of reading is transformed into terrifying episodes in accountability in which the final meaning of texts and of language is the province of the father. In addition to his required reading, Mill mentions his "private reading" of Mitford's Greece only to note that "my father had put me on my guard against the Tory prejudices of this writer" (9). Similarly, after reading Latin treatises on scholastic logic, Mill tells us that he was forced to give to his father, each day, in their walks together, "a minute account of what I had read," and was required to answer his "numerous and searching questions" (12). Hence what he learned from the elder Mill, among other things, was how to dissect a bad argument with logic: a skill that forms "exact thinkers, who attach a precise meaning to words and propositions, and are not imposed on by vague, loose, or ambiguous terms" (13). The same lesson, we are told, was learned by reading Plato, whose work constrains the "man of vague generalities . . . either to express his meaning to himself in definite terms or to confess that he does not know what he is talking about" (15). Finally, the fear of using words whose meanings have not been properly defined is connected to Mill's overwhelming sense of failure as a pupil and, hence, as a son:

> I remember at some time in my thirteenth year, on my happening to use the word idea, he asked me what an idea was; and expressed some displeasure at my ineffectual efforts to define the word: I recollect also his indignation at my using the common expression that something was true in theory but required correction in practice; and how, after making me vainly strive to define the word theory, he explained its meaning, and showed the fallacy of the vulgar form of speech which I had used; leaving me fully persuaded that . . . I had shewn unparalleled ignorance. (20)

That Mill's earliest recollections of spoken and written language are presented in terms of his subjection to his father is elaborated further in his description of the exercises in elocution, which were part of his education. Of all the things he was made to do, Mill tells us, there was nothing in which he failed so miserably as in his efforts to read aloud to his father, who "had thought much on the principles of reading." The "rules" of "modulation," Mill writes, were "strongly impressed" upon him, and he was taken "severely to task for every violation of them" (16). Thus even when Mill is speaking he is really listening; for it is his father who, in the son's account, defined not only the books to be read but also the manner in which they were to be read and discussed. But if James Mill seemed to exercise complete control over the terms of discourse, there was, Mill tells us, one sphere in which he was left to explore the fantasies of his imagination: "A voluntary exercise to which throughout my boyhood I was addicted, was what I called writing histories. . . . My father encouraged me in this useful amusement, though, as I think judiciously, he never asked to see what I wrote; so that I did not feel that in writing it I was accountable to any one, nor had the chilling sensation of being under a critical eye" (10). However, Mill notes, he later destroyed all the papers he had written "in contempt of (his) childish efforts" (10). Moreover, these exercises in youthful creativity paled in comparison to that great *History of India*, the text of which John Stuart read aloud to his father as the elder Mill corrected the proofs of his monumental manuscript in the year 1817.

The effect of an education that stressed the analytic over the poetic uses of language was to deprive Mill of those literary modes of expression he would later rediscover in his reading of Romantic poetry, specifically Wordsworth. The young Mill's sporadic attempts at self-imagining through the writing and reading of verse, he notes, were crushed by his father's derision of most English poetry. Indeed, it was more than the "spontaneous promptings" of Mill's "poetical ambition" that were destroyed by turning an exercise "begun from choice" into one "continued by command" (11). The instrumental approach of his father to language, the son recounts, was but part of his more general contempt "for passionate emotions of all sorts, and for everything which has been said or written in exaltation of them" (31). Hence, Mill wrote in a 1833 letter to Thomas Carlyle, the poet's boundless capacity for feeling, especially love, was completely lacking in himself; and consciousness of this lack only heightened the pain associated with willing what could not be willed: "I can do nothing for myself and others can do nothing for me; all the advice which can be given, . . . is, not to beat against the bars of my iron cage."[18]

Mill's measured criticism of his father and of his education bears the traces of the anxiety of authorship spoken of at the beginning of this essay. Assessing his relation to the required books, specific meanings, and circumscribed textual world of his childhood, Mill is torn between exalting and doubting the excellences of the paternal figure. On the one hand, Mill represents himself as the product, legacy, and beneficiary of his father's efforts. This point is underscored, significantly, in a passage in which the author of the Life repeats James Mill's last words to him upon leaving his "father's house for a long absence" at age fourteen:

> I remember the very place in Hyde Park where, . . . he told me that I
> should find, as I got acquainted with new people, that I had been

taught many things which youths of my age did not commonly know; and that many persons would be disposed . . . to compliment me upon it. . . . He wound up by saying, that whatever I knew more than others, could not be ascribed to any merit in me, but to the very un- usual advantage which had fallen to my lot, of having a father who was able to teach me, and willing to give the necessary trouble and time. . . . I felt that what my father had said . . . was exactly the truth . . . and it fixed my opinion and feeling from that time forward. (22)

On the other hand, Mill also explicitly criticizes his father's method, which sacrificed, among other things, affect at the altar of reason. Some of these, more tempered, critiques are woven into the fabric of the published text, but the most damning of them are to be found in the rejected leaves of the *Autobiography*. Here we are told that James Mill's "children neither loved him, nor, with any warmth or affection anyone else" (33 n. 3); that John Stuart's "was not an education of love but of fear" (33 n. 3); and that the pedagogical consequences of utilitarianism included a form of moral (as well as physical) enervation: "I acquired a habit of leaving my responsibility as a moral agent to rest on my father, my conscience never speaking to me except by his voice" (33 n. 3).

Mill's overly punitive and severe internalization of paternal authority, however, cannot be understood apart from another representation of his father, found as well in the rejected leaves: an image of James Mill as the victim of an ill-assorted marriage and of his eldest son as the unfortunate child of an unloving mother. It is to Harriet Burrows, then, that I next turn in my reading of Mill's life story. For in naming, criticizing, and then cross- ing out the mother, Mill's subtext tells us something about the place of de- sire in his account of a life whose stated intent it was to pay back a "debt" by offering himself as an example for the reader.[19]

The Absent Mother

Noting that Mill's autobiography represents the author's birth as analogous to that of a book only begins to unravel the meaning of his self-introduction to the reader. Retelling the tale of the author's reinscription of himself within Oedipal law acknowledges but has yet to explain the meaning of the mother's absence. Indeed, our discussion so far would seem to affirm a fa- miliar reading of Mill as a prodigal son, whose struggle for language might be read as symptomatic of the "anxiety of influence" outlined by critics such as Harold Bloom.[20] In other words, as Marlon Ross writes in a related con- text, Mill might be said to be caught in a generational "tug-of-war" with his father, in which "only the strong man wins, for only he can create himself despite the father's overriding claims of insemination, authority, and paternal possession."[21] On this reading, writing is the process through which Mill would do battle with the father who made him; but, as Bloom recognizes, any notion of conquest is illusory; for "the son wins self-possession only tentatively, if at all, in the same way that he may realize that he has made himself who he is *only* because he could not be what his father has already become."[22]

In contrast to a reading that would situate Mill, and the question of authorship, strictly in relation to paternal authority, literary and familial, feminist theories of writing and language acquisition offer a different angle from which to speculate on Mill's narrative account of his education. By focusing on the pre-Oedipal period, which precedes the child's entry into the symbolic order of language, American literary critics such as Margaret Homans and French theorists such as Julia Kristeva and Luce Irigaray have stressed the centrality of the loss (or, on Irigaray's account, the overt murder) of the mother to the emergence of the male speaking subject.[23] The abyss that separates subject and object, to which, for example, Mill alluded in his letter to Carlyle about Man's capacity to love, is that of a man and his absent mother. Following Jacques Lacan, these feminists have argued that language is founded on the figurative substitutes for the originary unmediated relationship to a pre-Oedipal maternal figure.[24] As Freud demonstrated in his account of the child's *Fort!/Da!* game, language is, among other things, a means for both mastering and replaying the mother's absence.[25] But the symbolic rendering of the lost object, as Homans puts it, which requires the absence of the object, also permits its controlled return: "What the son searches for, in searching for substitutes for the mother's forbidden body, is a series of figures, someone like his mother."[26] Figuration, then, allows the son to flee from the mother and the lost referent, the literal, with which she is identified. In our "predominant myth of language," argues Homans, "the presence of the mother's body," of the literal, would make figurative meaning unnecessary, "it would hypothetically destroy the text."[27] Thus, the "feminine" in language is the absent referent that makes possible and engenders figurative structures of literature. The "woman," writes Homans, must remain forever out of reach in order for male authors "to speculate forever on how to reach her, or to replace her with their own abstractions."[28]

This abbreviated account of language acquisition proves very useful to an exploration of the workings of the Oedipus myth in John Stuart's narrative of his childhood. For if James Mill is presented to us as an exalted, almost superhuman figure, we might well wonder about the meaning of this larger-than-life portrait in Mill's written self. From a slightly different angle, then, one could argue that the unusual description of Mill's birth, in which the mother is refused by not being represented, works not only to reinstate the author as son but also to shore up the identity of James Mill as father: in short, to affirm paternity. The exaltation of the father figure, wrote Freud in his "Family Romances," occurs when the child realizes that "*pater semper incertus est,* while the mother is *certissima.*"[29] In Mill's account, however, that affirmation is even more curious; for in what amounts to a textual self-genesis, Mill's prose works to deny as well the fact that he is not the product of writing but of coitus, not of intellect but of desire. Indeed, in the *Autobiography* language reconstructs what Freud called the intolerable fact of parental sexual intercourse to make it more acceptable to the author.

The theme of sexual desire in Mill's autobiography is often articulated in terms of the son's efforts to explain the inconsistency of his father's life and his politics, that is, the fact that the size of James Mill's family stood in flagrant contradiction to his theoretical Malthusianism. Mill himself leads the reader in this direction when he writes that his father, "with no resources but the precarious one of writing in periodicals, . . . married and had a large family; conduct than which nothing could be more opposed, both as a matter of good sense and of duty, to the opinions which, at least at a later period of life, he strenuously upheld" (*Autobiography,* 4). Accordingly, it is the father's desire that is problematic and hence male sexual desire that must be accounted for and explained. Although Mill's life story does not provide the extended critique of male sexuality found in his political writings, it does suggest at least one way of accounting for statements such as the following: Something in the "merely physical subjection to their will as an instrument, causes them (husbands) to feel a sort of disrespect and contempt towards their own wife which they do not feel towards any other woman, or any other human being."[30] For if Mill's feminism would focus on what he held to be the barbaric nature of male sexuality, the *Autobiography* situates the demon of (hetero)sexual "instinct" in relation to the author's mother—a figure whose swollen body stands as more than what Christine Di Stephano calls "a pregnant reminder of her husband's illicit desires and behavior, which had little legitimate space within the frame of his rationalist Utilitarianism."[31] What Mill's account of his birth and his childhood reconstructs and in effect denies, I would add, is not only the embarrassing fact of the father's recurring desire but also the mother's.[32]

That Mill can hardly mention sexuality without condemning it, and, with it, the men who force themselves on their wives is one of the more curious if commonly acknowledged aspects of his feminism.[33] Indeed, there is little room in Mill's theory for a notion of sexual desire that is not masculine and invasive. Human instincts, he argues, are the dangerous, natural impulses that Mill believed the progress of civilization would eventually contain, if not eradicate, through the triumph of reason and, specifically, through the rational extension of political equality to women.[34] In Mill's account, the political and economic subjection of women is the cultural product of their subjection to male sexual instinct. The image of woman in Mill's political writings as the passive and helpless victim of male desire, however, is complicated by the *Autobiography*'s subtext, in which the acknowledged absence of gender equality in the Mill household is but a pretext for explaining the father's unfortunate situation in being married to a woman to whom "he had not, and never could have supposed that he had, the inducements of kindred intellect, tastes, or pursuits" (4 n. 2). This sentence, which follows the passage on the size of James Mill's family, quoted above, is an indirect reference to the mother; and, like all other references to the mother, it was crossed out and finally deleted from the published manuscript. The price of James Mill's marriage to such a woman, however—which included the enormous financial burdens of a large family and the "extraordinary energy which was required to lead the life which he led"—was paid not once but twice; the second time by his eldest son: "A man who, in his practice, so vigorously acted up to the principle of losing no time, was likely to adhere to the same rule in the instruction of his pupil. I have no remembrance of the time when I began to learn Greek" (5). That this passage is preceded by a reference to Mill's mother is significant. For it is the loss of the mother that is replayed in the subtext of Mill's narrative account of language acquisition, which begins with a painful memory of learning Greek under the tutelage of his father. At the same time, that the first textual trace of maternal negation, that is, the explicit because written crossing-out of the mother, occurs at a point in the manuscript where Mill acknowledges his entry into the symbolic order of language suggests as well not so much the loss as the overt murder of the mother suggested by Irigaray. It is a murder, however, fraught with ambivalence. Like the book, which, as a figurative substitution for the maternal body, allows Mill both to deny that his mother (and her desire) was necessary to his birth and to replace her with a more sanitary figure, learning Greek presupposes the mother's absence while permitting her controlled return within the symbolic order of paternal law. But this loss or murder of the mother is, as we have seen, not without its destructive consequences. What is lost with the death of mother is the unmediated communication with others, the ability to merge identities in a (pre-Oedipal) universe of feeling.

The argument about Mill's own subjection to his father comes full circle when we attend to the rejected leaves of his autobiography. But Mill's ambivalence or reluctance to "pronounce whether I was more a loser or gainer by his severity" (32) is managed in a long, deleted passage that follows—a passage in which the father is forgiven for his deficient moral relation to his children, his "lack of tenderness," for he too was unloved. "In an atmosphere of tenderness and affection," we are told, James Mill "would have been tender and affectionate":

> That rarity in England, a really warm hearted mother, would in the first place have made my father a totally different being, and in the second would have made the children grow up loving and being loved. But my mother with the very best intentions, only knew how to pass her life in drudging for them. Whatever she could do for them she did, and they liked her, because she was kind to them, but to make herself loved, looked up to, or even obeyed, required qualities which she unfortunately did not possess. (33)

The literature on the marriage of James and Harriet Mill agrees, for the most part, with John Stuart's assessment.[35] James Mill's attitude towards his wife is commonly portrayed as one bordering on complete indifference if not contempt. Although we know from a variety of letters, written by friends of the Mills, that James Mill played tyrant in his home, when considering John Stuart's representation of his mother, we still need to consider the complex role played by the imagination and fantasy in the construction of personal narrative.

By attending to the ways in which Mill's prose manages the loss of the mother, we can read Mill's melancholia, recounted in his famous "mental crisis" at age twenty, in terms of a loss of "narcissistic supplies" rather than strictly as an Oedipal narrative. For the superego, as Thomas Weiskel has written in his account of Wordsworth, is likewise "a precipitate of the mother as well as the father, and its displeasure may thus be manifested not only in the fantasy of castration but also in the sense of loss—of self-esteem."[36] But by telling the reader "I neither estimated myself highly nor lowly; I did not estimate myself at all" (*Autobiography*, 21), Mill seems to underscore a reading of his life in which the father is the central figure whose powerful presence prohibits any attempt at self-invention. Thus, his crisis might be read in terms of the liberating effect that the reading of Marmontel's *Memoirs* had upon the young Mill, specifically the passage that, Mill writes, "relates the father's death, the distressed position of the family, and the sudden inspiration by which he, then a mere boy, felt and made them feel that he would be everything to them—would supply the place of all they had lost" (85). Apart from the "rescue fantasy" suggested by Mill's text,[37] a strict focus on the patricidal wish in this passage overlooks the more troubling problem of self-consciousness with which Mill concludes the episode: the absence of genuine feeling, of true happiness, in a world whose "objects of human desire" had been dissolved by the "influence of analysis" (*Autobiography*, 84). Instead of searching for happiness as an object in itself, Mill writes, "Let your self-consciousness, your scrutiny, your self-interrogation exhaust themselves" on something external to it; only then will you "inhale happiness with the air you breathe, without dwelling on it or thinking about it, without either forestalling it in the imagination, or putting it to flight by fatal questioning" (86).

Mill's "cultivation of the feelings" sought an unmediated connection to others through poetry and music. That Mill identified Wordsworth as the poet whose writings made him aware of the existence of genuine feeling is significant. Although Mill may not have read *The Prelude*, in which the poet recounts the "mute dialogues" which he held with his mother as an infant, Wordsworth's poetry had a profound effect upon the author of the *Autobiography*. Indeed, in reading the "famous Ode," Mill writes, he found that "he (Wordsworth) too had had similar experience to mine" (90). Wordsworth's poetry, Mill tells us, allowed him to recapture that "real, permanent happiness in tranquil contemplation"; something of that "first freshness of youthful enjoyment of life" (90); that "sympathetic and imaginative pleasure, which could be shared in by all human beings; which had no connection with struggle or imperfection" (89); in short, a world in which language offered the (illusory) possibility of crossing the abyss between subject and object, a world without difference and separation.

Not surprisingly, then, in his essay on marriage, Mill echoed Wordsworth's longing for those lost dialogues. Motherhood, Mill insisted, is not about doing but about being: "It is not by particular effects, but imperceptibly and unconsciously that she (the mother) makes her own character pass into the child; that she makes the child love what she loves."[38] But Mill's depiction of such a blissful state, and the acts of figuration that engender it, is only possible if the illusion that we might have access to some originary ground of meaning is sustained.[39] And central to this illusion, as I now conclude, is Mill's "Harriet Taylor," that other figure whose "presence" in Mill's narrative requires her absence as subject.

Conclusion

The *Autobiography*, I have suggested, is not so much, as it represents itself, an account of Mill's education at the hands of his father. Rather, as Mary Jacobus has written of *The Prelude*, it is "an educational treatise directed at the missing mother."[40] That Mill drafted his autobiography in the years 1853–1854, years in which his mother fell gravely ill and finally passed away, may be but a crude indication of the possible links between Mill's project of writing his Life and the mother who gave him life.[41] More significant, perhaps, is that although the *Autobiography* seems to confirm the author's identity as the indebted son of the author of the "History of British India" by denying the place of the mother in creation, the text works primarily to affirm a myth of self-possession. For by reducing the debt to his father to the life of the mind, Mill's prose reconstructs what he owes to his parents (his birth) in terms that can be repaid through the act of writing itself. But if the infidelity involved in adopting intellectual positions on political questions contrary to the teachings of his father are legitimated, in part, by replacing the inner "voice" of his father with that of "Harriet Taylor," so too is the potential *re*fusion with the mother through fusion with his wife mediated by an unusual conjugal relationship—a marriage that will produce not children but books, and a relationship that will cultivate not sexual passion but elevated ideas of human community.

On 6 March 1851, shortly before his marriage to Harriet Taylor, Mill wrote a lengthy letter in which, among other things, he divested himself of the "odious powers" of any "right" to his wife's "person" and "property" (*Correspondence*, 168). But Mill's insistence that his wife would retain "in all respects whatever the same absolute freedom of action, & freedom of disposal of herself . . . , as if no marriage had taken place" (168) needs to be squared with his desire to abnegate any separate sense of self, to "merg(e) . . . the entire being with that of another, which is the characteristic of strong passion" (EDRL, 621–622). Mill's refusal to participate in the social practices of coverture entailed, not only a relinquishment of his claim to Taylor's body, but also an insistence that the "renunciation of any separate existence" be both "spontaneous" and "equally complete on both sides" (EDRL, 621). He found inspiration for such union in the romantic rhetoric of androgyny, in a poetic language of inclusion that promised to reconcile the grammar of opposites that was sexual difference.

"A great mind must be androgynous," wrote Coleridge.[42] Similarly, Mill asked rhetorically in a letter to Carlyle: "Is there really any distinction between the highest masculine and the highest feminine character?"[43] The "first-rate" people of both sexes, Mill answered, seemed to combine the highest masculine and the highest feminine traits in perfect harmony.[44] By the "higher natures," Mill wrote in his essay on marriage, I mean those characters who have "the greatest capacity of feeling happiness, and of bestowing it."[45] To be both the "natural object" and the giver of "love," Mill adds, is the crux of an identity that can "promote the greatest possible happiness of all who are within the sphere of (its) influence."[46] The reference to his wife was echoed in the *Autobiography*, in a passage in which Taylor is portrayed as a woman of "boundless generosity, and a lovingness ever ready to pour itself forth upon any or all human beings who were capable of giving the smallest feeling in return" (113). But the love that Mill experienced in the presence of Taylor was more than a substitute for that which he claimed to have neither felt nor received from his mother, as some critics have suggested.[47] The link between happiness and love, which Mill drew time and again in his writings, was central to the myth of self-possession described by Freud in his 1914 essay on narcissism. "To be their own ideal once more, in regard to sexual no less than other trends," wrote Freud, "as they were in childhood—this is what people strive to attain as their happiness."[48]

Language acquisition, as I have argued, marks indelibly the birth of the speaking subject in a universe of difference, a world in which, as Blake wrote, one may hope only for an "organized innocence"[49] but never again complete or originary innocence. But if writing signified this impossibility, so too did it offer the illusion of crossing the gap that marked human separateness. When Mill, as quoted above, writes that he is not "fit to write on anything but the outskirts of the great questions of feeling & life," he echoes Wordsworth's concern at the beginning of *The Prelude* that, as Geoffrey Hartman notes, he "cannot decide whether he is fit to be a poet on an epic scale."[50] Like Wordsworth, Mill "cannot find his theme because he already has it: himself."[51] Mill shared with the poet the weight of self-consciousness, of a passion that is "murderous to dissect."

Taylor, I have suggested, was the trope that linked the ratiocinative world of Mill's father and the repressed desires of and for his mother. To ask whether Mill's representation of "Harriet Taylor" succeeds in avoiding the dangers posed by the one-sided (female) abnegation of self is to raise the problem of androgyny as a completion of the male ego.[52] Despite Mill's concern with establishing Taylor as a subject in her own right, the *Autobiography* tells a different story—one in which Mill incorporates the "feminine" by choosing, as Freud writes, "a sexual ideal after the narcissistic type which possesses the excellences to which he (the male subject) cannot attain."[53] That Mill saw Taylor as the embodiment of "perfect disinterestedness," a rare condition that his political theory sought to attain, is of some relevance here. In a passage deleted from the published text of his autobiography, Mill wrote that his wife's "strong feeling" on the social position of women, in short, her feminism, "was the effect of principle and not of any desire on her own part to mingle in the turmoil and strife of the occupations which the dominant sex has hitherto reserved to itself" (EDRL, 621). What is contested by Mill in this image of his wife, whose intellect he credits for his political writings, is a far more problematic idea of her as someone whose own desire for recognition through action in the world would undermine the *Autobiography*'s idealized image of Taylor as a woman of complete "unselfishness." Although the political issues raised by Mill's idealization of Taylor are far too complex to examine here, readers of the *Subjection of Women* will recognize the links between Mill's benevolent image of his wife and his rather sentimentalized notion of how female suffrage would effect a kind of cultural husbandry of patriarchal society.

To return to the question of authorship and signature with which we began—if Mill's "Harriet Taylor" is but a feminized version of himself, so too does she mark the discursive space in the *Autobiography*, between the writer and his absent mother, that cannot be crossed but the illusion of which must be sustained if the project of writing is to succeed in affirming the author's identity. "Whenever I look back at any of my own writing of two or three years previous," Mill wrote in his diary in the year of his mother's death, "they seem to me like the writing of some stranger whom I have seen and known long ago" (*Correspondence*, 198). Although Mill accounts for this distance in terms of the gap between the "enlargement of his ideas and feelings," which he owes "to *her* (Taylor's) influence," and his inadequate "powers of execution" (198), the "stranger" that confronted Mill as reader of his own life was, perhaps, nothing other than that haunting maternal figure, one whose absence in the writing spoke powerfully to her presence in the unconscious.

NOTES

1. John Stuart Mill, "Early Draft Rejected Leaves," in *Collected Works*, ed. J. M. Robinson and Jack Stillinger (Toronto: University of Toronto Press, 1972), 1: 617. Henceforth cited in the text as EDRL. The epigraph to this chapter is from EDRL, 612.

2. John Stuart Mill to Thomas Carlyle, 5 July 1833, *The Earlier Letters of John Stuart Mill*, ed. Francis E. Mineka, in the *Collected Works*, 12: 163. On the same point, see John Stuart Mill, *Autobiography*, ed. Jack Stillinger (New York: Houghton Mifflin, 1969), 122. Henceforth cited in the text as *Autobiography*.

3. John Stuart Mill and Harriet Taylor Mill, *Their Correspondence and Subsequent Marriage*, ed. F. A. Hayek (Chicago: University of Chicago Press, 1951), 193. Henceforth cited in the text as *Correspondence*.

4. The recent speculative literature on Harriet Taylor's contribution to Mill's writings and her influence on his thinking is fairly consistent. Whereas earlier biographers and critics, such as Packe and Hayek, granted Taylor a legitimate, if "feminine" place in Mill's intellectual development, contemporary readers are more likely to deny Taylor any role at all or to blame her for those parts of Mill's work which seem inconsistent or problematic. For Gertrude Himmelfarb, who claims that the liberalism of *On Liberty* is far too "absolutistic and simplistic," the problem lay not with Mill but with Harriet Taylor: "This was his wife's way of thinking." See *On Liberty and Liberalism: The Case of John Stuart Mill* (New York: Alfred A. Knopf, 1974). Bernard Semmel praises Himmelfarb's "brilliantly argued" hypothesis of the two Mills: the one influenced by Taylor and the other "much sounder Mill." See *John Stuart Mill and the Pursuit of Virtue* (New Haven: Yale University Press, 1984), 5 n. 4. Alan Ryan portrays Taylor as rather spoiled and "bored" by her marriage to John Taylor: "It seems clear that Harriet was put out by the fact that her husband was no Shellyesque hero, though she aspired to be a romantic heroine." See *J. S. Mill* (London: Routledge & Kegan Paul, 1974), 49. In comparison, Michael St. Packe's portrait of Taylor as a woman who had "given up her manly ambition to . . . express herself in a more feminine way through her effect on him (Mill)" seems harmless. See Packe, *The Life of John Stuart Mill* (New York: Macmillan, 1954), 140. see also 237, 315–316, 348, and 371.

5. See Linda M.-G. Zerilli, *Images of Women in Political Theory: Agents of Culture and Chaos* (Madison: University of Wisconsin Press, 1992).

6. As I am concerned with the question of Mill's self-representation in this essay, I do not examine the letters written by Taylor to Mill, nor do I speculate on the rewriting of the *Autobiography*, some of the revisions of which are in Taylor's hand. In the face of critical hostility to Taylor, needless to say, such an analysis would be both useful and informative.

7. John Stuart Mill, "Essay on Marriage and Divorce," in *Essays on Sex Equality*, ed. Alice S. Rossi (Chicago: University of Chicago Press, 1970), 69.

8. Christine Di Stephano, "Rereading J. S. Mill: Interpolations from the (M)Otherworld," in *Discontented Discourses: Feminism, Textual Intervention, Psychoanalysis*, ed. Marleen S. Barr and Richard Feinstein (Urbana: University of Illinois Press, 1989), 163.

9. On the importance of the maternal subtext in male writing, see Coppelia Kahn, "Excavating 'Those Dim Minoan Regions': Maternal Subtexts in Patriarchal Literature," *Diacritics* 12, no. 2 (1982): 32–41.

10. I am indebted to an essay by Gayatri Chakravorty Spivak on Wordsworth for this point. Spivak, however, reads Wordsworth's myth of self-possession in terms of his refusal of paternity. See Spivak, "Sex and History in *The Prelude* (1805): Books Nine to Thirteen," *Texas Studies in Literature and Language* 23 (Fall 1981): 324–360.

11. Quoted in Hayek's introduction to the *Correspondence*, 15.

12. John Stuart Mill to George Makepeace Towle, 13 September 1869, *The Later Letters of John Stuart Mill*, ed. Francis E. Mineka, in the *Collected Works*, 17: 1641.

13. Mill would seem to extend the eighteenth-century notion that an autobiography ought to be instructive. See Patricia Spacks, *Imagining a Self: Autobiography and Novel in Eighteenth-Century England* (Cambridge: Harvard University Press, 1976).

14. On the ways in which "feminine figures seem to bear" a male author's "anxiety of authorship" and his fear of being rewritten by the reader, see Sonia Hofkosh, "The Writer's Ravishment, Women and the Romantic Author—The Example of Byron," in *Romanticism and Feminism*, ed. Anne K. Mellor (Bloomington: Indiana University Press, 1988), 93–114.

15. *James and John Stuart Mill: Father and Son in the Nineteenth Century* (New York: Basic Books, 1975), 3.

16. See, "Screen Memories," *The Standard Edition of the Complete Psychological Works of Sigmund Freud*, ed. James Strachey et al. (London, 1953–66), 3: 322. On the same point, see Thomas Weiskel, *The Romantic Sublime* (1976; reprint, Baltimore: The Johns Hopkins University Press, 1986), 170.

17. Spacks, *Imagining a Self*, 3.

18. John Stuart Mill to Thomas Carlyle, 9 March 1833, *The Earlier Letters of John Stuart Mill*, in *Collected Works*, 12:143.

19. It should be noted that portions of Mill's early draft were marked for deletion in the hand of Harriet Taylor. But Mill, of course, made the final decision on what to include in the manuscript.

20. Harold Bloom, *The Anxiety of Influence: A Theory of Poetry* (London: Oxford University Press, 1967).

21. Marlon Ross, "Romantic Quest and Conquest: Troping Masculine Power in the Crisis of Poetic Identity," in Mellor, *Romanticism and Feminism*, 27. Although Ross is critical of Bloom's patriarchal poetics, he persists, nonetheless, in reading the cultivation of a specifically feminine sensibility in terms of the Oedipal struggle between fathers and sons.

22. Ibid.

23. Irigaray argues that the mother ("femme-mere") is not simply lost but mur-

dered. Irigaray contests Freud's reading of the birth of culture in his *Totem and Taboo*. See Luce Irigaray, *Le Corps-a-corps avec la mere* (Ottowa: Pleine Lune, 1981), 15–16. I am indebted to Margaret Homans's introductory essay in her book *Bearing the Word* (Chicago: University of Chicago Press, 1986), 2, for this reference. Among numerous other writings, see especially, Homans, *Bearing the Word*, especially chap. 1; Luce Irigaray, *This Sex Which Is Not One*, trans. Catherine Porter and Carolyn Burke (Ithaca: Cornell University Press, 1985); and Julia Kristeva, *Desire in Language* (New York: Columbia University Press, 1980); and *Tales of Love*, trans. Leon S. Roudiez (New York: Columbia University Press, 1987).

24. See Jacques Lacan, "The Mirror Stage," "The Signification of the Phallus," and "The Function and Field of Speech and Language in Psychoanalysis," especially 65–68, in *Ecrits*, trans. Alan Sheridan (New York: W. W. Norton, 1977).

25. Sigmund Freud, "Beyond the Pleasure Principle," in *Standard Edition*, 18: 14–17. See Lacan's discussion of Freud in "The Function and Field of Speech," in *Ecrits*, 65.

26. Homans, *Bearing the Word*, 9.

27. Ibid., 4. Homans adds: "This possibility is always, but never more than, a threat, since literal meaning cannot be present in the text: it is always elsewhere."

28. Ibid., 2.

29. Sigmund Freud, "Family Romances," in *The Complete Psychological Works of Sigmund Freud* (London: The Hogarth Press, 1959), 9: 239.

30. John Stuart Mill, *Principles of Political Economy*, ed. J. M. Robson, in *Collected Works*, 3: 373. Mill is referring here to the working class.

31. Di Stephano, "Rereading J. S. Mill," 164.

32. On the problem of representing maternal desire, see Julia Kristeva, "Motherhood According to Giovanni Bellini," in *Desire in Language*.

33. On Mill's feminism, see Susan Moller Okin, *Women in Western Political Thought* (Princeton: Princeton University Press, 1979); Zillah Eisenstein, *The Radical Future of Liberal Feminism* (New York: Longman, 1981); Jennifer Ring, "Mill's *The Subjection of Women*: The Methodological Limits of Liberal Feminism," *The Review of Politics* 47, no. 1 (January 1985): 27–44; and Julia Annas, "Mill and the Subjection of Women," *Philosophy* 52 (1977): 179–194.

34. See John Stuart Mill, *The Subjection of Women*, in *Essays on Sex Equality; Political Economy*, in *Collected Works*, vol. 3.

35. See Mazlish, *James and John Stuart Mill*; Packe, The Life of John Stuart Mill; and Josephine Kamm, *John Stuart Mill in Love* (London: Gordon & Cremonesi, 1977), 13.

36. *The Romantic Sublime*, 102. On the same point see Julia Kristeva, *Black Sun: Depression and Melancholia*, trans. Leon Roudiez (New York: Columbia University Press, 1989).

37. Sigmund Freud, "Contributions to the Psychology of Love," in *Sexuality and the Psychology of Love*, ed. Philip Reiff (New York: Collier Books, 1963), especially 56–57.

38. "Essay on Marriage," 76.

39. See Homas, *Bearing the Word*, 4.

40. Quoted in Marlon Ross, "Romantic Quest and Conquest," 51 n. 17.

41. Mill declined to be the executor of his mother's will and refused (until Taylor convinced him otherwise) to accept his share of the maternal inheritance. Mill seems unable to reach a decision on these matters without consulting his wife. Even more curious is his reluctance to claim his mother's more personal belongings, such as her furniture. See *Correspondence*, 209–211.

42. Quoted in Alan Richardson, "Romanticism and the Colonization of the Feminine," in Mellor, *Romanticism and Feminism*, 20.

43. John Stuart Mill to Thomas Carlyle, 5 October 1833, *Earlier Letters*, in *Collected Works*, 12: 184.

44. Ibid.

45. "Essay on Marriage and Divorce," 68.

46. Ibid.

47. See, for example, Kamm, *John Stuart Mill in Love*, especially chap. 2.

48. Sigmund Freud, "On Narcissism: An Introduction," 100.

49. Quoted in Geoffrey Hartman, "Romanticism and Anti-Self-Consciousness," in *Romanticism and Criticism*, ed. Harold Bloom (New York: W. W. Norton, 1970), 49.

50. Ibid., 53.

51. Ibid.

52. For a critique of the politics of androgyny in romantic thought, see Alan Richardson, "Romanticism and the Colonization of the Feminine," especially 19.

53. "On Narcissism: An Introduction," 101.

◆ KALI A. K. ISRAEL ◆

Style, Strategy, and Self-Creation in the Life of Emilia Dilke

For her . . . the burden and complexity of womanhood were not enough; she must reach beyond the sanctuary and pluck for herself the strange bright fruits of art and knowledge. . . . Thus we behold her, a memorable figure . . . reaching out with "a fastidious yet hungry ambition" for all that life could offer the free and inquiring mind and confronting her feminine aspirations with the real world of men.

—*Virginia Woolf, "George Eliot"*

Memorials and Memories—"Complete and Unique"

After her death in October 1904, Emilia Dilke was memorialized as an "exceptional woman" by a diverse group of mourners.[1] *The Women's Trade Union Review*, the journal of the Women's Trade Union League, grieved as "her colleagues in the work to which she devoted the larger part of her life and the choicest powers of her fine intellect," regretting the loss of "one . . . fitted, as few human beings . . . to fill the post of leader in a crusade against the tyranny of social tradition and the callousness of social indifference." Letters of mourning from dozens of individuals and organizations in the Labour movement followed, interspersed with plans for a memorial fund to support the League's work, and her funeral was attended by representatives of the Trades Union Congress and the Miners' Federation and such trade-union luminaries as Mary Macarthur, Ben Tillett, and Margaret Bondfield. Their testimonials spoke of trade unionism as "[her life's] chief enthusiasm, its ruling aim and purpose."[2]

A year after her death, an anonymous article appeared in the *Quarterly Review*, entitled "The Art-Work of Lady Dilke."[3] The writer intersperses a discussion of Dilke's works of art history with extravagant praise for her as "probably the equal in intellect" to Jane Austen, Macaulay, and Charlotte Brontë, and long laments that Lady Dilke should have spent her energy on anything but the practice of art history. She had "sacrificed precious hours and months of a too brief life to a benevolent mission which might have been fulfilled by others," neglecting her "unique vocation."[4] Her trade-unionist and feminist work was thus considered as an unfortunate distraction from her more exalted intellectual labors. But both organized labor and this admirer of Lady Dilke's art history agreed on one thing—the fullness of the life.

In his account of her last days in his "Memoir" of Lady Dilke,[5] Sir Charles Dilke too conveys an image of a woman of diverse interests and activities, although he does not represent them as conflicting. Virtually on her deathbed, Lady Dilke chats about politics as she opens a letter "from Tokio, thank[ing] her for . . . [her work] for the Japanese wounded, and widows and orphans," then "jot[s] down notes on some tapestries" she had recently seen, referring occasionally to thick volumes of art history. Sir Charles concludes: "My wife had two sides to her intellectual life. . . . I alone shared both lives."[6]

However, unlike those who perceived only one aspect of Lady Dilke, Sir Charles contends that her life was complete and consistent; made up though it was of "two apparently distinct spheres of activity . . . there were those who knew that the two lives were one." Implicit and explicit in Dilke's memoir is an argument that it was this multifaceted wholeness of her work and her "personality" that rendered her so extraordinary. All her activities were marked, he says, by her "overmastering sense of duty, and an unfailing courage—little short of sublime."[7]

In evidence, Charles Dilke offers the plaudits of French friends. "She had it all—beauty, bounty of heart, high intelligence, simplicity. How could anyone not cherish this special woman, so absolutely complete and unique?" Dilke further offers, from one of Lady Dilke's "great friends": "We other women have enough need for forces sufficient for our double burden, that of our task and that of our husbands. You have spent yourself in this mission more than any other."[8] Lady Dilke's greatness, therefore, encompasses her feminine role as wife as well as her activities as a public figure in her own right, and all these tasks are shouldered with grace and accomplished with success.

Obviously, Charles Dilke and his sources rest their claim for the value of Lady Dilke's life and work on her status as a thoroughgoing "exceptional woman." Dilke's "Memoir" mingles tones of love and grief with pride that this rare creature should have loved him, supporting his burdens in addition to her own; his own status becomes that of "exceptional man" by association.[9] But the combined import of his memoir and the testimonials and obituaries of others is to present a somewhat static picture of Emilia Dilke, who was and always had been exceptional, "absolutely complete and unique."

This fixing of the subject into a heroic position is generic to obituaries and family memoirs, but it is particularly jarring in Lady Dilke's case. It is startling both as it conceals a life of nearly ceaseless movement and transformation, and as it reveals to us Emilia Dilke's status as an icon, cultural figure, and image. It is pointless to ask if any of these descriptions of her are "true"; all are partial, even as they claim to represent the wholeness of their subject. Instead, we should question how a Victorian woman of an undistinguished middle-class and provincial background drew such tributes as an icon of fully realized womanhood.

In this essay, I consider Emilia Dilke's earlier years, her girlhood and first marriage, as she struggled to establish an identity and a vocation for herself, and the work she produced. The issues I address arise from the questions: how did a Victorian middle-class woman construct a means of access to knowledge and formal learning? What sort of self did a woman need to create in order to undertake intellectual work, to assemble an intellectual identity, to be "an intellectual"? What is this process of self-creation? Where do we locate the self that creates and the selves that are created? This is unambiguously the story of a woman creating a career for herself, a career that struggled with and drew on Victorian (male) ideas about work, vocation, and self-creation.[10] But ambiguities reside in the meanings of *creation* and *self-fashioning,* and in the relationships between the stories Lady Dilke drew upon, wrote, and lived.

There are vast literatures on Victorian women and on the Victorian theme of "vocation" and a developing literature on the historical creation of identity, which explicate the relationship between the theme of self-creation in Victorian middle-class culture and the specific "selves" created and recreated in/by/of some individual lives.[11] It seems clear that some middle-class Victorian women drew on the representations of female (and male) lives found in novels and other collections of "characters" to (re)make themselves. These arrays of other "selves" could serve as more than static iconic models of positions into which to form the self; the very multiplicity of such representations raised the possibility of constructing a "repertoire," a range of roles, which both constrained and allowed movement.[12] Movement from one role to another might serve strategic (though not necessarily conscious) purposes, historical agency in Joan Scott's sense, "action taken in specific contexts, but not entirely autonomously or without constraint."

As Scott suggests, these actions and their contexts then "create and con-
solidate identities," which themselves contribute to the formation of new
constraints, new discourses, new grounds for narrative and action.[13] These
possibilities and limitations were rendered more dynamic by the fluidity
of the categories of "self" and "character" and by the very category of
"woman" in Victorian culture. The assemblage "female self-creation" is so
volatile precisely *because* each term—woman, self, and creation—is so ambiguous within Victorian bourgeois discourse.

The ability of some women to generate mobility among images does not
amount to freedom nor to a high level of choice *relative to men of their own
class,* nor should movement among fictional and fictionalizing positions be
conflated with the social experiences of occupying multiple and contradictory subject positions. The experience of contradiction in psychic subjectivity and in daily *material* and physical life—and these two levels are
indivisible—was not chosen but *militated* by the contradictions of a classed,
raced, and gendered social and economic order. The sort of movement I
suggest may approximate Teresa de Lauretis's hopeful formulation of "a
gendered and heteronomous subject" who, while "subject-ed to social constraint" is "yet subject in the active sense of maker as well as user of culture,
intent on self-definition and self-determination," but the possibilities of
circulation and change are generated by the very social contradictions that
constitute their limits.[14]

Emilia Dilke's construction and representation of two positions in her
career, first as ultrafeminine wife of a don and then as aspiring intellectual,
display such constrained self-creation. During her childhood, education,
and first marriage, she plotted and enacted three fictions: imagining
marriage as a working partnership; representing herself as an exotic and
fluid Other; and creating a self as an authoritative expert. Rebelling against
the position of decorative or domestic helpmeet to Great Men, she defined
herself as flamboyantly Other than the male intellectual and social model,
while simultaneously creating for herself a role as an autonomous scholar in
pursuit of total knowledge, subversively but dangerously mirroring the
male pattern of learning. In both of these strategies, Lady Dilke's attraction
to Renaissance ideals and nineteenth-century liberal humanism enabled and
thwarted her aspirations to independent vocation and wholeness.

In using such terms as "story" and "plotting," I suggest that Dilke's life,
as much as her work, can fruitfully be seen in terms of narrative, but not
that she possessed a full, Machiavellian consciousness or control of her own
actions and meanings. Her use of multiple narratives allowed her to transform her self in the face of contradiction and impasse, although such movement exacted a price in real pain and generated new contradictions. But her
changes were attempts to deal with problems of forging both an intellectual

identity and an intellectual and social *role* in a society profoundly hostile to independent female intellectual vocation.[15]

Bourgeois women faced a double burden in Victorian plots of self-creation; their needs for identity and for social role are intricately intertwined and placed even women of comparative privilege in a difficult double bind. To fail to achieve a sense of self, identity, and integrated personhood, however fictionalized, was, by the terms of the middle-class *Bildungsroman*, to be a *failed person;* yet the achievement of this sense of coherent individual purpose, vocation, and identity outside of the roles of mother, wife, and sometime muse could only be precarious and unofficial for women. To "succeed" at all laid individual women open to the charge of being *failed women.* This gap between liberal humanist notions of the self and of women was complicated by the almost complete lack of social roles: paid jobs and official positions for independent women. The discursive as well as material power of these dilemmas is illustrated by the inability of the Victorian middle class to conceptualize an *independent, married woman.*

Let us begin by considering Lady Dilke's own retrospective thematicization of her inner development, in an essay of 1897 innocuously and deceptively entitled "The Idealist Movement and Positive Science. An Experience."[16]

"An Incomplete Soul"

This essay, published in *Cosmopolis*, frames and conceals its autobiographical content within a generalized discussion of the problem of conflicts between religious and "scientific" forms of knowledge, specifically in reference to the problem of education and the dilemmas of young people.[17] Dilke begins on a high intellectual and spiritual note, quoting St. Augustine on "the whole duty of the spiritual life," and continues with elevated and general thoughts about the current limits of education, replete with quotations from Heine and Browning. Finally, she introduces the possibility of speaking of her own life, diffidently suggesting "that the experience even of . . . 'an incomplete soul' may have some interest for, or be of some use to, those who share its aspirations and desires."[18]

The woman so widely lauded as complete and fully developed here covertly proclaims herself "an incomplete soul"; this phrase is neither mere rhetoric nor meant only in a theological sense. Rather, it is crucial to understanding Emilia Dilke's sense of her own development and of the costs entailed by her struggles. This phrase not only suggests a continuing journey in the soul's development but also its renunciations and losses. This soul is incomplete not only because it is "unfinished," not only because "identity is a shifting ground, not a permanent accomplishment,"[19] but also because of past *subtractions* from itself. Yet this soul—distanced and presented as an un-sexed "it"—is able to make a claim against isolation by conceiving openly of the existence of others "who share its aspirations and desires."[20] Here is Lady Dilke's reply to the designation of her life as finished, "complete and unique."

After a general discussion of religion versus "science" (read: positivism), in which are buried clues to her own history, Lady Dilke presents "a frag-ment of self-history . . . by one well known to me," in which guise she presents a passage of autobiography.[21] The anonymous "friend" is *male.* Lady Dilke may have felt that this change of gender would not only disguise her own voice but might also lend the story a "wider" significance and weight, taking her "story" beyond the framework of the "Woman Ques-tion" as her audience of the 1890's might conceive it. More disturbingly, this sex change in the speaker, as well as the distancing device of "my friend" hints at the continual problem even for women of recognized and highly public intellectual stature in speaking as experts about their own lives.

Emilia Dilke presents the tale of a young man, brought up in the High Church and deeply religious in his youth. He read widely in "St. Augustine and others of the Fathers" and in the theology of the English Reformation, through which he became interested in ecclesiastical history and developed a historicist conception of religion. Although "his" reading was "directed solely by the desire to find confirmation and support of the principles in which he had been instructed," with no thought of rebellion, his own views "slowly materialised" and "gradually assumed less and less of an emotional character." He gave up church practices but retained the ethical system of Christianity, and was eventually persuaded to Comtism as a system to re-place religion.[22]

Emilia Dilke's own life was not such a story of autonomous intellectual self-development.[23] Born in 1840 in Ilfracombe, Devonshire, to Major Henry Strong and Emily Weedon Strong, she was baptized Emily Francis and known as Francis (the masculine spelling of Francis, after her god-father, was deliberately retained and emphasized). Her father was a retired army officer; his family background was to some extent "American," as his father had settled as a colonist in Georgia, but the Strongs were loyalists during the American Revolution and returned to Britain.[24] After serving in India for sixteen years, Henry Strong eventually became manager of the London and County Bank in Oxford, and Francis grew up in Iffley, south of Oxford on the Thames. Little is known of Emily Weedon but that she was younger than Henry, was intensely religious in a respectable High Church way, and was somewhat appalled by her daughter's independence, both in Francis's artistic pursuits and in her eventual Puseyite religious fervor.[25]

Francis was educated at home by a governess, Miss Bowdich, and by contact with Oxford society. Miss Bowdich was very well educated for a private governess of her time, teaching Francis Latin and Greek as well as French and the rudiments of German, a linguistic education quite exceptional for women in the 1850s. Gertrude Tuckwell later described Miss Bowdich as "a darling old lady," very devout and gentle, by no means a "strong-minded" woman except in her intellectual reach. Francis was educated with her two younger sisters, Marian and Ethel; all learned history, geography, arithmetic, and probably modern languages, but only Francis studied classics.[26] According to Charles Dilke, Miss Bowdich was not in great sympathy with Francis's artistic leanings because she did not feel confident to teach her. Dilke also claims an absence of strong family tendencies toward art in his wife's family, but it is clear that her father was encouraging; an amateur artist who exhibited locally and in an amateur exhibition in London, he was involved in Oxford "artistic" society and apparently proud of his daughter's skill.[27]

As a young girl, Francis was a favorite of several Oxford families like that of Dr. Henry Acland; her position as a young, pretty, and bright "pet" in the liberal society connected with the university may have given her a deceptive sense of the place for women in Oxford society. Eleanor Smith, an intimate of the Aclands and a widely respected and formidable bluestocking, would later become her closest confidante. More important in her childhood and youth was Acland's sponsorship in her studies of drawing; through him, she was brought to the attention of Ruskin, who admired her drawings from the Ashmolean casts. At the urging of Acland and Ruskin, who impressed upon her the importance of anatomical studies, she prevailed upon her parents to allow her to study art in London at South Kensington Art School, beginning at the age of nineteen.[28]

In London, she associated with amateur and professional artists, both Academicians and members of the Pre-Raphaelite Brotherhood; she was a frequent guest at Little Holland House, where she was a favorite of Watts. In this milieu, Francis Strong began to engage in a style of self-representation which would continue during her first marriage. She dressed in clothing modeled on the Italian Renaissance, in rich colors and odd designs, and she was addressed by Watts and others as "Francesca."[29] Also during this period, she first became friends with George Eliot, and after Francis's marriage the intimacy of the two women was marked by letters addressed "Madre" and "Figliuolina."[30] Obviously, this self-dramatization, a rather tame blend of romantic Italianism and bohemian artiness, was not unusual in the Little Holland House set, but for women it offered unusual opportunities for experimentation and fluidity in self-presentation.

During these years she remained devoutly religious, disturbingly so to some of her fellow students, including the young Charles Dilke, but, as the *Dictionary of National Biography* inimitably phrased it, "At the same time her youthful spirits ran high and her outlook on life betrayed independence,"[31] an independence most notably displayed by Francis's successful demands to be allowed to draw from the nude, a highly prestigious element of art education almost universally denied women. Living and moving independently and engaging in a lively social life, Francis Strong seems a "new woman" before her time,[32] The sole discordant element in this picture was her intense religiosity and the extremity of her conception of the duty of self-mortification, drawing upon the intense religious drama of Tractarianism. Charles Dilke is at some pains to stress that Francis's religious ideas were themselves a kind of rebellion into penitence, renunciation, and spiritual purpose; but her Puseyism struck him and other friends at South Kensington then as oddly fanatical and incongruous in one otherwise high-spirited, fun-loving, and contemptuous of the dicta of feminine decorum.[33] But neither rebelliousness nor religiosity could resolve the ambiguity of the future for a young woman of her talent and temperament.

Enforced Courses: Work and Marriage

In "The Idealist Movement and Positive Science," Lady Dilke moves smoothly from her "friend's" early education and loss of religious faith to his embrace of positivism, with no discussion of external events in his life. She constructs a continuity for his intellectual and emotional development: "[T]he fulfillment of . . . [Comtist principles] demanded too a self-abnegation as complete as that exacted by the 'Imitatio Christi.' "[34] In the "friend's" intellectual and spiritual development, only his own mind and decisions determine and necessitate this self-abnegation. In Francis Strong's life, external events, although of her own choosing, intervened decisively to precipitate this move to Comtism. On 10 September 1861, she married Mark Pattison.

Pattison had become Rector of Lincoln College, Oxford, in January 1861; though a clergyman, he was among the few Oxford dons allowed to marry.[35] Francis Strong thus became part of an early generation of faculty wives, a position very different from that of the bright young daughter of a local family or that of the occasional "bluestocking" on the fringes of Oxford intellectual society.[36] Her position was anomalous and somewhat perilous in any case, but it was rendered more difficult by two factors—her own personality and Mark Pattison's.

At the time of their marriage, Francis Strong was twenty-one; Mark Pattison was forty-eight and prematurely aged.[37] As his *Memoirs* both reveal and conceal, he had suffered through an appalling childhood and difficulties with colleagues at Oxford; considered in light of the history of his marriage, his own rebellion against the rigidly patriarchal structure of his father's house was ultimately unsuccessful, as he himself became a less powerful shadow of his tyrannical—and ultimately mad—father. The eldest of thirteen children, eleven of whom were girls, Mark had dominated within his family both by masculine privilege and by his access to learning. In a series of relationships with his sisters, he had accepted their affection in return for his advice and admonitions on their need to educate themselves; however, these relationships splintered each time one of the sisters failed to meet Mark's need for undivided loyalty. Exacerbated by the violent deterioration of his father's sanity and his mother's physical health, Mark felt for the women of his family love, contempt, guilt, rage, and disappointment. Wounded by other betrayals in Oxford, Mark Pattison's intellectual brilliance was shadowed, and he was notorious throughout Oxford for his miserliness, bitter wit, dourness, self-pity, and quickness to rage, although he was also, especially with women, capable of enormous charm and emotional eloquence. Tellingly, in his *Memoirs* he was to lament the loss of his Yorkshire childhood's "cosy and patriarchal life . . . where I never saw any one but my father and sisters . . . more pleasant to me than the society of my equals."[38]

Above all, Mark Pattison was a formidable intellect; he described his life as one devoted entirely to learning. His own loss of religious faith and turn to historicism and positivism was quickly reproduced in Francis Strong Pattison. She clearly did not feel herself liberated by this turn away from the Christian church. Rather, as the "fragment of self-history" reveals, Comtism matched the "Imitatio Christi" as a bulwark for those "under the impression of the paramount moral obligation of self-sacrifice. The determination, therefore, to work out the Comtist system in daily life brought no change into [my] conception of the standard of duty."[39]

The marriage puzzled contemporaries and may still baffle, especially given the lack of information about their brief "courtship." But "The Idealist Movement" guardedly and cryptically suggests some of the reasons that the independent Francis Strong should become a don's wife, and the wife of a don both charismatic and controlling. Lady Dilke writes with deceptive generalities of those "in whom a very real desire to learn truth, and be true to it, co-exists with the weakness of wishing to be thought advanced." Marriage into Oxford represented access to the intellectual life of the day, while marriage to one of the notorious contributors to *Essays and Reviews*, certainly might have appeared a path to the latest, most enlightened thought.[40] Francis Strong's sense of the difficulty of achieving a social role as a woman artist may have left her adrift and somewhat frightened by her "exceptional" status as a young woman with no socially defined future outside of marriage.

In this light, we might look at this marriage as a half-consciously adopted strategy toward unclear goals. Continuing as a young woman alone in London and Oxford seems not to have been an alternative for Francis Strong, perhaps because of family pressures, perhaps because of her own fears about the marginality of such a situation. Her family, especially her father, were quite extraordinarily supportive of her goals *as a young art student,* but some limit may have been reached as she approached age twenty-one.

In a very early fragment, probably written upon her sister Rosa's marriage in the early 1850s, Francis Strong expressed her wish "to be humble and quiet . . . & a comfort to you & Mama instead of a trouble."[41] She seems not to have fully succeeded in these aims during her adolescence, but in her marriage, Francis may have followed Rosa's lead. To Francis, Rosa was both an example of proper decorum, obedience, humility, and quiet and an illustration of the limits of family permissiveness. Rosa was herself both beautiful and talented as a young girl. She studied voice with "Torriglioni" *away from her family* in Jersey; her teacher apparently wanted her to become a professional singer, but Henry and Emily Weedon Strong would not allow it. The limit of a good daughter's artistic self-development was the point at which the possibility of public performance was broached. Rosa's examples were probably important in providing Francis with images of female self-development and self-abnegation, and even of marriage to a scholarly cleric, one with whom "it was sometimes an effort [for her] to keep pace" in intellectual matters.[42] It was to Rosa that Francis Strong wrote poignantly, shortly after her engagement, "My own dear sister . . . I feel now as if I loved & knew more of you than I ever thought possible to me I don't know how it was but what an Ishmaeliteish position I always held at home and amongst my nearest relatives during my vacations from London."[43]

Although bright and gifted, Francis Strong doubted her potential to be a serious artist, and even women who sought such a career faced nearly insuperable obstacles.[44] Most marriageable men might well have looked like depressing prospects; the most obvious candidates would have been members of the "squirearchy," and men of her father's class: middle-level professionals, army officers, or the provincial clergy. None of these groups were likely to offer husbands who would support their wives' intellectual aspirations or social and political concerns. Against a backdrop of these men, Oxford dons could well have looked more appealing, as they claimed to value learning and the life of the mind, and Mark Pattison, like George Butler and Henry Fawcett, was avowedly liberal and a supporter of women's education.

Writing of her "friend," Lady Dilke in "The Idealist Movement" observed, "There is a critical moment, when the mind gains consciousness of its own independence, and the growing activity of the reasoning powers begins to cause a not unnatural distrust of the emotional impulses, so that their leading is questioned and rejected."[45] And one marries Mark Pattison? Pattison in abstract might have been a rational option, a path to intellectual fulfillment and participation in society. Emilia Dilke seems to imply, thirty years later, that she married Pattison in an almost ascetic turn to the life of the mind, with a belief that hers would be a marriage, if not of equals, at least one of partnership and personal intellectual growth. She envisioned a marriage of minds, with scarcely a thought of the body. In the abstract, this strategy seems plausible; however, Pattison in the flesh and Oxford in daily life represented an ever-increasing demand for self-abnegation, service to men of intellect, and marginality in social settings. But if Francis Strong had "emotional impulses" against this marriage, she overrode them.

Mark Pattison was the author of a volume on Milton, and his expectations of his wife's role in his intellectual work, although always ambivalent, was not unpredictable. He certainly encouraged, even required, that she should work diligently at her own studies; he assisted her in her Greek and Latin and guided her reading in theology and philosophy. However, he expected her principal concern to be his work, his household, and his health. Although proud of her progress and "cleverness," he became increasingly angry with her intellectual independence, separate social and intellectual milieu of "bohemian" artist friends, and willingness to spend time away from him, pursuing her own researches. Three novels that stand in some relationship to the Pattison marriage, George Eliot's *Middlemarch*, Rhoda Broughton's *Belinda*, and Robert Liddell's *The Almond Tree*, occultly memorialize this aspect of the Pattison menage by depicting the young wives of elderly scholars who are expected, after their husbands' deaths, to complete the scholars' work along lines established by the husbands.[46]

In Lady Dilke's own later fiction, the older husband is not a scholar but a doctor-scientist who marries a naïve young girl. "The Physician's Wife" was published in 1886, two years after Pattison's death, but was written earlier.[47] Lady Dilke describes the early days of this marriage, and the character of the old man:

> [A]t first she was not ill-pleased to watch the wonders of his laboratory, and . . . to do his errands; but gradually her gaiety forsook her, and her life grew irksome to her. . . . Now, in the sight of this man, Science, pursued for her own sake, was the one absolute good, and dwelling much with his own thought he had come to be uplifted with zeal, believing that in truth science had yielded to him the deepest secrets of nature, and that he was thus marked out from all other men. . . . So it came to pass, that whilst he himself worshipped Science as the true principle and lamp of life, he demanded of all those

who approached him the recognition in him of that deity which, so to speak, should be revealed to them in his person.[48]

Early in the Pattison marriage, Francis placed herself under Mark's tuition, rightly perceiving him as far more learned than herself, and perhaps not yet seeing the need for control which infected all of his relationships with young women.[49] Francis began both by assisting Mark in his own work on the Reformation and on the rise of philology, aiding his research during their honeymoon in Vienna, and by undertaking semi-independent studies under his direction. Charles Dilke gives a chilling description: "There was no personal resistance to the influence over her of her husband. His mind and learning deserved the surrender of the educational direction of a young girl, however gifted, to his mental and philosophical control, and he obtained it. Although full of love of personal liberty, she had an unusually disciplined reverence for Authority as represented by those she thought really competent in ability and learning."[50] As Francis Pattison later wrote that this reverence for "Authority" extended to all aspects of her marriage; of her difficulty in disagreeing with even Mark's wildest allegations about her motives and desires, she confided in Eleanor Smith, "[I]t does get worse—" & I *do* think the more blame one takes to oneself (wh[ich] is what I've been always doing for the sake of peace) the worse he gets. I think it is better for him that I had never gone on that line but I was too young [to] not feel somehow guilty whenever a person so much my superior in every way chose to think so."[51]

This reverence for authority was increased, as we have seen, by her "conversion" to positivism, which claimed the status of science, and its ethical standards, which virtually prohibited self-definition and rebellion against Mark Pattison. "The Physician's Wife" presents the doctor's conflation of "Science" and his self; he "deem[ed] that he saw all men truly and all things truly, since, his passions [were] wholly drawn into the service of Science." Further, in the early days of the marriage, the doctor overcame his wife's misgivings by being "merciful"; "by his wonderful tongue, he so charmed her ears that she, believing the melancholy which arose in her to be sinful, fought with herself, striving to put the passion of her balked desires into the daily services demanded of her. Her nature was, however, too strong for her will, and her life became very bitter to her."[52] As represented here, the husband's authority was not merely legal and intellectual, but "scientific," and, as a science was granted all the authority of religion, rebellion was both wrong and sinful. But, Charles Dilke argues, "[Mrs. Pattison] kept, however, an imaginative side and part of life, in which Mark Pattison was hardly allowed to share."[53] However cynically we might assess Dilke's motives, as he implies that *he* shared her life more fully, his assertion is verified by a consideration of Francis Pattison's life at Oxford. She continued to draw and paint, but, more important, she maintained contact with friends from London, including George Eliot, to whom she guardedly suggested the emotional struggles she endured in submitting to Oxford and the rigidity of her marriage.

Mark Pattison made one fatal error if his conscious aim was to control and harness his young wife's intellectual energies; he advised her to choose her own subject for study, a field on which she would become an authority.[54] Mark Pattison was immersed in the Reformation and the history of formal learning, religion, and classical scholarship, and he modeled himself on his vision of German scholarship; Francis, however, chose the Renaissance and the history of art, especially in relationship to the organization of politics and culture, and immersed herself in the history and culture of France.[55] By defining her interests, in several senses, as different from his, Francis Pattison opened a space for her own authority; echoing Mark Pattison's endless insistence on the importance of knowledge, study, and research, she could both justify leaving Oxford and refuse to subordinate her work to his own.

This establishment of a semi-independent intellectual life did not resolve Francis Pattison's problems. Rather, she also enacted other strategies to define and create herself as an intellectual woman and an active participant in society, distinguishing herself from the bluestocking wife of a Great(er) Man. Indeed, "The Idealist Movement" implies that this immersion in learning, insofar as it was an accommodation to Mark Pattison's standards of learning and knowledge, was insufficient to sustain her self-identification as independent and different. It in no way solved the problems of creating a real and valued role for her in the larger society.

In "The Idealist Movement," we find Emilia Dilke's embittered memories of this period, which focus the issue of the difference between work and vocation; she saw her life as one of toil without satisfaction or meaning:

> I began to be aware, as my powers and character matured, that my whole nature fought against the self-imposed yoke. I became aware of an intense desire for the enjoyment of life—not in any limited or common sense, but a desire for knowledge and experience in every direction, utterly incompatible with the ideal of entire self-renunciation . . . ; but I regarded the protest of my own nature as immoral, and strove yet more earnestly to suppress it. Casting about for help in the path which appeared to me hateful, but right, I sought to cheat myself by forcing the very passion with which I desired other things into the one outlet that I believed to be authorised, carrying this so far as to feign pleasure in these enforced courses.[56]

The strains she endured, attempting to live by an ethical code that demanded extremes of self-abnegation and conformity with the demands of her husband, the enforcer of those courses, are evident. In "The Physician's Wife," the young wife tries to conceal her pain from the frankly sadistic eyes of her husband; "there was now bred in her the cowardice of the slave, so she gave no outward sign, though her *rage* and her anguish became greater with each day."[57]

Emilia Dilke looked back on this part of her life with memories of "the horror of the monotony, the narrowness and pressure of my immediate surroundings . . . and when I sought to put away the horror as a mood truly sinful, it would return with redoubled force. Then it would seem to me as if all the capacity for pleasure, all the energy which prompted me to ask for the widest possibilities of life, were tied and bound as with chains." Images of confinement and tyrannical authority multiply, conjoined with her own intense sense of guilt. It was not only the dynamics of a bad marriage but of a whole social code that bound her, inflecting her predicament with gendered meanings. Francis Pattison was indeed caged by male authority—that of religion and its Comtist guise, that of her husband, and that of the masculine academic power, authority, and sterility that Oxford represented and embodied; it was no wonder that she saw no escape. As she wrote later, her life was ordered by the pattern of the "Imitatio Christi"; she only eventually saw that this book "fails us as soon as the sense of duty to oneself comes to form a part of one's conception of duty to others."[58] This notion was to become the central concept in Francis Pattison's development away from Oxford.

This move away depended on the development of a sense of intellectual and vocational selfhood in the world, which would necessarily take time to develop. During these years of learning and struggle and gradual self-education, during the 1860s especially, Francis Pattison also employed a more dramatic technique for self-preservation and re-creation, one that harkened back to her student days and made her a peculiarly individual figure in Oxford society.

French Femininity on the Isis

[I]n France alone woman has had a vital influence on the development of literature. . . . The women whose tact, wit, and personal radiance created the atmosphere of the Salon, where literature, philosophy, and science, emancipated from the trammels of pedantry and technicality, entered on a brighter stage of existence.

—*George Eliot, "Woman in France: Madame de Sablé"*

Residents of Oxford during the 1860s and early 1870s were far less likely to discuss in their memoirs and memories Francis Pattison's hours of study than to remember, dazedly, the impression she created in Oxford social life. As the wife of the Rector of Lincoln, she was necessarily a social leader of sorts, but her status was not at all defined by her participation in parish teas or calls on other marginalized women. Rather, Francis Pattison created something new at Oxford, a social life that encompassed both Mark Pattison's friends and her own, including scholars and artists of the day. She developed, much to the chagrin of Oxford traditionalists, a salon of sorts and offended many dons with the deliberate introduction of a more "feminine" style into the staid university, but a femininity, like that of earlier *salonières* coupled with intellect and high culture.[59] Mrs. Pattison deliberately meant to counter the sterility of Oxford's scholarly masculinity, and her parties emphasized to traditionalists the changing social conditions around them. Mrs. Pattison was neither a desexualized bluestocking nor an acceptably matronly academic wife.[60] Her salon, therefore, emphasized both the new heterosexuality of Oxford society and the changing position of women in Britain as a whole; her ominous activities for women's suffrage and university education only made matters worse.[61]

Mark Pattison's views on these activities seem to have been mixed at best, although he enjoyed enacting the role of glowering intellectual and his access to young people, especially young women, whom he quizzed and implored to develop their minds.[62] But her salon was attractive to many younger men, and it marked the increasing integration of Oxford and London intellectual society. Francis Pattison's defiant self-creation as a *salonière* was only partially successful as a strategy to refuse the dictates of Oxford male society, its own perils entangled with its subversive quality. Defying Oxford, she represented herself as the apotheosis of gendered behavior, the exotic, flamboyantly feminine, and disturbingly artificial Other.

Mary Arnold (later Mrs. Humphrey Ward) wrote in her memoirs of the vivid impression made upon her by both of the Pattisons:

> I was much at Lincoln in the years before I married, and derived an impression from the life lived there that has never left me. . . . From 1868 to 1872, the Rector, learned, critical, bitter, fastidious, and "Mrs Pat", with her gaiety, her picturesqueness, her impatience of the Oxford solemnities and decorums, her sharp restless wit, her determination *not* to be academic, to hold on to the greater world of affairs outside—mattered more to me perhaps than anybody else.[63]

Mark Pattison was one of the most perfect embodiments of the "academic" style Oxford ever produced. He saw his whole life as entirely a story of the pursuit of learning, but Francis Pattison's intellectual ambitions were less confident and less easily accommodated within the male model of the university. Mark Pattison's vaunted Germanic "universal knowledge," though desirable to her, both in theory and practice, excluded women trapped between social convention and desire. Francis's desire to create at Oxford an atmosphere both intellectual and social prefigures her attempts to recast the intellectual and political connections of art and social life.

The difference in the Pattisons's ages was emphasized by their personal styles. Francis was considered extremely beautiful, and she was very close in age to many of the young men she entertained; her "salon" allowed her a respectable way of maintaining contact with young men of similar interests while she tested the boundaries of decorum for married women. In a possibly apocryphal story an undergraduate of Lincoln arrived late at breakfast, proffering the excuse, "Sorry I'm late . . . but I've been to the gym, watching Mrs. P learn fencing to polish off her husband."[64] This combination of athleticism, youthful high spirits, and high intellectual standards made her salon intriguing; Taine was staggered by her youth and vivacity during his visit to Oxford and wrote admiringly of her as "le 'leading light' de la société féminine d'Oxford," and recalled her startling youth as she stood against an old stone wall, her expression "presque mutin."[65] She drew young men apart to share her French cigarettes under the starlight in cosy tête-à-têtes in the College gardens.[66] Richard Claverhouse Jebb captures her scandalous charm:

> [Mrs Pattison] is difficult to describe. . . . She is very clever: she has tenderness; great courage; and an exquisite sense of humour. In manner she is inclined to be brusque, though, by that instinct which women of a fine strain never lose under any vagary, she never fails in perfect taste; she is joyous, and affects a certain specially Oxford type of feminine fastness, which it would take too long to define, except by saying it is based upon the jocose ease of cultivated youths;—she talks of art and books and philosophies,—yet rather about them than of them;—but to any one who can clearly see her whole nature in one view, she is most captivating. . . . We have just been sitting in the open air in the court, under the starlight, and Mrs Pattison and I have been smoking her particular cigarettes—made for her in Paris by somebody. She is a connoisseur.[67]

Despite her own later writings describing her pain and frustration, and the eventual collapse of her health in 1869, the contemporary testimony describes Francis Pattison's vivacity, dedication to work, and, above all, her development of a personal style to mirror her interests in art and France.[68]

It is possible to summarize this personal style by examining a painting of Mrs. Pattison done by her friend Lady Pauline Trevelyan in 1864.[69] Mrs. Pattison is shown painting a panel of sunflowers for the circular atrium of the Trevelyan house at Wallington. The gold of the sunflowers matches her hair, which is in an intricate braid around her face and loose down her back.

She is wearing a Renaissance style dress of green brocade, seated with a curtain half-drawn to reveal her. Both the dress and the curtain are strewn with gold fleur-de-lys, emblematic of her work in French art.[70] This portrait was, according to Charles Dilke, among the most faithful pictures of his wife, although modified in accordance with Pre-Raphaelite standards of beauty. Dilke quotes J. E. C. Bodley that "her exterior aspect was not that which is popularly associated with the bluestocking . . . she seemed to impart a reminiscence of the canvas of Boucher and Van Loo, which she celebrated as the types of the *Grand siècle* when the highest forms of feminine intelligence were not yet divorced from exterior signs of feminine grace."[71]

Mary Arnold described both her own impression and that of George Eliot on seeing Mrs. Pattison at Oxford:

> [S]uddenly at one of the upper windows [of Lincoln] appeared the head and shoulders of Mrs Pattison, as she looked out and beckoned smiling to Mrs Lewes. It was a brilliant apparition as though a French painting by Greuze or Perroneau had suddenly slipped into a vacant space in the old college wall. The pale pretty head blonde cendrée; the delicate smiling features and white throat, a touch of black, a touch of blue, a general 18th century impression as though of powder and patches. Mrs Lewes perceived it instantly.[72]

These impressions of Frenchness and of an aristocratic bearing which conflicted with Oxford middle-class convention are repeated in other reminiscences, although the painters vary. Emilia Dilke seems to have settled on a Renaissance style after having experimented with other periods, and she remained willing to vary her style. A vivid portrayal of a more modern look appears in Stephen Gwynn's description of the dying Mark Pattison in Oxford,

> drawn in a bath-chair by a shambling menial, lying more like a corpse than any living thing I have ever seen. And yet there was a singular vitality behind that parchment covered face: something powerful and repellent. Beside him walked his wife, small, erect, and ultra Parisian, all in black with a black parasol—I did not know then how often Frenchwomen thus enhanced the brilliance of a personality: still less did I know how few but Frenchwomen could do it. But there . . . was the gift of style. . . . [H]er presence conveyed detachment for her convoy with an emphasis that absence alone could never have given.[73]

This "French" style must be understood in the larger context of the social and sexual subtexts of "Frenchness" in mid-Victorian England. Those who commented upon it, including her second husband, knew Mrs. Pattison was already becoming an authority on French art and architecture, and they associate her personal style with her identity as an art historian; however, this is not simply an elision of self with object of study.[74] It also served to make even more vivid and apparent to observers her sense of difference and detachment from the world around her, as Gwynn astutely perceived. Mrs. Pattison found Oxford stifling, later referring to it as "that hole," and neither her salon nor her scholarly work could reconcile her to it.[75]

Her artistic self-presentation did more than suggest a need to mark her difference from her surroundings; it drew attention to her gender. Unmistakably "feminine," her style made it impossible for observers to "erase" her sex in dealing with her intellectuality. Rejecting any grudging tolerance of masculinized and caricatured "bluestockings," Mrs. Pattison focused attention on her fashionableness, her unconventionality, her body, and its feminine masquerades. By choosing a French style in particular, Francis Pattison played off the English associations of Frenchness with sexuality in an already sexually charged and volatile social setting. Hellenism was also a flourishingly outré and sexually meaningful form of theatrical self-presentation, desirable to Francis Strong, but off-limits for women.[76] Specifically male and laden with "perverse" subtexts, it presented problems for historical identification for women. But a woman could turn to the French past and find other sexed and gendered alternatives to Oxford monasticism. Exploiting the outlandishness of her status as a woman of intellect and politics in Oxford, Francis Pattison camped femininity to undercut the fixity of sex. She may have provoked outrage by assuming a vivid yet fluid gender/sexual identity, but she made herself mobile and she fascinated. Emphasizing her gender in elaborately "artistic" dress and manner, she covertly suggested that gender itself is a matter of act and artifice, of convention, aesthetics, and perception.

Above all, Francis Pattison's costuming and enactments blur the boundaries between her positions as an artistic creator, art object, and professional scholar and commentator on artistic subjects, an elision which drastically undercuts positivist epistomologies in general and fixed gender identities in particular. Her style asserted the Renaissance possibility of "making one's life into a work of art,"[77] the possibility of control even in the impossibility of freedom. This almost-Foucauldian gesture may be self-delusive, but the self that deludes, the self that is fooled, and the self that is presented as if to delude others cannot be separated and stabilized. The fiction of control, of self-creation, cannot be opposed to a nonfictional, essential inner self. The body and mind that Mrs. Pattison (re)presented in the fancy dress of French femininity could not exist "outside" of masquerade, although the masks might vary.[78] There was no way out of representation, of being read, but the deployment of the self in multiple texts might well help create a way out of Oxford.

Francis Pattison's simultaneous self-shaping as an autonomous intellectual also drew on her understanding of past cultures, including the forbidden Greek and the liberatory and transgressive themes they might embody. Indeed, Francis Pattison's turn to the Renaissance can be seen as a way of combining classicism with religious studies.[79] In the continental Renaissance she found ideas and inspirations in her rebellion against Mark Pattison and Oxford and legitimation of her quest for female self-creation. These ideas mediated her movement from life as a trapped wife whose self-representation was as a scintillating but dependent cultural object to a new role as a cultural authority.

Authority and Expertise: The Exceptional Woman and Total Knowledge

Lady Dilke covertly and obliquely wrote the story of her turn to the Renaissance in "The Idealist Movement." Her "friend" came to the Renaissance through study of the Reformation and embraced "the Aristotelian conception of the satisfaction of all the energies as offering a complete and splendid theory of life." Emilia Dilke continued:

> To conceive of such a theory . . . was to conceive of a justification of revolt. It was light in the darkness . . . it seemed to him as if a true man should demand, as of right, all pleasure, all knowledge, life at full stretch between morn and night. "The system," he says, "of which I felt the wheels grinding all around me . . . added to my intolerance. I appeared to myself to have been robbed, to have robbed myself, of life. . . . It was something so new to one such as I, to recognise that the individual had rights, had a right to live in the development of his own nature, to satisfy his own aspirations, to possess himself.[80]

This fiery sense of revolt that the Renaissance validated did not lead Mrs. Pattison out of her marriage and Oxford and into a free life. Rather, her discovery of the Renaissance had the opposite effect at first, as she buried herself deeper in study. But in the Renaissance, Francis Pattison found a model for the inclusive intellect, which lived in the world even as it engaged in intellectual work, and an image of the search for complex and total knowledge which included reason, culture, emotion, intuition, and movement, a model of learning which might include women among its subjects and its objects. Failure to achieve this model's goals would not diminish the grandiosity of her ambition to make herself a *donna universala*.

Emilia Dilke's work on French art extended from the fifteenth century to 1800; at the time of her death she was contemplating a volume on the nineteenth century. Her linguistic and historical range was astonishing, and she assumed substantial historical knowledge on the part of her reader. As Colin Eisler notes, "To this day, no other scholar can be said to have been so profoundly cognizant of five hundred years of French art as this English-woman, who was largely self-educated in the fields of her professional activity."[81] Frequently reiterated are the two convictions that informed her entire oeuvre: that the development of art should be considered in all of its aspects and in a social and historical context; and that art and morality are separate matters and should not be conflated.

Many mid- to late-century scholars were attempting to historicize art, but Dilke was bold in making explicit connections between the organization of social and economic forms and the state of the arts through exhaustive research into the material culture and political relations of an era. She studied the work of art (in the double sense of the object and the process of its making) in secular, material, and public settings that included women as makers and thinkers as well as images. She insisted that the art of an age be considered in all of its aspects. A study of painting should also consider the development of sculpture, furniture, decoration, architecture, and other aspects of artistic and "craft" endeavors. This encyclopedic ambition reflected both her aspiration to complete knowledge and her conviction that change in the arts was profoundly related to changes in the social order. "The aesthetic perceptions adjust themself with sensitive instinct to find the means of translating" the new "moral aspect of things into corresponding aspects of colour and of form."[82] She grounded these moral developments in a social and materialist analysis of the relations of economics, power, and the state to the development of culture.

In her historical and critical separation of matters of aesthetics from morality and ethics, Lady Dilke broke from one dominant tendency in Victorian art history, advocated by her mentor, Ruskin. Reviewing Ruskin's *Lectures on Art*, she states forcefully her position:

> Art itself is neither religious nor irreligious; moral nor immoral; useful nor useless; if she is interpreted in any one of these senses by the beholder, is she to bear the blame? Not one of these qualities are essential to find art, and as to perfecting the ethical state, that by means of art comes to pass, not by "direction of purpose", but by her constant presence indirectly refining our perceptions, and rendering them more delicate and susceptible.[83]

Lady Dilke here "splits" art and intellectual work from historically grounded conventions. She fears enslaving "art" and the "individual" to transient convention. Art ought not be directly didactic, but educative of the self, perhaps feminizing as it renders one "delicate and susceptible," yet liberating one from convention into (masculine) agency. The Renaissance individual whom she posited as the model for human development, like the aesthetic ideal of contemporary Hellenism, is ambiguous both in its gender and its relation to history.[84]

Although she agreed with Ruskin that a just society might produce great art, she lacked his optimism and denounced his vision of utopia as a "Social Science Association Arcadia."[85] While art history should include not only all aspects of the arts but also the social development in which they occurred, context should not determine the judgment of the art itself. Asserting that "art . . . is only truly herself in giving pleasure," Lady Dilke wanted to save her own pleasure in art and to combine that desire with full knowledge of social misery and injustice. In her life, she united such pleasure with knowledge and action in the social sphere. In her historical practice, this balance was less easily achieved. For example, she connected her criticisms of French painting of the *grand siècle* to corrupt social and political conditions, oscillating between Ruskinian social analysis and pure aestheticism.

In her *Art in the Modern State* (1888), Emilia Dilke provides a history of the Académie Royale in the seventeenth century. Her central thesis is that under Richelieu and Colbert we find the genesis of "modern political and social organization," in so far as "all the disturbing complexities of our present economical situation were formulated and constructively dealt with by the rulers of France in 'the grand siècle.'" Lady Dilke did not approve of all these "constructive" solutions but argued that they are historically comprehensible. Ultimately, however, the development of the absolute state in France was both destructive to individual liberty and damaging to the development of the arts. She emphasizes the social creation of art and the power of political conditions, but above all stresses the damage to the creative individual, faced with obstacles and temptations that society ought not create. The Renaissance is constantly invoked as a lost moment of possibility, tragically foreshortened.[86]

As a history of patronage and the creation and maintenance of images by powerful institutions, Colin Eisler characterizes this work as a "brilliant" study of "what lurks beneath the surface of art, a study of the use by power of seduction and display."[87] Dilke traces the effects of the institutionalization and commoditization of "high" culture. She praises some artists, notably Claude and Poussin, and does not derogate the skill of others, but above all she denounces the use of art as propaganda in the service of Louis xiv and his court as a betrayal of the Renaissance. In the *grand siècle,* she found

Nothing but little pictures, mean thoughts, frivolous compositions, "propres au boudoir d'un petit maitre, faires pour des petits abbés, des petits robins, des gros financiers ou autres personnages sans moeurs et d'un petit goût"! We have stepped from the great stage to the puppet show . . . and to these charming littlenesses, prettinesses, emptinesses which make up the glorified upholstery of Boucher, of Baudoin, or Fragonard. . . . Brilliant, indeed, were many of these men; all too fascinating the idylls of their theatrical Arcadia, the powdered charms of their voluptuous nymphs; Yet, looking back, we see the elder days were other.[88]

This denunciation of the influence of the market on art in seventeenth-century France may reflect on similar practices in nineteenth-century Britain; both "bourgeois" periods are tacitly and explicitly juxtaposed to Dilke's idealized Renaissance.[89] Certainly contemporary paintings never drew the warmth of her responses to Renaissance art. But in reviewing the early Impressionists, her quite negative comments seem at least interested, as she saw in Manet and others a difference, an attempt to break from a sterile tradition; however alien she found their work, she believed that "it is . . . to them that the future belongs."[90]

The future held everything: art and "democracy." The Renaissance was crucial because it had "transferred art from the service of religion to that of the Prince—an idealized conception of man . . . [it] has formed the bridge needed to cross the gulf between faith in the unknown and service to the known."[91] The Renaissance had been eclipsed and suppressed because it had "failed to obtain social and political expression" and the individual was reduced by "arbitrary government," but "now for the last hundred years the protest against the suppression of the Renaissance has been gathering strength. To fight against it is as irrational as to become its fanatical apologist; it requires neither advocacy nor apology, it is an inevitable transformation—an historical evolution."[92]

Appraisals

Emilia Dilke succeeded in achieving wide knowledge, beyond most of the scholarly patterns of her day; her work also included consideration of women artists and issues of social organization that directly affected women. She became an "authority" on art and culture, transcending by manipulating the narratives of her time. But the end of the story was not an utterly integrated identity; those disparate obituaries return to haunt us. Could one really live out a Renaissance alone? What about women for whom the future, the full new Renaissance, could only come too late?

Lady Dilke wrote, during the composition of her first volume of art history:

All depends on whether one can keep [contemporary political and economic questions] in relation to the whole of life. One cannot write these chapters of modern history without trying to form one's own opinion on the questions of the day, and that inspires one with the wish to try at least to find the bond which must exist somewhere between the fine arts themselves and the current of national life. So it seems to me that even the little bit of work one tries to do one's self must gain in value.[93]

Here is Lady Dilke in control of multiple intellectual activities, asserting the value of even the attempt to encompass contemporary politics and Renaissance art. At other times, a more despairing tone appears, acknowledging the confines of gender. Responding to a friend's concern that her art historical work suffered because of the energy she spent on other activities, she replied:

Yet I gain something. Ordinary life widens the horizon for men. Women are walled in behind social conventions. If they climb over, they lose more than they gain. It is therefore necessary to accept the situation as nature and society have made it, and to try to create for one's self a position from which *on peut dominer ce qu'on ne peut pas franchir.* [One can dominate (or look over) what one cannot pass through.][94]

This passage is ambiguous as to the reasons for limitations on women's lives; although "nature" is invoked, the real force confining women is "social convention." During the years that these ambivalent and sometimes pathetic letters were written, Lady Dilke was intensely involved in activity aimed at securing the rights of women of all classes on many fronts, despite her difficulty in establishing firmly the basis of women's oppression. She fought for the diminution of oppressive conditions and herself lived a life that transgressed the Victorian social code of femininity.

In her intellectual work as well, there is ambivalence and protest, especially in repeated analogies between the absolute state and the patriarchal family, analogies which help define Dilke's feminist politics.[95] She stresses that there are historical reasons why the family and the state exist as they do, but that the cost is too high for the individual. Change must occur if society is to survive and because of the "law" of progress. She meant at the end of her life to trace the development of art's social relationships from the Greeks to the present, in terms of a widening conception of democracy and knowledge. "To the Greek, certain types only were worth the full honour of perfect expression. To the modern artist all forms of life are sacred."[96]

Hidden in this tendency to argue that the future emancipation of social classes and individuals was inevitable was an argument that the emancipation of women was also historically necessary. Insofar as her political argument against the absolute state rested on an analogy to the patriarchal family, her arguments against that state's arbitrary power could be inverted to serve in an argument against patriarchal control of women. Thus, despite lip service to "nature," Lady Dilke lived as though the constraints on women's lives were purely the products of "social convention," which could be understood historically and changed by collective action. Her scholarly documentations of far-reaching social and cultural change implicitly contained a message of hope for women, but the emphasis on the *longue durée* meant that the individual, that central figure in her conception of the Renaissance, must often be lost.

Emilia Dilke's impatient desire for history and complete knowledge, which encompassed social, political, aesthetic, and economic conditions, embraced the development of all branches of French arts and aspired to the totality of human culture from ancient Greece to the present, could generate despair. "Quelque-fois je pense même que le plus bel usage que l'on puisse faire de sa propre vie serait de se vouer à tout savoir, à se rendre maitre—au moins dans sa signification générale—de tout ce que l'esprit humain a conquis sur tous les térrains:—mais, j'ai quarante ans, et c'est trop tard."[97] This mixture of grandiosity of ambition and exhaustion of resources derives from Mark Pattison, Oxford, and the gendered universe of middle-class society. It is increased by Lady Dilke's desire for female peers and feminist support. This wish for an intellectually supportive community of women links the seemingly disparate branches of her life.

While Emilia Dilke was able to work with and for other women and male feminists for feminist and Radical goals politically, in her intellectual work and her unappeasable desire, she was more isolated and deviant. As a young woman, she attempted intimate friendships with other intellectual and artistic women. Abroad, she sought female friends who shared her interests, but found only a few. After a visit to Rome, she wrote of the special value of female society there: "The *warm* sympathy of so many active minded liberal intelligent *women* creates an atmosphere wh is all the pleasanter for its rarity," which she contrasts to the icy "city of learning," drawing on her century's great text of female intellectual desire. "Do you know I got terribly *cowed* all those years in Oxfd,—they were a variation of Corinne's experiences in Northumberland. Poor Corinne!"[98]

The lack of institutional positions for women intellectuals made Dilke dependent on the help, advice, friendship, and resources of male colleagues. However generously given, these could not diminish her sense of isolation. Despite the perceived openness to women of art history as a field, Lady Dilke's situation was highly anomalous. Few other women art historians' work at that time shared Dilke's *scholarly* standards, modeled on the increasingly rigorous Oxford scholarship; her work is more clearly "academic" than that of most of her contemporaries, male or female. Art history, as a field barely beginning to be professionalized, was simultaneously accessible to women and dangerous as a ground that men were claiming and institutionalizing as a masculine domain. Further, the assertion of a sense of vocation and self-consciousness as one doing meaningful work was fraught with symbolic and material difficulties. Neither in her own society nor in the Renaissance could Lady Dilke have found many models for such a female life. However she made herself, Emilia Dilke could not overcome the contradiction, fundamental to Victorian middle-class society, between the very terms of her self-definition, woman intellectual.

As a later sponsor of young "New Women," Dilke reiterated to them her theme of Renaissance womanhood, arguing for female autonomy and pursuit of total knowledge on the basis of the duty and the *pleasure* of intellectual and spiritual development for the self. This pursuit of knowledge was necessary that women might act in the world, and that middle-class women reformers in particular might move society towards "democracy" rather than simply enacting the role of Lady Bountiful in their interventions in the lives of the working class. It might also create female communities and networks which might bring together high intellectual standards and passionate feminist commitment.

Her own creation of a career for an educated feminist woman had been improvisatory, employing borrowed ideas from fiction and history to resist the roles of wife and helpmeet, inspiring muse, or intellectual dilettante. First by flaunting her femininity in male-dominated Oxford, then by redefining the terms of intellectual work to legitimate her own scholarship, Lady Dilke claimed to be both other than and more inclusive than her society. Appropriating the Renaissance for her own ends, she paid the price of feeling that she lived her life behind the walls of the present. But she tried to see beyond that which she could not pass through and staked her hopes on a general movement of society that might free other women.

Bibliography of Emilia Dilke's Books

As E. F. S. Pattison

The Renaissance of Art in France, 2 vol. (London: Kegan Paul, 1879).

Claude Lorrain, sa vie et ses oeuvres (Paris: Rouam, 1884).

As Emilia Dilke

The Shrine of Death and Other Stories (London: George Routledge, 1886).

Art in the Modern State (London: Chapman and Hall, 1888).

The Shrine of Love and Other Stories (London: George Routledge, 1891).

French Painters of the Eighteenth Century (London: George Bell, 1899).

French Architects and Sculptors of the Eighteenth Century (London: George Bell, 1900).

French Furniture and Decoration of the Eighteenth Century (London: George Bell, 1901).

French Engravers and Draughtsmen of the Eighteenth Century (London: George Bell, 1902).

The Book of the Spiritual Life, with a Memoir of the author by Sir Charles Dilke (London: John Murray, 1905).

NOTES

I am grateful to the 1986 Rutgers graduate seminar in women's history, especially Suzanne Lebsock; to Angela V. John, for many wonderful conversations about the problems of writing exceptional lives; to Daniel A. Harris, Cora Kaplan, the Rutgers Gender Group, the Interdisciplinary Feminist Seminar of the University of Essex, the Gender Studies Program at Thames Polytechnic, and George Levine and the 1988–1989 fellows of CCACC for listening and responding to pieces of this work. Special thanks to Paul B. Israel, John Gillis, and Judith Walkowitz for their sustained attention and patient criticism of this essay and the larger project of which it is a part.

1. Regarding *names:* "Lady Dilke" was christened Emily Francis Strong. During her first marriage (1861–1884) she was "Mrs. Mark Pattison" socially but she signed her published writing "E. F. S. Pattison." During her second marriage, to Sir Charles Wentworth Dilke (1885–1904), she was addressed as "Lady Dilke." Her private correspondence is signed "Emilia Dilke," "Emilia F. S. Dilke," or "E. F. S. Dilke." Although her books of fiction had "Lady Dilke" on the title page, her articles and reviews were often signed "Emilia F. S. Dilke." I shall refer to her as "Lady Dilke" or "Emilia Dilke" except in specific contexts in which another name applied. The initials EFS, EFSP, and EFSD are used in these notes. MP = Mark Pattison, CWD = Charles Wentworth Dilke (1843–1911).

2. *Women's Trade Union Review (WTUR)* 56 (January 1905): 1; obituary and "appreciations" of EFSD, 1–19. EFSD was president of the Women's Trade Union League (WTUL) from 1886 until her death; she had been involved with its foundation and its Oxford branch from 1874. The League was founded in 1874 as the Women's Protective and Provident League; for its history, see Gladys Boone, *The Women's Trade Union Leagues in Great Britain and the United States* (1942; New York: AMS Press, 1968); Sarah Boston, *Women Workers and the Trade Unions* (London: Davis-Poynter, 1980); Harold Goldman, *Emma Paterson* (London: Lawrence and Wishart, 1974); Sheila Lewenhak, *Women and Trade Unions: An Outline History of Women in the British Trade Union Movement* (London: Ernest Benn, 1977); Norbert C. Soldon, *Women in British Trade Unions, 1874–1976* (Dublin: Gill and Macmillan, 1978); and Rosemary Feurer, "The Meaning of 'Sisterhood': The British Women's Movement and Protective Labor Legislation, 1870–1900," *Victorian Studies* 31 (Winter 1988): 233–260.

3. "The Art-Work of Lady Dilke," *Quarterly Review* 205 (October 1906): 439–467. The unknown author was probably male; leading suspects are D. S. MacColl or J. E. C. Bodley. See Phyllis Helen Bodley, "'For Remembrance' of J. E. C. Bodley," unpublished manuscript, 6 vols., donated in 1953; MS. Eng. misc. d.357, Bodleian Library, Oxford University [henceforth Bod.]. See also J. R. Shane Leslie, *Memoir of*

J. E. C. Bodley (London: Jonathan Cape, 1930). For MacColl, see D. S. MacColl, "Rhoda Broughton and Emilia Pattison," *Nineteenth Century* 137 (January 1945): 28–33.

4. "Art-Work," 339–340, 442–443. The writer deplores EFSD's failure to restrict her energies to writing art history after having spelled out that *women* of genius in particular ought to confine themselves; of "that small band of Englishwomen who . . . have proved that feminine intellect, in its highest development, is on a par with that of man . . . the less extended the area in which they have worked, the greater the excellence of their achievement." It is on the basis of the excellence *for women* of limited scale and limited output that Austen and Brontë are on a "higher level" than George Eliot; Elizabeth Barrett Browning is a greater poet *because* she wrote about English social conditions from Rome, rather than immersing herself in English social activism. The author also asserts EFSD's uniqueness as the other women "won their fame in the realm of imagination," while EFSD's "will rest on her mastery of the positive facts and tendencies of history"; he therefore dismisses both her fiction and her more ephemeral art criticism. By this focus on her "technical knowledge of the fine arts" and her ideas about aesthetics and the social production of art, he locates EFSD's true peers in *France:* Madame de Staël and Madame de Sevigne, the latter being "the only woman whose learning, breadth of view, and powers of critical observation" would have been fully adequate to EFSD's task. The implication was not only that EFSD was a Frenchwoman *manquée,* but that EFSD was not quite adequate to the task she chose because of her birth.

5. Charles Dilke, "Memoir," in Emilia Dilke, *The Book of the Spiritual Life* [henceforth *BSL*], 1–128; see bibliography. The memoir is followed by a series of short essays, collectively titled "The Book of the Spiritual Life," and two short stories. A somewhat different manuscript with annotations by J. R. Thursfield is in the British Library, London [henceforth BL], Add. Mss. 43946.

6. *BSL*, 126, 127.

7. *BSL*, 116, 128.

8. "*Elle avait tout—beauté, bonté de coeur, haute intelligence, simplicité. Comment ne pas chérir cette femme d'élite si absolument complète et unique*" (*BSL*, 127; quoting "the Marquise de Sassenay"). "*Nous autres femmes nous avons tant bésoin de forces pour suffire au double fardeau, de notre tâche, et de celle de notre mari. Vous vous êtes dépensée à cette mission plus qu'aucune autre*" (*BSL*, 127, quoting Marie Thérèse Ollivier, wife of French politician Emile Ollivier; the original, dated "1897" by another hand, is BL, Add. Mss. 43908, fol. 227ff.).

9. CWD's status as an exceptional, feminist man did not derive entirely from his association with EFSD. See Roy Jenkins, *Sir Charles Dilke, A Victorian Tragedy* (London: Collins, 1958); rev. ed., *Victorian Scandal: A Biography of the Right Honourable Sir Charles Dilke* (New York: Chilmark Press, 1965); and Olive Banks, *The Biographical Dictionary of British Feminists, vol. 1: 1800–1930* (New York: New York University Press, 1985), 66–68. CWD was well placed to recount EFSD's past; they wrote each other nearly daily during the last ten years of her first marriage and he knew her as a girl. Although he walked a fine line in attempting to give a true, as well as heroic, picture of EFSD's life while maintaining some discretion about her first marriage, he is generally reliable.

10. See Rachel Blau DuPlessis's *H. D. The Career of That Struggle* (Bloomington: Indiana University Press, 1986), especially her discussion of women writers' struggles with and for "[f]our kinds of authority . . . cultural authority, authority of otherness/marginality, gender authority, and sexual/erotic authority," each of

which "is particularly inflected with a woman's race, class, and social condition" (xiii). I would add issues of intellectual authority, professional authority, and feminist authority, that is, the authority to speak not only as a woman but with and (problematically) for other women.

11. See especially Deborah Epstein Nord, *The Apprenticeship of Beatrice Webb* (Ithaca: Cornell University Press, 1985); Nina Auerbach, *Ellen Terry: Player in Her Time* (New York: W. W. Norton, 1987); and *Woman and the Demon: The Life of a Victorian Myth* (Cambridge: Harvard University Press, 1982); and Carla Peterson, *The Determined Reader: Gender and Culture in the Novel from Napoleon to Victoria* (New Brunswick: Rutgers University Press, 1986).

12. See Auerbach, *Woman and the Demon*, chap. 6 and epilogue, especially 187–188. I employ the term "role" consistently in its theatrical, not its sociological, sense.

13. Elaine Abelson, David Abraham, and Majorie Murphy, "Interview with Joan Scott," *Radical History Review* 45 (Fall 1989): 51–52.

14. "Issues, Terms, and Contexts," in *Feminist Studies/Critical Studies*, ed. Teresa de Lauretis (Bloomington: Indiana University Press, 1986), 10. Cf. Chris Weedon, *Feminist Practice and Poststructuralist Theory* (Oxford: Basil Blackwell, 1987), 95.

15. See Deirdre David, *Intellectual Women and Victorian Patriarchy: Harriet Martineau, Elizabeth Barrett Browning, George Eliot* (Ithaca: Cornell University Press, 1987), 1–26. See also Susan J. Leonardi, *Dangerous by Degrees: Women at Oxford and the Somerville College Novelists* (New Brunswick: Rutgers University Press, 1989), 1–45.

16. *Cosmopolis* 7 (September 1897): 643–656; henceforth cited as "Idealist Movement."

17. For EFSD on the education of young women, see Gertrude Marian Tuckwell, "Reminiscences" [henceforth GMT, "Rem."], unpublished manuscript with annotations, Trades Union Congress Library, London, esp. chaps. 5–11 and 18. See also Beatrice Webb's diary for 18 September 1889 for an extremely hostile recognition of this role, in *The Diary of Beatrice Webb. vol. 1: Glitter Around and Darkness Within*, ed. Norman and Jeanne MacKenzie (London: Virago, 1982), 294.

18. "Idealist Movement," 643–644, quoting St. François de Sales.

19. Abelson, Abraham, and Murphy, "Interview with Scott," 45, 51.

20. "Idealist Movement," 644.

21. "Idealist Movement," 650; some passages also appear in *BSL*, 145, 166–167; see also *BSL*, 117–118.

22. "Idealist Movement," 650.

23. See CWD's account of EFSD's religious history, BL Add. Mss. 43932, fol. 137ff. Cf. Jenkins, *Sir Charles Dilke*, 94–95. For EFSD's "mature" religious views, see *BSL*, 139–230, 145–155, and 173–183.

24. *BSL*, 3; for EFSD's family, see *BSL*, 1–2, and the more detailed draft in BL Add. Mss. 43946, fols. 3–6.

25. GMT, "Rem.," A24f, refers to Emily Weedon as "an Oxford girl"; *BSL*, 4, 9.

26. GMT, "Rem.," A15–16. EFS's elder sisters, Rosa and Henrietta, were considerably older, as was her brother, Owen, who was educated for the army.

27. BL Add. Mss. 43946, fol. 6ff; the catalogue *Exhibition of Oxford Amateur Art, June 1851* (Oxford: printed I. Shrimpton, 1851) lists "Capt. Strong, London and County Bank" as the treasurer for the exhibit; he also exhibited 18 pictures, one of which was the "prize" to be auctioned off for charity; see Bod., G. A. Oxon b. 113(62). See also Christopher Wood, *Dictionary of Victorian Painters*, 2d ed. (Woodbridge, Suffolk: Antique Collectors' Club, 1978), s.v. "Strong, H., fl. 1840."

28. *BSL*, 5, 7.

29. *BSL*, 4–5; see Watts's letters to EFSD, BL Add. Mss. 43908, passim.

30. For George Eliot's letters to EFSP, see BL Add. Mss. 43907, fol. 24–79; *BSL*, 16–17. See also Nina Auerbach, "Artists and Mothers: A False Alliance," in *Romantic Imprisonment: Women and Other Glorified Outcasts* (New York: Columbia University Press, 1985), especially 177–183.

31. *BSL*, 8–12; see also BL Add. Mss. 43946, fol. 13ff. The author of EFSD's *DNB* entry was Sidney Lee, a friend of both Dilkes.

32. Cf. Martha Vicinus, *Independent Women: Work and Community for Single Women, 1850–1920* (Chicago: University of Chicago Press, 1985). EFS was too young for most of Vicinus's "options" for an independent female life and rather worldly for the Anglican sisterhoods. Ironically, MP's sister was a heroine of one of these nursing sisterhoods; see Jo Manton, *Sister Dora: The Life of Dorothy Pattison* (London: Methuen, 1971).

33. *BSL*, 9, 11–12; BL Add. Mss. 43946, fol. 13f.

34. "Idealist Movement," 651.

35. On MP, see his own *Memoirs*, introduction by Jo Manton (1885; Fonthill, Sussex: Centaur Press, 1969); Manton, *Sister Dora*; and the works of V. H. H. Green: *Oxford Common Room: A Study of Lincoln College and Mark Pattison* (London: Edward Arnold, 1957); *The Commonwealth of Lincoln College, 1427–1977* (Oxford: Oxford University Press, 1979), chap. 17 and appendix 9; and *Love in a Cool Climate: The Letters of Mark Pattison and Meta Bradley, 1879–1884* (Oxford: Oxford University Press, 1985). I am indebted to the Reverend Dr. Green for his extremely kind assistance and advice about the Pattison Papers. See also John Sparrow, *Mark Pattison and the Idea of a University* (Cambridge: Cambridge University Press, 1967); and Betty Askwith, *Lady Dilke: A Biography* (London: Chatto & Windus, 1969). For MP's election and Lincoln College, see Green, *Oxford Common Room*, chaps. 4–9, and C. P. Snow's novel, *The Masters* (New York: Charles Scribner's Sons, 1951), author's "note."

36. See William Tuckwell, *Reminiscences of Oxford* (London: Cassell, 1900), 7–10. In the 1870s there was an influx of younger women when Fellows of Colleges were allowed to marry.

37. See Green, *Oxford Common Room*, 156; and *Love in a Cool Climate*, plates following 142; and Askwith, *Lady Dilke*, plates following 86.

38. MP, *Memoirs*, 117; note the absence of MP's mother in this description. See Green, *Love in a Cool Climate*, for the warmer side of MP, but Green underplays the concern with power in MP's relationships with young women; see also Manton, *Sister Dora*, passim.

39. "Idealist Movement," 651.

40. "Idealist Movement," 646; cf. Belinda Churchill's reasons for marrying the Reverend Dr. Forth in Rhoda Broughton's *Belinda* (1883; London: Virago, 1987); the novel is partially based on the Pattison ménage.

41. Bod., Mss. Pattison 140, item 4; on Rosa's more conservative generation and temperament, see GMT, "Rem.," A59.

42. GMT, "Rem.," A43, A272f. William Tuckwell became a lively "Radical Parson" activist and supporter of women's rights.

43. Bod., Mss. Pattison 140, fol. 10–11, n.d.

44. On Victorian women artists, see Pamela G. Nunn, ed., *Canvassing: Recollections by Six Victorian Women Artists* (London: Camden Press, 1986); and Nunn, *Victorian Women Artists* (London: The Women's Press, 1987).

45. "Idealist Movement," 648.

46. Mark Pattison, *Milton* (1879; London: Macmillan, 1909). James Glucker makes much of an alleged relationship between MP's treatment of Milton's marriage and MP's own, especially regarding divorce (MP, *Milton*, chap. 5); see his "The Case for Edward Casaubon," *Pegasus* [University of Essex Classical Society Magazine] (November 1967): 7–21, especially 16–17. While correct in arguing for the importance of reading MP's works for their potential autobiographical content, Glucker neglects the possibility that this content is itself shaped by narrative conventions; he is utterly seduced by the possibility of collapsing *all* the plots in MP's work, together with those of *Belinda, Middlemarch*, and Robert Liddell's *The Almond Tree* (London: Jonathan Cape, 1938), into a grand story ("art") which "life" must, perforce, have imitated. Glucker's contribution must be seen in the context of "the *Middlemarch* wars"—the extended debate in print over the relationship between that novel and the Pattisons. For MP's pride in EFSP's "cleverness," see, e.g., Bod., Mss. Pattison 132, fol. 19v (MP's diary, 28 July 1879); for his resentment of her artistic studies and "art friends," see fol. 16v (MP's diary, 1 June 1879) and fol. 17v (9 June 1879). For MP's "stigmatizing" of EFSP's "'bohemian' friends," see Bod., Mss. Pattison 118, fol. 28ff. (EFSP to Ellen Smith, 14 December 1875); for his resentment of her absence from Oxford, see fol. 24ff. (EFSP to Ellen Smith, 9 August 1875).

47. "The Physician's Wife," in Emilia Dilke, *The Shrine of Death and Other Stories* (London: George Routledge, 1886). On these stories, see *BSL*, 93–95 and BL Add. Mss. 43906, fol. 32ff. (CWD to EFSP, 3 March 1885).

48. EFSD, *Shrine of Death*, 40. This story is extremely rich as a source of EFSP's conception of her first marriage. The young girl and one of the doctor's assistants fall in love, which amuses the old man "for he thought the passions of youth matters of small importance" (43). Finally, the young lovers fall into each other's arms, but the young man thinks better of this tie, takes his gun to go hunting in the hills and think "how he might leave her" (48). The old man sees him return and laughs at his impotence; the youth "remembered he had not so much as fired a single shot" (49), is "shame[d] and anger[ed]" into telling the wife he is leaving. He departs because "before all on earth his mother was sacred to him, and for her sake he would not abide there, nor could he face her with the girl at his side" (49–50). She is shocked and dazed; seeing the gun and thinking to kill herself, she hears the old man laughing and sees "the distorted features of the physician convulsed with malicious merriment" at the window (51). She shoots him, refuses the return of the faithless youth, and eventually dies alone in the castle, having—unconvincingly—come to understand more the old man's love of science; "his very cruelty arose out of devotion to ends beyond the common aims of men" (54–55). She was buried in a "nameless grave" (55), but the inscription on her grave-cross, "Dites-moi un Pater" (56), served as an example to other women whose lives were "torture" (55).

49. See Green, *Love in a Cool Climate*, and Mary Arnold Ward's *A Writer's Recollections* (London: Collins, 1918), 102–111.

50. *BSL*, 19; cf. GMT, "Rem.," A26.

51. Bod., Mss. Pattison 118, fol. 22ff. (EFSP to Ellen Smith, n.d. [summer 1875]).

52. *Shrine of Death*, 41, 42.

53. *BSL*, 20. CWD places EFSP's fiction in this "side" of her life.

54. Cf. Ward, *Writer's Recollections*, 105.

55. See Michael Levey, *The Case of Walter Pater* (London: Thames & Hudson, 1978), 77, on the conflict of German learning—with its vision of encyclopedic com-

pleteness and rigorous method, "its very language suggested respectability, required hard work to master, and seemed to exclude the faintest possibility of anything frivolous being written in it"—and French culture, "a France not just of Gothic cathedrals and picturesque countryside known to Ruskin or to bourgeois dons during vacation tours, but of sophisticated beliefs in the arts for their own sake . . . there exuded a sense of unbridled passion which was at once exciting and evil." Levey argues that Pater combined "French aestheticism and German intellect." The same might be said of EFSD. But see her review of Pater's *Studies in the History of the Renaissance, Westminster Review* n.s. 43 (April 1873): 639–641.

56. "Idealist Movement," 651. The sexual connotations of the phrase "enforced courses" are obvious; cf. Bod., Mss. Pattison 60, fol. 91ff. (EFSP to MP, 21 January 1876), in which EFSP informs MP that her aversion to sexual relations was "now wholly beyond control." See also fol. 93ff. (EFSP to MP, n.d. [27 January 1876]).

57. *Shrine of Death*, 43; emphasis mine. See also "Idealist Movement," 651: This period was one of "much distress and suffering to [me] and to those about [me] . . . [although] it might have been thought—though falsely—that it was they [MP] rather than [me] who endured the chiefest pain," a clear allusion to MP's notorious predilection for self-pity.

58. "Idealist Movement," 651–652. Cf. Maggie Tulliver's reading of the "Imitatio" in *The Mill on the Floss* (book 4, chap. 3); see also Peterson, *The Determined Reader*, chap. 5. EFSP's copy of the "Imitatio" was given her by Eleanor Smith who recommended its teachings; according to CWD, EFSD carried the book everywhere; *BSL*, 10–11; "Idealist Movement," 651.

59. On first going up to Oxford, ca. 1916/17, Maurice Bowra was shown Lincoln College by an elderly Fellow who pointed out the Rector's Lodgings with the comment, "This was where *That Woman* used to have her parties" (Askwith, *Lady Dilke*, 97).

60. Cf. Josephine Butler, *Recollections of George Butler*, 2d ed. (Bristol: Arrowsmith, n.d.[1893]), pp. 86–116, especially 94–103.

61. Ward, *Writer's Recollections*, 152–153.

62. See, e.g., Bod., Mss. Pattison 130, fol. 72ff (MP diary, 23 Nov. 1873) on the horrors of entertaining; but MP chastised other young women, especially Somerville College students for looking dowdy or lacking social graces.

63. Ward, *Writer's Recollections*, 103.

64. Green, *Commonwealth of Lincoln*, 483; no source given.

65. Hippolyte Taine to Madame Taine, 4 June 1871 and 26 May 1871, *Hippolyte Taine, Sa vie et sa correspondence*, vol. 3, quoted in Askwith, *Lady Dilke*, 48–49; see also GMT "Rem.," A31.

66. See Askwith, *Lady Dilke*, chap. 5; William S. Peterson, *Victorian Heretic: Mrs Humphry Ward's "Robert Elsmere"* (Leicester: Leicester University Press, 1976), 65–73; Ward, *Writer's Recollections*, 102–111.

67. Jebb to "C. L. S.," 20 July 1873, quoted in Caroline Jebb, *Life and Letters of Sir Richard Claverhouse Jebb* (Cambridge: Cambridge University Press, 1907), 163–165.

68. Cf. Bertha Johnson, "The First Beginnings, 1873–1900," in *Lady Margaret Hall: A Short History* [also titled: *A Short History of Lady Margaret Hall*], ed. Gemma Bailey (Oxford: privately printed, 1923), 29: "There was a sense of strain in her talk at one time and a provoking frivolity at another, often when you specially wanted her to be serious and helpful."

69. On Pauline Trevelyan, see Raleigh Trevelyan, *A Pre-Raphaelite Circle* (Totowa, N.J.: Rowman and Littlefield, 1978). The picture, now in the National

Portrait Gallery, was drawn by Lady Pauline Jermyn Trevelyan, but the colors were painted in by Laura Capel Lofft, later Lady Trevelyan after Pauline's death.

70. A photograph of EFSP in this dress is in BL Add. Mss. 49612(b), item 1; on the back, CWD has dated it 1862.

71. *BSL*, 120. In fact, EFSP did not like Boucher.

72. Ward, *Writer's Recollections*, 109–110.

73. Stephen Gwynn, *Saints and Scholars* (London: Thornton Butterworth, 1929), 81–114; passage quoted, 81. Gwynn, clearly antagonistic towards MP, later co-wrote the authorized biography of CWD.

74. Colin Eisler, "The Six Lives of an Art Historian," in *Women as Interpreters of the Visual Arts*, ed. Claire Richter Sherman (Westport, Conn.: Greenwood Press, 1981), 147–180; Eisler find this elision disturbing (163).

75. Bod., Mss. Pattison 118, fol. 28ff. (EFSP to Ellen Smith, 14 December 1875). See also EFSD, "A Vision of Learning," in *The Shrine of Death*, 57–76.

76. *BSL*, 3–4, 121–122.

77. David Norbrook, "The Life and Death of Renaissance Man," *Raritan* 8, no. 4 (Spring 1989), 91.

78. A psychoanalytic formulation from cinema studies of the relations between femininity and masquerade is in Mary Ann Doane, "Film and the Masquerade: Theorising the Female Spectator," *Screen* 23, nos. 3–4 (1982): 87.

79. I am extremely indebted to Eliza Reilly for illuminating the connections between EFSD's Hellenism, her religiosity, and her embrace of the Renaissance.

80. "Idealist Movement," 652. For the Renaissance in the nineteenth century, see Wallace K. Ferguson, *The Renaissance in Historical Thought* (Cambridge: Harvard University Press, 1948); Peter Burke, *Culture and Society in Renaissance Italy, 1420–1540* (London: B. T. Batsford, 1972), 1–21; and Norbrook, "Renaissance Man," 93–100. In EFSD's narrative, the Renaissance renewed the "friend's" interest in classical studies, but no barrier of gender had deflected him earlier.

81. Eisler, "The Six Lives of an Art Historian," 147. A partial bibliography of EFSD's articles and reviews, compiled by Claire Richter Sherman, is appended to Eisler's essay (177–180). EFSD's languages included very fluent French, German, Italian, and Latin, and less fluent Greek, Spanish, Portugese, Dutch, Provençal, and Swedish; at time of her death, she was learning Welsh; *BSL*, 18, 121.

82. *BSL*, p. 83, quoting EFSD's 1883 *Academy* review of a Burlington House Exhibition.

83. EFSP, review of John Ruskin, *Lectures on Art* and *Catalogue of Examples, Academy* (10 September 1870): 305–306. See also EFSP, "Art and Morality" (review of Victor Laprade, *Le sentiment de la nature avant le Christinaisme* and *le sentiment de la nature chez les modernes*), *Westminster Review*, n.s. 35 (January 1869): 66–83.

84. But see her "Art and Mortality," 81, for a partial differentiation of her views from "aestheticism." See also EFSP's review of Pater: she complained that he wrote of the Renaissance as if it were "an air-plant, independent of the ordinary senses of nourishment . . . a sentimental revolution having no relation to the conditions of the actual world," and that "we miss the sense of the connection between art and literature and the other forms of life of which they are the outward expression, and feel as if we were wandering in a world of unsubstantial dreams." His polished phrases "are not history nor are they ever to be relied upon for accurate statements of simple matters of fact" (305). Her own brief discussion of the Italian Renaissance in "Art and Morality" stresses blood and "sensual indulgence" (80).

85. EFSP, review of Ruskin, p. 305.

86. Emilia F. S. Dilke, *Art in the Modern State* (London: Chapman and Hall, 1888), 1, 3–5, 137, 220.

87. Eisler, "The Six Lives of an Art Historian," 174. Eisler finds *Art in the Modern State* an "extraordinarily accomplished presentation . . . still unrivalled in its scope" which anticipates the work of Pevsner (64). Also compare EFSD's study of images to Margaret D. Carroll, "The Erotics of Absolutism: Rubens and the Mystification of Sexual Violence," *Representations* 25 (Winter 1989): 3–29.

88. *Art in the Modern State*, 144–45.

89. On the pervasiveness of this trope, see Helene Roberts, "Exhibition and Review: The Periodical Press and the Victorian Art Exhibition System," in *The Victorian Periodical Press: Samplings and Soundings*, ed. Joanne Shattock and Michael Wolff (Leicester: Leicester University Press, 1982), 79–108.

90. Passage quoted, *BSL*, 83; for Manet, see EFSP, "Summer Exhibition of the Society of French Artists," *Academy* 3, no. 49 (1 June 1872), 204–205; Askwith, *Lady Dilke*, 41–42. See also Kate Flint, "The English Critical Reaction to Contemporary Painting, 1878–1910," unpub. D. Phil. thesis, Brasenose College, Oxford, 1983.

91. *BSL*, 121–122; CWD is quoting papers left unfinished at EFSD's death.

92. *Art in the Modern State*, 222.

93. *BSL*, 54–55; probably to Ellen Smith, James Thursfield, or CWD, early 1880s.

94. *BSL*, 55. Trans. by CWD; the original is in the Muntz Papers, Nouvelles Acquisitions Françaises, Bibliothèque Nationale, Paris. Colin Eisler translates the final phrase, "One can master what one is not able to escape" ("Six Lives of an Art Historian," 176 n. 46).

95. See, e.g., *Art in the Modern State*, 28.

96. *BSL*, 122.

97. *BSL*, 20–21; "Sometimes I think (too) that the best use one could make of one's own life would be to devote oneself to knowing all, to make oneself [to be made] master—at least in its general significance—of all that the human spirit has conquered [achieved] in all fields [on all grounds];—but, I'm forty years old, and it's too late."

98. EFSP, probably to CWD, n.d. [ca. February or March 1881]. Cf. Ellen Moers, *Literary Women* (London: The Women's Press, 1978), 173–210.

Three Reconstructions

✦ IRVING HOWE ✦

The Self in Literature

No one has ever seen the self. It has no visible shape, nor does it occupy measurable space. It is an abstraction, like other abstractions equally elusive: the individual, the mind, the society. Yet it has a history of its own which informs and draws upon the larger history of our last two centuries, a time in which the idea of the self became a great energizing force in politics and culture.

Let us say that the self is a construct of mind, a hypothesis of being, socially formed even as it can be quickly turned against the very social formations that have brought it into birth. The locus of self often appears as "inner," experienced as a presence savingly apart from both social milieu and quotidian existence. In extreme circumstances, it may be felt as "hidden."

There is probably some continuity between the idea of the soul and that of the self. Both propound a center of percipience lodged within yet not quite of the body. Soul speaks of a person's relation to divinity, a participation in heavenly spark, while self speaks of a person's relation to both others and oneself—though soul may in part serve this function too. In these ideas of soul and self there is a dualism of self-consciousness that forms, I believe, a historical advance. And there is a similar link between the idea of the self and modern notions of alienation, since both imply a yearning for—with knowledge of a usual separation from—a "full" or a "fulfilled" humanity, unfractured by contingent needs.

Once perceived or imagined, the self implies doubleness, multiplicity. For what knows the awareness of self if not the self?: division as premise and price of consciousness. I may be fixed in social rank, but that does not exhaust, it may not even quite define, who I am or what I "mean." By asserting the presence of the self, I counterpose to all imposed definitions of place and function a persuasion that I harbor *something else,* utterly mine—a persuasion that I possess a center of individual consciousness that is active and, to some extent, coherent. In my more careless moments, I may even suppose this center to be inviolable, though anyone who has paid attention to modern history knows this is not so. To say that the world cannot invade the precincts of the self is to indulge in bravado, and yet, even while sadly recognizing this, I still see the self as my last bulwark against oppression and falsity. Were this bulwark to be breached, I would indeed be broken.

In the long past of modernity, there have been numerous prefigurings of selfhood. Hamlet spars with his sense of self, both cradling and assaulting it. Saint Augustine's *Confessions* have been called a "manifesto of the inner world," though I doubt that he postulated a self in a modern sense of the term. Jacob Burckhardt writes that by the end of the thirteenth century Italy was beginning to "swarm with individuality: the ban upon person-ality was dissolved."[1] But the ban upon that personality assuming historical initiative was not dissolved.

In the latter part of the eighteenth century, through the Enlightenment and Romanticism, a deep change begins in mankind's sense of its situation. In the Enlightenment educated Europeans experienced "an expansive sense of power over nature and themselves" (Peter Gay).[2] The self attains the dignity of a noun, as if to register an enhancement of authority. Earlier intimations of selfhood give way to the *idea,* or at least sentiment, of the self, slippery as that proves to be and susceptible to criticism as it will be-come. The idea of the self becomes a force within public life, almost taking on institutional shape and certainly entering the arena of historical conten-tion. For what occurs is not just a new perception of our internal space, but its emergence as a major social factor. Once, as in Hegel's phrase, we cele-brate "our existence *on its own account*" (emphasis added),[3] that is, being for being's sake, we have stepped into a new era.

So far as I can tell, the prominence of the self in the writings of that bril-liant intuitive psychologist, Denis Diderot, notably in *Rameau's Nephew* and *Jacques the Fatalist,* does not lead to any expectation or even desire for a fusion of self and role. The split between the two is accepted as a given. There can be no return to any "state of nature," whether taken to be histor-ical fact or tacit allegory. We may at first suppose that the *Moi* of *Rameau's Nephew,* that "honest soul" marked by a "wholeness of self," constitutes an image of ordinary, solid mankind, while the *Lui,* or the "disintegrated con-sciousness" about whom Diderot keenly remarks that "he has no greater opposite than himself," is a literary construct anticipating modes of charac-ter still to come. But the reality is quite the opposite. The very fact that Diderot's books were composed at the historical moment they were, sug-gests that it is "the whole man" who is the imagined creature, a figment of desire, while the nephew, reveling in chaos, approaches a condition of actuality.

Once the notion of the self becomes entrenched in Western culture, there follows an acceptance of multiplicity within being. There may also follow a sort of pride in what each of us regards as unique stampings of personality. The Enlightenment, writes Kant in *What Is the Enlightenment?*, signifies "man's emergence from his self-imposed minority": which is to say, signifies the possibility of autonomy and the probability of division. The release of historical energy through the Enlightenment means that the self will now come forth in confident aloneness, declaring its goal to be both a reformation of and an optimal distance from society. This also means that our frequently deplored alienation can be seen as a human conquest, the sign that we have broken out of traditionalist bonds. Psychologically: because the pain of estrangement can be seen as a necessary cost of the boon of selfhood—if we bemoan "deformed" selves we may be supposed to have a glimmer of "true" selves. And morally: because it is all but impossible to postulate a self without some intertwined belief in the good and desirable. For the self is not just an intuited supposition of a state of being; it is also a historically situated norm.

The self turns out to consist of many selves, as Walt Whitman happily noted: partial and fragmented, released through the liberty of experiment and introspection. It is also an interpretation of new modes of sensibility, and of interpretations, as we have often been informed, there need be no end. So I hasten to note just a few of these conflicting selves—songs, chants, and whispers:

♦ The self may evoke an original state of nature, not yet stained by history, as if all were still at rest in the garden. "I dared to strip man's nature naked," said Rousseau, and, naked, there emerged the features of goodness.

♦ The self does service as a heuristic category enabling criticism of modes of existence taken to be morally crippling.

♦ The self can be envisaged graphically, with "higher" and "lower" segments, or perhaps as fluctuating up and down between them, so that the two—some hold out for three—come to be seen as both intertwined and separable.

♦ The self becomes a lens of scrutiny with which to investigate psychological states, and is especially helpful for the study of anxiety, a condition that grows in acuteness as awareness of self increases.

♦ The self can become an agent of aggrandizement, an imperial expansion into a totality encompassing or obliterating the phenomenal world.

◆ Like all powerful ideas, the self can falsify itself through parody, become a masquerade of faked inspirations, hasty signals of untested institutions. Jacques Rivière writes keenly about this:

> There is nothing more deceitful than what is spontaneous, nothing more foreign to myself. It is never with myself that I begin; the feelings I adopt naturally are not mine; I do not experience them, I fall into them right off as into a rut . . . ; everybody has already travelled along them.

> My second thoughts are the true ones, those that await me in those depths down to which I do not go. Not the first thoughts alone are thinking in me; in the very depths of myself there is a low, continual meditation about which I know nothing and about which I shall know nothing unless I make an effort: this is my soul.[4]

◆ The self is an ideal possibility, sole resident of utopia—a notion enabling humanity to extend its moral capacities. Schiller writes: "Every individual human being . . . carries within him, potentially and prescriptively, an ideal man, the archetype of a human being."[5]

◆ The self implies an acceptance of the sufficiency of the human condition, so that divinities, myths, and miracles slip into obsolescence. Deism frees the mind from the puzzle of origins—God is granted primal power and then gently put to sleep—thereby clearing a path for human autonomy.

◆ As against atomistic theories positing a space "outside" of society, the self may be seen as a social formation, a corollary of advanced civilization. A character in Henry James's *Portrait of a Lady* remarks: "There is no such thing as an isolated man or woman. . . . What do you call one's self? Where does it begin? Where does it end? It overflows into everything that belongs to us—and then it flows back again."[6]

◆ The self entails a provisional unity of being, yet this occurs, if it does at all, during transformation and dissolution. For the self, as a felt presence, is inescapably dynamic, at once coming into and slipping out of being.

◆ The self (see Proust) creates a created self, manifested in works of art as a kind of double, different from yet linked to the putative empirical self.

◆ And in our own time, the self becomes a redoubt, the last defense against intolerable circumstances, precious even when lost. In Pasternak's novel, Dr. Zhivago writes in one of his poems:

> For life, too, is only an instant,
> Only the dissolving of ourselves
> In the selves of all others
> As if bestowing a gift—

Given this multiplicity of possible selves, is there any value in continuing to speak of "the self?" The question is of a kind that occurs in many contexts, as in the famous discussion of whether romanticism "exists" in view of the innumerable definitions proposed for it. The answer is provided by our experience: despite our awareness of how slippery a term "romanticism" is, we cannot avoid using it. Without such slippery terms, we cannot think.

✦ ✦ ✦

The versions of the self I have mentioned might be called interpretations in static cross-section. What gave them, historically, a tremendous charge of meaning and energy is that the idea of the self came to form a social and moral claim. A claim for space, voice, identity. A claim that man is not the property of kings, lords, or states. A claim for the privilege of opinion, the freedom to refuse definitions imposed from without. A claim advanced by all who had been herded into orders and guilds. A claim against the snobbisms of status. In sum, the claim advanced by a newly confident historical subject. And a claim upon whom? Upon anyone and no one, launched into the very air—though at a given moment perhaps chiefly against despised governments. This revolution in moral consciousness, with its steadily magnified complex of claims, is by no means completed; it never will be: it is the one truly permanent revolution.

That the idea of the self should be mobilized as a mandate for action is part of the development of the liberalism—both political and metaphysical—that comes to the fore in the late eighteenth century. Liberalism not just as social program or political movement, but as a new historical temper.

Liberalism in its heroic phase constitutes one of the great revolutionary events of our history. The richness of modern culture would have been impossible without the animating liberal idea. The self as a central convention of modern literature depends upon the presence of liberalism. The dynamic of plot in the novel, based as it is on new assumptions about human mobility, would be quite inconceivable without the shaping premises of liberalism.

All of these terms—self, liberalism, romanticism—have a way of melding into one great enterprise of renewal. "The deepest driving force of the liberal idea of the Enlightenment," writes Karl Mannheim, "lay in the fact that it appealed to the free will and kept alive the feeling of being indeterminate and unconditioned." This new moral and imaginative power promises a dismissal of intolerable constraints, speaks for previously unimagined rights, declares standard of candor and sincerity. For the whole of modern culture, liberalism release energies of assertion, often as energies of opposition. Without some such cluster of values and perceptions, how could the nineteenth-century novelist so much as have conceived a *Bildungsroman* in which the self attains itself through a progress within and against society, or struggles to escape the locked frames of social role?

◆　◆　◆

Let me now glance at a few central texts, starting with Rousseau's *Confessions*.

Not the whole of Rousseau, not the Rousseau whom Ernst Cassirer presents as the author of a coherent political philosophy, not the Rousseau of that problematic notion, "the general will"; but the Rousseau who said about himself that he was more changeable than "a Proteus, a chameleon."[7] If we choose to see Rousseau as moving from speculative thought to personal apologia, we can focus upon him as an exemplary and undisciplined—exemplary, in part, because undisciplined—personality, one of those whose tumult and self-penetrating chaos ushers in the modern age. William Hazlitt, a critic born sixty-five years after Rousseau, but of a romantic generation which could still read him as its contemporary, observed: "The only quality which [Rousseau] possessed in an eminent degree . . . was extreme sensibility . . . an acute and even morbid feeling of that which related to his own impressions. . . . He had the most intense consciousness of his own existence."[8] This "intense consciousness" was both a sign of the moral revolution being enacted in his time and what Jean Starobinski calls "a manifesto from the third estate, an affirmation that the events of his inner life . . . have an absolute importance."[9]

Saint Augustine confessed to God; Rousseau to a packed house, sometimes filled with enemies, sometimes with merely his own shifting selves. Saint Augustine hoped to make confession into a discipline; for Rousseau it would be an affirmation, at once humbling and flaunting. Saint Augustine sought to bend himself to Christ, Rousseau to justify the contortions of self to . . . anyone who might listen. Saint Augustine sought truth, Rousseau sincerity. Seeking truth, Augustine found, at the least sincerity; seeking sincerity, Rousseau unleashed a memorable persona with a lively touch of scandal. For Augustine, anything like the self would be a barrier to relation with God; for Rousseau the self is the public creation of a private face, sometimes a scolding judge before whom he pleads guilty with every expectation of going free.

Rousseau's *Confessions* opens with the declaration that he has resolved on "an enterprise which has no precedent." He will offer "a portrait in every way true to nature, and the man I shall portray will be myself."[10] A few sentences later occurs the crucial word "sincerity," that mode of feeling through which he, Jean-Jacques, at once "vile" and "noble," will bare his soul to the "Eternal Being!" A not inconsiderable project, and as I read this slippery character, he is quite aware of how improbable his "enterprise" is. Which only prods him, with a sort of malicious sincerity, to further displays of self, a subject of which he never tires.

Yes, he will be sincere, he will reveal the truth about his inner being, he will strip everything away to reach an essential self that the world has only glimpsed. It is unique, this self, he declares with a pride that to a Christian must seem appalling (as it did to Kierkegaard who in his *Journal* remarks that Rousseau "lacks . . . the ideal, the Christian ideal, to humble him . . . and to sustain his efforts by preventing him from falling into the reverie and sloth of the poet. Here is an example that shows how hard it is for a man to die to the world"[11]—something that a writer with one thing more to write will rarely do).

But the fact is that the more Rousseau reveals his turmoil, his inner conflicts, his misdeeds through the flaring chaos of his self, the more persuaded we are likely to be that, yes, he *is* unique; and still more odd, the more we are persuaded that never before was there anyone quite like this Jean-Jacques, the more we feel that this touching monster shares many traits with us; and oddest of all, the knowledge that there are contradictions here does not trouble us, we may even feel that this tangle of response approaches a sentiment (if not a statement) of truth.

Everything that can be said about the versions of the self in literature composed during the age of Proust, Kafka, and Beckett—"I wanted," says Hermann Hesse's Demian, "only to try to live in obedience to the promptings which came from my true self. Why was that so very difficult?"—has already been said by Rousseau. So it's not quite true, as historians of consciousness sometimes claim—I'll be making the same mistake in a few moments—that the self in literary representations has "disintegrated" over time. The self in Rousseau *begins* as a state of disintegration, a state it abides with ease, sometimes with a tear of shame or a smirk of remorse.

The writer who declares he will be utterly sincere, indeed, the first truly sincere voice in the history of mankind, ends as a virtuoso of performance. As Starobinski remarks, "The discovery of the self coincides with the discovery of the imagination: the two discoveries are in fact the same."[12] Programmatically to make a claim for sincerity may already entail an element of bad faith, may itself contain an alloy of insincerity (the reasons for this having been grasped by Rousseau himself in his attack on the theater).

Sincerity is not likely to make its appearance as an announcement. If it can be had at all, it must (Whitman again) sidle in as a portion of speech; always more halting and less articulate, surely less well-rounded, than Rousseau's wonderful prose. But why should his effort to reach an unprecedented sincerity have resulted in a performance in which "natural man" turns out to be a shifty historical actor? Because his enterprise yields the hubris of supposing that a human being, even one so keen as Rousseau, is capable of sufficient self-knowledge. Because it means replacing the fragments of candor with the fullness of program—and a program, be it "noble" or "base," signifies a performance undertaken to some outer measure.

Still, may not the partly sincere or even insincere performance of sincerity—this contrived public self—be in some way authentic? May this not actually be Rousseau's "true self," that is the only self available to him, as against the much-invoked "inner self" we have been taught to look for? May not, still further, the "true self" consist in the performance which is perhaps all we have in life?

Rousseau was quite sincere in his yearning for sincerity, but everything about him, especially the public being he had so artfully constructed, militated against that. As he shrewdly noticed, his downfall began the moment he published his first *Discourse*, since from then on, alas, it was all *up*hill, toward the construction of the most dazzling if frequently repulsive persona of the modern era. His vision of natural man was only a phantasm of civilized man, a compensation for having no escape from civilization and its not-unglorious discontents.

By now, Rousseau has found his place in literature. His thought seems hopelessly entangled by time and commentaries, but his figure looms brilliantly, our ancestor in division, who made his self into a myth of literary consciousness, quite as Bryon would and after him, Lermontov. There is no "real Rousseau to be ferreted out in research; the Rousseau of the writings is the salvage of time. If I may parody Wallace Stevens: The self is momentary in the mind, but in performance it is immortal.

✦   ✦   ✦

Brushing aside their enormous differences in style and temper, Hazlitt linked Rousseau and Wordsworth. He saw that the linkage was historical: whatever binds radically different personalities within a defining epoch, perhaps an overflow of consciousness variously mirrored. The self, for both Rousseau and Wordsworth, figures as creed, goal, burden, necessity, sometimes as token of revolution. Wordsworth, wrote Hazlitt, "may be said to create his own materials: his thoughts are his real subjects."[13] Even when placed against great historical events or a natural setting glowing with sublimity, his thoughts center upon the molding of self, that growth which enables him to claim identity ("Possessions have I that are solely mine, / Something within which yet is shared by none").

In his autobiographical poem *The Prelude* Wordsworth cultivates a historically novel sense of the self as emergent, internally riven, and therefore constantly open to misstep, yet finally providing a provisional security of being out of which he the poet, here representative of humanity, can look back upon his earlier years, measuring his personal history against the history of his time. If Rousseau's self is a virtuoso performance, Wordsworth's is a sober narrative. The self we discover in *The Prelude* seems more hooded and less volatile than that of Rousseau, but what the two writers share is a persuasion that this self, be it psychic actuality or mere shadow of desire, is not fixed in either unalterable nature or historical circumstance. It is created, nurtured, the mark of our freedom. The self is its own child.

Still, what can it mean, in the Wordsworthian climate, to say that man is his own creation? Partly this is a testimony to the powers of imagination, not always distinguishable from the powers of will. The entirety of Wordsworth's thought can be read as a meditation upon the interrelation, sometimes the bewildering mutual disguising, of imagination and will. To imagine a self beyond immediate reach, *to be able* to imagine such a self, is to prod the will to action; it is to awake from the metaphysical slumbers of the past; it is to assert a new history. Tacitly, then, *The Prelude* seems to signify a rejection of all those who dismiss the idea of the self as a mere fiction of unity. Wordsworth locates any possible unity of the self as an arena of conflict, buffetted by historical flux. It is this which prompts one to think of *The Prelude* as an epic of selfhood in which "the transitory Being," as Wordsworth refers to the contemplative "I," replaces the hero of traditional mythic quests.

Is there, however, in Wordsworth's view of things an "original self," an integral pre-historical being endowed by nature? We must beware of reducing a poem to a proposition; what Wordsworth cares about is the experience more than the idea of the self. Still, he does write as if the infant, not yet soiled by consciousness, awaits that fortunate fall which signals the growth of the self. Because not yet homeless, the infant is not yet burdened with self-awareness:

> No outcast he, bewildered and depressed:
> Along his infant veins are interfused
> The gravitation and the filial bond
> Of nature that connect him with the world.

The self carries the brand of alienation, the consciousness of consciousness, that which we have left after expulsion from the garden or after being torn from the mother's breast. There are intimations in *The Prelude* of the therapeutic notion that, as an endowment of nature, we may recover gifts of childhood in a journey through a series of false and inadequate selves—rather like the trial of a romance hero confronting a sequence of ordeals—and that this will culminate as a healing of self and unity of peace. But this journey is perilous, and it is to the perils that *The Prelude* introduces us. The poem can be seen as a chronicle of false starts and bewitched wanderings: from commonplace vanities to revolutionary intoxications; from the "unnatural self / The heavy weight of many a weary day / Not mine, and such as were not made for me," which is one consequence of the city's false sociality, to those treacheries the self can so cunningly generate ("Humility and modest awe, themselves / Betray me, serving often for a cloak / To a more subtle selfishness"). Nor is there any reason to suppose that in this *Bildungsroman* Wordsworth indulges a notion of a fixed, unitary self, ready like a premade box for instant use; he speaks rather of seeing himself at times as "Two consciousness, conscious of myself / And of some other Being."

Nor does the precious if fragile unity of being celebrated at the close of *The Prelude* constitute an end, for there is no end, only quest. This implies a quasi-religious, if hardly Christian, vision, finding its strongest imprint in the "spots of time," set pieces focusing upon lighted moments of memory. These "spots of time" evoke an achieved (not a given) capacity for the peace that might yet surpass understanding, through a loving submission to nature—yet (a Wordsworthian paradox) also through the activity of imagination. In J. V. Cunningham's words, this entails "the problem [of] the relationship of a man and his environment, and the reconciliation of these two in poetry and thus in life."[14]

The journey at rest but not concluded, there may follow what Geoffrey Hartman calls "the special consciousness that can bring a man home to himself"—a home not soon found, not without many confusions and misdirections, even to the journey's end.

There is a lovely passage in *The Prelude* about "the Boy," an apprentice in selfhood, who stands by "the glimmering lake" and blows "mimic hootings to the silent owls / That they might answer him." "A lengthened pause / Of silence" follows and the boy would yield himself to the environment, so that "the visible scene would enter unawares into his mind / With all its solemn imagery, its rocks, / Its woods, and that uncertain heaven." Like many other nineteenth-century writers, Wordsworth enacts a spiritualization of nature—and also an accommodation of nature to human ends—as the basis for a healing, which is also a questioning, of the self. And, note well, heaven remains "uncertain."

The interaction of nature and mind postulated by Wordsworth remains a difficulty, perhaps a mystery, for us and for him. It represents a desire, a yearning, in which it may be, as Geoffrey Hartman says, "nature [does] the best it can to act as Heaven's substitute."[15] Nevertheless, through this uncertain struggle, with the imagination as prompter, the self is formed.

I have read *The Prelude* largely in terms of Wordsworth's own perception of the formation of his self, but there is of course another reading, one that sees his strong valuation of selfhood as a consequence or sign of a displacement of political aspiration, a turning inward after the disappointment of political hopes—which makes the poem an anticipation of post-totalitarian literature in our own century, also charting journeys from public to inner life. At various points Wordsworth himself seems to endorse this reading, as a subtheme to his main one. These two ways of approaching Wordsworth's journey of selfhood can, with a bit of jostling, be reconciled, but what matters, in any case, is that the realization of self be seen as a consequence of costly journeys, whether toward revolutionary Paris or the poet's idyllic birthplace. The Wordsworthian theme, however placed, is that our inner existence can become a mode of heroism too, even if without sword and shield, and that it is we who can make it such.

◆   ◆   ◆

In no other writer does the idea of the self—the self as host and shaper of consciousness—attain such centrality as in George Eliot; and in no other writer does the self become the object of such severe moral scrutiny. The novels of the later George Eliot treat consciousness—for her, the very stuff of selfhood—as a gift; but then, in accord with her "religion of humanity," that gray solace for the fading of the gods, consciousness becomes a *project* for mankind. It is only consciousness that keeps us from slipping into the abyss of egotism and its nihilist reduction; yet, as if to recall that at heaven's gate there is a byway to hell, consciousness also comes to be its own intimate betrayer, breeding Wordsworth's "more subtle selfishness."

Egoism engulfs the self. The freedom that is the reward of consciousness swells into despotic possessiveness. If consciousness is indeed to serve as a solacing companion, it must now turn upon itself, ruthless in judgment. The "abstract individual" of the eighteenth century, gives way in George Eliot's novels to a social individual who exists only by virtue of the presence of others. To this acceptance of solidarity, the only alternative, as George Eliot graphically demonstrates, is the kind of moral monster—also a self, indeed, preeminently a self, as a fearful parody—who dominates her last novel, *Daniel Deronda*.

But is there not something terrifying in George Eliot's invocation of consciousness? Is that all? Nothing else beyond or within? Yes, that is all we have, replies the sibyl with her steely warmth, and precisely because she knows how weak a bulwark the self can be, she makes her fictions into muted calls for sympathy, hoping, as she puts it, to "mitigate the harshness of all fatalities."

◆   ◆   ◆

Those characters in *Middlemarch*—Dorothea, Lydgate, Casaubon—who serve as centers of consciousness also become, in consequence, its victims. Almost all of them yield to the low clamor of self which, by a turn of mischief, can also mask itself as a favorite of consciousness. Still, her characters wrest a few moments of insight, if only in grasping how sadly limited these can be. Her major characters think and, thinking, suffer.

The stress upon consciousness in her earlier novels had implied, I suppose, at least a partial attribution of positive moral value. How could she not have slipped into the assumption, so tempting to the secular mind, that a history of consciousness must display signs of progress? But in *Daniel Deronda* she faces up to the chasm between consciousness and value, self and ethic. Through the character of Grandcourt, that supercilious aristocrat who embodies a *system* of dehumanized relations and who, as she remarks in passing, is ruthless enough "to govern a difficult colony," she invokes the barbarism that shadows civilization as a double of the cultivated self. Grandcourt cannot be said to lack consciousness, he has it in abundance, yet he takes a peculiar pleasure in employing it for a "principled" brutality. The structured self here becomes a pleased witness of the very things George Eliot had supposed it would enable us to resist. In creating Grandcourt, this monster in and of civilization, George Eliot the novelist achieved a triumph, but at the expense of George Eliot the moralist, who must now acknowledge that before the spectacle of a Grandcourt consciousness— hers, ours—may be helpless.

Trapped in dilemmas to which her truth-seeking imagination has driven her, George Eliot turns in her novels to that sustained flow of commentary, at once impassioned and ironic, severe but not systematic, which forms the moral spine of her work. So commanding is the Eliot voice, we can readily suppose that the rendered consciousness of her characters is a tributary of the consciousness of their creator. The voice of George Eliot as narrator envelopes her characters in an arc of judgment and compassion. It is a voice that comes, so to say, to serve as the source of the characters' existence, the self that is the mother of all these imagined selves. George Eliot does for her characters, and perhaps for her readers too, what she has become convinced God can no longer do for humanity: she offers shelter.

◆   ◆   ◆

It is in Whitman's poetry, and especially "Song of Myself," that the idea of self takes on its most benign expressions and copious modes, a sort of luxurious, relaxed experimentalism accommodating both the private and the transcendent. Democratic man is transfigured into a democratic hero— "plumb in the uprights, well entreated, braced in the beams / Stout as a horse, affectionate, haughty, electrical." Whitman's images are plebeian, those, you might say, of an ecstatic carpenter. At once individual and "en-masse," Whitman's democratic hero, cast in American easiness, sees no problem in adopting numerous masks, venturing a wide variety of roles, and then skidding back to the solitary self.

"Song of Myself" carves out a transit between self and all that is non-self, between the Walt hugging secrets to his bosom, a furtive, somewhat deracinated bohemian at the margin of social life, and the assured self that enters into, merges with, and shares an easy moment with all other selves. But Whitman's notion of the self is sharply different from that of Rousseau, in that he has little taste for revelation or display, and different also from that of Wordsworth, in that he cares more for simultaneous enactments, shifty changes of role, than for a coherent, formative history. In Whitman the self serves as a normative supposition projecting the democratic hero who is of and with "the roughs and beards and space and ruggedness and nonchalance." Prototype of a "new order"—we have still to see it—in which "every man shall be his own priest" and carry himself "with the air . . . of [a person] who never knew how it felt to stand in the presence of superiors," this envisaged self yokes Protestant individuality with new-world friendliness and is treated by Whitman with humor, even mockery—as if to acknowledge the impudence of native visions!

Whitman is quite realistic about the place of the self in an urban world. The most fruitful of his persona has been described, though not with Whitman in mind, by Georg Simmel, the German sociologist, in his brilliant essay "The Stranger." If "wandering," writes Simmel,

> is the liberation from every given point in space and thus the conceptual opposite to fixation at such a point, the sociological form of "the stranger" presents the unity . . . of these two characteristics. . . . The stranger is being discussed here not . . . as the wanderer who comes today and goes tomorrow. He is, so to speak, the *potential* wanderer: although he has not moved on, he has not quite lost the freedom of coming and going.[16]

He who comes today and stays tomorrow, the *potential* wanderer "whose position in the group is fixed" yet "who imports qualities into it"[17]—is this not a sketch of the author of "Song of Myself"?

The self of the poem is fluid, defined by unwillingness to rest in definition, committed, with both an ingenuous faith and comic skepticism, to the belief in *possibility* which so delights and bedevils Americans. At times the

self of the poem comes to resemble a protean demigod, absorbing all creatures, who yet avoids grandiosity by the grace, rather infrequent among
demigods, of having a sense of humor. After one of his rhapsodic
catalogues, Whitman writes: "And these one and all tend inward toward
me, and I tend outward to them, / And such as it is to be of these more or
less I am." That *more or less* is priceless as an intimation of what I'd call Whitman's distancing fraternity.

At times the self of the poems sinks to an almost mineral tranquility, a
quasi-mystical dissolution of consciousness. The famous "oceanic" impulse that disturbs some readers because it seems to blur distinctions in
quality of being, is here acceptable because we see that the self of the poem
also acts out of a deep anxiety and loneliness. Reduce the cosmic straining of
"Song of Myself" from philosophical grandiosity to a common human
tremor, and Whitman's possession of all possible selves, like his corresponding withdrawal from them, becomes familiar.

"I have no mockings or arguments, I witness and wait." "Agonies are
one of my changes of garments." Such lines are spoken by a stranger in the
midst, planted in the very milieu from which he moves apart. In a splendid
phrase Whitman speaks of the "knit of identity," that is, the self composed
of a multitude of experiences, feelings, and intuitions, all braided into a
loose but clear unity. The self becomes an agent of potentiality, and Whitman, most amiable of pragmatists, tries on a range of new ones, yet keeps
returning to his own center: "I have pried through the strata and analyzed to
a hair / And counselled with doctors and calculated close and found no
sweeter fat than sticks to my own bones."

◆　　◆　　◆

The rejection of the self as mere mental consciousness finds its keenest nov-
elistic voice in D. H. Lawrence. He invites us to respond to his characters as
Ursula, in *The Rainbow*, responds to the life about her: "She could not understand, but she seemed to feel far-off things." These "far-off things" are
not only of immensities and absolutes, the "infinite world, eternal, un-
changing"; they are also close within, deep down, untapped. Lawrence said
he wanted to drop "the old stable ego," or what we call the coherent self,
and move toward "a stratum [of being] deeper than I think anyone has ever
gone in the novel."[18]

In *The Rainbow* he strives to represent states of being which his characters
feel to be overpowering yet find hard to describe. "There is another seat of
consciousness than the brain and nervous system," wrote Lawrence in a letter to Bertrand Russell, "there is the blood-consciousness, with the sexual
connection holding the same relation as the eye, in seeing, to the mental
consciousness. . . . This is one half of life, belonging to the darkness."[19]

Through metaphor and analogy, since he cannot find a denotative vocabulary for this "deeper stratum," Lawrence explores "the other seat of consciousness." Might this "other seat" be what we usually call the unconscious? Admittedly, the distinction between "blood-consciousness" and "the unconscious" is vague; if we could speak with clarity about such matters, there would be no need to speak at all. But I venture that there is a distinction of sorts between the two: because Lawrence spoke of a variant of consciousness, and because this "deeper stratum," unlike the unconscious, can now and again be reached by his characters on their own.

Through long, loping alternations of submission to and resistance against this "state of being," some of the Brangwens (the family in *The Rainbow*) know this "state" or at least can feel themselves in its grip. Acutely or drowsily, they sense that in some nether layer of consciousness there swirls a supply of energy, and that this energy is not to be controlled entirely by will or intelligence—on the contrary, these characters feel that fulfillment can come only through yielding to these deep-seated rhythms, rhythms in which they move toward union with another person and then withdraw into solitariness. Lawrence's characters live out the thrust and pull of the forces churning within themselves; sometimes throw up sterile barriers of resistance; but except for Ursula, who represents the third and youngest generation of Brangwens, they do not propose or think it possible to name these forces.

Naming things, identifying the deeper surges of instinctual life, becomes a possibility only for Ursula's generation, though by the previous or second generation, that of Will Brangwen, there is a groping after meanings that elude words. This wish to describe the inner actions of psychic life coincides with and may even be a consequence of a yearning to move "upward" spiritually, a yearning that can be felt even when Lawrence's characters are still in the drowse of sensual experience.

Naming things is something about which Lawrence feels sharp inner conflict. He sees the urge to name things as a striving after "higher" values, but also as a sign of the sickness afflicting an over-rationalized consciousness. He admires those who live in "another seat of consciousness than the brain and the nervous system," he even makes them into exemplars of his fiction; yet he is himself, like those characters, such as Ursula, who are closest to him, a creature of "the brain and nervous system." The writer who would abandon or at least minimize that "system" cannot help resorting to it. Lawrence writes most familiarly about characters who have entered what he calls "the finer, more vivid circle of life," the circle of mental consciousness. For only the latter are capable of so much as imagining "another seat of consciousness"—those already lodged there don't know or need to know it.

The "deeper" stratum Lawrence seeks to evoke consists of intervals in long swings of psychic-emotional energy, into "the darkness" and then back to the outer air. There are mergings with others, sometimes ecstatic, as if to break into the marrow of being, and sometimes sullen, as if in fear of losing identity; and then comes a bruised solitary apartness, the stuff out of which a self is formed.

Yet a reading of *The Rainbow* leaves one with a question: We can readily say that the solitariness of Lawrence's characters, their periods of withdrawal, are the stuff out of which a self is formed: that, after all, is a familiar notion to readers of the nineteenth-century novel. But may not the phase of merging into "the darkness" also be—not a blotting-out of self—but another way of renewing the self? May not Lawrence's enterprise be one of prompting a series of tentative, connected selves, available upon need and retracted when not? And may these not be present within a deeper stratum, call it "blood-consciousness" or the unconscious?

The Lawrence who would probe beneath mental consciousness is also the Lawrence who aspires to its "higher" levels. So the self is not obliterated. It may for a time be "lost," it may be transformed or immersed within some collective flow; but it returns, a witness to its subterranean adventures.

✦   ✦   ✦

I would have liked, if there were time, to look at the vicissitudes to which the idea of the self has been subjected in twentieth-century literature, through both monstrous expansion and radical shrinkage of characters, as well as through the manifestations—imperial, disintegrative, muffled—of the authorial presence. An extreme instance would be that of Samuel Beckett, in whose work occurs a dispossession or emptying-out of characters as selves, so that in a play like *Endgame* a world of feeling remembered and mourned for comes into juxtaposition with an emptied present, the "zero-level" condition in which Beckett's characters torment themselves. But in Beckett's work the self also emerges as an overpowering presence: his own voice, with its lucid speech and biting wit: "You must go on, I can't go on, I'll go on."

I approach the end, without having finished or, perhaps, being able to finish. In recent literary and, to some extent, political theory, the self has suffered demotion, even dispossession. I have tried to get a handle on this school of thought, but with shaky results. There is the problem of verbal opacity, which I find a formidable barrier. So I can only venture a few possible reasons for the demotion of the idea of the self.

✦ It is said that the idea of the self is phallocentric, a sign of traditional male domination. This claim is partly true, but since it is made through or as a historical approach, it is not in principle so different from the one I have been using here: namely, to see the self as a concept with its own history forming a narrative within history at large. If there is value to such an approach, then there is no reason why the idea of the self need remain phallocentric, no reason why it cannot be revised and extended to serve as a basis for rectifying the inequities of gender.

◆ The idea of the self, providing lonely moderns with "metaphysical consolation," is a notion, we are told, that a post-symbolic view of language—language self-subsistent, perhaps autonomous—can now dispense with. There is a philosophical tradition, reaching back to parts of Nietzsche, which rejects the idea of the self. But the evidence compiled by Stanley Korngold in his learned book about German literature seems decisively to show that in some version the idea of the self has been central to work of many major literary figures these past two centuries, and more problematically, that even Nietzsche, while at some points disdaining the idea of the self, inclines at other points to recoup a version of it. The self, it would appear, can be banished only by a banishing self. At least for purposes of literary discourse—I cannot enter the philosophical discussion—this historical evidence takes on significant weight.

◆ A fairly innocent reason for demoting the idea of the self is provided by Richard Poirier. Writing in a quasi-Emersonian vein, he argues that the very idea of the self, fixed because defined, blocks further vistas of possibility, closing off a "circle" in that endless sequence of "circles" that forms the schema of Emersonianism. One such possibility—but now Poirier seems to write in a Foucauldian vein—is "the abolition of the human," and the question whether this "is a good or bad idea," he adds, "is not to be decided by a show of hands."[20] Indeed not! Exactly what "the abolition of the human" might mean Poirier does not make crystal clear, nor do I suppose he can, although the nonchalance with which he puts forward the notion strikes me as breathtaking. But is it really true that to hold to an idea of the self is to foreclose on the endlessness of the Emersonian "circles"? Cannot our idea of the self expand with the expansion of those "circles" of possibility, perhaps now and then to reach an "oceanic sense" of a transindividual or collective self, and may it not also contract with the contraction of the "circles" into a grim acknowledgment of nothingness?

◆ Perhaps the most powerful assault on the idea of the self is one that identifies it, tacitly or explicitly, with the historical disabilities of humanist liberalism. I cite two telling passages from Michel Foucault:

> By humanism I mean the totality of discourse through which Western man is told: "Even though you don't exercise power, you can still be a ruler. Better yet, the more you deny yourself the ex-

ercise of power, the more you submit to those in power, then the more this increases your sovereignty." . . . In short, humanism is everything in Western civilization that *restricts the desire for power.* [emphasis in original][21]

And

It is a source of profound relief to think that man is only a recent invention, a figure not yet two centuries old, a new fold in our knowledge, and that he will disappear again as soon as that knowledge has discovered a new form.[22]

Foucault's first passage bears a distressing resemblance to the weary notion that "bourgeois democracy" is a mere façade for class domination. As for the second . . . well, we can only wait and see what the "new form" replacing man will be like. So far, most candidates have not been very attractive. But what interests me most is not so much the question, Why is this being said?, as the question, Why have these statements somehow become apparently plausible at this historical moment?

Have we reached a breaking point? Is it possible to argue the question of the self, especially with its more intransigent opponents? Do we not have here two sharply contrasting narratives of modern experience which can only be placed side by side in the hope of later enlightenment?

So let me declare my bias. The idea of the self has been a liberating and revolutionary step, perhaps the most liberating and revolutionary, toward the goal of a communal self-humanization. I will cite, for support or comfort, two utterly different writers. Karl Marx: "The critique of religion ends with the doctrine that *man* is the highest being for man, hence with the categorical imperative to overthrow all conditions in which man is a degraded, enslaved, neglected, contemptible being."[23] And in two lines of verse, Hölderlin:

Der Mensch will sich selber fühlen . . .
Sich aber nicht zu fühlen, ist der Tod.

Man wants to have a sense of self . . .
Not to have a sense of self is death.

NOTES

1. Jacob Burckhardt, *The Civilization of the Renaissance in Italy* (London: Phaidon Press, 1944), 81.

2. Peter Gay, *The Enlightenment: An Interpretation* (New York: Alfred A. Knopf, 1969), 2:3.

3. Cited in Lionel Trilling, *Sincerity and Authenticity* (New York: Harcourt Brace Jovanovich, 1972), 34.

4. Jacques Rivière, *The Ideal Reader* (London: Harvill Press, 1962), 26.

5. Friedrich Schiller, *On the Aesthetic Education of Man*, trans. E. M. Wilkinson and L. A. Willoughby (Oxford: Clarendon Press, 1967), 17.

6. Henry James, *The Portrait of a Lady* (1881; Boston: Houghton Mifflin, 1963), chap. 19.

7. Jean-Jacques Rousseau, "Second Dialogue," in *Rousseau, Judge of Jean-Jacques*, ed. Rogers Masters and Christopher Kelly (Hanover, N.H.: University Press of New England, 1990), 143.

8. William Hazlitt, "On the Character of Rousseau," in *The Round Table* (New York: Dutton, Everyman, 1936), 88.

9. Jean Starobinski, *Jean-Jacques Rousseau: Transparency and Obstruction* (Chicago: University of Chicago Press, 1988), 185.

10. Jean-Jacques Rousseau, *The Confessions*, trans. J. M. Cohen (London: Penguin Books, 1953), 17.

11. Starobinski, *Jean-Jacques Rousseau*, 384.

12. Ibid., 7.

13. William Hazlitt, "On Mr. Wordsworth's *Excursion*," in *The Round Table*, 112.

14. J. V. Cunningham, *Tradition and Poetic Structure* (Denver, Col.: Alan Swallow, 1960), 115.

15. Geoffrey Hartman, *Wordsworth's Poetry* (New Haven: Yale University Press, 1964), 215–216.

16. *The Sociology of Georg Simmel*, ed. Kurt Wolff (Glencoe, Ill.: The Free Press, 1950), 402.

17. Ibid.

18. *The Letters of D. H. Lawrence* (New York: Viking, 1932), 198.

19. *The Collected Letters of D. H. Lawrence*, ed. Harry Moore (New York: Viking, 1962), 178.

20. Richard Poirier, *The Renewal of Literature* (New York: Random House, 1987), 182.

21. Michel Foucault, *Language, Counter-Memory, Practise* (Ithaca: Cornell University Press, 1977), 221.

22. Michel Foucault, *The Order of Things* (New York: Vintage Books, 1973), 386–387.

23. Karl Marx, "Contribution to the Critique of Hegel's Philosophy of Right: Introduction," in *The Portable Karl Marx*, ed. Eugene Kamenka (New York: Viking, 1983), 119.

✦ AGNES HELLER ✦

Death of the Subject?

Before someone is buried, s/he needs to be first identified, lest the alleged corpse resume business right after the funeral. No autopsy has yet been performed on the thing or concept termed "subject" though its demise is taken for granted by many students of philosophy. Actually the concept "subject" is polysemic to the extent that it easily lends itself to unintended verbal and conceptual manipulation. An author can make a case against the subject in one of its interpretations, then shift the argument in direction of another, completely different interpretation, without even noticing the shift. No wonder, then, that readers and interpreters are often party to the construction of mistaken identity.

In the contemporary French (and German) debates the term "subject" takes any of the following meanings: point of view; individual; the "subject" of biography; the hermeneutical (meaning-constituting) subject; the subject who-comes-to-know (Erkenntnissubjekt); the subject of knowledge (Wissen); the political subject (both as *subjectum* and *subjectus*); the moral subject (again, both as *subjectum* and *subjectus*); person; personality; self; the mono-centered self; Ego; the man; self-consciousness; self-reflexivity; subject as Will; subject as Sovereignty; or simply the personal pronoun *I*. In addition, the term "subject" includes all cases of nonindividual, nonpersonal subjects, such as the Kantian Transcendental Subject, the Hegelian World Spirit, or the Fichtean *I*; furthermore, the personal, but nonhuman subjects such as God, and the so-called universal Subjects such as History, Humanism, Rights, Art, and the like. Finally, if something is asserted on "the subject," it is also meant to be asserted about "the subjective," "subjectivity," and "subjectivism." The referents of the

Previously published in Agnes Heller, *Can Modernity Survive?* (Berkeley and Los Angeles: University of California Press, 1990). Reprinted by permission.

term "subject" are slightly different in some cases, only remotely linked in some others, whereas sometimes they have absolutely nothing in common or are entirely unrelated. The adjective "subjective," and the nouns "subjectivity" and "subjectivism" are related to certain interpretations of the subject, whereas they are entirely unrelated to several others.

When the concept of subject is discussed, our first question should be about the kind of subject under discussion. For example, Jean-Luc Nancy acclaims, in *La partage des voix*, the "end of the subject" given that real man has been sacrificed (in modernity) to Subjects such as Philosophy, Peace, Science, Art, and History. Yet statements like "La voix de chacun est singulière" (everyone's voice is unique) and that "l'interpretation de l'universel est sa partition en voix singulières" (the interpretation of the universal consists of dividing it into unique voices) sounds rather like a confession of love for the subject and an expression of hope in its rebirth, rather than a gleeful obituary after its demise.

The thesis, the "end of the subject," is far from being new. Behaviorism embraced it a half-century ago and has been committed to it ever since. One of the greatest philosophical masterpieces of our century, Wittgenstein's *Philosophical Investigations*, can at least be interpreted as a statement on behalf of that thesis. The contemporary French wave, however, has very little to do with the Anglo-American tradition in spite of Lyotard's ample references to Wittgenstein's language-game theory. In the Anglo-American tradition, the disappearance of the subject has been an undramatic affair. Wittgenstein never made the existential dimensions of his philosophy explicit. In the strict behaviorist tradition, the subject has been dismissed as a mythological device of a prescientific manner of thought. It deserves mention that French structuralism, non-Marxist and Marxist alike, has also played out the card of a "scientific versus nonscientific" approach. The very assumption that there might be something such as an individual "subject," consciousness, or will, has been dismissed by structuralism as a fairy tale for grown-up children. The structuralists, particularly Althusser, condemned the "philosophy of the subject" as being guilty of humanism, in other words, as being unscientific, a long time ago.

The prehistory of the contemporary debate deserves a brief glance for obvious reasons. The political and philosophical formation of many participants of the new wave has taken place under the influence of Althusser. The "death of the subject" survived the demise of Marxism, and has reappeared in a completely new garb. Now the concept of the "subject" is not rejected for not being scientific enough, but rather for the opposite reason. In terms of the new scenario, it is the "subject" that has created the havoc of science and technology. For one reason or another, it is always the subject that has to exit.

Contrary to the drabness of behaviorism, the new wave of French ideology reintroduces the good old philosophical custom to present a thesis in the form of a historical fiction. There are quite a few philosophical narratives and metanarratives presently in the air. The speculative clout of these narratives are extremely divergent. Very briefly, I will refer only to the two most dominating clusters of narratives: the neo-Heideggerian and neo(post)-structuralist scenarios. Since each and every participant in the discourse presents his or her own version of the master narratives, I cannot do justice to any of them in enumerating certain major problems rather than themes. I need to add that, even if the narratives are fragmented, they remain fictions. Derrida is right in stating that there are nothing but fragments, I would only add that some can create the illusion of having presented the whole. Yet in (post)modern philosophical fictions this rarely happens.

The Heideggerian fiction of the death of the subject unfolds on three levels. The first level is mystico-speculative, the second is metaphilosophical, the third is meta-historico-political. Due to the constant interplay of the three levels, a wide territory is opened up for theoretical meditation. One can discuss the forgetfulness of Being, the Subject of metaphysics and its vicissitudes, and the doom which had been foisted upon the modern world by metaphysics in the form of technology (and democracy) in one breath. The more weighty a philosophy, the more divergent its interpretations, textual exegesis being perhaps the most subjective mode of interpretation. This is not meant as an abuse, for, at least in my view, "subjective" can have both positive and negative connotations depending on the context. The interpretations of Heidegger, which are sometimes textual exegeses of textual exegeses, can appear, among others, in the following composite fictions (in a deliberate simplification). First scenario: The subject as the brainchild of metaphysics disappears as soon as metaphysics is deconstructed; metaphysics is now being deconstructed, *ergo* the subject is now disappearing. Second scenario: The subject has been the brainchild of metaphysics; modern technology is the ultimate consummation of metaphysics in which the "forgetfulness of Being" comes to pass (albeit technology is also the manifestation of Being). In fact, the second scenario does not lend much support to the creed of the "death of the subject" for in its framework we are witnessing the exuberant presence or "actualization" of the subject rather than its final demise. Third scenario: Everything remains as above with the difference that the deconstruction of the subject of philosophy (metaphysics), and perhaps also the presence of the artwork, signal the coming end of the subject.

In all previous combinations (and they are more complex and more sophisticated than my brief parody would suggest) the "death of the subject" is meant as something "positive," if I am allowed to use a word from the metaphysical (and everyday) vocabulary. However, in the post-structuralist scenario the same term refers to something "dark," unwanted or "negative." Foucault himself, who played an eminent role in the development of the second scenario, has preserved an aloofness, a playful pretension of mere descriptive objectivity. And yet, the reader of the discourse on prisons, mental asylums, or sexuality gains a different, much more serious, emotional or intellectual experience. The negative evaluation of the "end of the subject" is not therefore a totally false or even vulgar conclusion drawn by the uninitiated.

Now we say "I speak" instead of "I think," so Foucault insists. The thinking person has "something" inside, whereas the person who says "I speak," has nothing. In Foucault's formulation, the being of language appears in the nonbeing of the subject alone. This is why, Foucault contends, the assertion "I speak" plays the same role in modernity as "I lie" did in ancient Greek thinking. Foucault does not provide us with a continuous story of a guilty metaphysics. In his later books, he rather draws a strongly complimentary picture of ancient Greek (and even Roman) "subjects" alias personalities. Still, on many occasions, "the subject," (and not only "man," an altogether different referent in Foucault's conceptual universe) assumes strongly negative connotations as being associated with "mastering" and "mastery," without any reference to the paradigm of "I speak." Here too the interpreter has a fairly broad hunting ground in investigating the demise of the subject.

I do not wish to address here the flaws of the master narratives. All philosophical fictions are flawed if read as real stories and not as allegories or metaphors as they should be. It is easy to point out that it took two thousand years for metaphysics to arrive at its supposed destination, which is modern technology. Thus the "connection" between the two events becomes so blown out of proportion that the pilgrimage of the Hegelian World Spirit looks a pedestrian travel story when compared with the Heideggerian myth of metaphysics. It is even easier to point out that we can devise alternative fictions aplenty with identical, abundant, or meager, empirical-historical support. The only question that remains open is the speculative yield of such alternative narratives. As a rule, the mere refutation of the empirical trustworthiness of master narratives generates a fairly poor speculative yield. Original counterfictions may bring more attractive results. There is no doubt in my mind that counterfictions will soon emerge when the narratives of the "death of the subject" are at least temporarily exhausted.

No philosophical statement can relativize itself. Most of the narratives of the "end of the subject" are simultaneously fictions of the "end of philosophy" with reference to the guilt of philosophy (or metaphysics) in producing the subject or in being Subject Incarnate. No one could ever imagine a scientific statement announcing the end of science or a religious statement heralding the end of religion; however, the emphasis on the "end of philosophy" fits smoothly into the tradition of philosophy; it is in fact the philosophical tradition *par excellence*. Since philosophers believe that there is only one philosophy, which is theirs, they must claim the end of philosophy in the same breath, and so they do. The only difference is that moderns, or at least some of the postmoderns, refrain both from claiming absolute truth and from suggesting the empty alternative that "truth is meaningless." Yet whatever they do, they remain within the confines of the philosophical language game. It is easy to prove this point. The best thinkers bring forth a world (a philosophical edifice) and furnish it with categories, the props of the game. They invite others for a visit. Those who enter this world will be at home in it. They will toss about the (existing) furniture, play the game according to the rules given; and interpret and modify the categories to the extent that the world of that particular philosophy permits. Those who enter the world of a philosophy accept the world's language as their natural tongue, they speak it and they think in terms of this tongue. They will be outraged if a person who has not joined the same world will declare that they are talking nonsense, that the things they refer to "do not exist," and the outrage will be justified. But the others will also have their point if some zealots of streamlined philosophical edifices exclude them from the world of speculation by confronting them with the alternative of either subscribing to the end of philosophy and of the subject or being stripped of the title "philosopher." True enough, one can interpret Heidegger as the enemy of the perpetual war in philosophy, and one can point out in harmony with him that works of art do not fight against one another. There is indeed a difference here: works of art do not fight even if artists do, but philosophies themselves, and not only philosophers, fight each other. The young Lukacs once suggested that works of art are closed worlds, cold stars that bring warmth to the recipients alone. In this capacity, they are the mirror images of our existential solitude. Philosophies, on the other hand, are mirror images of our unsocial sociability. The debate on the "end of philosophy" ends only within philosophy. As long as the fiction of "the end of" something, or, alternatively, the birth of something, continues, philosophy is alive and kicking.

Precisely because philosophy is the mirror image of our unsocial sociability, we do not choose a philosophy at random. In taking up a philosophical position, we take up a position within the network of unsociable sociability, of conflicts, alliances, abuses, loves, and friendships, that is, of affections and commitments. And precisely because philosophy is the mirror image of our unsocial sociability, we can indulge in letting our philosophical taste have the lion's share in the choice. One does not enthusiastically subscribe to a manifestly pedestrian philosophy even if it is consonant with one's commitment. One cannot help but admire speculative strength, and one is often carried away by it to the point where one's commitment starts to protest loudly. Certain contemporary authors, Habermas among them, identify philosophy too closely with the network of unsociable sociability. They tend to forget that it is just a mirror image, a metaphor, a game. On the other extreme, other philosophers tend to forget that philosophy is not devoid of moral and political commitment, precisely because it is the mirror image of our unsociable sociability. When a philosopher carries his enthusiasm for Heidegger to the extreme of making humanism the main culprit for Nazism, he definitively crosses the dividing line between a responsible and an irresponsible game. To assert that one of the interpretations of the subject, that of absolute creativity (autoproduction), can also result in totalitarianism is one thing, and to collapse autoproduction into humanism in toto is another. If a philosopher tampers with the interpretation of momentous political events, he needs to scrutinize his categories more thoroughly than otherwise. Autocreativity has been only one of the interpretations of humanism throughout modern history, and not even the major one. Without elaborating the alternative interpretations of the same concept, all of which have been on a collision course with Nazism, a philosopher sacrifices things that he as a person stands for, in order to win a point in the philosophical game.

Given that the slogan the "end of the subject" is mostly (rightly or wrongly) associated with another slogan "anything goes," I cannot help but briefly comment on the latter.

"Anything goes" can have several different meanings. One of them reads as follows: The language game called philosophy permits a great variety of new combinations; in principle, no gambit is excluded from the genre. Spectators (of philosophy) have no difficulty with this position. Philosophical actors can also subscribe to this version of relativism without endangering the survival of this unique species of imagination. On my part, I am prepared to accept this brand of relativism, provided a few fellow philosophers will join me by manifesting a similar readiness. The philosophical discourse is flooded by statements such as "one can no longer philosophize this way"; "the paradigm of language is the only paradigm of philosophy"; "the paradigm of consciousness is totally outdated"; and the like. Philosophy is still perceived, and not only by the zealots of "the end of the subject," as a kind of technological device, for example, a computer, which is easily outdated with the introduction of a new model.

"Anything goes" can also have the following meaning: one philosophy is as good or as bad as the other, none of them is more true than the other. No philosophical actor can possibly take up this position, and none ever have. One cannot fully commit one's personality, unleash one's imagination to bring forth a world in which creator and recipients can dwell alike, and yet assert about it that in this world "anything goes." Even if the content of a particular philosophy is relativistic, the language game termed "philosophy" itself is not. For, as it has been repeatedly pointed out, relativists consider relativism absolute truth. The "philosophical spectator" can be an accomplished and relativistic hermeneutician; but creative philosophers, while dwelling in the house of their own philosophy, never. Whether or not they constitute a Subject, whether they construct or deconstruct, is of very little relevance here.

Every time someone offers you a world in which you can dwell, a language which you can speak esoterically, a framework of speculation within which you can toy with many dominant and subdominant elements, you must be aware that you are not moving in the medium of the accomplished hermeneutician. Nor will you be an accomplished hermeneutician as long as you find satisfaction in toying with the dominant or subdominant elements of this world. This world is an individual, for you can identify it in its uniqueness. It is a meaning-carrying individual, which interprets (self-interprets) as well as lends itself to a great variety of, but not all possible interpretations. It is a (not mono-centered) self by virtue of its dominant and subdominant elements. And, insofar as it is modern, it is also a subject, for it bears the hallmark of contingency the constituents of which have been pulled together into a personal destiny. The subject in the text and the subject of the text together can be termed "dogmatism" or the "fixed point," the "center," the cachet, the birthmark—you name it. This is the subject I am going to discuss. More precisely, I am not going to discuss the subject of the philosopher as an actor (author), but the subject of men and women (which makes modern actorship and authorship possible in the first place). Whether this subject serves as a limit to relativism remains to be seen.

As already indicated, concepts like subject, subjective, subjectivity, and subjectivism need to be distinguished. For brevity's sake let me exemplify the issue by a few references to the history of modern philosophy. In the work of Kant and Hegel, the two main defendants in the trial against the Subject, the term "subjective" normally indicates inferiority in contrast with "objective." By contrast, it was Kierkegaard who threw down the gauntlet in the arena declaring truth subjective against the Hegelian stricture. And Kierkegaard was certainly not a champion of logocentrism. On the other hand, subjectivity is frequently identified with inwardness in Hegel as well. Subjectivism, as the cultivation of the subjective point of view, together with the claim of individuality to unrestricted self-realization, was associated with the romantic school. In contrast, subjectivism was strongly disapproved of by Hegel and Kierkegaard alike, for the latter's enthusiastic plea for subjectivity was not an endorsement of subjectivism. In the foregoing I restricted my brief references to the understanding of individual subjects prior to (or irrespective of) the differentiation between epistemological, moral, and political subjects. My own comments will follow later.

◆   ◆   ◆

Whatever is termed "subject" in contemporary philosophy, is certainly not conceived of as an empirical human universal, but as a real or imaginary entity, feature, attitude, propensity, something which happens to belong to occidental history or to the modern world. I accept this view as a starting point. Occidental or European history is a modern text that incorporates certain premodern traces or testimonies, and rejects or neglects others as antipodal. Since we share modern history, we cannot avoid being party to the exegesis of the modern text. One can attempt to transcend history in order to challenge the limits of our horizon. In fact, this is precisely what Heidegger and Derrida attempt. I am not joining them; rather I am attempting to clarify our own historical consciousness within the limits of our historical horizon.

Many of us are familiar with the novel (and the motion picture) titled *The World According to Garp*. Neither the novel nor the movie is of interest here, only the title. There is a person called Garp, as a consequence, there is also a world according to Garp. If there is a person called Joh Piper, there is also a world according to Joh Piper. There is a world according to every person who dwells here, in modernity. This is what I am going to call the *subject*.

The first autobiography was written by Augustine, and it was not about the world according to Augustine, but about the representative ascent to Truth. The first "European" autobiographies were the products of the period of the Renaissance. But Cardano did not describe the world according to Cardano, nor did Cellini portray the world according to Cellini. Each committed to paper the unusual, unique adventures that had happened to him in a world given to him. Rousseau's *Confessions* can already be characterized by us as "the world according to Rousseau." Yet Rousseau himself would have protested against such an enormous impertinence. His confessions were not those of a contingent person, but the testimony of a representative personality. The world, too, was meant to be representative, not just a world according to Jean-Jacques.

Let us cast a random glance on recent publications. The book market is flooded with life stories, stories of success and failure and much else. Friedrich Schlegel once said that everyone can write at least one good novel, his or her autobiography. I would date the emergence of the subject from this statement rather than from the Cartesian *cogito*. That everyone can write a (good) novel about him or herself is questionable if good is meant to stand for high artistic quality. But if "good" refers to engaging or even interesting reading, Schlegel proved to be a genuine prophet. If someone became only a minor celebrity as an actor or an actress, a singer, a director, a criminal, a businessman, a painter, a writer, a boxer, a baseball player, or even the son or daughter, sister or brother of one of the above, a politician of the smallest renown, or even his secretary or factotum, one expects them to write an autobiography. And if one cannot write, one's autobiography will be taped and transcribed by someone else. Can we attribute this thirst for autobiography to mere curiosity, to our irresistible desire to eavesdrop or to peek at windows? The thirst for gossip is old, but the general drive to write autobiographies (and biographies) is new. In addition, autobiographies are read even if one is completely ignorant of the field in which the author achieved his or her celebrity.

Modern autobiographies have a dual author. There is an *author of the* (written or taped) text who is at the same time the *author of his or her own life,* or, put more cautiously, who is supposed to be the author of his or her own life, as well as of his or her text. The dual authorship warrants the *truth-content.* The authors are expected to present the reader with a true world, in this dual sense. They are expected to be truthful, that is, to recount a "real" story (one is not supposed to present fiction as autobiography). They are also expected to present the world (or rather two worlds, an internal and an external one) as they saw and experienced it, as they have assessed it, and this is the world *"according to them."* Even the most pedestrian autobiography full of stereotypical banalities needs the make-believe of a world that is of the author's own making. In confirmation of Schlegel, men and women normally succeed in presenting a world "according to them" beyond all expectations. As it happens, they present themselves as subjects.

Is "the world according to Joh" the subject of Joh? Or rather, is Joh a subject who presents himself as such? Or is Joh a subject insofar as he presents himself in a specific, subject-related interpretation of the world?

The circumstances that there is a world according to (Joh) manifests that "there is a subject." Yet the world according to Joh is not the subject of Joh. The world is not a subject at all because there is no world according to the world, or, at least, such a proposition does not make sense in the framework of my present speculations. For "a world according to Joh" to exist, there must be a world in the first place. Joh, like all other human beings, was born into a meaningful human universe. He too, like everybody else, was destined by birth to be related to all other bodies by meaning. He received the network of meanings from his social universe. These meanings were embedded in, and mediated by, the norms and rules of ordinary language, the use of objects, and the customs of his environment. Joh, like all other Johs before him, started his life by elaborating on the meanings of the received meanings, in other words, by filling the received meanings with his personal experience. Objects were given to his inborn drives (like proper food to his hunger); yet he *developed* a taste of his own. He was taught how and when to manifest his innate affects (like fear), yet he *became* courageous or a coward. Tasks were given to him (for example, the cultivation of a spot of land), and he completed them well or badly. His best innate propensities developed or remained barren. Every Joh became thus a single person different from all others. Before learning the importance of sentences like "I think" or "I speak," he certainly learned the importance of the utterance "I feel." Every Joh is the navel of his own universe.

Had our occidental Joh been born a few hundred years ago (or probably less), he would have received not only the network of meanings, but also their general explanation without exception. He would have learned why everything is as it is and why it should be so; why the stars shine, why people die, and what happens to them after they die. He would have thus received a fairly complete map of the external and internal world. Had our occidental Joh been born a few hundred years ago, there would not have been a world "according to Joh," that is, there would have been no subject.

Let us proceed to the second question. Is Joh himself the subject we discuss? Is there a world "according to Joh" because Joh (the subject) manifests himself in this world? "Subject" can mean "being subjected to" or "subjecting something to." In the modern philosophical vocabulary "subject" is normally juxtaposed to "object." I could even add an unorthodox variation to the theme in rendering the meaning of the subject as "being related to something or someone." Yet no interpretation of the "subject," orthodox or unorthodox, can possibly identify it with Joh or with anyone else.

Joh is indeed "subjected to" several things. *What* he is subjected to (God, the sovereign, the constitution, the law of nature, the moral law) is a historical variable and, at least sometimes, open to interpretation and choice. But regardless of whatever Joh is subjected to, he is never identical with hisbeing-subjected-to. If Joh is a slave, he is not identical with himself-as-a-slave. If for no other reason, simply because he also subjects something to himself and is also related to something else. Hegel, in the celebrated chapter on masters and slaves in his *Phenomenology of Spirit* presented the model of this dialectical turn and twist.

Many things are indeed subjected to Joh; so are persons. *What* he subjects to his will is a historical variable and sometimes open to interpretation and choice. (A particular Joh subjects the land while tilling it, yet another Joh subjects his wives and children to his will, while a third Joh in another epoch will perhaps decide not to subject them.) But whatever Joh subjects to his will, he is never identical with the practice to his will, he is never identical with the practice of subjecting-to, if for no other reason, simply because he is also subjected to something, and because he also relates to something else.

The same could be asserted about Joh's "being related to something." Joh as subjecting something, being subjected to something, and being related to something *taken together* still *do not* add up to Joh. Joh thinks and talks, and, in particular, feels a great many things in conjunction with all three relations. If two Johs were to subject the same things to their will and if they were also subjected to the same powers as well as related to the same persons and things, they would still remain different persons, and not merely in their external appearances. Yet it is not this triviality I wanted to arrive at.

If Joh is not a subject, what *is* he then?

We can answer that he is a human person. This is a correct, but irrelevant, answer in our quest for the subject. Since we have begun this quest with the purpose of pinning down the subject in "the world according to Joh," the abstract identity of a person with all other persons cannot play a role in our inquiry, not even as the exemplification of what the subject is not. Only a theory of a collective Subject writ large needs to discuss human persons stripped of all their personal and cultural identification marks. And still, the sentences "Joh is a subject" and "Joh is a human person," are closely linked. More precisely, they are *historically* linked. There must be something in modern development that made both phenomena (subjecthood and personhood) appear, for otherwise one could not give a proper account of their simultaneous appearance. To this question I will shortly return.

The question: if Joh is not a subject, what *is* he then, still needs to be answered.

Space does not allow here to identify our Joh as a Frenchman, a merchant, and the like, nor to show that all such and similar identifications are ultimately irrelevant to our inquiry.

We have left our Joh (who had been thrown into a world by the accident of being born just then and there) at the stage where he started to cope with this accident and became such-and-such a single person different from all other single persons. He *is* a single person, he *is* this-and-this particular and unique person. This is what he actually is. But he can be(come) a unique person in two different ways. Becoming a unique person in one way or another makes a difference, or, more precisely, it makes *all the difference*. For the unique person can remain unique as a particular single being and can also become an individual or a personality.

Joh is either a particular single being or a unique personality (obviously, he can also be a mixture of both).

Joh is a particular single being and remains one in the process of dual identification. He identifies himself entirely with the world he takes for granted and he identifies himself entirely with himself as well. Put bluntly, he identifies himself with the two a prioris of his very existence: the genetic and the social. All his experiences are organized around the two a prioris. Since the latter are accidental, yet the person is unaware of their accidental character, the person himself becomes entirely accidental. By contrast, the individual unique person (personality) never identifies himself with the world as it is, nor does he identify himself entirely with himself. A personality reflects upon the world and himself. His experiences are synthetic in character for he synthesizes the two a prioris. This is the way he ceases to be accidental, and becomes his own destiny.

It would be the greatest blunder to identify the individual personality with the subject in any of the current interpretations of the latter. Certainly, the historical conditions of (especially early) modernity favored the self-development of personalities of this kind. It is also true, that the modus operandi of modernity does not impose as severe a constraint upon the development of personality as most premodern societies did. But all this does not lead up to the identification of "the subject" and the individual personality. The referents are different (for Joh *is* a personality but he *is not* a subject). In addition, there is no necessary connection between the two. There were many outstanding individuals in ancient societies, yet one could hardly characterize Oedipus or Moses as "subjects." When Hegel and many other thinkers of his time predicted the demise of personalities in the modern world, which seemed to them to be the time of the subject, they made a serious point. For one can associate the birth of the subject with the birth of pettiness. If one agrees with me that Joh's subject is the world according to Joh, then the subject can be tied both to a person of unreflected singularity and to that of individual personality. The lack of reflexivity, the complete self-identification as well as the total identification with the environment, in other words, narcissism and conformity, do not prevent any Joh from conjuring up a world "according to Joh." Experience teaches rather the opposite.

After having found out what Joh is and what he can become, it will suffice to repeat that he is not a subject. Yet even if this were true, could we still suggest that a person (this time we shall call her Jill) manifests or expresses herself *as* a subject in the world "according to Jill"?

Mentioning Jill *as* a subject is tantamount to presuming that Jill *has* certain features, faculties, or capacities that can be termed her subject. Spatial thinking normally places this "subject" of Jill inside the body of Jill.

That our conscious and unconscious "inside" is not homogeneous is so obvious that one could hardly find a primitive culture that would know it otherwise. Mythologies and other fictions explain this most fascinating and most commonly perceived wonder. Several maps of the soul have been drawn and provided by religions, psychologies, and philosophies alike.

The non-homogeneous character of our so-called interior is so self-evident that it can only be compared to the experience of seeing or hearing. We actually do not even need "to come to know" (*erkennen*) this phenomenon given that we know it (*kennen*). What we need to and what we in fact do receive from the representative fictions is *meaning*. Since we are bodies who are connected to all other bodies by meaning, we are surely connected also to our own body by meaning. It is from the standpoint of the above (provided) meanings that we understand or interpret our own "inside"; it is thus that we make sense of our pre-cognitive intuitions.

Jill, our next-door neighbor is in a predicament. Unlike her great-grandmother who understood herself as being composed of a mortal body and an immortal soul, she has no firm solace. Jill is bombarded by at least a dozen entirely different and competing interpretations of her "interior." Alas, each of them makes a certain sense; as a result, she has difficulties with figuring out what kind of map she is carrying inside. We can perhaps maintain that doing something *as* a subject, or manifesting oneself *as* a subject amounts to the following two-step procedure. First, one interprets one's own interior by a meaningful world view and draws up the map of one's interior by using an original draft of the world view in question. Second, one employs this "map" in the understanding of the world. The world according to Jill would then be a world that succeeds in making manifest the map Jill is carrying inside as interpreted and perceived by Jill herself.

Jill's predicament is modern; so is, as it has been assumed throughout, the subject. There is certainly a connection between Jill's predicament and the emergence of the subject. If there is no single meaningful world view (or a limited number of such world views) to provide us with a map for the understanding of the inside of all of us, if there is rather a market place on which any world view can be obtained and freely exchanged with all others, maps guiding us in discovering the meaning of the world, or for that matter, that of anything in the world, are no longer available. There is indeed a congruency between the contingency of the internal and the external maps. Yet there is no reason to believe that the external map will somehow express or manifest the internal map. The "world according to Jill," that is, the subject of Jill, can hardly be identified with the direct manifestation of the internal map Jill is carrying inside her body, not at least in her own perception.

The map of the interior can be termed the *self*. Since our spiritual interior has practically never been perceived as homogeneous, there has never been a mono-centered self, if we think in terms of the fixed centerpoint of a circle. But in a completely different interpretation, the term "mono-centered self" makes perfect sense. In terms of this interpretation, the map is hierarchically ordered, and the center is its most powerful agent. This can be a peak called Reason towering over the plains, or a tremendous waterfall termed Passions, which sweep away everything that gets in their way. The gist of the matter is, however, that *the center of the map of the self (be it reason, passion or something else) is not the center of the self: for the center of the self (around which the self is centered) is outside the self.* It is "in" the world. The center of the self is neither Reason nor Passion, but their main objects; everything can be that center if it is referred to by a possessive pronoun. Jill is not mono-centered; the center of her self is the person she loves, her child, her political commitment, her profession. *Everything that is mine can be one of the centers of my self;* though not everything that is mine is in the center of my self, or even on the periphery of my self. Only a few issues, people, things, goals, propensities that are mine can be the centers of my self. They become really mine exactly because they are one of the centers of my self. The "world according to Jill" will encapsulate these centers of Jill's self.

We know that Jill did not inherit a master map of the soul to guide her self-understanding. Nor did she receive from her ancestors a master narrative to guide her understanding of the world. Now we come to know about her third privation, namely that she did not inherit any ideal or real object as the center of her self, and in this sense, *nothing which is hers* is hers by right of birth. These three privations together amount to a cluster of open possibilities. The bunch of open, because indeterminate, possibilities *add up to contingency.* Modern men and women are contingent; they are also aware of their contingency. Mere possibilities are empty, yet they can be filled with a great, even infinite variety of contents. Mere possibility is the potential of personal autonomy, it is also the potential of a total loss thereof. Modern men and women are unstable and fragile, yet they seek a certain degree of firmness. They easily stumble into chaos, therefore they need at least a fragment of "cosmos" to make sense of their own lives and, possibly, render meaning to it.

Jill *is* Jill, a unique, particular person. A modern unique and particular person can develop two distinct attitudes to the world (including her own interior world): the attitude of unreflected singularity and that of an individual personality.

Since Jill does not receive the broad outlines of her destiny in her cradle, she has to destine herself to become an individual personality. To destine oneself is to choose oneself. As we know, the center of the self is not an item on the map of the soul; it is just the thing, the person, the cause we are involved in, beyond and above everything else. Choosing oneself thus means to choose the foci on which our personality begins to develop. By choosing ourselves (the centers of our self) we become what we are: this kind or that kind of individual personality.

Kierkegaard once said that if you do not choose yourself, you let others choose for you. If Jill fails to choose herself, she lets others choose for her. This was not the alternative of Jill's great-grandmother who had received her destiny (at least in its rough outlines) in her cradle. Great-grandmother Jill could have developed a reflective relation to herself and the tradition or she could have followed the tradition and those persons who embodied it (her father, husband, and priest) without reflection. At any rate, those others would have decided for her, the others-by-tradition, the noncontigent others; in final analysis tradition would have made all the decisions. Our modern Jill has been born as a bundle of empty possibilities. When she fails to choose herself, she lets other *contingent* persons choose for her. The end result, the narcissistic conformist, is well known.

Let me return for the last time to the problem of the centers of the self. I referred to those centers by the term "objects." "Object" stands here for a *being*-in-the-world and objects for "beings"-in-the-world where "being" is not writ large. Objects-in-the-world are related to subjects. Yet the center of the self is the center of the *self* and not of the "subject." The subject of Jill is (in our definition) the world according to Jill, not Jill as a person, not Jill's self, not Jill's personality (if she has one) or her unreflected singularity (if she failed to choose herself). The object is what appears in the center(s) of the self as being presented in the world according to Jill (her subject). The world according to Jill is the subject of Jill, and what appears at the center is the object(s). This(these) object(s) could be chosen by Jill, but Jill could also have failed to choose, and if she did, the objects of Jill would be chosen by others, not by Jill. But whether the first or the second is the case, there will certainly be a world according to Jill (a subject) and a centerpoint (or several centerpoints) of this world (objects). The subject-object relation is not an epistemological, but a historico-ontological relation.

Subject is the idiosyncrasy of the interpretation of human world-experience and self-experience under the condition of modernity. We are not subjects, we do not carry inside something that can be called "subject." Yet we manifest ourselves as subjects, and we cannot help it. We are destined to manifest ourselves as subjects (in modernity) for we are *not* destined to be or to become this or that, to understand the world exactly this way or that way: we are born as bundles of open and indeterminate possibilities. To manifest ourselves as subjects is neither a citation granted us by the World Spirit nor is it a curse from Heaven. It is certainly a difference. Manifesting ourselves as subjects makes us different from non-moderns. We can get rid of this difference only by getting rid of modernity itself. For the time being the death of the subject is not in sight.

Modern men and women manifest themselves as subjects (idiosyncratically). Regardless of whether they are (become) unreflected singularities or individual personalities, they manifest themselves as subjects alike. The world according to a conformist or a narcissist is a subject no less than the world according to a personality. But the equally idiosyncratic worlds are still different in kind. Jill chooses herself and thereby also her main involvements (objects). The world according to her will center on the issues of her involvements. Thus she gets as close as one ever can to what was once called subject/object identity. The other Jill, who let others choose for her, will manifest the "objects" of her self, these fragments of alien meanings, as firm and incontestable truths, whenever they support her narcissism, and as blatant untruths, whenever they affront her network of self-identification. What is idiosyncratic here (the world according to our second Jill) is the ever-changing character of the pendulum-like movement between unreflected identification (with others) and equally unreflected self-identification.

There are many narratives of the "end of the subject" and all of them are entirely idiosyncratic in the form they happened to be first told by their authors. Sometimes our epoch is compared, with very little justification, to Hellenism. In Hellenism, Stoicism, Epicureanism, Scepticism, and Platonism were followed by thinkers for more than a millennium. It was the common world that reigned supreme, in philosophy perhaps even more than in social and political life. But on our tree of philosophy no two leaves are alike; some leaves do not even resemble others. Sometimes one gets the impression that the fury of innovation has put what is now termed philosophy under a spell. Evil tongues explain this fixation with reference to fashion, competition, or the market!

In fact, many modern philosophies are being recycled, although in a remarkably idiosyncratic fashion. These recycled versions of the old participate in the world of idiosyncratic quasi-monads. Philosophical mininarratives are only quasi-monads because the sole quality that makes them monads is their idiosyncracy, their difference. Mininarratives are not closed, but open; they collide with one another, they combat, they are even sensitive to social change. This is how philosophy remains the mirror image of our unsocial sociability. Yet, the monads are also resistant to influence, their receptivity threshold is extremely high, and as a result, very little real discourse is going on among them (philosophies of discourse are no exceptions).

The narratives on the end of the subject are extremely strong statements about both personalities and subjects. The narratives encapsulate worlds according to the contemporary philosophers. They are subjects, moreover, they are *representative subjects*. The less we want them to be representative subjects, the more they become so. Not even philosophers can jump their own shadows.

✦ JULIA KRISTEVA ✦

Psychoanalysis and the Imaginary

When speaking about the imaginary in psychoanalysis, I am committed to a discourse that brings us as close as possible to the imagination: a discourse that I want to address to your own imagination, to provoke images in you—and an eventual acceptance of my conclusions beyond and because of your imaginary participation in my arguments. This means that I will try to be as concrete as possible and to tell you some stories that nourish the analytic theory but which the necessity of professional privilege and the tough metalinguistic ambitions of the theoreticians normally keep psychoanalysts from communicating to the public

The imaginary is generated by transference—by identification between patient and analyst (the strongest moment), just as it can be generated by identification between teacher and student, artist and muse, etc. What happens in transference? I will refer only to one aspect of this huge problem, which will bring me to the imaginary; what is transference time? I will differentiate three moments in it.

Transferences

1. One immediately thinks of the linear time of the patient's narrative: a time belonging to memory, which attempts to reconstruct the links, reestablish a continuity.

2. And then suspended time springs to mind, the zero time of silence—empty, blank from trauma or pleasure or dizziness, beyond the line of discourse. Lacan was brave—or exhibitionistic—enough to claim the right to this dizziness, this idiocy of pleasure that marks the patient's discourse at the same time as the analyst's listening.

3. Finally, and necessarily, we come to the time of interpretation: to give a meaning to memory, but also to the suspension of memory. To be within the line of discourse *and* in the blank of dizziness-pleasure, and then to come up again for an instant in an identity with a provisional meaning. A time belonging to resurrection.

There is a certain rejuvenation particular to transference and counter-transference that sometimes takes place quite perceptibly within the patient. But I will focus here on the analyst: through identification, the analyst assumes or assimilates the memory, as well as the pleasure-suspension of the patient's discourse: the line and the pause. As a result, temporality is multiplied, and analysts live several lives within one life. And yet the regenerative effect of transference seems to me to stem less from the plurality of time sequences than from what I've called suspension and resurrection: from pleasure beyond time and from the resurgence of a provisional meaning to that pleasure. When I speak of rejuvenation, you will no doubt think of that perpetually youthful look the analysts have, inhabited as they are by regression, adolescence, and even silliness—all more or less acted—and which never fails to strike in a gathering of analysts once the theoretical superego has been torn away. This rejuvenescence, which I attribute to the various temporalities intersecting in the transferential dynamic, appears most clearly, and quite logically, in what I would call the *explosive discourse:* in the *joke* as the quintessence of analytic speech, steeped in instinctual pleasure beyond time and "logically concluding" provisional. Freud calls this explosive discourse, *Witz,* and his own style evidently had it. I simply want to make clear which temporality it seems to me to rest upon: a temporality that, although a personal characteristic of the speaker, is nevertheless intrinsic to the very logic of the cure.

✦ ✦ ✦

If one accepts the varied temporality of the transferential dynamic, one is led to ask the following question: since speech, with its linguistic signs and their linking together, assures linear time and the memory in transference, then in what signs (other than silence) do the zero time of temporal suspension (the time of pleasure) and the resurrectional time of interpretation find their support?

Infralinguistic signs at once occur to me, as they seem to me to mark this zero time of pleasure: modulation or vocal intensity, phonic gesture or facial expression. All of them are to be taken into consideration, to be interpreted in the transference (this seems to me to be essential, particularly when dealing with sufferers of depression or melancholy).

But here I want to emphasize above all the appearance in certain cures of nonlinguistic signs (for example, images, photos, or paintings), which, as secret objects or projectiles, reveal *aggressively* this zero time of pleasure, but keep it apart from verbal expression. The discourse remains in the power of repression or splitting, and if one limits oneself to verbal communication only, one risks keeping the cure within the domain of defense and of the superego, of that which cannot be analyzed. Yet, taking into account these pictorial works can bring the split pleasure—for it is more a question of "splitting" than of "repression"—onto the manifest scene of transference and alter the transference itself. I speak of "the manifest scene of transference" because I believe that for as long as the implicit elements of the transference remain unnamed, there can be no analytical transference strictly speaking.

I have a patient who is a painter in his spare time, a draughtsman by profession, married but with no sexual relationship either marital or extramarital, masturbation being his only form of sexuality. He has a few intermittent somatic symptoms, like eczema and migraine. He came to me after his mother died, and for two years he left the deceased's apartment closed, without touching it, neither visiting it, nor even thinking of selling it, despite his financial difficulties. Now, his discourse on the couch was voluble, even well-informed about psychoanalysis. He did all the talking, he knew everything, he didn't expect anything from me. Masturbatory speech of complete infantile power, without silence—and yet it was continuous silence, without emotion or affect, even when he was speaking about erotic or phobic dreams or memories. I soon had the feeling that the secret lay in the space of the mother, of course, but at the same time in this means of translinguistic expression his paintings represented, which he used to show to his mother while she was alive. (He never exhibited or sold them, he always gave them to his mother.) During the transference, and because I took on the place of the mother, the patient (Didier) expressed the desire to show me his works. I accepted, and several sessions took place in which Didier displayed his photos and paintings: lying on the couch he showed them to me, showed them to himself, explained them to me, explained them to himself. The pictures represented bodies cut up, arms and legs floating, collages made from posters of well-known actors and actresses within the painting, the posters themselves cut up and rearranged by the patient. He spoke to me of the shapes and of the technical aim of his pieces, about his aesthetic sources and his style. His discourse was always neutral, but this time the neutrality was in the content, whereas for once the tone of his voice grew lively, as did his gestures and the color of his skin. I had the feeling I was watching the transferential time of the autoerotic pleasure in the presence of the mother—a time beyond time, removed from speech, now flowing into the actual cure.

It was my task to give meaning to it. I constructed in place of the aesthetic and formal discourse of the patient, the fantasy that was missing in the speech, but which seemed to me to be present in the dizziness of the pictorial display and in the excited voice. I talked about his masturbatory pleasure, about the fear of seeing his own member cut off, about how this fear was counterbalanced by cutting to pieces the two parents—the "actors" of the posters. Contrary to the silent complicity of his voyeuristic mother, I introduced an interpretative discourse that was the *discourse of perversion:* I grafted on it a perverse fantasy absent from the operative speech of the patient.

Result: he opened his mother's apartment and distributed her heritage. Didier found himself seduced ("amorously, not sexually, I don't dare," he said) by a young girl, an "almost teenager" from his office. His eczema was cured . . . by a trip to sunny Morocco.

To come back to the *fantasy-graft* I performed, and which many of our interpretations in the transference/countertransference perform: it is a resurrectional moment when pleasure and meaning are brought together for the analyst and, consequently, for the patient.

I was in the deadened time of his memory, a time frozen in a linear discourse, void of affect and steeped in the superego. I plunged into the beyond-time of his pictorial pleasure—worldless, full of violence and fecal matter (compare the colors and fragments he uses on his works), secret and aggressive, and of the cutting up of his own body as well as the maternal body: a time inscribed in images, but not in speech. Affect had remained signifiable in images—in return, speech could not signify affect. Finally, the interpretative discourse I held was that of perversion, a discourse that created the link between language void of affect and affect simply rendered in images.

I constructed fantasies: now instincts made image through speech, and I did this by reconstructing a meaning to the formalist and worldless images of Didier's works. Was the meaning I suggested mine? Or was it his? Didier accepted it.

The transferential dynamic demands of the analyst a veritable fantasy-construction: a passage through perversion to assure the flow between affect and language, sometimes passing through nonlinguistic signs. This dynamic of analytical perversion (a-perversion, since it is already named and analytical) is the other side of the explosiveness, of *Witz*, as shown to us by Freud. In other words, the *Witz* is the logical aspect, the a-perversion—the thematic aspect of the transferential dynamic, as long as it is capable of crossing through the various temporalities I mentioned at the beginning. The moral is: let ourselves be dizzied and let us look for meaning where there is no more language. How? By trusting our perversion and by making it apparent in discourse as far as it is the secret side of our wit (witticism, being witty).

This is the imaginary aspect—necessary and unavoidable—of the analytic interpretation.

◆   ◆   ◆

I turn now to another aspect of the role played by the imaginary in the rebirth of the subject during the analytic cure—its role in the acquisition and utilization of logical and grammatical norms.

Certain cases of slowness in language acquisition, or of difficulties in learning logical and grammatical categories, seem to have physiological causes that are difficult to identify, and even more difficult to treat on a somatic level. Yet, in the radial structure of the brain, these lesions, if minor, do not hinder access to the *symbolic,* provided we allow the child a wide and intense use of the *imaginary.*

I am using *symbolic* to indicate the practice of discourse according to the logical and grammatical rules of interlocution. I am using *imaginary* to refer to the representation of strategies of identification, introjection, and projection, which mobilize the image of the body, the ego and the other, and which makes use of primary processes (displacement and condensation).

The imaginary is, of course, dependent on the mirror stage. It constitutes the self-image of the subject in the process of formation, and, in order to do this, the imaginary mobilizes, through the play of the representations proposed to the child, the whole range of identifications: narcissistic identification accompanied by a hold over the maternal image or a reduplication of it; primary identification with the ideal father of the "personal prehistory" (Freud); secondary identification during the Oedipal stage and notably its variant, the hysterical identification with a phallic role, etc. The fact that it may be a kaleidoscope of images of the ego from which the subject of utterances comes into being should not allow us to forget the imaginary extends its effects as far as the phychical modalities preceding specular identification, that is to say, as far as the *phychical representatives of the affects* subject to the fluctuating rules of assimilation and rejection, of condensation and displacement. We can hypothesize that this imaginary level of *semiotic meaning,* as opposed to *linguistic signification,* is closer to the drives specific to the lower layers of the brain, and could serve as a relay between these layers and the cortex governing linguistic performance, thus constituting supplementary cerebral circuits in a position to remedy possible bio-physiological deficiencies. This is why, in a child who has no active use of symbolic communication—and in whom the exact passive comprehension retained is uncertain—the imaginary is a means of access: if not immediately to linguistic signification, then, at least, and to start with, to the meaning of more archaic affective representations, and to their dramaturgy, which continues to dwell in him, to torment him or to afford him pleasure.

I am thus making a distinction between, on the one hand, the instinctual and affective meaning organized according to primary processes and indicated by secondary vectors often different from language (sound, melody, rhythm, color, odor, etc.), which I call semiotic; and on the other hand, *linguistic signification,* which finds realization in linguistic signs and their syntactic and logical organization, and which requires certain biological and psychical conditions in order to occur. Certainly, the imaginary, as it is understood in imaginative or fictional works, stems from linguistic signification, and cannot be dissociated from grammar and logic. Yet, it is not this level that is specific to the imaginary strategy in the effectiveness it has (as I see it) at the center of the cure of children. On the contrary, looking beyond linguistic performance, it is the *psychical prerequisite conditions* that interest me in the conception of the imaginary: conditions that do not seem to be innate in certain children, or that have been damaged during intrauterine life or at birth, and which the therapist could attempt to bring into being precisely through the use he is able to make of the imaginary.

I will go one step further. The difficulties to which I am referring— difficulties in gaining access to the symbolic that mean that some children have no natural and spontaneous access to *signification* although they still have access to meaning—give rise to a depression that may be more or less recognized and more or less serious in these children. Now, where language is concerned, a depression is characterized by the denial of the symbolic. "Language doesn't count, your signification doesn't matter to me, I'm not one of you, I'm withdrawing, I'm not even fighting you like a child suffering from character neurosis would, I'm not cutting the ties of meaning like an autistic child would. No, imprisoning you in my unutterable meaning is killing me." This is what the child with "linguistic problems"—often a depressed child not recognized as such—seems to be saying. Because he doesn't use the symbolic, the young "infans," who prolongs the period of babyhood well beyond the canonical age, buries himself in the crypt of his unsignified affects, exasperating those around him, exasperating himself, or taking pleasure in this hiding place, without, however, allowing the adult to recognize the secret signals of his infralanguage of distress and regression. Neither autistic, nor suffering from character neurosis, these children are more likely to give the impression of being seized by a phobic inhibition that hampers access to discourse: as if language frightened them, whereas what frightens them is perhaps their depression at being unable to use it, at being incompetent in the world of other speakers, at being "bad speakers." The task of the therapist is thus double: on the one hand, he becomes an analyst in order to bring about the desire (and of course the desire to speak) that lies behind the inhibition and depression; on the other hand, he becomes a speech therapist in order to facilitate paths *specific* to the child in question (for whom he has understood that "universals" don't occur universally), and to help him acquire linguistic categories that will enable him to give symbolic realization to his being as a subject.

Precipitating cognitive requirements (in our terminology, symbolic requirements) onto such an economy is not only useless; it censors the situation in which this "infans," with meaning but without *signification,* finds himself, a situation where he has no alternative but to elaborate in the imaginary the semiotic conditions necessary for access to discourse. After all, it is the economy of the imaginary that brings the subject of utterance into existence, and so this economy is the psychical prerequisite for language acquisition.

I would like to clarify these remarks with a few brief clinical indications.

I had been acquainted with Paul's neurological difficulties from the time of his birth, and at the age of three he was still unable to utter a single word, only some echolalia where a few unidentifiable pseudoconsonants could just be discerned. He couldn't stand dialogue between his parents, and of course refused to accept the exchange of words between the therapist and his mother, these situations sending him into dramatic states of screaming, tears, and distress rather than rage. I was able to interpret these reactions as an Oedipal refusal of the sexual relation between his parents and, by extension, of any verbal exchange thought to be erotic between two adults from which Paul felt himself excluded.

Not only did this interpretation have no effect on him; very quickly it seemed to me premature. I began to think that Paul was refusing a signifying chain he was incapable of managing, and *perception,* or should I say the precocious *consciousness,* of this incapacity was devalorizing him, depressing him, inhibiting him through fear. I decided to communicate with him, but also with his mother, by using the means available to him: *singing.* The operas we improvised, which must have appeared ridiculous to any possible spectators, certainly carried the *signification* that I wanted us to exchange, but they also carried the meaning of the representatives of affects and instincts coded in the melodies, rhythms, and accentuation, which were more (if not exclusively) accessible to Paul, which were his element. "Come and see me" (do-re-mi); how are you (do-ti-la), etc. Gradually, through this vocal game, which was actually multidimensional (semiotic and symbolic), the child overcame his inhibition and started to vary his vocalizings more and more.

At the same time, he began to listen to a large number of records and to reproduce the melodies and gradually the words. I felt as though I were tuning a musical instrument, getting to know him, and making more and more unexpected and complex possibilities surge forth from this resonant body. Thus, through our "Opera," we developed the precise articulation of phonemes while singing, without there being any technical work on pronunciation, strictly speaking, but rather by counting on the possibility and pleasure of articulating and hearing oneself in the melody. Once sure of knowing how to pronounce while singing—therefore able to control his breath, sphincters, motor functions, body—Paul agreed to use his phonemes, already established in the opera, henceforth in everyday speech, and this with a precision in his articulation that few children possess. The singer had become a speaker.

I shall not talk to you about the actual analytical work we did, but I do insist upon the fact that it cannot be dissociated from the arrival of language that it favored.

Some problems arose during the following stages, which once again the imaginary enabled us to solve. One example among others: *the distinction between first and second person personal pronouns, I/you, me/you.* The confusion in this case revealed Paul's dependence on his mother, and the participation of the young woman who was unable to detach herself from her child—a narcissistic prosthesis invested in the depression she had suffered due to her son's deficiencies—was the key to the cure. Yet, the crucial point of the distinction *I/you* was Paul's identification with Pinocchio (the character from the famous children's tale), particularly in the episode where the little boy saves his father Gepetto from the jaws of the whale Monstro. "Help, Pinocchio," begged the old man. "*I*'m coming, *Father,* wait for *me,* don't be afraid, *I*'m with *you,*" replied Paul. This story allowed the child not only to dominate the voracious whale, but to cease to be the victim. Paul took his revenge on the father. He could now say "I," provided that he no longer felt threatened with engulfment or castration. The "you," that is the sign by which Paul—the poor child, the victim—was designated, was another in this tale. This unfortunate soul, the dreaded other ("you") which fused with the bad part of Paul, could now be somebody else and receive love, for in the tale it was Gepetto, the benevolent and gifted father, who was the victim. Through this displacement of the suffering upon another signifier (Gepetto) the other ("you") could be separated from the self ("I") and given a different name from oneself. At the same time, Paul took on the role of the hero, and only in this way was he able to refer to himself with "I" rather than a "you" coming from his mother's lips. In addition, the "you" had its place, which was no longer confused with bad "I": it was the place of the other ("Gepetto"), not the other as impotent child, but, with and through the acknowledged misfortunes associated with this victim position, the "you" indicated the role of a dignity certainly in danger but sovereign and king (*you* was another hero, the other of the hero) with whom Pinocchio could converse as one equal to another, that is, as one different person to another.

I have only given you a few brief elements of my conversations with Paul, but a number of conclusions can be drawn from this information.

Discourse is a complex psychical affair that cannot be reduced to the dimension of grammatical categories and their combination, a dimension I have called *symbolic*. It also comprises the *semiotic* modality, which is extraneous to language, but in which the psychical representatives of the affects unfold, and with them, the dramaturgy of the desires, fears, and depressions that make sense to the child but that do not manage to enter the coded signification of everyday language.

In order to hear this infralinguistic semiotic sense, the analyst-cum-speech therapist needs to have an optimal maternal ear. I put my faith in Paul's mother, or rather she convinced me of the existence of meaning in her child, because she said that she understood him, and she used to answer him without his having spoken to her. I adopted her way of listening and of deciphering this meaning. In this day and age, when science is able to make almost any woman a childbearer, let us try to revalorize the *maternal role,* which manages to ensure a path towards signification for the child (despite the fact that mothers often use the child as a narcissistic prosthesis, a counterphobic object, or a provisional antidepressant).

In generating the language we know in fact as maternal, the mother is often alone, and she relies on therapist-teachers, especially when neurological difficulties arise to complicate the in itself already problematic passage from meaning to signification in all speaking beings. In the best of cases, the mother arrives with the meaning; it is up to us to find the signification. Which is to say that our role is more than maternal: through identification with the mother-child relation, we recognize and often anticipate the meaning of what is not said; however, through our ability to hear the logic of buried affects and blocked identifications, we allow the suffering to emerge out of its tomb. Only in this way can the signifier we use—the signifier of everyday language—cease to be a devitalized envelope that the child cannot assimilate, and become invested with meaning for a subject whose second birth, after all, we have accompanied.

Rare are the mothers who manage single-handed to give signification to the unutterable meaning of their handicapped children, because their own unutterable suffering, present or past, clings to it. When this naming occurs, we must seek the help of the third party that encouraged it (it could be ourselves, or the father, or some other third person who led the mother herself to recognize, name, and lift her unspeakable depression) before supporting her child as he travels similar paths. For even if the causes of the depression in one (the child) are essentially biological and in the other (the mother) are psychical, the result where language is concerned is similar: we find the same inability to translate psychical representatives of the affects into verbal signs.

In reality, the imaginary plays the role of theatrical director of the psychical conditions that underlie grammatical categories. The imaginary prevents language, which is sometimes acquired through imitation or forced by parroting, to act as an artifice for use of a false self. Despite his backwardness, Paul never presented the symptoms of the "as if" personality, and all his performances—modest in the beginning and "beneath his age"—were striking in their authenticity and in his child's ability to use them creatively.

Finally, the *time* of the imaginary is not that of speech. It is the time of the story, of the "mythos" in the Aristotelian sense: the time where a conflict arises and is resolved into an outcome, that is to say a way out, a path for the subject of speech to follow. It is a tortuous time, which encompasses the non-time of the unconscious, the tiresome repetition of the eternal recurrence, the sudden eruption of suffering that can assume the face of anger, and lastly the bright spell of comprehension against which the earlier conflict can be seen differently from the way it appeared initially, in the confusion of the unutterable—this conflict appears now as a latent project, as an implicit advancement towards a goal. But in the internal labyrinths of this imaginary time, how many dark nights of expectation and exasperation? Until the time of speech (of the symbolic) arrives, the linear time of syntax (*subject/predicate*) where he who speaks positions himself to advance the representation of an act that is the act of judgment. Yet, since in hearing the utterance by the child of this luminous time of judgment, we are comforted, let us not forget—when it becomes blurred, when the child suddenly hides from us, once again, this syntactic signification of judgment we believed to have been already established once and for all—let us not forget how to find once more the labyrinth of imaginary time. For, by marking time inside him once again with a new imaginary graft, the imaginary will be able to help us clear the logical impasse where the child has been blocked.

Paul used the tenses of verbs (*present, past,* and *future*) correctly in conjugation and grammatical exercises. But when he told himself a story, he always used the *present,* the adverb alone indicating that he actually saw himself in a *before,* a *now,* or an *after,* but that his personal expression of the verbal system had not yet assumed this distinction. "Before, I am a baby, he said, "now, I am grown up; afterwards, I am a rocket pilot." The categories of tense remained established in the abstract for he could recite them in conjugations, but they didn't occur creatively in Paul's speech. It was with *tales of metamorphoses* that we were able to integrate the use of temporal shifters in Paul's discourse.

And so, to take but one example, there was *Sleeping Beauty*. The princess was sixteen years old when the Wicked Fairy put her to sleep; a hundred years went by; and she was awakened from her slumber by the love of the prince, to find herself at the same age, still with all the youthful freshness of her sixteen years, but not in the same era. This theme of resurrection, where a character finds herself unchanged but living and transposing her past across the caesura of sleep into a new context, unknown and surprising, enables us to measure the passing of time. The child identifies with the past childhood of Sleeping Beauty ("she was"); he later identifies with the massive zero time of her sleep, which perhaps also represents the stagnation of the present moment where in his difficulties he is marking time not understanding ("she is sleeping"); and finally he identifies with the time of her revival, which amounts to a project, to a future life, a life that is, however, already realized ("she is coming back to life through love, she will live") without any threat of separation, but on the contrary with the reassurance of the future as reunion, as resurrection. Even more precisely, it seemed to me that it was the distinction the fairy tale makes between a present-hiatus or a confusional present (sleep) and a present launching, act, and realization (waking up), the first receding into the past, the second opening the future life, which was the real trigger, positioning the past and the future, and allowing Paul to travel on the path of temporal categories.

You will notice that these stories, which structure the subject and thus create the conditions necessary for linguistic categories, are love stories. Let us consider this for a moment, and remember it whenever a child—or somebody else—with unutterable meaning comes to see us.

The imaginary here is the language of the love relation—solid and nevertheless distant—that the analyst establishes with his patient.

◆   ◆   ◆

After having given you these imaginary examples and coming to the conclusion about the importance of love enabling us to produce them, let me end with a more abstract statement.

To posit the existence of a primal object, and even of a Thing or of a prelinguistic meaning anterior to signification, which is to be conveyed through transference into a new capability—isn't that the fantasy of a melancholy theoretician enamored of a lost paradise?

Certainly, the primal object, the thing in itself—the meaning beyond signification that always remains to be conveyed—this ultimate cause of conveyability, exists only for and through discourse and the already constituted subject. Because what is conveyed is already there, the conveyable can be imagined and posited as in excess and incommensurable. Positing the existence of that other language and even of an other of language, indeed of an outside-of-language, is not necessarily setting up a preserve for

metaphysics or theology. The postulate corresponds to a psychical requirement that Western metaphysics and theory have had, perhaps, the good
luck and audacity to represent. That psychical requirement is certainly not
universal; Chinese civilization, for instance, is not a civilization of the conveyability of the thing in itself, nor of the prelinguistic; it is rather one of
sign repetition and variation, that is to say, of transcription.

The obsession with the primal object, the object to be conveyed, assumes
a certain appropriateness (imperfect, to be sure) to be considered possible
between the sign and, not the referent, but the nonverbal experience of the
referent in the interaction with the other. I am able to name truly. The
Being that extends beyond me—including the being of affect—may decide
that its expression is suitable or nearly suitable. The wager of conveyability
is also a wager that the primal object can be mastered; in that sense it is an
attempt to fight depression (due to an intrusive pre-object that I cannot give
up) by means of a torrent of signs, which precisely aims at capturing the
object of joy, fear, or pain. Metaphysics, and its obsession with conveyability, is a discourse of a pain that is stated and relieved on account of
that very statement. It is possible to be unaware of, to deny the primal
Thing, it is possible to be unaware of pain, to the benefit of signs that are
written out or playful, without innerness and without truth. The advantage
of those civilizations that operate on the basis of such a model is that they are
able to mark the immersion of the subject within the cosmos, its mystical
immanence with the world. But, as a Chinese friend recognized, such a culture is without means of facing the onset of pain. Is that lack an advantage or
a weakness?

Westerners, on the contrary, are convinced that they can convey the
mother and the archaic pre-language—they believe *in her,* to be sure, but in
order to convey her, that is, to betray her, transpose her, be free of her. Such
melancholy persons triumph over the sadness at being separated from the
loved object through an unbelievable effort to master signs in order to have
them correspond to primal, unnameable, traumatic experiences.

Even more so, and finally, the belief in conveyability ("mother is nameable, God is nameable") leads to a strongly individualized discourse, avoiding stereotypes and clichés, as well as to the profusion of personal styles.
But in that very practice we end up with the perfect *betrayal* of the unique
Thing (the *Res divina*). Why is assigning a name a betrayal? Because if all the
fashions of naming are allowable, the verbal reality, the Thing postulated in
itself becomes dissolved in the thousand and one ways of naming it. The
posited conveyability ends up with a multiplicity of possible conveyances.
The Western subject, as potential melancholy being, having become a relentless conveyer, ends up a confirmed gambler or potential atheist. The
initial belief in conveyance becomes changed into a belief in stylistic perfor-

mance for which the near side of the text, its other, primal as it might be, is less important than the success of the text itself.

Thus, if the belief in a prelinguistic reality is metaphysical, it ends up with a profusion of the imaginary, of infinite possibility for play.

Question: does Western religion integrate this lucidity, is it a Divine comedy? Or is the imaginary lucidity alien to religion, its opposite, its enemy?

Allow me to leave you with the choice: how are we to answer those questions?

✦ CONTRIBUTORS ✦

SARANE SPENCE BOOCOCK is currently a professor in the Rutgers University Department of Sociology. Before coming to Rutgers in 1976, she was a staff sociologist at the Russell Sage Foundation, and has also taught at Yale University, University of Southern California, Johns Hopkins University, and Hebrew University of Jerusalem, Israel. She is the author of *An Introduction to the Sociology of Learning, Simulation Games in Learning*, and *Turning Points: Historical and Sociological Essays on the Family* (with John Demos). Her most recent work involves cross-cultural analyses of childhood and child care.

MARTIN E. GLOEGE is enrolled in the Graduate English program at Rutgers University. He is completing his dissertation on "postmodern" identities in the fiction of Thomas Pynchon, Toni Morrison, and Philip K. Dick.

AGNES HELLER is Hannah Arendt Professor of Philosophy at the New School for Social Research, the Graduate Faculty. She was a student of Georg Lukacs before her political expulsion from Hungary in 1958. She is the author of many books, including *A Theory of Feelings* (Van Gorcum, 1979), *The Power of Shame* (Routledge, 1985), *General Ethics* (Basic Blackwell, 1979), and *Can Modernity Survive?* (University of California, 1990).

IRVING HOWE is Distinguished Professor Emeritus at the Graduate Center of the City University of New York. He is the author of many books of literary and social criticism, among them *Politics and the Novel, The Decline of the New, World of Our Fathers, Thomas Hardy, Socialism and America*, and *Selected Writings, 1950–1990*. He has recently been named a MacArthur Fellow.

KALI A. K. ISRAEL wrote her essay in this volume while a doctoral candidate in history at Rutgers University; her dissertation was titled "Drawing from Life: Art, Work, and Feminist Politics in the Life of Emilia Dilke (1840–1904)." She is now an assistant professor of history at the University of Cincinnati; her research interests are women, intellectual culture, and the gendering of struggles over the meanings of the past in the Victorian era.

JULIA KRISTEVA is Professeur de Linguistique attachée au Department de Littérature "Science des Textes et Documents" de l'Université de Paris VII. Her recent works include: *Pouvoirs de L'Horreur* (Tel Quel, 1980), *Histories D'Amour* (L'Infini, 1983), and *Soleil Noir* (Gallimard, 1987).

DENNIS K. MUMBY is assistant professor of communication at Purdue University. He studies power and discourse in institutional contexts, and he is currently researching postmodern feminist approaches to organization studies. His book, *Communication and Power in Organizations*, was published by Ablex in 1988.

JACKSON LEARS is professor of history and the graduate director of history at Rutgers University. He is author of *No Place of Grace: Anti-Modernism and the Transformation of American Culture. 1880–1920*, and the forthcoming book, *The Wand of Increase: American Advertising and American Culture*. He is interested in exploring the intersections between intellectual and social experience in modern American culture.

GEORGE LEVINE is Kenneth Burke Professor of English and the director of the Center for the Critical Analysis of Contemporary Culture at Rutgers University. His most recent book is *Darwin and the Novelists* (Harvard University Press), and he is currently working on "Dying to Know," a study of the tradition of scientific objectivity as it affects the literary imagination.

JAN LEWIS is associate professor of history and the chair of history at Rutgers University–Newark. She is author of *The Pursuit of Happiness: Family and Values in Jefferson's Virginia*, published by Cambridge University Press. Her forthcoming works include: *Mother's Love: The Construction of an Emotion in 19th Century America* and *Mothers as Teachers: Education and the American Family*.

LOUIS A. SASS is an associate professor in the Department of Clinical Psychology in the Graduate School of Applied and Professional Psychology at Rutgers University. He is completing two books: *Madness and Modernism*, to be published by Basic Books, and a book on Wittgenstein and the Schreber Case, to be published by Cornell University Press. He is also coeditor of *Hermeneutics and Psychological Theory*, published by Rutgers University Press. He is interested in phenomenological approaches to mental disorders and the philosophy of psychology and psychoanalysis.

LINDA M.-G. ZERILLI is an assistant professor of political science at Rutgers University. She is author of *Images of Women in Political Theory: Agents of Culture and Chaos* (1992). She is interested in feminist theory, historical political theory, American politics, and comparative politics.